DO PRISONS MAKE US SAFER?

DO PRISONS MAKE US SAFER?

The Benefits and Costs of the Prison Boom

Steven Raphael
and
Michael A. Stoll
Editors

Russell Sage Foundation
New York

Library of Congress Cataloging-in-Publication Data
Do prisons make us safer? : the benefits and costs of the prison boom.
p. cm.
Includes bibliographical references and index.
ISBN 978-0-87154-860-3 (alk. paper)
1. Prisons—United States. 2. Prison administration—United States
3. Corrections—United States. I. Russell Sage Foundation.
HV9469.D75 2009
365'.973—dc22   2008036245

Text design by Genna Patacsil.

RUSSELL SAGE FOUNDATION
112 East 64th Street, New York, New York 10065
10 9 8 7 6 5 4 3 2 1

Contents

	About the Authors	vii
	Acknowledgments	ix
Chapter 1	Introduction *Steven Raphael and Michael A. Stoll*	1
PART I	PRISON BOOM CONTEXT	
Chapter 2	Why Are So Many Americans in Prison? *Steven Raphael and Michael A. Stoll*	27
Chapter 3	The Origins of Mass Incarceration in New York State: The Rockefeller Drug Laws and the Local War on Drugs *David F. Weiman and Christopher Weiss*	73
PART II	THE BENEFITS AND COSTS OF THE PRISON BOOM	
Chapter 4	The Impact of Prison on Crime *Shawn D. Bushway and Raymond Paternoster*	119
Chapter 5	The People Prisons Make: Effects of Incarceration on Criminal Psychology *Amy E. Lerman*	151
Chapter 6	Ever-Increasing Levels of Parental Incarceration and the Consequences for Children *Rucker C. Johnson*	177

Chapter 7   Footing the Bill: Causes and Budgetary
               Consequences of State Spending on Corrections   207
               John W. Ellwood and Joshua Guetzkow

Chapter 8   Collateral Costs: Effects of Incarceration on
               Employment and Earnings Among
               Young Workers   239
               Harry J. Holzer

PART III   ARE WE AT A SOCIALLY OPTIMAL LEVEL
               OF IMPRISONMENT?

Chapter 9   Assessing the Relative Benefits of Incarceration:
               Overall Changes and the Benefits on the Margin   269
               John J. Donohue III

               Index   343

About the Authors

STEVEN RAPHAEL is professor of public policy at the University of California, Berkeley.

MICHAEL A. STOLL is professor and chair of public policy in the School of Public Affairs, and associate director of the Center for the Study of Urban Poverty at the University of California, Los Angeles.

SHAWN D. BUSHWAY is associate professor of criminology and criminal justice at the State University of New York, Albany.

JOHN J. DONOHUE III is Leighton Homer Surbeck Professor of Law at Yale Law School.

JOHN W. ELLWOOD is professor of public policy at the Goldman School of Public Policy, University of California, Berkeley.

JOSHUA GUETZKOW is assistant professor in the Department of Sociology at the University of Arizona.

HARRY J. HOLZER is professor of public policy at the Georgetown Public Policy Institute at Georgetown University.

RUCKER C. JOHNSON is assistant professor at the Goldman School of Public Policy, University of California, Berkeley.

AMY E. LERMAN is assistant professor in the Department of Politics and the Woodrow Wilson School of Public and International Affairs at Princeton University.

RAYMOND PATERNOSTER is professor of criminology and climinal justice at the University of Maryland.

DAVID F. WEIMAN is Alena Wels Hirschorn '58 Professor of Economics at Barnard College, Columbia University.

CHRISTOPHER WEISS is director of the Quantitative Methods in the Social Sciences Program at the Institute for Social and Economic Research and Policy (ISERP) at Columbia University.

Acknowledgements

The roots of this book can be traced to a 1999 research project initiated by the Russell Sage Foundation. Under the leadership of Eric Wanner, the president of Russell Sage, a mandate from the foundation's Future of Work Advisory Council, and the intellectual leadership of David Weiman, a working group of leading scholars was formed to address key research and policy questions regarding mass incarceration in the United States. A number of important, innovative, and influential studies emerged from this project—in particular, studies that address the labor market consequences of mass incarceration. We were fortunate to be part of this group. Our involvement had a profound impact on our research agendas and influenced much of our thinking regarding the criminal justice issues presented in this book and socioeconomic inequality more broadly. Naturally, a key concern that undergirded much of this work was the question of whether the growth in mass incarceration met the crime-fighting objectives of policy makers and society at large. More specifically, we became interested in whether this policy experiment brought with it a set of unintended consequences that may have overridden many of the benefits accruing to society from incarcerating a large and growing population of mostly young, less educated, minority men. That question is one that we wrestled with and could not dismiss; ultimately, it prompted us to pursue this project.

With tremendous support and encouragement from Eric Wanner and key advice and council from Aixa Cintron at Russell Sage, this project came into being. The foundation provided generous funding for our work, which, among other things, made possible the organizing of the initial conference in 2006. This event brought together the authors of the chapters in the volume and leading scholars in the field, who served as critical discussants and, more generally, helped us address and untangle the key questions raised by this project. Our scholar discussants provided invaluable comments on earlier drafts of the papers and guidance as to the general direction of the volume. In this regard, we thank Julie Berry Cullen, Jeffrey Grogger, Michael Jacobson, Daniel Nagin, Anne Piehl, Michael Tonry, Jeremy Travis, and Peter Reuter for all their efforts in this regard. The papers are much improved as a result. Moreover, comments from anonymous reviewers tremendously improved the organization, readability, substance, and quality of the chapters in the book.

Of course, we would be remiss if we did not acknowledge the efforts of Suzanne Nichols at the Russell Sage Foundation in moving this volume from conceptualization to production. As always, Suzanne kept the trains running on time, provided steady council and editorial expertise, and cracked the whip when necessary, all with the goal of strengthening and enhancing the quality of the volume. We are grateful to her for her efforts.

Finally, we thank our families for putting up with us—our long workdays, our sometimes absent minds, and our obsession with excellence—during this project. So we extend our gratitude and love to Kelly, Antonio, and Ariana and to Kenya, Emera, Samina, and Myla for their patience and understanding, and their love.

Steven Raphael
Michael A. Stoll

Steven Raphael
and
Michael A. Stoll

1 | Introduction

Do prisons make us safer? This question is central to the debate about the great American experiment in imprisonment that the country has undergone over the past twenty-five years. Over this period, the incarcerated population has swelled in the United States, such that incarceration is becoming a relatively common experience for many American men. This is particularly true for relatively less-educated, prime-age minority men for whom the chances are better than not of serving some time in a state or federal prison over the course of their lives, and for whom the likelihood of being incarcerated on any given day is often comparable in magnitude to the likelihood of being gainfully employed.

The debate over the impacts of the recent prison boom in the United States has been pointed (Donohue, chapter 9, this volume; Zimring and Hawkins 1988; DiIulio 1996). Some argue that prisons make us safer and that we should expand their use even further. This argument posits that prisons reduce crime and therefore make us safer by serving as a deterrent to potential criminality and by incapacitating those who commit and are likely to commit crimes. By way of evidence, some point out that today's crime rates are appreciably lower than in the past. Indeed, declines in crime rates have occurred for all serious felony crimes, with pronounced decreases in the most serious violent offenses. Moreover, the largest declines in victimization rates have occurred among low-income households and minorities.[1] To the extent that the prison boom of recent decades is responsible for these crime trends, one can argue that the policy shifts driving the increases in incarceration rates have generated a tangible and quite equitably distributed benefit.

On the other hand, some oppose the growth in imprisonment on the grounds that the costs far outweigh the potential crime-reducing benefits.

They point to empirical research suggesting that the crime prevention bought by a small increase in incarceration has declined considerably as the incarcerated population has grown, as well as the growing evidence of the collateral consequences of imprisonment, including depressed labor-market opportunities for ex-offenders, an erosion of family and community stability among high-offending demographic groups and high prison-sending communities, the legal disenfranchisement of former inmates in a number of states, and the acceleration of the transmission of communicable diseases such AIDS among inmates and their nonincarcerated intimates, among other factors (Western 2006).

Moreover, the amount of public resources devoted to maintaining the currently incarcerated as well as to monitoring and servicing the previously incarcerated via community corrections is higher than at any point in the past. In 2005, U.S. state governments spent $65 billion on corrections alone, roughly $220 per U.S. resident. Adjusted for inflation, per capita expenditures on corrections have increased 2.8 times relative to per capita spending in 1982 (Bureau of Justice Statistics 2008a). Moreover, these expenditures do not account for the increased resources in policing and adjudication that certainly accompany a larger incarcerated population, factors that certainly contribute to the overall costs of increasing incarceration rates. The high costs of incarcerating such large numbers may also impact public spending in other areas. Surely there are many competing priorities (for example, public education or tax relief) that are to some degree displaced by corrections expenditures.

The juxtaposition of these sides in the current debate begs the question of whether the benefits that the nation has derived from dramatically increasing the incarceration rate exceed the costs. In other words, the key concern in this debate should not only be whether prisons make us safer but also whether the marginal benefits in crime reduction of imprisonment outweigh the economic and social costs of expanding the ranks of the imprisoned or formerly imprisoned.

In the past, evaluating this latter question has been difficult because the evidence needed to answer it has been mixed, poorly understood, difficult to address, or just largely unavailable. In addition, a related yet substantively different question concerns whether the net benefit to society could be increased by increasing or even decreasing the incarceration rate relative to its current level—that is, are we currently at a social optimum. Answering these two questions requires both a clear articulation of the forces behind the mass increase in incarceration of recent decades and a careful evaluation of how this increase has impacted the social outcomes that we have outlined. Addressing these questions also requires a careful analysis of how, at the margin, small changes from the status quo are likely to impact crime rates, socioeconomic inequality, state budgets, and other factors.

The chapters in this volume aim to answer these and other related questions regarding the various costs and benefits of recent developments in U.S. corrections policy. Many of the chapters provide new empirical findings pertaining to the causes and consequences of incarceration. Several distill large bodies of existing research pertaining to the relationship between incarceration and crime and the potential collateral consequences of having served time for inmates and their families. In general, the volume seeks to answer the following four questions:

- What explains the increase in incarceration rates over the past three decades?

- How has society benefited from this increase?

- What are the costs of the increase?

- Are we at, below, or above the socially optimal incarceration rate?

There is a sense among many that incarceration rates in many U.S. states have reached unsustainable levels. In many instances, prison populations have outstripped available capacity, and states are under logistic and, in many instances, legal pressure to find alternatives to incarceration or to devise more efficient uses of existing correction resources. The larger purpose of this volume is to provide a framework for thinking about such potential changes that is rational, based on the evidence, and grounded within the historical context of the recent evolution of U.S. correctional systems.

RECENT INCARCERATION TRENDS AND THE INCIDENCE OF INCARCERATION

We first characterize recent incarceration trends and the degree to which the incarcerated are concentrated among certain subgroups of the U.S. adult population. Over the past three decades the U.S. prison incarceration rate has increased to unprecedented levels. Prior to the mid-1970s, the incarceration rate was stable, hovering in a narrow band around 110 inmates per 100,000. Thereafter, however, the incarceration rate increases precipitously. Between 1975 and 2005, the prison incarceration rate more than quadrupled, from a rate of 111 to 488 per 100,000. By 2005, the point-in-time population of state and federal prisoners stood at slightly over 1.4 million inmates.

State and federal prisons hold those convicted for a felony offense who are sentenced to a year or more, as well as parole violators and probation violators who may ultimately serve less than a year on any given prison admission. In addition to these inmates, however, there are many who are held in local and county jails, either while awaiting adjudication, while serving time on a sentence of less than a year, or while serving time on a prison sentence in a local jail due to overcrowding in state facilities. Between 1980 and 2005, the total population in U.S. jails quadrupled from 183,988 inmates to 747,529. The jail population increased by slightly more than three times relative to the resident population (an increase in inmates per 100,000 residents from approximately 81 in 1980 to 252 in 2005).

Behind this steady increase in incarceration rates are large flows of inmates into and out of the nation's prisons and jails. By construction, the annual flow out of U.S. jails should be several times the point-in-time jail population, given the many very short stays in local jails and the fact that longer terms are generally limited to inmates sentenced to less than a year. What is perhaps more surprising is the number of inmates that are released from and admitted to prison each year. While there are certainly many prisoners that are serving very long sentences in the nation's penitentiaries (inmates that are most likely to be captured by point-in-time snapshots of the prison population), there are many more U.S. residents who serve relatively short spells in prison or who cycle in and out of correctional institutions serving sequential short spells over substantial portions of their adult lives. Most tellingly, annual admissions to U.S. prisons have consistently hovered around one-half the size of the prison population, while roughly half of all inmates are released in any given year. In recent decades, admissions have consistently exceeded releases, resulting in sustained increases in incarceration rates.

The increasing incarceration rates do not reflect a general increase in the likelihood of becoming incarcerated, but a concentrated increase in the incarceration risk for well-defined subsegments of the population. First, while incarceration rates have risen for both genders, the overwhelming share of these increases is accounted for by increased rates for men. This is not surprising considering that men consistently account for over 90 percent of the incarcerated population in current and past decades. Within the adult male population however, the increase in incarceration risk has been further concentrated among relatively young men (ages twenty-five to forty), minority men (black men in particular), and less-educated men.

Tables 1.1, 1.2, and 1.3 demonstrate how the likelihood of incarceration has changed for adult males by race, level of educational attainment, and age. The figures in the table are based on tabulations of the 1980 and 2000 Public Use Microdata Samples (PUMS) of the U.S. Census of Population and Housing. The decennial census enumerates both the institutionalized as well as the noninstitutionalized population. Within the institutionalized population, one can separately identify individuals residing in nonmilitary institutions. This category includes inmates of federal and state

Table 1.1   *Estimates of the Proportion of Men Eighteen to Fifty-Five Engaged in a Productive Activity, Noninstitutionalized and Idle, and Institutionalized by Race-Ethnicity from the 1980 and 2000 PUMS Files*

	1980	2000	Change, 2000–1980
Non-Hispanic White			
Employed or in school	0.899	0.878	–0.021
Idle	0.093	0.109	0.016
Institutionalized	0.008	0.014	0.006
Non-Hispanic Black			
Employed or in school	0.758	0.673	–0.085
Idle	0.206	0.239	0.033
Institutionalized	0.037	0.089	0.052
Non-Hispanic Asian			
Employed or in school	0.918	0.859	–0.059
Idle	0.079	0.135	0.056
Institutionalized	0.003	0.006	0.003
Hispanic			
Employed or in school	0.845	0.744	–0.101
Idle	0.140	0.226	0.086
Institutionalized	0.014	0.030	0.016

Source: Tabulated from the 1980 and 2000 Census Public Use Microdata Samples. Men in the armed forces are included in the "Employed/In School" category.

prisons, local jail inmates, residents of inpatient mental hospitals, and residents of other nonaged institutions. As the institutional populations in the last two categories are trivially small relative to the incarcerated, the institutionalization rate measured in this manner provides a close approximation to the population in prisons and jails. We use residence in a nonmilitary institution as the principal indicator of incarceration. Previous research (Raphael 2005) demonstrates that estimates of the incarcerated population based on residents in nonmilitary group quarters in the census are quite close to incarceration totals from alternative sources.[2]

Each table presents the proportion of the respective population that is engaged in a productive activity (either employed, in school, or in the military), the proportion that is noninstitutionalized but idle (not employed, not in school, and not in the military), and the proportion institutionalized. All data pertain to men eighteen to fifty-five years of age. Table 1.1 presents overall estimates for men for four mutually exclusive race-ethnicity groupings. The proportion incarcerated increased for all groups of men between 1980 and 2000. However, the absolute increase is largest for non-Hispanic black men and Hispanic men. The 2000 census indicates that roughly 9 percent of the adult black male population was incarcerated on any given day. The comparable figures for other groups are 3 percent for Hispanics, 1.4 percent for whites, and 0.6 percent for Asians.

Table 1.2 reveals that the proportion incarcerated has increased the most for the least educated men, and that this education-incarceration relationship differs substantially across racial groups. Among white men in 2000, those without a high-school diploma are more than twice as likely to be institutionalized relative to those with a high-school degree, with 4.5 percent of the former and approximately 2 percent of the latter institutionalized in 2000. Moreover, white male high-school dropouts experienced the largest increase in institutionalization rates between 1980 and 2000 (2.4 percentage-point change, compared with a 1.3 percentage-point increase for white high-school graduates, and a 0.4 percentage-point increase for those with some college education).

These changes as well as the levels are small in comparison to what is observed for black men. Between 1980 and 2000, the percentage of black men with less than a high-school degree that are institutionalized on any given day increased from 5.7 percent to 20.6 percent. For black male high-school graduates, the percentage institutionalized increased from 2.7 percent to 8.7 percent. Even among black men with some college education, the incarceration rate increased by over two percentage points. In fact, the changes observed among this group of black men are comparable in magnitude to the changes observed among white high-school dropouts.

By comparison, the changes in institutionalization rates among Asian men are small, as are the changes among Hispanic men. The relatively low institutionalization rates among Hispanic men are consistent with recent research by Kirsten Butcher and Anne Morrison Piehl (2006) demonstrating the relatively low levels of incarceration among recent immigrants (levels that are particularly surprising given the much lower levels of educational attainment).

Table 1.3 parses the data further for the least educated by age. For high-school dropouts and those with a high-school diploma, the table presents the distribution of each group across the three possible states by race-ethnicity and by three age groups (eighteen to twenty-five, twenty-six to thirty-five, and thirty-six to forty-five). While not true in all instances, the proportion institutionalization is greatest for men between twenty-six and thirty-five within each education-race group. The most startling figures are those for black men in 2000. Among black men, roughly one-third of high-school dropouts between twenty-six and thirty-five are incarcerated on a given day—a number comparable to the proportion of

Table 1.2 Estimates of the Proportion of Men Eighteen to Fifty-Five Engaged in a Productive Activity, Noninstitutionalized and Idle, and Institutionalized by Race-Ethnicity and Education from the 1980 and 2000 PUMS Files

	Non-Hispanic White		Non-Hispanic Black		Non-Hispanic Asian		Hispanic	
	1980	2000	1980	2000	1980	2000	1980	2000
Less than High School								
Employed or in school	0.794	0.698	0.658	0.430	0.804	0.699	0.793	0.667
Idle	0.185	0.257	0.285	0.364	0.186	0.278	0.188	0.297
Institutionalized	0.021	0.045	0.057	0.206	0.010	0.023	0.020	0.036
High-School Graduate								
Employed or in school	0.895	0.835	0.776	0.630	0.889	0.793	0.864	0.734
Idle	0.099	0.146	0.197	0.284	0.106	0.195	0.124	0.232
Institutionalized	0.006	0.019	0.027	0.087	0.005	0.012	0.011	0.035
Some College								
Employed or in school	0.941	0.911	0.866	0.794	0.952	0.880	0.927	0.855
Idle	0.054	0.079	0.110	0.156	0.046	0.115	0.065	0.126
Institutionalized	0.005	0.009	0.024	0.050	0.002	0.005	0.007	0.019
College or More								
Employed or in school	0.963	0.947	0.917	0.890	0.958	0.913	0.943	0.892
Idle	0.035	0.051	0.073	0.096	0.041	0.087	0.053	0.101
Institutionalized	0.002	0.002	0.011	0.014	0.000	0.000	0.004	0.007

Source: Tabulated from the 1980 and 2000 Census Public Use Microdata Samples. Men in the armed forces are included in the "Employed/In School" category.

Table 1.3 Estimates of the Proportion of Men Eighteen to Fifty-Five Engaged in a Productive Activity, Noninstitutionalized and Idle, and Institutionalized by Race-Ethnicity and Education from the 1980 and 2000 PUMS Files

	Less Than High School							
	Non-Hispanic White		Non-Hispanic Black		Non-Hispanic Asian		Hispanic	
	1980	2000	1980	2000	1980	2000	1980	2000
Age 18 to 25								
Employed or in school	0.784	0.797	0.604	0.473	0.791	0.794	0.760	0.703
Idle	0.188	0.161	0.314	0.307	0.192	0.164	0.212	0.257
Institutionalized	0.028	0.041	0.081	0.221	0.017	0.043	0.028	0.039
Age 26 to 35								
Employed or in school	0.783	0.683	0.634	0.343	0.783	0.655	0.807	0.672
Idle	0.186	0.249	0.281	0.336	0.207	0.311	0.170	0.289
Institutionalized	0.032	0.069	0.085	0.321	0.010	0.034	0.023	0.039
Age 36 to 45								
Employed or in school	0.823	0.666	0.726	0.423	0.845	0.685	0.824	0.645
Idle	0.161	0.286	0.240	0.387	0.150	0.301	0.165	0.318
Institutionalized	0.016	0.047	0.034	0.191	0.005	0.013	0.011	0.038

High School Graduates

Age 18 to 25								
Employed or in school	0.872	0.843	0.742	0.634	0.871	0.848	0.844	0.760
Idle	0.121	0.136	0.229	0.281	0.123	0.140	0.145	0.206
Institutionalized	0.007	0.021	0.029	0.084	0.007	0.012	0.012	0.034
Age 26 to 35								
Employed or in school	0.900	0.845	0.780	0.624	0.888	0.769	0.874	0.726
Idle	0.093	0.131	0.184	0.259	0.104	0.213	0.111	0.231
Institutionalized	0.007	0.024	0.036	0.117	0.008	0.019	0.015	0.043
Age 36 to 45								
Employed or in school	0.926	0.845	0.827	0.635	0.913	0.785	0.898	0.725
Idle	0.069	0.137	0.156	0.280	0.085	0.208	0.094	0.244
Institutionalized	0.005	0.018	0.017	0.085	0.001	0.007	0.008	0.032

Source: Tabulated from the 1980 and 2000 Census Public Use Microdata Samples. Men in the armed forces are included in the "Employed or In School" category.

this subgroup that is employed. The comparable figure for black men with a high-school degree is approximately 23 percent. More generally, the institutionalization rate increased for all subgroups of less-educated young men. However, the patterns for black males are particularly severe.

The patterns depicted in tables 1.1, 1.2, and 1.3 are conservative estimates of the changes in incarceration for these groups, given that we are limited to data from the 2000 census. Since the time period when the data underlying the PUMS was last collected (approximately April 1999), the prison and jail populations have continued to grow, albeit at a slower rate. Between 1999 and 2006, the point-in-time prison population increased by roughly 270,000 inmates (a 20 percent increase), while over the same period the local jail population increased by 160,000 inmates (a 26 percent increase). By contrast, the U.S. population grew by roughly 8 percent over this time period. Thus it is likely that the 2010 census will reveal even more stark patterns.

In addition, tables 1.1, 1.2, and 1.3 display only the proportion incarcerated on a given day. Another relevant set of facts for understanding the importance of a prior incarceration in impacting self-sufficiency is the proportion of men who have ever served time. Given the high turnover in U.S. prisons, the drastic increases in incarceration rates experienced over the last three decades has left in its wake an increasingly large population of former inmates. The Bureau of Justice Statistics estimates that approximately 3 percent of white male adults, 20 percent of black male adults, and 8 percent of Hispanic male adults have served prison time at some point in their lives (Bonczar 2003). In an analysis of administrative records from the California Department of Corrections, Steven Raphael (2005) estimates that at the end of the 1990s, over 90 percent of black male high-school dropouts, and 10 to 15 percent of black male high-school graduates have served prison time in the state. Becky Pettit and Bruce Western (2004) estimate that for all African American men born between 1965 and 1969, the proportion who have been to prison by 1999 was 20.5 percent overall, 30.2 percent for black men without a college degree, and 58.9 percent for black men without a high-school degree.

Thus, this empirical tour of census and prison-population data has revealed the dramatic growth in imprisonment in the United States over the past twenty-five years. In particular, less-educated minority men are considerably more likely to be incarcerated currently than at any time in the past, partly because of the racial disproportionality of the prison experience. Because of the fluidity of prison populations, the population of non-institutionalized former inmates has grown continuously and now constitutes sizable minorities, and in some instances majorities, of certain subgroups of American men. Much of this growth is the direct consequence of policy choices made by society at various levels that has resulted in stiffened penalties for specific offenses and in expanded sets of infractions deemed worthy of a spell in prison. Thus, the increase in the imprisoned as well as the growth in ex-offenders represents a policy experiment of sorts, in that it reflects both a break with the past as well as a consequence of public choice.

SCOPE AND METHOD

What are the effects of this policy experiment of increased imprisonment? Do the potential benefits of this policy shift toward more imprisonment outweigh its potential costs? The chapters in this volume aim to provide the information needed to better address these questions. Of course, in doing so, we are not able to capture all of the costs and benefits that are likely produced by this experiment, but we certainly hope to capture most and especially the major ones. How did we identify relevant benefits and costs? To decide what issues to examine, we established criteria that included whether there is substantial coverage in the literature of a particular benefit or cost, as well as the importance of these in the global context of the impacts of imprisonment. For instance, there is a substantial body of work on collateral consequences of mass incarceration on families and communities (Patillo, Weiman, and Western 2004; Braman 2004; Travis and Waul 2004; Mauer and Chesney-Lind 2003) and its impact on racial inequality (Western 2006). There is less research on the intergenerational consequences of increased use of prisons. Moreover, much recent work has focused on the labor-market prospects of ex-offenders (Bushway, Stoll, and Weiman 2007) and the policy barriers such as legal disenfranchisement of former inmates and their impact on civic participation (Manza and Uggen 2006). There is also much work on the crime-imprisonment connection (Jacobson 2005; Currie 1998).

The cost factors included in this volume are related to these, but we focus on those that have received less attention while being tremendously important and having measurable direct consequences on society. We focus on questions concerning whether prisons themselves have criminogenic effects on inmates, the extent of the association between parental incarceration and childhood outcomes (especially criminogenic outcomes), as well as the extent to which state budgets are affected by rising prison expenditures. Yet, by including these cost factors, we do not claim that other direct or indirect costs of incarceration are unimportant. Quite the contrary, we believe that they are.

We also believe that many of the factors impacted by imprisonment are themselves interrelated. For instance, we focus on the impacts of imprisonment on employment because of the importance of economic factors more generally. The employment of ex-offenders is an important factor in determining their postrelease outcomes (Raphael and Weiman 2007). But as Harry J. Holzer (chapter 8, this volume) notes, even among those who do not recidivate, employment outcomes are correlated with (and perhaps causally related to) health and other measures of their own well-being. Employment prospects and outcomes after incarceration thus appear to be major determinants of whether or not ex-prisoners "reenter" civil society successfully. Reduced employment and earnings of fathers certainly reduce the family incomes of their children and may have important intergenerational effects well beyond those measured here. The lost employment in neighborhoods and communities likely weakens employment networks and, more broadly, norms about work that suggest wider negative impacts.

These same criteria also partly account for the different methods used by the authors in this volume. Some authors address the central question in their chapters using new empirical inquiries, while others rigorously summarize existing literature. What distinguishes these methods of inquiry is whether there is substantial work in the area of concern. For example, Shawn D. Bushway and Raymond Paternoster (chapter 4, this volume) address the question of whether and the extent to which incarceration impacts crime rates. There is a substantial though varied literature in this area, so they critically evaluate the existing literature in relation to the general purpose of the book. Amy E. Lerman (chapter 5, this volume), on the other hand, uses unique prison data to examine the potential criminogenic impacts of imprisonment because this area of inquiry is largely understudied.

Still, while these methods of inquiry differ, the results are equally important as we attempt to answer the central questions of the book, especially in illuminating whether or not we are at a socially optimal level of incarceration given its benefits and costs. Indeed, in the concluding chapter of the book John J. Donohue III (chapter 9, this volume) uses many of the estimates and costs concepts provided by authors in this volume to carefully consider this question of optimality (that is, do the benefits equal the costs of imprisonment).

PLAN AND SUMMARY

The book is divided into three parts. Chapters 2 and 3 set the stage conceptually for the subsequent chapters. This section documents and explores the factors behind the unprecedented increases in incarceration occurring over the past three decades. Chapters 4 through 8 focus on benefits and costs of incarceration. Finally, chapter 9 seeks to address whether we are at a socially optimal level of imprisonment given the benefits and costs of incarceration.

Before evaluating the potential benefits and costs of U.S. imprisonment, it is important to understand the factors that drove the rapid increase in incarceration rates over the past twenty years. In chapter 2, Steven Raphael and Michael A. Stoll directly examine the question of why there are so many Americans in prison and why the incarceration rate increased so dramatically in such a short time period. As is noted in chapter 2, a nation's incarceration rate is determined both by the criminal behavior of its residents as well as by policy choices made by the electorate, elected officials, and representatives of the criminal-justice system. The relationship between criminal behavior and incarceration is simple and mechanical: the more people engage in criminal activity, the greater the proportion of the population at risk of "doing time." The determinants of criminal behavior, however, are complex and multifaceted and may include economic conditions, demographic characteristics, the incentives created by the criminal-justice system, and the institutional supports for individuals with a high propensity to offend.

On the policy side, choices defining which offenses are punishable by incarceration along with the pronounced severity of the punishment play a key role in determining the overall incarceration rate. The greater the scope of activities deemed deserving of a prison spell, the higher the fraction of the population that will be incarcerated. Moreover, longer sentences holding offense type constant will result in more prisoners. Again, however, the determinants of both the scope and severity of prison sentences are complex and often involve multiple branches of the U.S. criminal-justice system.

Using data primarily on population growth in state prisons, they find two principal changes that bear directly on growth in the incarceration rate and that provide a relative accounting of various behavioral and policy contributors to incarceration growth. First, they find that conditional on the violation that led to the prison sentence, the average time one can expect to serve has increased considerably in the United States. But, in the aggregate, increases in time served are not readily observable. That is, the average prisoner entering today will not serve more time on a given prison spell than the average prisoner admitted twenty-five years ago. The reason for this apparent anomaly is that the composition of prison admissions across violation or offense type has shifted decisively toward less serious offenses, with particularly large increases in the proportion of admissions accounted for by drug offenses and parole violations. All else held equal, this trend should have led to a decrease in average time served among the nation's prison inmates. But when comparisons of actual time served for recently admitted inmates are made relative to prison inmates admitted in decades past who have committed similar offenses, the authors observe quite large increases in actual time served. Their estimates suggest that this fact alone (increasing time served holding constant offense severity) explains about one-third of recent incarceration growth.

Second, in recent decades the rate at which inmates are admitted to prison has increased considerably, with overall prison admissions per capita more than doubling since 1979 and admissions per reported crime more than tripling. The lion's share of this increase in prison admissions is driven by a very large increase in the likelihood of being sent to prison conditional on being arrested for a serious crime. Both of these results suggest that changes in criminal-justice policy (in either scope or severity of punishment) can explain most of the increase in U.S. incarceration rates. As a result, Raphael and Stoll further note that a smaller proportion of the increase in prison admissions and, in turn, a smaller portion of the overall increase in incarceration is driven by increases in criminal behavior. They are unable to identify the exact policy changes that drove the increase, but speculate that a variety of policies have contributed (including minimum mandatory sentencing and truth-in-sentencing policy changes).

Raphael and Stoll's analysis provide compelling evidence that the rise in the nation's incarceration rates was driven principally by policy changes and not changes in behavior of individuals. These changes beg the question of what political and economic factors were influential in shifting criminal-justice policy. In chapter 3, David F. Weiman and Christopher Weiss address this question by examining the political economic roots of this new U.S. criminal-justice regime using New York's Rockefeller Drug Laws as a case study. Their analysis focuses on the war on drugs in the state of New York from the early 1970s to the early 1990s to illustrate their argument that the dramatic surge in incarceration rates especially among inner-city minority populations depended on critical decisions made at the local level—by mayors, police commissioners, and district attorneys and judges—in implementing and hence enforcing the sentencing policies enacted in state and federal capitols. They argue that the importance of grassroots rather than higher-order policies explains the significant lag between adoption of the notorious Rockefeller Drug Laws in 1973 and the surge in New York incarceration rates fueled by felony drug convictions and commitments after 1980. They show that the New York experience follows the national trends at least until the early 1990s, because the drug policies of the state, and especially of New York City, were forged in the same turbulent political economic crucible that shaped criminal-justice polices nationwide.

Their arguments regarding the war on drugs' influence in making criminal-justice policy more punitive are supported through historical analysis and perspective. They track trends in U.S. incarceration rates over the century before 1980 using comprehensive enumeration of the prison population by the census bureau. Their data show evidence of the relative stability of incarceration rates, except the period of acceleration in incarceration in the 1920s and 1980s. They argue that common political economic factors driving these changes are the war on drugs. They track changes in the percentage of inmates incarcerated on "moral" offenses between 1910 and 1980, where these respective periods roughly translate into the categories of public order and drug crimes. They show that between 1910 and 1923 the share of prisoners convicted on "moral" offenses jumped from 5.5 to 17.3 percent, an almost parallel increase to the surge in imprisoned drug offenders during the 1980s. This evidence is consistent with past work that has shown similarities between the legal wars against alcohol and drugs.

The major potential benefit of increases in incarceration is crime abatement. In the short term, incarceration is likely to reduce criminal activity by incapacitating active offenders and deterring those who would otherwise offend in the absence of an incarceration risk. Increased imprisonment could also prove socially beneficial if in fact prison helps rehabilitate those with strong criminal tendencies. In chapter 4, Shawn D. Bushway and Raymond Paternoster examine whether these policy reforms have led to these anticipated outcomes. As they note, sentencing policy in modern society is driven by two main approaches: retributive and instrumental philosophies. The former refers to "just desserts" or punishment that should be proportionate to the harm of that crime, while the later refers to approaches that reduce the harm of crime by reducing crime itself. In both approaches however, incarceration is just one of the tools used by policymakers to achieve these competing goals. Yet, the research evidence of whether these approaches are working differ dramatically.

For the purposes of our inquiry, the instrumental approach to crime is of greatest concern. Following the logic of this approach, Bushway and Paternoster in part focus on four main goals of incarceration as an instrumental approach to punishment and crime reduction: the short-term goals of deterrence and incapacitation, and the long-term goals of specific deterrence and rehabilitation. Each of these concepts represents a distinct theoretical process by which prison can lead to reduced crime. General deterrence posits that the threat of punishment immediately leads to less crime. Incapacitation is based on the notion that offenders cannot commit crime in larger society while in prison. Specific deterrence suggests that the experience of prison leads to changes in the perceptions about the cost of punishment such that the individual makes a different choice when faced with the same decision. Finally, rehabilitation says that the experience of prison (or the programs experienced in prison) leads to reductions in criminal propensity.

In comprehensively reviewing the voluminous literatures in these areas, Bushway and Paternoster note the fundamental problem in generating a causal estimate of increased incarceration on crime: the simultaneity between crime rates and prison rates. When crime goes up, policymakers can respond by increasing prison rates; but, at least theoretically, when prison rates go up, crime goes down. This simultaneous relationship between prison and crime means that a null finding at the aggregate level implying no relationship between crime and prison could be misleading. Despite this, they find evidence that the probable elasticity of prison and crime is somewhere in the –0.2 to –0.4 range (see also Donohue, chapter 9, this volume), meaning that a 10 percent increase in incarceration will lead to a 2 to 4 percent reduction in crime rates. While they note that this elasticity is in the region where the costs and benefits of increased imprisonment are exactly balanced, recent evidence suggests that it has been decreasing in recent years, as incarceration levels have increased. This suggests very little empirical support for increased incarceration at the aggregate level as a crime control strategy. However, they note that while aggregate level impacts of imprisonment on crime are important, more attention should be paid to the individual level impacts of imprisonment. For these they argue, the literature on deterrence in criminology, though rare, is clear that changes in perceived punishments lead to decreased crime, but that its effects vary across individuals.

But what about the costs of incarceration? While many of these costs (such as the direct monetary costs of incarceration) are obvious, many are not. One of these potential costs is that incarceration itself could lead to increased criminality, despite the literature discussed by Bushway and Paternoster that suggest the potential rehabilitative experience of prison (or the programs experienced in prison) could lead to reductions in criminal activity after release. In chapter 5, Amy E. Lerman examines the effects of prison conditions on inmates. Specifically, she investigates a very little studied, yet important, question of whether incarceration in different types of prisons can have criminogenic consequences. She uses unique survey data from the California Department of Corrections and Rehabilitation (CDCR) to address this question. The use of this data is important since CDCR oversees the third-largest prison system in the world, second in size only to the federal Bureau of Prisons and the Chinese national correctional system.

Of course, it is very difficult to identify the causal effect of imprisonment on criminal propensity, since they can be simultaneously determined. Presumably, those incarcerated may have such tendencies to begin with. Of course, the key question is whether imprisonment increases or intensifies these above the levels at time of prison admittance. Lerman uses a regression discontinuity design to overcome this problem to assess these effects of prison culture on inmate criminal psychology. The CDCR places inmates into a particular security level based on a numerical classification score. If an inmate's score falls within a certain range, he is placed in the corresponding security level. The regression discontinuity takes advantage of the fact that, assuming there is a certain amount of randomness in the calculation of the score, assignment of a value just above or below the cutoff point should approximate randomization; the only variable that should be discontinuous at the threshold is the security level to which an inmate is assigned. With this placement method, it is possible to estimate the effect of being placed in a higher relative to a lower security level.

The findings in chapter 5 indicate that there is a significant adverse effect on prisoners of placement in a higher-security prison. But the effect does not appear significant in the sample as a whole. Instead, the effect of security placement appears only for those with little or no prior criminal involvement—those who have the fewest prior jail commitments, arrests, convictions, or probations. These findings suggest that the move towards more punitive prisons over the past few decades may have had undesirable consequences. If incarcerating individuals in more punitive prisons leads them to adopt antisocial attitudes, this may result in detachment from prosocial networks, a further deterioration of adherence to social and legal norms, and ultimately a greater likelihood of recidivism following release.

In chapter 6, Rucker C. Johnson explores another far less-documented consequence of incarceration: the increase in the proportion of children who grew up with a parent incarcerated at some point during their childhood. This phenomenon has a clear racial implication as well, as black children are far more likely than white children to have a parent involved in the criminal justice system. This contributes to the growing gulf between the early-life experiences of white and black children, and the profound effects on their later-life socioeconomic attainments. The key question he explores is, What are the effects, if any, of parental incarceration on child outcomes, including early antecedents of youth crime?

Johnson examines this and other related questions using data from the Panel Survey of Income Dynamics (PSID). He first produces nationally representative estimates of the prevalence of parental incarceration for children born between 1985 and 2002, by race and socioeconomic status. He then focuses on examining the consequences of parental incarceration on children's outcomes. He finds at the general level that the prevalence rates of parental incarceration at some point during childhood are significantly larger than point-in-time estimates, so that cumulative profiles of risk show more prevalence of this phenomenon than simply examining this question at one point in time. More significantly, he finds that 20 percent of black children had a father with an incarceration history; among black children with fathers who did not graduate from high school, an alarming 33 percent had fathers with an incarceration history (much higher than those for whites and much higher than prediction using non–nationally representative samples).

More importantly, Johnson finds a strong correlation between children from families with an incarceration history and children's behavioral outcomes: they have worse outcomes than those from families without an incarceration history. He employs several different empirical strategies to distinguish whether this correlation emanates primarily from observed and unobserved disadvantaged childhood-environment characteristics as opposed to causal effects of parental incarceration. The findings are remarkably similar across all of the empirical model specifications and suggest that parental incarceration exposure leads children to develop greater behavioral problem trajectories. He further speculates on the extent to which parental incarceration exacerbates racial disparities in childhood and in early adulthood outcomes.

Of course, one of the potential and obvious costs of growing incarceration is its impact on state budgets. In 1980, states spent an average of about $280 million on corrections, or about $60 per person. By 2000, states were spending $1 billion on average, or about $164 per capita (Ellwood and Guetzkow, chapter 7, this volume). What determines the growth in state spending on prisons? Does this level and change of spending on corrections impact spending on other budgetary categories, such as education, welfare, or health? John W. Ellwood and Joshua Guetzkow examine these and other related questions using data from state budgets and multivariate models in chapter 7.

Ellwood and Guetzkow show that while average levels of state spending on prisons has grown, they mask a great deal of variation across the states. In 2000, the five states that spent the most on corrections expended 2.6 times more per capita than the five states that spent the least on their corrections systems. Moreover the percentage of state budgets devoted to corrections spending also varies a great deal across states. However, state spending on corrections is positively associated with the percentage of the state population that is black and the incarceration and violent-crime rates, while it is negatively associated with state budgetary processes that set funding targets.

However, very few predictors are associated with changes in state spending on corrections over time. They find that the presence of requirements for performance measurement at the state level is associated with a lower rate of growth of state corrections spending between 1988 and 2000, but the presence of a performance management system and a budget that set out these performance measures is associated with increased spending on corrections over this period.

Most importantly, Ellwood and Gueztkow find that state spending on corrections crowds out spending on other budgetary categories. However, counter to expectations, such state spending only negatively impacts spending on welfare, while other budgetary categories such as education and health are largely unaffected.

In chapter 8, Harry J. Holzer critically evaluates the literature on whether and how incarceration affects employment prospects. A key reason to focus on the effect of incarceration on employment is because these effects are extremely important and directly affect a whole host of other factors that correlate with incarceration, including reoffending, recidivism, and other important and well-studied social factors like health status, community well-being, civic participation, and voting behavior (Raphael and Weiman 2007).

However, at least theoretically, the impact of incarceration on employment could be positive or negative. By deterring crime and perhaps by fostering additional educational attainment among prisoners, incarceration may have positive effects. But, by reducing work experience, labor-market contacts, and incentives to work (especially among those with child-support arrearages), incarceration could have negative effects on labor-force activity. The likely negative effects of incarceration on employer demand compound this likelihood, though it is unclear whether or not these effects are large enough to actually translate into lost earnings.

Holzer summarizes and evaluates a wide spectrum of research in this area employing alternative data sources and empirical methodologies, characterizing the research findings in terms of the estimated magnitudes of the effects of prior incarceration on future employment prospects. The object in doing so is to attempt to reconcile conflicting results and generate a useful summary of results from the literature in this area. Also, he identifies key methodological challenges in estimating the effect of incarceration on employment and earnings for each of the different methodologies employed to examine this question. Holzer identifies an important question of what is the appropriate counterfactual to examine this question, especially for those studies that use administrative data and "before-after" methodologies. Much of the literature using this data and approach find a zero effect of incarceration on subsequent employment and earnings (Holzer, chapter 8, this volume). Much like the arguments developed by Shawn D. Bushway, Michael A. Stoll, and David F. Weiman (2007), he notes that the before-after incarceration approach likely understates the effect of incarceration on subsequent employment and earnings. This is because such an approach does not take into consideration the likely upward trajectory of employment and earnings profiles during young-adult to prime-age working years of even less-educated men who are never incarcerated.

In sum, he concludes that while "credible" empirical evidence is mixed, much of it points to negative effects of incarceration on the subsequent employment and earnings of ex-offenders. Further, given reduced employment prospects, recidivism rates of released offenders are likely to be affected in a negative direction, which in turn impose further costs on society (in the form of both crime and incarceration expenditures). Policies designed to reduce these collateral costs, either through direct reductions in incarceration rates or through their negative effects on subsequent earnings, might generate positive benefits to the ex-offenders and to society more broadly.

Given its potential costs and benefits, it is possible that many states have reached incarceration levels that are beyond the social optimum. Using a variety of different yet relevant estimates and methodological approaches, John J. Donohue III addresses this question in chapter 9 by carefully constructing a benefit-cost analysis of incarceration levels. To help determine the socially optimal level of incarnation, five questions must be answered:

1. What is the magnitude of any incarceration-induced drop in crime?

2. What is the monetized value of this decrease in crime?

3. What is the marginal cost of incarceration needed to generate these marginal benefits in crime reduction?

4. Does this cost-benefit calculus suggest that a certain level of incarcerations is efficient?

5. Could a reallocation of resources to alternative crime-fighting strategies achieve the same benefits at lower social costs?

But, as Donohue argues, these are difficult questions to address, thus making conclusions drawn from these types of studies problematic.

After considering various cost-benefit estimates and the variation in their ranges given different assumptions and methodologies, Donohue does in fact conclude that it is very difficult to provide clear insight regarding the optimal level of incarceration. But he finds that such an exercise helps one to think systematically about what the relevant marginal costs and benefits of incarceration are. In doing this and thinking about what the optimal crime-fighting policy is, more discussion and thought should be directed at the following questions:

1. Should utility of prisoners or their families count?

2. Should utility of victim families count (although perhaps this is implicit in willingness to pay estimates)?

3. Should pure transfer costs be included in the cost of crime?

4. Should the important issue of murder victimization be treated in a more nuanced way to reflect the different social costs attending the deaths of those involved in criminal behavior?

Donohue suggests that if one includes a broader conceptualization of the costs associated with incarceration, such as the criminogenic effects of imprisonment itself as well as the collateral costs of imprisonment to individuals and communities, the conclusion drawn from such cost-benefit studies is likely to be that we have gone beyond the optimal incarceration level. Moreover, if one looks beyond a narrow cost-benefit calculus of incarceration to consider alternative crime-fighting approaches such as preschool enrichment strategies or other educational options, there is reason to believe that alternatives to incarceration might well appear more socially attractive than our current heavy reliance on incarceration as the predominant crime-fighting strategy.

Donohue's insights provide much support for what we observe to be the key punch line of this book: the current marginal benefit of crime reduction derived from incarceration might not outweigh the growing social and economic costs to society of added imprisonment. That is, the recent expansion of the prison system has likely been fueled by incarcerating growing numbers of those who could be viewed, as some have argued, as marginal offenders, or those who engage in and are caught for lesser offenses. These individuals likely pose less of a threat to society than those who commit more serious crimes.

Incarcerating these marginal offenders comes at great cost. These costs not only include the expenses associated with policing and adjudicating the offense, and building, maintaining, and supervising a prison cell to hold the prisoner. They also include the costs that prison itself could heighten one's propensity to offend, that children of the incarcerated and formerly incarcerated are more likely to commit crimes and go to prison, as well as a host of other costs to society such as reduced productivity through lowered employment and the opportunity costs to society of spending greater shares of public budgets on prisons, in addition to many other factors. If it is the case that the crime reducing benefits of incarceration are less pronounced for these marginal offenders, then the costs of incarceration may indeed exceed the benefits.

If our conclusions are on point, then society would be better off reducing its use of incarceration as a crime-fighting strategy in favor of other methods in this current environment. Certainly, the results from chapter 2 indicate that the growth in incarceration was driven principally by policy decisions made by society and much less by changes in criminal behavior of those in society. This suggests that policy choices as well as other factors will be important vehicles to achieve this goal. What might these other options be?

Fortunately, the chapters in this volume offer some explicit policy prescriptions to help deal with the more negative influences of imprisonment on important social and economic outcomes, even though most focus on the impacts of various crime policies in particular. In many instances, their analyses and policy ideas address those issues that come up at many stages of the criminal-justice system. As Donohue suggests, if we widen the conceptualization of the costs associated with incarceration or look at alternatives to incarceration to achieve the same benefit, we might be better off as a society to reduce the level of incarceration. But what avenues we pursue to achieve this remains an open question. Certainly, the ideas from chapters 2 and 3 suggest that sentencing and enforcement policy would be most appropriate place to look because changes in these policies were the primary drivers of the initial changes in incarceration levels. But how one does this is the central question, especially in times when political support for "get tough policies" remains widespread, and when political asymmetries remain a reality (that is, it is politically easier to get "tough" on crime than to get "soft" on crime).

The ideas in chapters 5 and 6 suggest that even small changes in sentencing and prison placements could have beneficial effects in reducing the collateral harm of imprisonment. Johnson's study identifies less-documented unintended negative consequences for children of incarcerated parents. To the extent that imprisoning parents may cause greater deviant behavior and crime in following generations—thus contributing to intergenerational transmissions of criminal involvement—criminal justice and sentencing policy may wish to consider these as potential negative externalities. The result of this classification may allow courts to treat parenthood as an extenuating factor in sentencing as a direct result of concerns about the child's well-being. This consideration could open the door for a more extensive range of services and supports including family- and child-support services when parental incarceration does occur.

Lerman suggests that changes in prison-placement methods could have beneficial effects as well. In deciding how to allocate inmates across prisons with respect to their level of security, she warns against blind use of even the most sophisticated modern risk-assessment instruments. These instruments predict the level of risk of the offender and the appropriate security level of imprisonment as a form of community corrections. She argues that practitioners should instead address the ways in which institutionalization impacts particular attitudes related to crime and criminality, which in turn may ultimately help decrease risk factors among those leaving prison, and more effectively manage community-based monitoring and treatment.

Postrelease policy or program reforms should also help smooth the ex-inmates transition to society, which should help mitigate collateral costs to individuals and communities. In chapter 8, Harry J. Holzer strongly advocates for programs to support prisoner "reentry," both before and especially right after their release. Successful programs rely on labor-market "intermediaries" to improve the access of offenders to employers, to improve offender basic skills or work readiness, and to provide employers with more accurate information about their recent work-related activities. Other state and federal policies might also be useful in this regard. Limiting unreasonable employment and occupational licensing restrictions should be encouraged, and state-level child-support policies should be reconsidered as well. This could include readjusting or even forgiving arrearages for men meeting their current orders. Finally, more effective tax credits and bonding should be provided to employers to offset the negative impacts of criminal history on their labor demand and Earned Income Tax Credit (EITC) extension for low-income men could be considered as well to help offset at least some of the negative incentive effects of incarceration.

NOTES

1. The Bureau of Justice Statistics estimates that the violent victimization rate per 1,000 persons twelve and older declined from 33 in 1992 to 13.6 in 2005 for African Americans. The comparable figures for whites are 16.9 and 6.5 (Bureau of Justice Statistics 2008b).
2. To gauge the validity of using the census data in this manner, in previous research Raphael (2005) compares estimates of the institutionalized population from the census to estimates of the incarcerated populations from other sources by race. While the census estimates are slightly larger than estimates of the incarcerated population from the Bureau of Justice Statistics, the disparities are quite small relative to the overall incarcerated population. The difference likely reflects the very small remaining inpatient population in U.S. mental hospitals.

REFERENCES

Bonczar, Thomas P. 2003. "Prevalence of Imprisonment in the U.S. Population, 1974-2001." Bureau of Justice Statistics Special Report, NCJ 197976. Washington: U.S. Department of Justice.

Braman, Donald. 2004. *Doing Time on the Outside: Incarceration and Family Life in Urban America*. Ann Arbor, Mich.: University of Michigan Press.

Bureau of Justice Statistics. 2008a. *Key Facts at a Glance*. http://www.ojp.usdoj.gov/bjs/glance/tables/expgovtab.htm.

Bureau of Justice Statistics. 2008b. *Serious Violent Victimization Rates by Race, 1973–2005*. http://www.ojp.usdoj.gov/bjs/glance/tables/racetab.htm.

Bushway, Shawn, Michael A. Stoll, and David F. Weiman. 2007. *Barriers to Reen-*

try? The Labor Market for Released Prisoners in Post-Industrial America. New York: Russell Sage Foundation.

Butcher, Kirsten F., and Anne Morrison Piehl. 2006. "Why Are Immigrant Incarceration Rates So Low? Evidence on Selective Immigration, Deterrence, and Deportation." Working paper. New Brunswick, N.J.: Rutgers University.

Currie, Elliot. 1998. *Crime and Punishment in America.* New York: Owl Books.

DiIulio, John. 1996. "Prisons Are a Bargain, By Any Measure." *New York Times,* January 16, A19.

Jacobson, Michael. 2005. *Downsizing Prisons: How to Reduce Crime and End Mass Incarceration.* New York: New York University Press.

Manza, Jeff, and Christopher Uggen. 2006. *Locked Out: Felon Disenfranchisement and American Democracy.* New York: Oxford University Press.

Mauer, Marc, and Meda Chesney-Lind. 2003. *Invisible Punishment: The Collateral Consequences of Mass Imprisonment.* New York: New Press.

Patillo, Mary, David F. Weiman, and Bruce Western. 2004. *Imprisoning America: The Social Effects of Mass Incarceration.* New York: Russell Sage Foundation.

Pettit, Becky, andBruce Western. 2004. "Mass Imprisonment and the Life Course: Race and Class Inequality in U.S. Incarceration." *American Sociological Review* 69(April): 151–69.

Raphael, Steven. 2005. "The Socioeconomic Status of Black Males: The Increasing Importance of Incarceration." In *Poverty, the Distribution of Income, and Public Policy,* edited by Alan Auerbach, David Card, and John Quigley. New York: Russell Sage Foundation.

Raphael, Steven, and David F. Weiman. 2007. "The Impact of Local Labor Market Conditions on the Likelihood That Parolees Are Returned to Custody." In *Barriers to Reentry? The Labor Market for Released Prisoners in Post-Industrial America,* edited by Shawn Bushway, Michael Stoll, and David Weiman. New York: Russell Sage Foundation.

Travis, Jeremy, and Michelle Waul. 2004. *Prisoners Once Removed: The Impact of Incarceration and Reentry on Children, Families and Communities.* Washington, D.C.: Urban Institute Press.

Western, Bruce. 2006. *Punishment and Inequality in America.* New York: Russell Sage Foundation.

Zimring, Franklin, and Gordon Hawkins. 1988. "The New Mathematics of Imprisonment." *Crime and Delinquency* 34(4): 425–36.

PART I

Prison Boom
Context

Steven Raphael
and
Michael A. Stoll

2 | Why Are So Many
Americans in Prison?

The United States currently incarcerates its residents at a rate that is
greater than any other country in the world. Aggregating the state and
federal-prison populations as well as inmates in local jails, there were 737
inmates per 100,000 U.S. residents in 2005 (International Centre for Prison
Studies 2007). This compares with a world average of 166 per 100,000 and
an average among European Community member states of 135. Of the
approximately 2.1 million U.S. residents incarcerated in 2005, roughly 65
percent were inmates in state and federal prisons, while the remaining 35
percent resided in local jails.

Moreover, current U.S. incarceration rates are unusually high relative
to historical U.S. figures. For the fifty-year period spanning the 1920s
through the mid-1970s, the number of state and federal prisoners per
100,000 varied within a ten- to twenty-unit band around a rate of approximately 110. Beginning in the mid-1970s, however, state-prison populations grew at an unprecedented rate, nearly quadrupling between the
mid-1970s and the present. Concurrently, the rate of incarceration in local
jails more than tripled.

Why are so many Americans incarcerated? Why did the incarceration
rate increase so much in such a short time period?

A nation's incarceration rate is determined both by the criminal behavior of its residents as well as by policy choices made by the electorate,
elected officials, and representatives of the criminal-justice system. The
relationship between criminal behavior and incarceration is simple and
mechanical: the more people that engage in criminal activity, the greater
the proportion of the population at risk of doing time. The determinants
of criminal behavior, however, are complex and multifaceted. Public policies defining which offenses are punishable by incarceration along with

the pronounced severity of the punishment also play a key role in determining the overall incarceration rate. Clearly, the greater the scope of activities deemed deserving of a prison spell are the higher the fraction of the population that will be incarcerated. Moreover, holding offense type constant, longer sentences will result in more prisoners.

The past twenty-five years have witnessed several shocks to the likely behavioral determinants of incarceration as well as many drastic policy changes pertaining to the scope and severity of punishment. Changes in illicit drug markets, the deinstitutionalization of the mentally ill, the declining labor-market opportunities for low-skilled men, changes in sentencing policy, and a more punitive community corrections system are all commonly offered as explanations of recent trends. This chapter seeks to sort out these competing hypotheses and to offer a comprehensive evaluation of the sources of the increase in U.S. incarceration rates.

We focus primarily on the growth in state-prison incarceration, though we often analyze variation in the overall incarceration rate inclusive of federal prisons and jails. Over the last two and a half decades, we observe two principal changes that bear the lion's share of responsibility for growth in the nation's incarceration rate. First, conditional on the violation that led to the prison sentence, average time served has increased considerably. Second, the likelihood of being sent to prison conditional on committing a crime has increased substantially. These facts suggest that changes in sentencing policy along the extensive margin (defining the difference between offenses meriting incarceration and those that do not), as well as along the intensive margin (determining average time served), explain most of the increase in U.S. incarceration rates. A relatively small proportion of the overall increase in incarceration is attributable to increases in criminal behavior (at most, 17 percent of overall growth).

We begin by presenting a simple model of the steady-state incarceration rate. The model is used to outline an empirical decomposition that permits attributing relative importance of changes in sentencing policy and changes in criminal behavior in understanding the increase in incarceration rates. We then present estimates of the key component statistics (time served by offense, admissions rates, crime rates, and so on) needed to perform the decomposition.

Next, we analyze the possible effects of several potential shocks to criminal behavior. In particular, we explore and quantify the potential contribution of changing demographics, the deinstitutionalization of the mentally ill, the declining value of real wages earned by less-skilled men, and the influence of recent drug epidemics. In all, the collective influence of these factors is minor relative to the impact of changes in sentencing and corrections policy choices.

INCARCERATION GROWTH IN THE UNITED STATES: A SIMPLE MODEL

Over the past three decades, the U.S. prison incarceration rate has increased to unprecedented levels. Figure 2.1 displays the number of state and federal prison inmates per 100,000 U.S. residents. Prior to the mid-1970s, the incarceration rate was stable, hovering around 110 inmates per 100,000. Between 1975 and 2004, the prison incarceration rate more than quadrupled, from a rate of 111 to 484 per 100,000. The annual incarceration rate increased by an average of 15.7 inmates per 100,000 per year during the 1980s, 16.8 inmates per year during the 1990s, and 3.1 inmates per year during the first few years of the twenty-first century.

Behind this steady increase in the incarceration rate are large flows of inmates into and out of the nation's prisons. While there are certainly many prisoners serving very long sentences in the nation's penitentiaries (inmates most likely to be captured by point-in-time snapshots of the prison population), many more U.S. residents serve relatively short spells in prison and cycle in and out of correctional institutions serving sequential short spells over substantial portions of their adult lives. As demonstrated by Jeremy Travis (2005), nearly all inmates are eventually released from prison, most within five years of admission. Most tellingly, annual admissions to U.S. prisons have consistently hovered around one-half the size of the prison population, while roughly half of all inmates are released in any give year. In recent decades, admissions have consistently exceeded releases, resulting in sustained increases in incarceration rates.

To broadly characterize the policy and behavioral forces driving the increases in figure 2.1, here we present a simple model of steady-state incarceration rates that helps illuminate the basic determinants of the size of this institutional population. Let c_{it} be the number of crimes per capita of type i ($i = 1, \ldots, I$) committed in year t, and let p_{it} be the corresponding number of prison admissions per crime committed. The latter parameter measures the incarceration risk per criminal act. Let θ_{it} be the proportion of prison inmates incarcerated at the beginning of year t for commission of crime i who are released over the course of the year.

The probability that a nonincarcerated person is sent to prison in year t for committing crime i is given by $c_{it}p_{it}$, while the proportion flowing into prison for this crime is given by one minus the beginning-of-period overall incarceration rate, times this transition probability. The proportion of the population convicted of this crime that is flowing out of prison over a year is the starting incarceration rate for crime i multiplied by the release rate θ_{it}. The average release rate also provides a proxy measure for the amount of time that the typical inmate serves during a given spell in prison. The higher the release rate, the lower the average time served. A

Figure 2.1   *Prisoners in State or Federal Prison per 100,000 U.S. Residents, 1925 to 2004*

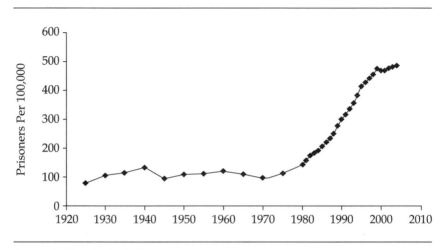

Source: Authors' calculations.

simple approximation is that the average time served is equal to one divided by the release rate.[1] Thus, a release rate of 0.5 corresponds to an average time served of two years, while a release rate of 0.33 corresponds to an average time served of three years.

In the implicit steady state at time t, the equilibrium incarceration rate for committing crime i is approximately equal to the transition probability for the flow rate into prison divided by the sum of the admissions and release rate transition probabilities,[2] or

$$Inc_{it} \approx \frac{c_{it}p_{it}}{c_{it}p_{it} + \theta_{it}} \qquad (2.1)$$

In practice, the transition probability into prison ($c_{it}p_{it}$) for a given crime will be a very small number, while the release rate θ_{it} will be relatively large. Thus, approximating the denominator by $1/\theta_{it}$ and making use of our approximation of time served, the steady-state incarceration rate for crime i can be rewritten as

$$Inc_{it} = E(T_{it})c_{it}p_{it} \qquad (2.2)$$

where $E(T_{it})$ is the expected value of time served. Finally, the overall steady-state incarceration rate is derived from the crime-specific incarceration rates by summing over i, giving

$$Inc_{.t} = \sum_i E(T_{it})c_{it}p_{it} \tag{2.3}$$

Equation 2.3 provides a simple accounting identity that is helpful in thinking through the potential sources of the patterns in Figure 2.1. Assuming that crimes are homogeneous within categories i, there are three potential sources of increase in the incarceration rate, two of which are determined by policy and one by behavior (although, of course, these three components may react to one another). Beginning with the policy determinants, increases in the expected value of time served for any or all of the crimes will increase the steady-state incarceration rate. Thus, sentence enhancements, truth-in-sentencing policies that dictate that inmates must serve larger fractions of their maximum sentences, or changes to parole policy that lowers the release probability conditional on time served will all increase incarceration rates through $E(T_{it})$. Indeed, the 1980s and 1990s witnessed many such changes to state as well as federal sentencing policy. Thus, such an expansion of the incarceration rate along the intensive margin is likely to be important (Raphael and Stoll 2007).

Second, increases in the likelihood that committing a given crime results in a prison admission will also increase the incarceration rate. Here, more intensive policing, increases in arrest rates, and a greater propensity to punish a given crime with incarceration will all increase the incarceration rate through the values of p_{it}. Simple comparisons of prison admissions per crime suggest that enforcement, prosecutorial, and sentencing policies have shifted decisively toward generating more admissions per crime committed.

Finally, changes in criminal behavior operating through the crime rate will impact the overall incarceration rate. Since the late 1970s, the United States has experienced several shocks that may have altered the distribution of the behavioral predisposition of U.S. residents toward criminal activity. For example, changing demographics and levels of educational attainment (tending toward less criminal activity), declining earnings prospects at the bottom of the earnings distribution (tending toward more crime), the continued deinstitutionalization of the mentally ill (tending toward more crime), and the introduction and diffusion of crack cocaine and crystal methamphetamine (tending toward more crime) have all occurred over the last three decades.

A simple method for decomposing the change in incarceration rates between two periods into a component attributable to policy change and a component attributable to behavioral change is as follows: Define time periods t = 0 and t = 1, between which the incarceration rate, the expected time served parameters, and the admissions per crime parameters all increase. Define the counterfactual crime rates, $c_{i1}*$(for $i = 1, \ldots, I$) as the crime rates that would have occurred in period 1 had the policy parameters not changed between periods 0 and 1. These counterfactual crime rates will differ from actual crime rates in period 1 due to the fact that under the sentencing parameters in period 0, the incarceration rate would be lower. A lower incarceration rate translates into smaller deterrence and incapacitation effects of prison on crime, and thus, more crime.

The change in the overall incarceration rate over this time period is given by

$$Inc_{.1} - Inc_{.0} = \sum_i E(T_{i1})c_{i1}p_{i1} - \sum_i E(T_{i0})c_{i0}p_{i0} \qquad (2.4)$$

The counterfactual incarceration rate that would have occurred had the policy parameters not changed is given by

$$Inc_{.*} = \sum_i E(T_{i0})c_{i*}p_{i0}, \qquad (2.5)$$

where the counterfactual crime rate for crime is multiplied by the corresponding spell length and admissions probability for year zero and then summed over all crimes. Adding and subtracting equation 2.5 to the right-hand side of equation 2.4 gives the final decomposition

$$Inc_{.1} - Inc_{.0} = (Inc_{.1} - Inc_{.*}) - (Inc_{.*} - Inc_{.0}) \qquad (2.6)$$

The first term on the right-hand side of equation 2.6 provides the extent to which the changing policy parameters increase the incarceration rate above and beyond the counterfactual change that would have occurred regardless. The second component displays what would have been observed had policy remained constant. Thus, the first term provides the estimate of the contribution of changes in criminal-justice policy, while the second term provides the contribution of changes in criminal behavior.

TRENDS IN THE BEHAVIORAL AND POLICY DETERMINANTS OF INCARCERATION RATES

Our simple model relates the steady-state incarceration rate to crime rates, average time served, and the likelihood of doing time conditional on committing a crime. Each of these broad components has changed in recent decades. We document these changes and use our empirical model to provide a rough decomposition of the growth in incarceration into policy and behavioral components.

Basic Trends

Table 2.1 provides estimates of all of the needed elements to calculate the steady-state incarceration rates in equations 2.3, 2.4, and 2.5 and the decomposition in equation 2.6. The first two columns present estimates of the time that an inmate admitted in either 1984 or 2002 can expect to serve on a given admission by reason for admission. These numbers come from synthetic cohort estimates of the time-served distributions for inmates admitted in 1984 and 1998 presented by Steven Raphael and Michael A. Stoll (2007), based on data from the National Corrections Reporting Program.[3] Over the time period analyzed, there are notable increases in the expected value of time served for all categories (on the order of 30 percent, but as high as 50 percent for larceny and other violent offenses, 64 percent for other property offenses, and nearly 80 percent for sexual assault). Even for inmates admitted for a parole violation (those not admitted with a new term for a new offense), average time served increased by 13 percent.

The next two columns present estimates of the number of prison admissions per 100,000 by offense category—that is, the joint product of the admissions per crime and the crime rate (cp).[4] With the exception of murder and burglary, there are increases in the overall admissions rate for each category. The most notable increases occur for drug crimes (from 7.73 to 43.93 per 100,000) and parole violators (from 20.48 to 80.75 per 100,000).

To split these overall admissions rates into crime rates and admissions per crime, one must divide the overall admissions rates by some measure of criminal offending for each year. For seven of the offense categories listed (murder, rape, robbery, assault, burglary, larceny, and motor-vehicle theft), the Federal Bureau of Investigations Uniform Crime Reports (UCR) provide estimates of the number of crimes per 100,000 reported to the police. We make use of these data for these crimes. To measure offending for drug crimes, we use the number of drug arrests per 100,000 for each year.[5] To measure crime rates for other violent crimes, other property crimes, and other crimes, we first estimate the average admissions per crime for each of the seven offenses with UCR crime-rate data (by dividing the admissions rate by the crime rate). These admissions-per-crime figures are used to approximate admissions per crime for the offenses lacking data on crime rates.[6] In combination with the total admissions rate for each of these offenses, the imputed admissions-per-crime rate allows us to back out crime rates for each of these addi-

Table 2.1 Comparison of Expected Time Served, Prison Admission Rates, Incarceration Risk per Crime, and Crime Rates for the United States by Type of Criminal Offense, 1984 and 2002

	Expected Value of Time Served in Years ($E(T)$)		Prison Admissions per 100,000 (pc)		Crime Rate per 100,000 (c)			Prison Admissions per Crime Committed (p)	
	1984	2002	1984	2002	1984	2002	2002 Counterfactual	1984	2002
Murder	6.49	8.13	5.47	4.98	7.92	5.63	6.95	0.69	0.89
Rape	2.98	5.30	4.35	7.70	35.71	33.11	42.01	0.12	0.23
Robbery	3.13	3.80	12.51	9.97	205.44	146.12	207.38	0.06	0.07
Assault	2.01	2.86	5.00	12.03	290.23	309.54	309.50	0.02	0.04
Other violent	2.30	3.47	1.72	3.53	21.34[a]	35.65[a]	44.45[c]	0.06[e]	0.10[e]
Burglary	1.99	2.48	19.08	14.21	1263.70	747.22	1,034.25	0.02	0.02
Larceny	1.44	2.17	13.93	17.83	2791.30	2,450.72	2,915.05	0.00	0.01
Motor vehicle	1.42	1.87	0.99	2.79	437.11	432.91	564.38	0.00	0.01
Other property	1.52	2.49	3.01	4.98	828.26[a]	725.46[a]	904.65[c]	0.00[f]	0.01[f]

Drugs	1.63	2.11	8.73	43.93	264.31[b]	469.68[b]	469.68[d]	0.03	0.09
Other	2.92	2.27	12.45	20.26	138.37[a]	184.18[a]	229.67[c]	0.06[g]	0.07[g]
Parole violators	1.27	1.44	20.48	80.75	—	—	—	—	—

Source: Time-served estimates come from Raphael and Stoll (2007). Each value is rescaled so that the expected value of time served is equal to the value implied by the national prison release rate for the year described. Prison-admissions rates are estimated by applying the distribution of admissions by offense category estimated from the 1984 and 2002 NCRP files to the overall national admissions rates. Crime rates are based the Uniform Crime Reports unless otherwise noted. Counterfactual crime rates are estimated using crime-specific incapacitation and deterrence effect estimates of incarceration on crime taken from Johnson and Raphael (2007).

[a] Crime-rate estimates based on imputed admissions per crime and the observed admissions rates.

[b] Crime rates for drug crimes are equal to the number of adult arrests for drug crimes per 100,000 U.S. residents.

[c] Assumes a 25 percent increase in offending above the 2002 level (equal to the 2002 admissions weighted sum of the predicted increase above 2002 for the seven part 1 offenses).

[d] Set equal to the arrest rate for 2002.

[e] Based on average admissions per crime committed for nonhomicide violent crimes by year.

[f] Based on average admissions per crime committed for nonburglary property crimes by year.

[g] Based on the weighted average admissions per crime for all crimes by year.

tional categories. A baseline crime rate for parole violations cannot be measured.

The data indicate that crime has been declining for most categories, although there are a few categories with slight increases between 1984 and 2002. The table displays substantial declines in crime rates for murder, rape, robbery, burglary, larceny, motor-vehicle theft, and the other property crime variables. The notable exception is for drug crimes, where drug arrests increase by nearly 80 percent. By contrast, the number of prison admissions per crime (estimates of p_{it}) increase uniformly over the time period.

The sizable increases in the expected values of time served as well as the increases in the admissions-crime ratio indicate that sentencing and enforcement policy are key driving forces behind the increasing incarceration rates displayed in figure 2.1. To more precisely decompose these changes, however, we need estimates of the counterfactual crime rates that would have occurred had the policy parameters remained constant at their 1984 values. To construct these counterfactual crime rates, we use the crime-specific estimates calculated by Rucker C. Johnson and Steven Raphael (2007) of the number of crimes prevented per prisoner incarcerated (the joint incapacitation and deterrence effects) to calculate what these crime rates would have been under this counterfactual scenario.[7] We first calculate the disparity between the incarceration rate in 2002 and 1984, and then we multiply this difference by estimates of the number of crimes per 100,000 prevented by incarcerating the average inmate. We then add this hypothetical prevented-crime total to the base crime in 2002. These numbers should be thought of as what the crime rate would be in 2002 were policymakers to reduce the incarceration rate to 1984 levels.[8] For drug crimes, we simply use the observed arrest rate as the counterfactual path.[9]

The counterfactual crime rates in table 2.1 suggest that had policy not changed, 2002 crime rates would have been closer to the 1984 levels, with some increases and some decreases. In particular, we would have still observed declines in the murder, rape, robbery, burglary, motor-vehicle crime, and other crimes rates. However, these declines would have been smaller than what actually occurred.

Decomposing the Changes into Policy and Behavioral Determinants

Table 2.2 presents estimates of the overall steady-state incarceration rate as well as rates by offense category for 1984 and 2002. The table also provides the counterfactual incarceration rate that would have been observed had sentencing policy not changed (that is, the rate described by

Table 2.2   Estimates Change in Steady-State Incarceration Rates, Overall and by Commitment Offense, and Calculation of Counterfactual Incarceration Rates Holding Policy Parameters Constant to 1984 Values

| | Implied Steady-State Incarceration Rates | | | Change, 1984 to 2002 | |
	1984	2002	2002 Counterfactual	Difference, 2002–1984	Difference, 2002 Counterfactual–1984
Murder	35.52	40.43	31.25	4.91	-4.27
Rape	12.98	40.81	15.27	27.84	2.29
Robbery	39.15	37.91	39.52	-1.23	0.38
Assault	10.03	34.36	10.70	24.33	0.67
Other Violent	3.97	12.24	6.46	8.27	2.49
Burglary	37.97	35.22	31.08	-2.75	-6.89
Larceny	20.02	38.62	20.90	18.60	0.89
Motor vehicle	1.41	5.22	1.82	3.81	0.41
Other property	4.57	12.41	4.99	7.85	0.42
Drugs	14.20	92.58	25.23	78.38	11.03
Other	36.30	45.94	60.26	9.63	23.95
Parole violators	26.05	116.38	—	90.34	—
Overall or total change in steady state	242.15	512.13	—	269.97	—
Overall or total change in steady state less parole violators	216.11	395.74	247.47	179.63	31.36
Actual overall incarceration rate	190.08	484.87	—	294.78	—

Source: Authors' calculations. See equations 2.1 through 2.3 in the text for the expressions for the steady-state incarceration rates.

equation 2.5). The last three rows of the table provide estimates of the overall steady-state incarceration rate, the steady-state incarceration not inclusive of those serving time for parole violations, and the actual incarceration rate for each year. The steady-state model predicts an incarceration rate of 242 per 100,000 in 1984 and 512 per 100,000 in 2002, for a total increase of 270 per 100,000. Relative to actual incarceration rates, the steady-state model overpredicts (more so in 1984 relative to 2002). These overpredictions are due to the fact the actual incarceration rates in each year deviate from steady-state rates, due to the fact that in each year the incarceration rate is in the process of converging to the higher steady state.[10] However, the predicted change in steady-state incarceration rates of 270 per 100,000 is quite close to the actual change of 295, thus providing a good ballpark approximation of actual trends.

The third column in table 2.2 presents estimates of the counterfactual incarceration rates by offense, overall, and overall excluding parole violators. The numbers suggest that under the sentencing and enforcement parameters of 1984, the 2002 incarceration rate would not have increased appreciably. In fact, for some crime categories there are small, predicted declines, and there is little change for others. Under this counterfactual scenario, the nonparolee incarceration rate is estimated at 247 per 100,000, only slightly more than the steady-state rate of 216 per 100,000 in 1984. Note, as this difference pertains to the behavioral component of the decomposition in equation 2.6, a counterfactual increase of 33 suggests that no more than 17 percent of the increase in nonparolee incarceration rates is attributable to behavior, with the remaining 83 percent attributable to stiffer, more punitive policy.

The data in table 2.1 can be utilized further to characterize the relative importance of sentencing-policy changes along the intensive and extensive margins. Specifically, the steady-state incarceration rate of 242.15 for 1984 is tabulated by calculating the product of time served and admissions by category in 1984 and then summing over crime categories. That is,

$$Inc_{1984} = \sum_{i=1}^{I} E(T_{i1984})c_{i1984}p_{i1984}$$

A comparable calculation was used to arrive at the steady-state incarceration rate of 512.13 for 2002. To isolate the importance of changes in time served, we calculate what the steady-state incarceration rate would have been had the expected value of time served remained at 1984 levels while admissions rates followed their observed empirical path. This counterfactual incarceration rate is given by the equation,

$$Inc_c = \sum_{i=1}^{I} E(T_{i1984})c_{i2002}p_{i2002}.$$

This calculation yields a steady-state incarceration of 417.57 per 100,000, a difference relative to the steady state for 2002 of approximately 95. In other words, had expected time served not increased between 1984 and 2002, the nation's incarceration rate would have been lower by 95 persons per 100,000. This constitutes roughly 35 percent of the overall increase in incarceration rate. Thus, with 35 percent of the increase attributable to expansion of incarceration along the intensive margin, and roughly 83 percent attributable to policy changes overall, roughly 48 percent of the overall increase in incarceration can be attributed to a greater propensity to incarcerate given the crime committed.

What About Parole?

The prison admissions rates in table 2.2 indicate that prison admissions due to parole violations have increased tremendously between 1984 and 2002, becoming by far the numerically most important source of prison admissions in recent years. In 1984, the number of parole admissions per 100,000 was relatively similar to the number of prisoners admitted for burglary (approximately 20 per 100,000 for each category). By 2002, the admissions rate for parole violators increased to slightly over 80, more than four times the admissions rate for burglary and nearly double the admissions rate for drug crimes.

Certainly, a large portion of this increase in parole admissions is driven by a growing population of parolees under the close scrutiny of parole officers. Returning a parolee to custody in many states is a much easier task than sentencing someone anew to prison, since parolees are technically serving the remainder of their sentence in the community and thus their partial liberty can be revoked without a new conviction (Petersilia 2003). However, in recent years the rate at which parolees are returned to custody has increased while the average severity of the conviction offense for those on parole has likely decreased. Specifically, between 1980 and 2003 the proportion of parolees nationwide that are returned to custody over the course of a year increased steadily from approximately 13 percent to 29 percent. Meanwhile, the average inmate (and by extension the average parolee) was older (and thus less criminally prone) and admitted to prison for offenses that generally receive shorter sentences (Raphael and Stoll 2007). In conjunction, these two facts suggest that parole policy has become tougher and thus is a key source behind the policy-driven increase in prison admissions.

While it is quite difficult to put a precise number on the relative contribution of changes in parole-failure rates, we can perform some simple simulations that permit a characterization of the likely order of magnitude of the effect of changes in parole policy on increasing incarceration growth. Specifically, we first perform a base simulation of the evolution of overall incarceration rates driven by changes in the transition probabilities between noninstitutionalization, prison, and parole. We then use the underlying model to simulate an alternative counterfactual incarceration rate under the assumption that the parole-failure rate remained at the 1984 level.

Specifically, we calculate the 1981 incarceration rate by first calculating the proportion of the noninstitutionalized population flowing into prison during 1980, the proportional flow from parole failures, and the proportional flow from 1980 prisoners that are not released from custody, and then summing these three components. The 1981 proportions on parole, not on parole, and not incarcerated can be calculated in a similar manner. Repeating these calculations for 1982 (using the calculated proportions for 1981) and for subsequent years would then provide the aggregate incarceration rate as a function of the sequence of observed admission and release rates.[11] Figure 2.2 presents a comparison of the simulated national incarceration rate using this iterative process for the period from 1980 to 2003 with the actual annual prison incarceration rates for these years. While the simulated incarceration rate increases by slightly more (to 504 per 100,000), the differences between the simulated and actual rates are never more than 5 percent and are often smaller.[12]

Using this simulation process, we then perform a counterfactual simulation designed to answer the following question: Assuming the rate at which parolees are returned to custody is held at its 1980 value, what path would the national incarceration rate have followed between 1980 and 2003? The results from this hypothetical simulation along with the base simulation are also displayed in figure 2.2. The simulations suggest that had the parole-failure rate remained constant, the incarceration rate in 2003 would be roughly 20 percent lower than that actually observed. Thus, changes in parole policy have clearly been an important source of growth in admissions over the past few decades.

POTENTIAL SOURCES OF CHANGES IN CRIMINAL BEHAVIOR

Having pinned down the overall likely contribution of behavioral shifts, we turn our attention to specific factors that are external to the criminal-justice system that may have altered the average criminality of the American public. In particular, we look at four topics: the nation's changing de-

Figure 2.2   *Actual Incarceration Rate, Incarceration Rate Simulated from Empirical Transition Rates, and the Simulated Incarceration Rate Holding Parole Failure Rates to the 1980 Level*

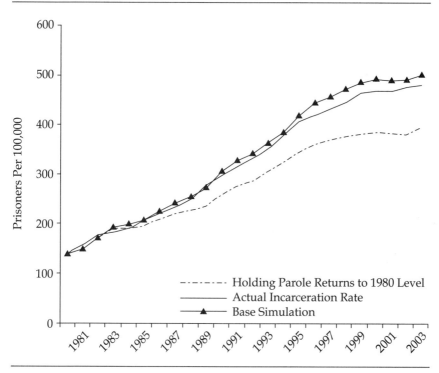

Source: Authors' calculations.

mography, the potential role of the deinstitutionalization of the mentally ill, changes in the legitimate labor-market opportunities available to low-skilled men, and shocks to drug markets in the United States—in particular, the introduction of crack cocaine.

Changing Demographics

In recent decades, we have observed several important demographic changes that bear directly on criminal offending and changes in incarceration rates. First, the proportion of the population that is foreign born has increased substantially, a pattern generally associated with lower incarceration rates (Butcher and Piehl 1998, 2006).[13] Second, the population has aged.[14] Since the likelihood of committing a crime decreases with age, this demographic shift should have also decreased crime and incarceration.

Finally, American adults have become more educated—an important trend considering that education is generally associated with lower offending and a lower likelihood of incarceration (Lochner and Moretti 2004).

The associations between these demographic factors and the likelihood of being incarcerated are evident in the tabulations in table 2.3. The table uses data from the 1980 and 2000 Public Use Microdata Samples (PUMS) of the U.S. Census of Population and Housing to calculate the proportion of men between eighteen and sixty-five years of age that were residing in institutionalized group quarters on the day of the census. From 1980 on, the lion's share of the nonelderly in such institutions are either in prison or jail.[15] Black men, men less than forty years of age, and the least educated men are the most likely to be institutionalized, with uniform increases in these rates between 1980 and 2000.

The nation's recent demographic trends have shifted population across these subgroups in a manner that should have decreased incarceration. In other words, the increases that we have experienced have bucked demographic trends given the correlations between these dimensions and the likelihood of being in prison or jail. This is most evident when looking at the distribution of the nonelderly adult male population across the subgroups defined by the categories in table 2.3. To demonstrate this fact, we first split the nonelderly adult male population into eighty demographic subgroups defined by the complete interaction of the four race-ethnicity groups, the five age groups, and four educational attainment groups used in table 2.3. Next, we use the 1980 PUMS data to calculate the proportion institutionalized for each group, and we then rank these groups by their institutionalization rates from lowest to highest. Finally, we compare the distribution of the male population across these eighty ranked groups in 1980 and 2000.

Figure 2.3 presents the results of this exercise. The figure presents the cumulative proportion of the male population in these eighty demographic groups ranked from least to highest institutionalization rates for 1980 and 2000. The distribution for 2000 is everywhere to the left of the distribution for 1980, indicating that the adult male population has shifted decidedly toward lower-offending demographic groups. The implications of this shift are made explicit in figure 2.4. The figure presents actual institutionalization rates for 1980 and 2000 as well as a hypothetical calculation giving what the institutionalization rate would have been in 2000 had the rates for the eighty individual groups not changed while at the same time the distribution of men across groups shifted as in figure 2.3. For all men and for men defined by race-ethnicity, the institutionalization rate in 2000 would have declined relative to that for 1980.

Note that we have only characterized the direction of the effect on in-

Table 2.3 The Proportion of U.S. Males Eighteen to Sixty-Five Institutionalized by Race-Ethnicity, Age, and Education, 1980 and 2000

	White		Black		Other		Hispanic	
	1980	2000	1980	2000	1980	2000	1980	2000
All	0.008	0.013	0.033	0.084	0.010	0.014	0.014	0.029
Age								
18 to 25	0.010	0.017	0.045	0.107	0.014	0.018	0.018	0.033
26 to 30	0.009	0.016	0.050	0.121	0.011	0.022	0.015	0.033
31 to 40	0.007	0.017	0.033	0.106	0.009	0.014	0.015	0.033
41 to 50	0.006	0.011	0.016	0.062	0.004	0.011	0.009	0.024
51 to 65	0.008	0.007	0.017	0.029	0.008	0.006	0.007	0.013
Education								
High School dropout	0.019	0.040	0.047	0.185	0.020	0.041	0.019	0.035
High School grad.	0.006	0.017	0.027	0.081	0.013	0.020	0.010	0.034
Some college	0.004	0.008	0.023	0.015	0.005	0.010	0.009	0.019
College graduate	0.002	0.003	0.008	0.047	0.002	0.002	0.004	0.008

Source: Tabulated from the 1980 and 2000 5 Percent Public Use Microdata Samples from U.S. Census of Housing and Population.

Figure 2.3   *Comparison of the Distribution of the U.S. Male Population Eighteen to Sixty-Five Across Demographic Groups Defined by Age, Education, and Race After Ranking Groups from Lowest to Highest According to Their 1980 Institutionalization Rates*

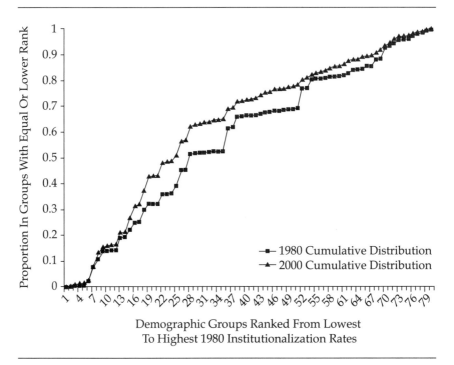

Demographic Groups Ranked From Lowest
To Highest 1980 Institutionalization Rates

Source: Authors' calculations.

carceration of the shifts in the distribution of the male population across groups defined by age, education, and race-ethnicity. Other demographic factors have also changed that are likely to have reduced the average criminality of the American public. First, the increasing proportion of foreign-born individuals tends to reduce crime as documented in the research of Kirsten F. Butcher and Anne Morrison Piehl (1998, 2006). An additional factor that has received much attention that we have not addressed is the impact of abortion legalization on changes in the composition of the population beginning around 1990. John Donohue and Steven Levitt (2001) hypothesize that the legalization of abortion has shifted the composition of those born toward wanted pregnancies and away from unwanted pregnancies. To the extent that children born under the latter category are more

Figure 2.4   *Actual Male Institutionalization Rates for 1980 and 2000 and Hypothetical Rates Using 2000 Population Shares and 1980 Institutionalization Rates*

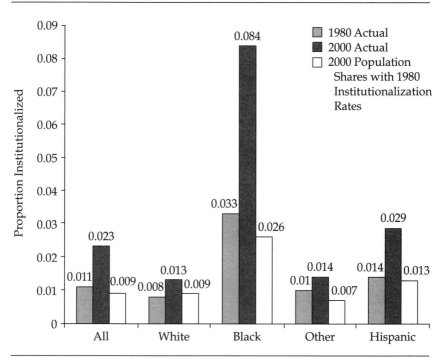

Source: Authors' calculations.

likely to commit crimes as a young adult, legalization should have had a lagged effect on criminal behavior, a supposition consistent with aggregate movement in violent-crime and property-crime rates.

Overall, the combination of these factors, as well as additional research findings, indicates that demographic trends should have reduced incarceration, all else held equal.

The Deinstitutionalization of the Mentally Ill

According to the BJS, there are nearly 300,000 mentally ill inmates in U.S. prisons and jails (Ditton 1999). These inmates account for 16 percent of state prisoners, 7 percent of federal prisoners, and 16 percent of local-jail inmates. Considering that roughly 2.8 percent of the adult pop-

Figure 2.5   *Prisoners per 100,000 Mental Hospital Inpatients per 100,000, and Total Institutionalized per 100,000, 1930 to 2000*

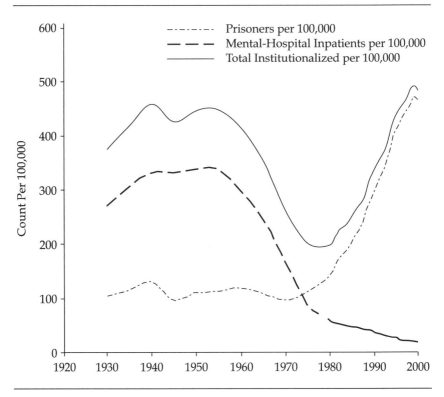

Source: Authors' calculations.

ulation suffers from severe mental illness over the course of a year (Torrey 1997), these figures indicate an incarceration rate for the mentally ill considerably greater than that of the general population. By contrast, by the end of the twentieth century there were roughly 60,000 inpatient residents in state and county mental hospitals. Thus, the population of incarcerated mentally ill is nearly five times the inpatient mental-hospital population.

That the incarcerated mentally ill population exceeds the inpatient population of mental hospitals is a relatively new development. In fact, as of midcentury, the number of mental-hospital inpatients per 100,000 U.S. residents greatly exceeded the overall prison incarceration rate. This fact is illustrated in figure 2.5. The figure presents state and county mental-hospital inpatients per 100,000, state and federal prisoners per 100,000, and the sum of these two series for each year between 1930 and 2000.[16] Through the 1950s, the mental-hospital inpatient rate was approximately three times the prison-incarceration rate. Beginning with the deinstitutionalization of the mentally ill in the 1960s, the inpatient rate declines precipitously, falling below the incarceration rate in the mid-1970s and continuing to decline thereafter.

Most notably, the overall institutionalization rate (defined as the sum of prisoners per 100,000 and inpatients per 100,000) at in the late 1990s was not high by historical standards. While the overall rate declines with deinstitutionalization, growth in state- and federal-prison populations more than compensates for this decrease by the late 1990s. The juxtaposition of these two trends begs the question of whether the mentally ill have been transinstitutionalized from mental hospitals to prisons and jails. If so, the deinstitutionalization of the mentally ill may have contributed to growth in U.S. incarceration rates.

Several studies have attempted to estimate the extent to which the mentally ill move between hospitals and correctional institutions. Lionel Penrose (1933) is perhaps the first to raise this issue. Data on eighteen European countries revealed a negative correlation between the size of the prison and mental-hospital populations. George B. Palermo, Maurice B. Smith and Franklin J. Liska (1991) find significant negative correlations between the size of mental-hospital population and prison and jail population in the United States over the period 1926 to 1989.

At least one recent study by Bernard E. Harcourt (2006) argues that, given trends in mental-hospital population counts, the explosion in the U.S. prison population may be more illusory than real. His study documents the inverse correlation between the two populations at the national level and tests for a negative association between total institutionalization and homicide rates. Harcourt writes,

> As a practical matter, empirical research that uses confinement as a value of interest should use an aggregated institutionalization rate that incorporates mental hospitalization rates. At a theoretical level, these findings suggest that it may be the continuity of confinement—and not just the incarceration explosion—that needs to be explored and explained. (1751)

Despite this research, there are several reasons to believe that the deinstitutionalization of the mentally ill plays only a minor role in explaining the massive increases in incarceration rates depicted in figure 2.1. Prime among these reasons is the large compositional differences between those

Table 2.4   *Distribution of Institution and Noninstitutional Populations Across Age Groups, Race-Ethnicity Groups, and Gender, 1950 Through 1980*

	1950			1960		
	Mental Hospital	Prison and Jails	Non-insti-tutional	Mental Hospital	Prison and Jails	Non-insti-tutional
Age groups	100%	100%	100%	100%	100%	100%
<10	0.85	0.84	19.51	0.43	0.03	22.03
10 to 17	1.06	11.10	11.51	1.66	2.85	14.21
18 to 25	5.31	27.54	12.13	5.03	30.01	9.86
26 to 30	6.32	17.28	8.19	4.30	16.38	6.13
31 to 35	8.02	12.88	7.54	5.94	13.76	6.73
36 to 40	8.40	8.69	7.45	7.36	11.86	6.90
41 to 45	8.34	7.23	6.53	8.32	8.39	6.39
46 to 50	11.16	5.24	6.08	9.52	6.40	5.89
51 to 55	11.69	4.08	5.20	10.11	4.78	5.28
56 to 64	18.54	3.25	7.75	18.61	4.50	7.71
65+	20.30	1.88	8.10	28.72	1.03	8.88
Race-Ethnicity	100%	100%	100%	100%	100%	100%
White	87.62	62.20	87.99	85.03	58.86	86.63
Black	10.52	33.40	9.90	12.73	35.57	10.47
Other	0.43	1.26	0.43	1.00	1.87	0.89
Hispanic	1.43	3.14	1.68	1.24	3.69	2.01
Gender	100%	100%	100%	100%	100%	100%
Male	52.55	90.79	49.60	53.23	95.10	49.01
Female	47.45	9.21	50.40	46.77	4.90	50.99
Population Estimate (000)	621	315	151,274	698	356	178,247

who are incarcerated in the late 1990s and those who were the inpatients of mental hospitals at midcentury.

Prison and jail inmates in the United States are overwhelmingly male, disproportionately minority, and are relatively young. The same cannot be said for mental patients at midcentury. Table 2.4 uses data from the PUMS census files for 1950 through 1980 to characterize mental-hospital inpatients, prison and jail inmates, and the noninstitutionalized.[17] In 1950, there are several notable differences between the inpatient population

	1970			1980	
Mental Hospital	Prison and Jails	Non-insti-tutional	Mental Hospital	Prison and Jails	Non-insti-tutional
100%	100%	100%	100%	100%	100%
0.57	0.15	18.48	0.73	0.04	14.77
3.59	3.43	16.18	6.26	2.23	13.69
9.09	39.67	12.76	14.63	43.15	14.80
6.13	16.67	6.43	9.18	21.66	8.41
5.75	11.24	5.50	9.02	12.90	7.41
6.50	9.15	5.51	6.91	7.65	5.97
8.04	6.69	5.85	6.95	4.60	5.06
8.02	5.34	5.90	5.81	2.67	4.91
9.00	3.29	5.28	7.76	2.41	5.20
18.33	3.35	8.11	12.52	1.63	8.54
24.99	1.03	10.00	20.24	1.06	11.24
100%	100%	100%	100%	100%	100%
82.80	54.67	85.52	79.40	47.14	81.50
15.45	40.29	11.03	17.15	42.65	11.65
0.93	1.82	1.18	1.95	5.14	3.41
0.82	3.23	2.27	1.50	5.07	3.45
100%	100%	100%	100%	100%	100%
55.95	94.84	48.45	60.79	94.10	48.37
44.05	5.16	51.55	39.21	5.90	51.63
440	341	202,257	246	461	226,024

Source: Tabulates from the 1950, 1960, 1970, and 1980 1 percent Public Use Micro Data Samples from the U.S. Decennial Censuses of Population and Housing.

and correctional population. First, the mental-hospital population is considerably older, with larger proportions over forty years old; the population that is sixty-five years and older is more than ten times the comparable figure for the correctional population. Second, the proportion that is black or Hispanic is not appreciably larger than the comparable proportions for the noninstitutionalized population, while minorities are very much overrepresented in prisons and jails. Finally, nearly half of the mental-hospital population is female, while in 1950 only 9 percent of

Figure 2.6   *Institutionalization Rates, All Adults and Adult Men by Race-Ethnicity*

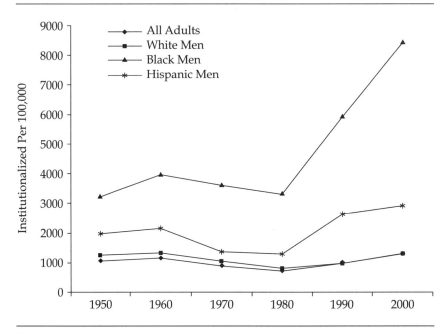

Source: Authors' calculations.

those in prison or jail were women. By 1980, this proportion declined to 6 percent.

Between 1950 and 1980, the mental-hospital inpatient population became younger, more minority, and more male, although the elderly and women still constitute larger proportions of the population of mental-hospital inpatients than they do of prison and jail inmates. These changes suggest that deinstitutionalization proceeded in a nonrandom fashion.

The limitations of deinstitutionalization as a major contributor to growth in incarceration are best illustrated by looking at overall institutionalization rates (combining mental-hospital, jail, and prison populations) by demographic subgroups. Figure 2.6 displays overall institutionalization rates for adult men between eighteen and sixty-five years of age by race-ethnicity using data from the PUMS files for 1950 to 2000. For the latter two years (1990 and 2000), the data do not permit separately identifying mental-hospital inpatients and prison and jail inmates. Nonetheless, the mental-hospital population in these years is trivially small rela-

Figure 2.7   *Institutionalization Rates for All Adults and For Adult Women by Race-Ethnicity, 1950 to 2000*

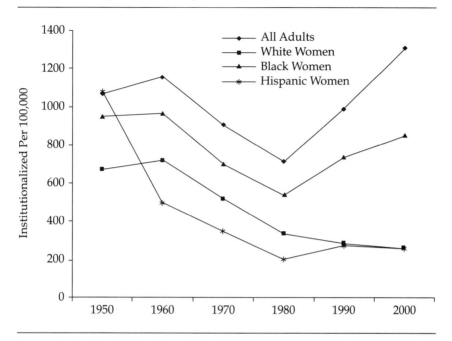

Source: Authors' calculations.

tive to correctional population, and thus the overwhelming majority of the institutionalized in these years are in jails or prisons. The most notable pattern in this figure is the large increase in the overall institutionalization rate for black men (the group that has contributed the most to increases in incarceration since 1980). Prior to 1980, the peak institutionalization rate for this group was slightly less than 4,000 per 100,000. By 2000, this rate exceeded 8,000. For white and Hispanic men, overall institutionalization rates more closely mimic the time path of overall institutionalization rates for all adults.

Figure 2.7 presents comparable results for women. Here, the most notable fact is the large sustained decline in the overall institutionalization rate of white women (a demographic group that constituted a sizable portion of the mental-hospital inpatient population in 1950). Hispanic women also experience large declines in overall institutionalization rates, while the time path for black women mimics the time path for all adults.

This group-specific analysis can be used to place an upper bound on the potential contribution of changes in the inpatient population on prison and jail growth. We perform this analysis in table 2.5. The first column presents the number of mental-hospital inpatients per 100,000 adults between eighteen and sixty-five years old for men and women by race and ethnicity in 1980. The second column presents the change in the overall institutionalization rate between 1980 and 2000 for each group using data from the census. Note that because the census data do not permit separately identifying prison, jail, and mental-hospital populations in each year, these changes show the net increase after accounting for further deinstitutionalization post-1980. The third column presents the maximum proportional contribution of deinstitutionalization to increases in the incarceration rate for each group. We calculate this figure by simply dividing the inpatient rate in 1980 by the change in institutionalization between 1980 and 2000. For white women, we set this rate at zero because overall institutionalization declined. For other women, we set this rate at one because the inpatient rate in 1980 exceeds the increase in institutionalization between 1980 and 2000.

The fourth column presents the absolute increase in the number institutionalized for each group, with the total population in correctional institutions increasing by roughly 1.3 million between 1980 and 2000.[18] The next column presents estimates of the contribution of deinstitutionalization assuming that the mental-hospital population is reduced to zero and that the transinstitutionalization rate is one for one. The final column presents similar estimates assuming a transinstitutionalization rate of one new prisoner per 100,000 for every two-person decline in the number of mental-hospital patients per 100,000.

The larger of the two estimates suggests that deinstitutionalization contributed at most 255,702 individuals to the growth in the nation's prison and jail populations. This would constitute roughly 20 percent of growth between 1980 and 2000. However, this estimate is certainly too large, as the mental-hospital population in 2000 was not zero (it was actually closer to 60,000), and because many of those in mental hospitals in 1980 were elderly or were individuals unlikely to commit serious felonies. Assuming a transinstitutionalization rate of 0.5 yields a contribution of 127,851 (roughly 10 percent of the increase).

An alternative method of pinning down the contribution of deinstitutionalization would be to directly estimate this transinstitutionalization rate and use this figure to estimate the likely contribution. This is the strategy employed by Raphael (2000). The study uses state-level data for the period 1971 to 1996 to estimate the effect of the state mental-hospital inpatient rate on the state prison incarceration rate. After adjusting for state and year fixed effects and observable covariates, the model yields a transinstitutionalization rate of approximately –0.15. When combined

Table 2.5   Assessing the Maximum Possible Contribution of Deinstitutionalization to Growth in Prison and Jail Incarceration Between 1980 and 2000

	Mental-Hospital Inpatients per 100,000 (1980)	Change in Institution-alization per 1000,000 (1980 to 2000)[a]	Maximum Possible Proportional Contribution of Deinstitu-tionalization[b]	Actual Absolute Change in Population Institutionalized (1980 to 2000)	Absolute Contribution of Deinstitutionalization With Transinstitu-tionalization Rate of 1[c]	Absolute Contribution of Deinstitutionalization with Transinstitu-tionalization Rate of 0.5[c]
Men						
White	157	479	0.33	328,326	107,207	53,604
Black	323	5,120	0.06	584,251	36,836	18,418
Other	148	68	1.00	47,738	47,738	23,869
Hispanic	83	1,631	0.05	294,197	14,958	7,479
Women						
White	91	−73	0.00	−33,066	0	0
Black	134	311	0.43	48,786	21,000	10,500
Other	25	15	1.00	7,816	7,816	3,908
Hispanic	51	57	0.89	22,692	20,147	10,073
Total	—	—	—	1,300,740	255,702	127,851

Source: Authors' compilation.
[a]Figures provide the change in the total institutionalization rate between 1980 and 2000.
[b]Maximum proportion contribution is set to 1 when the change in institutionalization rate exceeds the 1980 mental-hospital inpatient rate.
[c]Tabulations assume that complete deinstitutionalization between 1980 and 2000.

with the decline in the number of mental-hospital inpatients per 100,000, this rate implies that deinstitutionalization increased the state incarceration rate by roughly 18 per 100,000 between 1971 and 1996 (roughly 5 percent of the increase in incarceration rates over this time period).

Thus, our upper-bound estimates indicate that deinstitutionalization accounted for no more than 10 percent of the increases in incarceration in recent decades. Research that attempts to directly estimate the transinstitutionalization rates suggests an even smaller role (5 percent).

The Effects of Increasing Earnings Inequality

The increase in U.S. incarceration rates since the mid-1970s coincides with profound changes in the distribution of earnings and income. Beginning in the mid-1970s, wage inequality increased greatly, with real absolute declines in the earnings of the least skilled workers and stagnating wages for workers at the center of the wage distribution (Autor and Katz 1999). Coincident with these changes in the earnings distribution are pronounced declines in the labor-force participation rates of less-skilled men (Juhn 2003). In particular, the labor-force participation and employment rates of relatively less-educated black men have dropped precipitously (Raphael 2005).

The potential connection between these labor-market changes and the increase in incarceration is relatively straightforward. The wage that one's time can command in the legitimate labor market represents the opportunity cost of allocating one's time toward other uses, such as participating in crime, taking leisure, engaging in home production, and so on. The lower one's potential earnings, the more attractive are criminal opportunities with income-generating potential. For individuals who are amoral and risk neutral, the necessary and sufficient conditions for committing a crime are that the expected return to devoting a small amount of time to crime must exceed both the value placed on free time (one's reservation wage) as well as potential legitimate earnings should this time be supplied to the labor market. For those morally averse to criminal activity and averse to risk, participating in criminal activity requires that the difference between the expected returns to crime and returns to legitimate work exceed a threshold that is increasing in the degree of moral as well as risk aversion.[19] Regardless, the likelihood of engaging in criminal activity (or stated differently, one's supply of time to criminal pursuits) should increase as potential earnings in legitimate employment decline.

Declining wage offers for the least skilled workers will induce a greater proportion to participate in crime, as those who are more risk averse and who are the least morally predisposed toward relative to those already engaged in criminal activity crime are peeled out of the legitimate labor market and into criminal activity on the margin. This relatively larger pool of criminals increases the fraction of the group at risk for incarceration and, holding the incarceration risk constant, increases the incarceration rate.

There is now considerable evidence that economically motivated crime increases with unemployment and decreases with average wages, especially the average wages of low-skilled workers. For example, Steven Raphael and Rudolf Winter-Ebmer (2001) find consistently positive effects of higher unemployment rates on property crime in an analysis of state-level panel data covering roughly the last quarter of the twentieth century. Using similar data, Eric D. Gould, Bruce A. Weinberg, and David B. Mustard (2002) find that property crime decreases with increasing wages. Jeff Grogger (1998) models the decision to participate in crime as a function of the wages one could earn in the labor market using microdata from the 1979 National Longitudinal Survey of Youth (NLSY79); he finds that a 10 percent increase in wages decreases the likelihood of participating in income-generating criminal activity by roughly 2.5 percentage points. As a final example, Richard B. Freeman (1987) finds that those youth who believe that they could earn more on the streets than in legitimate employment are more likely to engage in criminal activity.[20]

With regards to the question at hand, it is possible to formally characterize the chain of effects linking wage declines to incarceration, and then to glean estimates of these various effects to provide a rough assessment of the potential importance of increasing earnings inequality. To see this, suppose that the proportion of the population that engages in crime, c, is a decreasing function of wages (that is, $c = c(w)$ where $c'(w) < 0$). Assuming only one type of criminal offense, the steady-state incarceration rate will thus be given by the equation

$$Inc = \frac{c(w)p}{c(w)p + \theta},$$
(2.7)

where we express the proportion engaging in crime as a function of wages in the legitimate labor market. The change in the incarceration rate caused by a small change in wages can be found by differentiating equation 2.7 with respect to wages. Doing so gives,

$$\frac{\partial Inc}{\partial w} = \frac{\partial Inc}{\partial c} \cdot \frac{\partial c}{\partial w} = \frac{\theta}{(cp + \theta)^2} \cdot p \cdot \frac{\partial c}{\partial w}$$
(2.8)

The final expression in equation 2.8 indicates that the effect of a small change in wages on the incarceration rate can be broken down into three components from right to left. First, a change in wages will impact the proportion of men supplying time to criminal pursuits (accounted for by the term $\frac{\partial c}{\partial w}$). Second, this increased criminality will generate new admissions to prison, as some proportion of new offenders (given by the parameter p) will be caught and incarcerated.

Finally, the impact of the increase in prison admissions on the incarceration rate (generated by $p\frac{\partial c}{\partial w}$) will be magnified by the amount of time an imprisoned offender is likely to serve. This magnification factor derives from the term $\frac{\theta}{(cp+\theta)^2}$. Note that in practice the product cp is likely to be a relatively small number (less than 0.003), while the release rate, θ, is likely to be relatively large. These two empirical facts imply that the magnification factor should be approximately equal to the ratio $1/\theta$. This term provides a relatively accurate approximation of the expected value of time served. Thus, longer average times served (or lower release rates) result in greater likely effects of a change in wages on the overall incarceration rate.

We use equation 2.8 to provide a rough approximation of the potential impact of changes in the national wage structure on the overall incarceration rate. Specifically, let $i = (1, \ldots, I)$, index I racial groups; and let $j = (1, \ldots, J)$, index J educational-attainment groups. For subgroups of men defined by race and educational attainment, we estimate how much lower the 2000 incarceration rate would have been had the average wages of the group not declined between 1980 and 2000. Specifically, we tabulate the estimates

$$\Delta I\hat{n}c_{ij} = \frac{\theta}{(cp+\theta)^2} \cdot p \cdot \frac{\partial c}{\partial \ln w_{ij}} \cdot d\ln w_{ij}, \tag{2.9}$$

where we have substituted the natural log of wages for wage levels, and where $d\ln w_{ij}$ gives the change in the average log wages for group ij between 1980 and 2000. Because average wages decline for those groups experiencing the largest increase in incarceration, the calculation in equation 2.9 provides us with an estimate of what the incarceration rate in 2000 would be if wages were restored to their earlier levels.

With the group-specific calculations in equation 2.9, we can estimate the proportion of the increase in incarceration attributable to changes in the wage structure. Specifically, taking a weighted average of the group-specific incarceration-wage effects would give

$$\Delta \hat{I}nc = \sum_i \sum_j M_{ij} \Delta I\hat{n}c_{ij},$$

(2.10)

where M_{ij} is the proportion of adult males accounted for by demographic group ij. Equation 2.10 gives the overall effect of changes in the wage structure on the 2000 incarceration rate, accounting for the proportional representation of the different race-education groups among the adult male population. Comparing the group-specific changes from equation 2.9 to actual increases in incarceration provides an estimate of the proportional contribution of changes in labor-market opportunities for each group. Comparing the weighted change in equation 2.10 to the overall change in male incarceration rates provides an overall estimate of the effect of economic changes.

Estimating equations 2.9 and 2.10 requires that we choose values for the parameters in these equations. Beginning with the term $\dfrac{\partial c}{\partial \ln w}$, the only estimate of the responsiveness of criminal participation to changes in wages that we are aware of is provided by Grogger (1998). He estimates that the effect of a change in the natural log of hourly earnings (hence the substitution to log wages in equation 2.9) on the likelihood of engaging in income-generating activity is approximately –0.25. Note that this estimate pertains to a NLSY79 sample from 1980 of males between fifteen to twenty-two years of age not enrolled in school or the military, where disadvantaged minority men were oversampled. This particular demographic group is likely to be the most predisposed towards criminal activity, and thus the estimated responsiveness will certainly be on the high side when applied to older and more educated men. As this is the only estimate we have to work with, our calculations presented below should be interpreted as upper-bound estimates.

To estimate the likelihood of being caught and incarcerated, one could pursue a number of potential strategies. Here we look to those who admit to engaging in criminal activity, and we assess the likelihood that they serve time during a given period. The 1980 survey question that is used to gauge criminal participation in the study by Grogger (1998) inquires about the extent to which one's income over the previous year came from illegal activity. Taking those who indicated any income from crime as the base population, the proportion interviewed in prison or jail at the time of the 1980 survey provides an indicator of the likelihood of being caught and incarcerated. Figure 2.8 presents the proportion of NLSY79 male respondents interviewed in prison or jail by their self-reported relative proportion of income derived from criminal activity. The figure clearly reveals that those more engaged in crime are more likely to end up incarcer-

Figure 2.8   *Proportion of NLSY79 Male Respondents Interviewed in Prison or Jail in 1980*

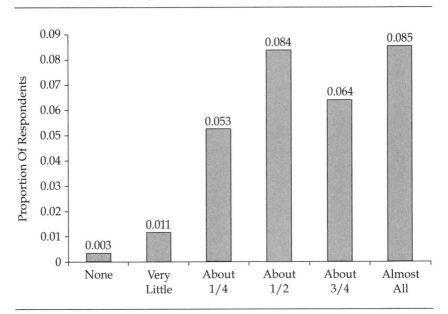

Source: Authors' calculations.

ated. However, the average incarceration probability across all those engaging in crime is relatively low (0.02), as the majority of respondents (75 percent) who report income from crime report very little income from crime.

We take 0.02 as an estimate of the likelihood of ending up in prison or jail for those who commit income-generating crimes in 1980.[21] As the ratio of prison admissions to crimes committed has roughly tripled between 1980 and the present, we assume that the risk of incarceration in 2000 for those engaged in income-generating crimes is 0.06.[22]

The magnification factor, $\dfrac{\theta}{(cp+\theta)^2}$,will increase as the release rate decreases (alternatively stated, it will increase as the expected value of time-served increases). The overall release rate in the late 1990s was roughly 0.50, indicating an estimate of a magnification factor of two. However, those offenders coaxed into criminal activity by declining wages are likely to commit fewer and less serious crimes relative to those already incarcerated. Thus, we assume that such marginal offenders that end up in prison or jail serve no more than 1.5 years on average.

Finally, we use the results of Chinhui Juhn (2003) as estimates of the changes in average log wages by race and educational attainment. Juhn presents estimated changes in the legal opportunity cost of crime for white men and black men by educational attainment.[23] For Hispanic men and other men, we assume that the changes in the wage structure experienced by black men with similar levels of educational attainment apply.

The results of this exercise are presented in table 2.6. The first column presents estimates of the change in log wages between 1979 and 1998 for men by race and ethnicity (approximately equal to the proportional change in wage levels). The numbers document the well-known erosion of the legal opportunity cost for the least skilled men. The second column presents group-specific estimates of the effects of these wage changes on group-incarceration rates (corresponding to equation 2.9). For each race-ethnicity group, we also estimate an overall change by taking the average of the effects by educational attainment weighted by the proportion of the group's representation at each education level. These overall figures suggest that changes in the wage structure increased the 2000 incarceration rate by 0.001 for white males, 0.002 for black males, 0.003 for Hispanic males, and 0.001 for other males.

Column 3 of table 2.6 presents estimates from the 1980 and 2000 censuses of the actual change in the proportion of males institutionalized by race-ethnicity as well as by race-ethnicity and education (taken from table 2.3). Note that these figures pertain to men in either jail or prison. This seems like a reasonable benchmark as the NLSY79 data used to calculate the risk of incarceration are based on whether the respondent is interviewed in prison or jail. The final column presents the ratio of the predicted wage effects on incarceration to the actual changes.

The results suggest that changes in the wage structure account for 23 percent of the increase in incarceration among white men, 4 percent of the increase among black men, 21 percent of the increase among Hispanic men, and 33 percent of the increase among other men. For all men, estimating equation 2.10 suggests that changes in the wage structure accounts for roughly 13 percent of the increase in incarceration. The disproportionate contribution of black male incarceration to overall growth pulls this estimate disproportionately toward the lower number for blacks.

Changes in Drug Markets

The second half of the twentieth century witnessed the rise and fall of several illicit drug epidemics. Each of these epidemics entails separate

Table 2.6 Estimates of the Effect of Changes in Earnings Opportunities on Male Incarceration Rates (Jail and Prison Incarceration Combined)

	ΔLn Wage Offers, 1979 to 1998[a]	Predicted Effect of Wages on Percent Incarcerated $(-\hat{inc}_{ij})$[b]	Actual Change in Incarceration Observe in the Census[c]	Proportion of Increase Attributable to Change in Ln(Wages)
White men				
< High school	−0.26	0.006	0.021	0.28
High school	−0.14	0.003	0.011	0.28
Some college	−0.04	0.001	0.004	0.21
College plus	0.13	−0.003	0.001	−2.95
All white men	—	0.001[d]	0.005	0.23
Black men				
< High school	−0.24	0.005	0.138	0.04
High school	−0.11	0.002	0.053	0.05
Some college	−0.04	0.001	0.024	0.04
College plus	0.04	−0.001	0.007	−0.12
All black men	—	0.002[d]	0.051	0.04

Hispanic men				
< High school	−0.24	0.005	0.016	0.34
High school	−0.11	0.002	0.024	0.10
Some college	−0.04	0.001	0.010	0.09
College plus	0.04	−0.001	0.004	−0.21
All Hispanic men	—	0.003[d]	0.015	0.21
Other men				
< High school	−0.24	0.005	0.021	0.26
High school	−0.11	0.002	0.007	0.34
Some college	−0.04	0.001	0.005	0.18
College plus	0.04	−0.001	0.000	0.00
All other men	—	0.001[d]	0.004	0.33

[a]Figures in this column are estimates of changes in wage opportunity costs accounting for labor-market dropouts (Juhn 2003). We assume that the changes in wage offers by education for black men apply to these other two race-ethnicity groups.
[b]The predicted effect of changes in wages on incarceration is calculated by multiplying the likelihood of being sent to prison conditional on engaging in criminal activity (we assume 0.06), the magnification factor (1.5), the effect of a change in ln wages on criminal participation (estimate of −0.25 from Jeff Grogger 1998), the actual change in the natural log of wages, and −1.
[c]Based on figures reported in table 2.3.
[d]The change in incarceration figure in these cells is the sum across education groups of the product of the proportion of males in the group of the given education level multiplied by the predicted change in incarceration for the race-education group.

subcultures of use and sales, idiosyncratic economic relationship and market organizations, and particularly pathways by which drug use and sales likely impacted crime and incarceration. During the 1960s and 1970s, intravenously injected heroine was the hard drug of choice among urban users in American inner cities. During the late 1970 and 1980s, recreational use of powder cocaine, inhaled or freebased, became popular and widespread. The introduction of crack cocaine in the mid-1980s greatly increased cocaine use in relatively poor minority neighborhoods and is commonly cited as a key determinant of the spike in violent crime occurring between the mid-1980s and the early 1990s. Finally, with the waning of the crack epidemic, marijuana use among criminally active youth increased substantially during the 1990s (Johnson, Golub, and Dunlap 2000).

The effects of these individual drug epidemics on incarceration growth operate primarily through an impact on crime. Moreover, the introduction of a new drug can be thought of as a behavioral shock to the criminality of a nation's residents. Bruce Johnson, Andrew Golub, and Eloise Dunlap (2000) present three avenues by which specific drug epidemics are likely to impact criminality; they provide a useful framework for thinking about the consequences of recent drug epidemics for crime and incarceration. First, each drug has unique psychopharmacological effects on users that may impact aggression, heighten a sense of paranoia, or alter other psychological factors that could predispose one towards violence. Second, users may turn to income-generating crime to support their habits. Such "economic-compulsive" criminal behavior may take the form of drug dealing, robbery, or burglary. Finally, as drug transactions are not governed by the legal system (that is, there are no formal mechanisms for contract enforcement and the protection of property rights), violent crime is likely to arise in the process of settling disputes, protecting market share, and in collecting payments.

The timing of the crack epidemic along with the particular connections between the market for crack and violence suggests that this particular behavioral shock may have been an important behavioral contributor to growth in incarceration. First, while the exact timing of the beginning of the epidemic is uncertain, two careful studies of this question date the introduction of crack to 1984 at the earliest, with sales and use spreading throughout the country by 1988 (Grogger and Willis 2000; Fryer et al. 2005).[24]

Second, the psychopharmacological effects of crack cocaine are more likely, relative to other drugs, to predispose the user toward violence. In contrast to heroin and marijuana, which are depressants, cocaine is a stimulant that induces hyperactive states.

Third, the number of transactions per user is particularly high for crack cocaine, reflecting its sale in small, relatively inexpensive quantities.[25] A higher frequency of contact between dealers and users increases the number of opportunities for violence. Each contact carries a risk of the user victimizing the dealer, the dealer victimizing the user, or a third party bent on robbery victimizing the user, the dealer, or both.

Finally, the structure of the crack-cocaine market was such that many young men were effectively employed by drug-selling operations in various capacities (MacCoun and Reuter 2001), with competing organizations often engaging in violent confrontations with one another over market share. At least one author (Grogger 2000) has hypothesized that the waning of violent crime during the 1990s was driven in part by a greater level of cooperation among drug-selling gangs and a greater propensity to rely on nonviolent means for settling turf conflicts.

Despite the timing of the epidemic and the clear connections between crack and violent crime, there are reasons to believe that the potential role of crack cocaine in explaining the explosion in incarceration growth is limited. First, the decomposition of the increase in prison admissions indicates that changes in criminal behavior explain a relatively small portion of the increase in incarceration. Second, the crack epidemic has diminished since 1990, while the incarceration rate has continued to grow. Finally, the one study (Fryer et al. 2005) that attempts to estimate the effect of crack-cocaine usage on prison admissions finds no evidence of an impact. We reproduce their basic finding here. Specifically, we match the crack-cocaine index measured at the state level by Roland G. Fryer and colleagues (2005) to state-level data on overall prison admissions per 100,000, new commitments per 100,000, and admissions due to returns to custody per 100,000. We restrict the data to the period from 1985 to 2000, due to the fact that the authors have little confidence in the signal associated with variation in their index prior to 1985. We then use these data to estimate a series of linear regression models where the key dependent variable is the state-level prison admissions rate and the key explanatory variable is the crack index.

Table 2.7 presents these results. The first row of numbers provides the coefficient on the crack index from a simple bivariate regression of the specific prison admissions rate on the index. The next row presents the same coefficient estimates after adding a complete set of state fixed effects. The inclusion of these fixed effects means that the effect of crack is being estimated using variation that occurs within states over time in the intensity of crack usage. The final specification adds a complete set of time fixed effects. This is perhaps the most important specification because these fixed effects remove all year-to-year changes in incarceration and crack usage that are common across states. In essence, this final regression estimates the effect of the introduction of crack by assessing

Table 2.7   *Estimated Marginal Effects of Variation in the State-Level Crack Index on Prison Admissions per 100,000 State Residents Based on State-Level Panel Data Covering the Period 1985 Through 2000*

	Total Admissions Rates	New Commitment Rate	Returns to Custody per 100,000
No state or year effects	11.83	6.22	7.63
	(2.59)	(1.59)	(1.79)
State effects only	14.71	10.49	4.65
	(2.40)	(1.51)	(1.35)
State and year fixed effects	–6.24	–0.57	–7.81
	(2.32)	(1.62)	(1.38)

Source: Standard errors are in parentheses. Figures in the table are the coefficient on the crack index taken from Fryer and colleagues (2005).

whether admissions rates increased earlier in states where crack appeared first (these results also correspond to the models estimated by Fryer and colleagues [2005]).

Beginning with the total admissions rates, there is a significant positive association between admissions and the crack index (as is evident from the simple bivariate regression coefficient), there is a somewhat larger positive estimate when we only use variation within states, but there is a significant negative effect when time effects are included in the specification. The largest estimate of the effect of crack on prison admissions (the coefficient of 14.71 in the model with state fixed effects only) predicts that the change in the crack index increased prison admissions between 1985 and 2000 by approximately 14 admissions per 100,000. As the actual rate increased by 114 over this period, the largest estimate in the first column of table 2.7 suggests that crack explained no more than 12 percent of the growth in prison admissions over this time period.

This certainly is an overestimate, however. The fact that the marginal effect of the intensity of crack usage does not survive adjusting for common year-to-year shifts casts serious doubt on this estimate. The results in the final row indicate that states where the intensity of crack use increased above and beyond the average increase for the nation experienced declines in the prison admissions rate. While this result may be biased by a reverse causal effect of prison on the crack epidemic (the explanation offered by Fryer and colleagues), the large disparity between the estimated impact of crack when omitting year effects and the effect when including these effects suggests that crack cocaine has played a minor role.

CONCLUSION

Why then are so many Americans in prison? We find that the answer to this question lies mostly with the collective series of policy innovations at the state and federal level. In other words, so many Americans are in prison because through our collective public choices regarding sentencing and punishment, we have decided to place so many Americans in prison. For those who would have been sentenced to prison in the past, we have increased the amount of time that such offenders will serve. For many other less-serious offenders, we now punish with a prison sentence rather than an alternative, less punitive sanction that would have been applied in the past. Collectively, changes in who goes to prison (expansion along the extensive margin) and for how long (expansion along the intensive margin) explain 80 to 85 percent of prison expansion over the last twenty-five years. Thus, the characterization by William Spelman (2000) of the doubling of the prison population between the mid-1970s and 1980s, and then the doubling once more through the late 1990s, as one of the largest policy experiments of the century is indeed correct.

To be sure, we do find evidence that there have been changes to some of the underlying fundamental determinants of criminal behavior that have militated toward higher criminal activity. With regard to shocks that are likely to have increased crime, the severely mentally ill are much less likely to be institutionalized today than in the past, a factor likely to contribute to some violent crimes and public-order violations. Moreover, the labor-market prospects of low-skilled men, especially low-skilled minority men, have deteriorated considerably since the mid-1970s. Finally, the introduction of crack cocaine in the mid-1980s clearly wreaked havoc on American inner cities, contributing substantially to youth homicide and likely contributing to growth in the incarceration rate.

Nonetheless, we have shown that the likely behavioral impact of each of these shocks is small. There is also evidence of demographic shifts that, all else held equal, should have reduced criminal offending as well as incarceration rates. Specifically, the U.S. population has aged, the percentage of immigrants has increased (a factor associated with lower crime and incarceration rates), and U.S. adults have become considerably more educated. All of these shifts would have decreased crime and incarceration had incarceration rates not increased within demographic groups defined by age, race, and education groups. Moreover, research by the economists John Donohue and Steven Levitt (2001) pertaining to the crime-abating effects of legalized abortion suggests another factor likely to have reduced the overall tendency towards criminal behavior among the noninstitutionalized (and perhaps, even the institutionalized) public. In conclusion, while there were some quite visible shocks to criminal behavior and to public order, there were many less visible underlying changes in the nation's demography that tended to counter the effects of the former on crime rates. In the end, it is not surprising that we find that behavior plays a small role in explaining the increase in the nation's incarceration rate.

NOTES

1. This approximation would be exact when the distribution of actual time served follows an exponential distribution.
2. The incarceration for crime i in year t is equal to the sum of new admissions between $t-1$ and t plus surviving inmates from the previous period, or

$$Inc_{it} = c_{it}p_{it} (1 - Inc_{it-1} - Inc_{i`t-1}) + (1 - \theta_{it}) \, Inc_{it-1},$$

where $Inc_{i`t-1}$ is the incarceration rate in time period $t-1$ for all crimes other than crime i. With sufficient time and stability in the transition parameters, the steady-state proportion incarcerated for crime i settles to

$$Inc_{it} = \frac{c_{it}p_{it} - c_{it}p_{it}Inc_{i`}}{c_{it}p_{it} + \theta_{it}}.$$

In practice, the second term in the numerator will be extremely small (less than or equal to $1/100{,}000$). Thus, the approximation in equation 2.1 applies.
3. Raphael and Stoll (2007) use admissions and releases data from the National Corrections Reporting Program to estimate the proportion of inmates admitted in a given year that are then released over subsequent years. We assume that after 1998, the time-served distribution remained constant. This latter assumption is likely to result in conservative estimates of the average time served, as many sentence-enhancement policies are adopted post-1998.
4. We generated these overall admissions rates by first tabulating the distribution of admissions across these categories using the prisoner admissions files from the 1984 and 2002 NCRP data, and then distributing total admissions for the states (available from the National Prison Statistics database) across these categories using these distributions. This imputation assumes that the admissions distribution for states not reporting to the NCRP is similar to the admissions distributions for states that do.
5. Certainly, the number of drug crimes is much greater than the number of drug arrests. However, since the incarceration rate depends on the product of the overall admissions rate (given by the crime rate multiplied by admis-

sions per crime), this simple imputation will not impact our inference regarding the causes of the changes in the incarceration rate. Regarding the implicit attribution of the entire change in arrests to changes in behavior, this will certainly bias upwards the estimate of the contribution of behavior to incarceration growth. There have been concerted efforts to step up enforcement of drug laws and to punish drug offenders more severely.

6. For other violent crimes, we estimate the admissions-per-crime variable using the average admissions-per-crime values for nonhomicide violent crime, using the composition of prison admits for that year as weights. For other property crime, we use the average of the admissions-crimes ratio for larceny and motor-vehicle theft. For other crimes, we use the overall average admissions-crime ratio weighted by the proportional distribution of admissions in each year for the seven offenses with observable crime rates.

7. Johnson and Raphael (2007) estimate the joint incapacitation and deterrence effects of putting someone away for a year using a state-level panel of crime and incarceration rates. The estimates adjust for the endogeneity of prison in crime regressions and arrive at estimates that are consistent with the some of the larger crime-abating effects in the extant literature (for example, Levitt 1996). The counterfactual crime rates in this chapter are based on the crime-specific effects from Johnson and Raphael unless otherwise noted.

8. Again, this should bias our estimates of the change in behavior upwards. This is because any increase in crime would generate some increase in incarceration, which would mitigate the added crime of such a prisoner release.

9. In addition, since Johnson and Raphael (2007) only provide crime-prevention estimates for the seven offenses in the UCR, we apply the proportional change for these offenses above the 2002 level to the three offenses that are not included in the UCR (that is, other violent crimes, other property crimes, and other crimes).

10. Johnson and Raphael (2007) model this dynamic adjustment process and show that, given the typical parameter sizes for prisoner release and admissions rates in the United States, a typical shock will induce a four- to six-year adjustment process between equilibrium.

11. More formally, define the vector P_t as

$$P`_t = \lfloor P^1_t \ P^2_t \ P^3_t \rfloor, \quad where \quad \sum_j P^j_t = 1$$

where the index values indicate the three potential states of not in prison and not on parole (j = 1), in prison (j = 2), and on parole (j = 3). Define the matrix T_t as

$$T_t = \begin{bmatrix} T^{11}_t & T^{12}_t & T^{13}_t \\ T^{21}_t & T^{22}_t & T^{23}_t \\ T^{31}_t & T^{32}_t & T^{33}_t \end{bmatrix}, \quad where \quad 0 \le T^{ij}_t \le 1, \quad \forall i, j, \quad and \quad \sum_j T^{ij}_t = 1, \quad \forall j.$$

The proportional distribution of the U.S. population across the three states in any given year can be rewritten as a linear function of the state distribution in the previous year and the transition probability matrix,

$$P^`_{t+1} = P^`_t T_t.$$

Similarly, the subsequent distribution of the population can be tabulated by applying the next matrix of transition probabilities to the first calculation, or

$$P^`_{t+2} = P^`_t T_t T_{t+1}, \text{ and so on.}$$

12. The disparity between the simulation rates and the actual incarceration rates is likely the result of measurement error in admissions and releases. Note that the structure of the calculations ensures that errors cumulate over the years of the simulation.

13. In 1970, foreign-born individuals accounted for 4.7 percent of the U.S. population. By 2000, the percentage that was foreign born increased to 10.4 percent. During these three decades, the resident immigrant population increased by 16.2 million, accounting for roughly one-quarter of overall population growth (U.S. Census Bureau 2001).

14. Our tabulations of the 1980 and 2000 Public Use Microdata Samples of the U.S. Census of Population and Housing indicate that for men between eighteen and sixty-five years of age, average age increased from thirty-eight to forty for non-Hispanic whites, from thirty-five to thirty-seven for non-Hispanic blacks, from thirty-five to thirty-seven for non-Hispanic Asians, and from thirty-four to thirty-five for Hispanics.

15. Raphael (2005) presents a detailed comparison of the incarceration estimates using these data and estimated correctional populations from the Bureau of Justice Statistics.

16. Data on inmates in state and county mental hospitals through 1970 were drawn from findings of George B. Palermo, Maurice B. Smith, and Franklin J. Liska (1991); post-1970 data were drawn from findings of Steven Raphael (2000).

17. For each of the census years, one is able to distinguish those in mental hospitals from those in correctional institutions using the detailed group quarters variable.

18. Note that the overall mental-hospital population declined over this period. Because those in nonmilitary institutionalized group quarters are predominately prisoners, jail inmates, and mental-hospital inpatients, this implies that the net change is a lower bound for the absolute increase in the number of jail and prison inmates.

19. Grogger (1998) presents one of the clearest microtheoretical expositions of these ideas. The author presents a model of time allocation between criminal activity, legitimate work, and leisure, where it is assumed that the return to crime diminishes with the amount of effort devoted to crime. With risk-

neutral and amoral decision-makers, committing a crime requires that the return of the first hour of criminal activity exceeds potential wages and the individual's reservation wage. The model also predicts that many will find it optimal to both work in the legitimate labor market and engage in criminal activity. This latter result follows from the assumption of decreasing returns to crime.

20. Fagan and Freeman (1999) provide a detailed summary of existing research regarding the interaction between work and criminal participation conducted through the mid-1990s.

21. With an annual incarceration risk of 0.02 and assuming no desistence among this population as they age, one can simulate the fraction that will eventually be interviewed in prison or jail over the course of the panel. Specifically, the likelihood of not having been incarcerated after t periods is given by 0.98^t. For any given period, one minus this calculation provides an estimate of the fraction that has ever served time. By 1996, the proportion of men who admit to engaging in income-generating crime in 1980 who are interviewed in prison or jail at least once is roughly 0.11 (consistent with the tabulations presented by Freeman [1996]). Assuming no desistance and a 2 percent annual incarceration risk, roughly 30 percent should have been interviewed in prison or jail. While criminal activity is likely to have declined with age, this overestimate is also likely to indicate that our assumed incarceration risk parameter is perhaps too high. Thus, similar to the estimate of wage responsiveness that we employ, the assumed risk of incarceration further reinforces our interpretation of these figures as upper-bound estimates.

22. We explored several alternative strategies for estimating p. One possibility is to estimate the amount of crimes reported to the police that would be generated by the typical prison inmate, and then to estimate the likelihood of being caught and incarcerated for this amount of crime. Johnson and Raphael (2007) estimate that the average inmate incarcerated between 1979 and 2002 reduced index crimes reported to the police by approximately 3.5 (the effect on overall crime is closer to 10 given underreporting). Because reported crimes are likely to generate police actions leading to an arrest and conviction, one estimate of the likelihood of incarceration is to estimate the likelihood that such an average prisoner would be caught and convicted again if released. With an average admissions-crime ratio of approximately 0.019, the likelihood of being caught and incarcerated for committing four index crimes in one year is approximately 0.074 (calculated as $1 - (1 - 0.019)^4$). Certainly, the marginal offender drawn into crime is not likely to engage in criminal activity with the intensity of the average prison inmate. Thus our slightly more modest choice of 0.06 seems justified.

A further alternative is to make use of the stylized fact presented by Levitt and Venkatesh (2001) that roughly one-third of the sixteen heads of the Chicago drug gang that they studied were in prison at any given time. Since all sixteen men can be accurately described as full-time criminals (that is, $c = 1$), the incarceration equation 2.1 for this group can be written as $0.33 = p / (p + \theta)$. With an estimate of the release probability, one could back out the annual risk of incarceration for these full-time criminals. The release probability for all inmates in 2000 was slightly less than 0.50, corresponding to an expected time served of two years. It seems reasonable to assume that the leaders of a violent drug gang are likely to be serving somewhat longer sentences than the average inmate. If we assume a release probability for this group of 0.33 (corresponding to an expected time served of three years), then the annual incarceration risk would be equal to 0.16. Thus, our estimated risk of 0.06 implies that the incarceration risk for a marginal offender is roughly 40 percent the incarceration risk for a full-time criminal. While these are clearly speculations, this seems like a reasonable approximation.

23. Juhn's 2003 published study does not include estimates of adjusted changes in hourly log wages for those with some college education but no degree. However, the author provided us with these additional tabulations.

24. Grogger and Willis (2000) use data from the Drug Awareness Warning System (DAWN) on cocaine-related emergency-room visits as well as a survey of police chiefs in large cities to date the onset of the crack epidemic for different urban areas. Roland G. Fryer and colleagues (2005) use data from the DAWN, data on Drug Enforcement Administration (DEA) cocaine seizures, newspaper citations on crack-related stories, cocaine arrests, and cocaine deaths to construct a single index. Both date the beginning of the crack epidemic to between 1984 and 1985.

25. Crack cocaine in its powder form is derived by dissolving cocaine in water, mixing it with baking soda, and boiling (Grogger and Willis 2000). The resulting "rocks" are smoked, concentrating cocaine in the bloodstream and brain at a particularly fast rate. This causes a short intense high followed by an intense depression and possibly desperation caused by the rapid decline in cocaine levels (Johnson, Golub, and Dunlap 2000).

REFERENCES

Autor, David H., and Lawrence F. Katz. 1999. "Changes in the Wage Structure and Earnings Inequality." In *Handbook of Labor Economics*, edited by Orley Ashenfelter and David Card. Amsterdam: Elsevier.

Butcher, Kirsten F., and Anne Morrison Piehl. 1998. "Recent Immigrants: Unexpected Implications for Crime and Incarceration." *Industrial and Labor Relations Review* 51(4): 654–79.

———. 2006. "Why Are Immigrant Incarceration Rates So Low? Evidence on Selective Immigration, Deterrence, and Deportation." Working paper. New Brunswick, N.J.: Rutgers University.

Ditton, Paula M. 1999. "Mental Health and Treatment of Inmates and Probationers." Bureau of Justice Statistics Special Report, NCJ 174463. Washington: U.S. Department of Justice.

Donohue, John, and Steven Levitt. 2001. "Legalized Abortion and Crime." *Quarterly Journal of Economics* 116(2): 379–420.

Fagan, Jeffrey, and Richard B. Freeman. 1999. "Crime and Work." *Crime and Justice: A Review of Research* 25: 225–90.

Freeman, Richard B. 1987. "The Relationship of Criminal Activity to Black Youth Employment." *Review of Black Political Economy* 16(Summer/Fall): 99–107.

———. 1996. "Why Do So Many Young Americans Commit Crimes and What Might We Do About It?" *Journal of Economic Perspectives* 10(1): 25–42.

Fryer, Roland G., Paul S. Heaton, Steven D. Levitt, and Kevin M. Murphy. 2005. "Measuring the Impact of Crack Cocaine." NBER working paper 11318. Cambridge, Mass.: National Bureau of Economic Research.

Gould, Eric D., Bruce A. Weinberg, and David B. Mustard. 2002. "Crime Rates and Local Labor Market Opportunities in the United States: 1979–1997." *Review of Economics and Statistics* 84(1): 45–61.

Grogger, Jeff. 1998. "Market Wages and Youth Crime." *Journal of Labor Economics* 16(4): 756–91.

———. 2000. "An Economic Model of Recent Trends in Violence." In *The Crime Drop in America*, edited by Alfred Blumstein and Joel Wallman. Cambridge, UK: Cambridge University Press.

Grogger, Jeff, and Michael Willis. 2000. "The Emergence of Crack Cocaine and the Rise on Urban Crime Rates." *Review of Economics and Statistics* 82(4): 519–29.

Harcourt, Bernard E. 2006. "From the Asylum to the Prison: Rethinking the Incarceration Revolution." *Texas Law Review* 84: 1751–86.

International Centre for Prison Studies. 2007. *World Prison Brief.* London, U.K.: Kings College.

Johnson, Bruce, Andrew Golub, and Eloise Dunlap. 2000. "The Rise and Decline of Hard Drugs, Drug Markets, and Violence in Inner-City New York." In *The Crime Drop in America*, edited by Alfred Blumstein and Joel Wallman. Cambridge, UK: Cambridge University Press.

Johnson, Rucker C., and Steven Raphael. 2007. "How Much Crime Reduction Does the Marginal Prisoner Buy?" Working paper. Berkeley, Calif.: University of California, Berkeley.

Juhn, Chinhui. 2003. "Labor Market Dropouts and Trends in the Wages of Black and White Men." *Industrial and Labor Relations Review* 56(4): 643–62.

Lochner, Lance, and Enrico Moretti. 2004. "The Effect of Education on Criminal Activity: Evidence from Prison Inmates, Arrest, and Self Reports." *American Economic Review* 94(1): 155–189.

Levitt, Steven D. 1996. "The Effect of Prison Population Size on Crime Rates: Evidence from Prison Overcrowding Legislation." *Quarterly Journal of Economics* 111(2): 319–51.

Levitt, Steven D., and Sudhir Venkatesh. 2000. "An Economic Analysis of a Drug Selling Gangs Finances." *Quarterly Journal of Economics* 115: 755–89.

MacCoun, Robert, and Peter Reuter. 2001. *Drug War Heresies: Learning from Other Vices, Times, and Places.* Cambridge, U.K.: Cambridge University Press.

Palermo, George B., Maurice B. Smith, and Frank J. Liska. 1991. "Jails Versus Mental Hospitals: A Social Dilemma." *International Journal of Offender Therapy and Comparative Criminology* 35(2): 97–106.

Penrose, Lionel. 1933. "Mental Disease and Crime: Outline of a Comparative Study of European Statistics." *British Journal of Medical Psychology* 18: 1–15.

Petersilia, Joan. 2003. *When Prisoners Come Home.* Oxford, U.K.: Oxford University Press.

Raphael, Steven. 2000. "The Deinstitutionalization of the Mentally Ill and Growth in the U.S. Prison Population: 1971–1996." Working paper. Berkeley, Calif.: University of California, Berkeley.

———. 2005. "The Socioeconomic Status of Black Males: The Increasing Importance of Incarceration." in *Poverty, the Distribution of Income, and Public Policy*, edited by Alan Auerbach, David Card, and John Quigley. New York: Russell Sage Foundation.

Raphael, Steven, and Michael A. Stoll. 2007. "Why Are So Many Americans in Prison." *National Poverty Center* working paper 07-10. Ann Arbor, Mich.: National Poverty Center.

Raphael, Steven, and Rudolf Winter-Ebmer. 2001. "Identifying the Effect of Unemployment on Crime." *Journal of Law and Economics* 44(1): 259–84.

Spelman, William. 2000. "The Limited Importance of Prison Expansion." In *The Crime Drop in America*, edited by Alfred Blumstein and Joel Wallman. Cambridge, U.K.: Cambridge University Press.

Torrey, E. Fuller. 1997. *Out of the Shadows: Confronting America's Mental Illness Crisis*. New York: John Wiley and Sons.

Travis, Jeremy. 2005. *But They All Come Back: Facing the Challenges of Prisoner Reentry*. Washington, D.C.: Urban Institute Press.

U.S. Census Bureau. 2001. *Profiles of the Foreign Born Population in the United States: 2000*. P23-206. Washington: U.S. Government Printing Office.

David F. Weiman
and
Christopher Weiss

3

The Origins of Mass Incarceration in New York State: The Rockefeller Drug Laws and the Local War on Drugs

From the vantage point of the early 1970s, noted criminologists Alfred Blumstein and his colleagues (Blumstein and Cohen 1973) could point to the remarkable stability in the U.S. incarceration rate since 1925 as well as comparable evidence from several other developed industrialized countries (figure 3.1).[1] Despite the economic, political, and social turbulence over the previous half century (including the Great Depression, hot and cold wars, and the civil rights movement), the U.S. incarceration rate hovered around 107 prisoners per 100,000 people. Generalizing on this comparative historical experience, they regarded the relative size of the prison population as a social norm and hypothesized a homeostatic social mechanism that adjusted the severity of punishment and the very limits of criminal behavior to maintain it. This process of adaptation, they argued, would occur on the margins of the criminal-justice system, namely, for nonviolent victimless crimes and for less serious offenders—cases in which policymakers and criminal-justice authorities could exercise greater discretion. To illustrate their point, they cited the Comprehensive Drug Abuse Prevention Act of 1970, which liberalized the classification of and punishments for drug violations, which had contributed to soaring felony drug arrest rates in the 1960s (Peterson 1985; Courtwright 2004).

Recent historical experience, as is well known, has treated the stability-of-punishment hypothesis harshly. Since the mid-1970s, but especially during the 1980s and 1990s, the U.S. incarceration soared and has neared 500 inmates per 100,000 people (or .5 percent of the total population) according to the most recent estimates (see figure 3.2; Sabol, Minton, and Harrison 2007; Pew Center on the States 2008). To explain this radical departure from the prior trend, Alfred Blumstein and Allen J. Beck (1999) conducted a simple empirical exercise that decomposed the growth in

Figure 3.1   *Prison and Total Incarceration Rates, 1925 to 1975*

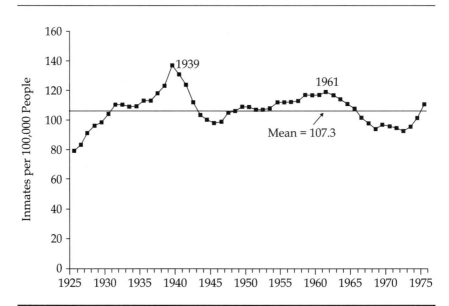

Source: Pastore and McGuire (2006, tables 6.1.2006 and 6.28.2006).

incarceration rates into two sources: higher crime rates and more punitive criminal-justice polices. Their results certainly suggested a clear break from the past. In all but one crime category, the policy variables accounted for nearly 90 percent of the increase in incarceration rates (Boggess and Bound 1997).

Analyzing changes in state-level incarceration rates over the same time period, David F. Greenberg and Valerie West (2001), as well as Katherine Beckett and Bruce Western (2001), have statistically corroborated the more decisive impact of "get tough" criminal-justice policies and more conservative "law-and-order" politics relative to that of increases in serious violent crime (Western 2006; Guetzkow 2006). On the policy front, they single out two key innovations: a new regime of determinate structured sentencing and the war on drugs. Since the mid-1970s, state and federal legislation has significantly curtailed the discretion of judges and parole boards in setting prison sentences and terms, steadily increasing the likelihood and length of a prison term for a felony conviction. The war-on-drug policies also operated at the more grassroots or local levels.

Figure 3.2   *Prison and Total Incarceration Rates, 1950 to 2005*

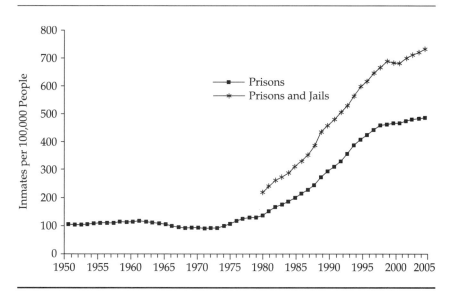

Source: Pastore and McGuire (2006, tables 6.1.2006 and 6.28.2006).

The aggressive policing and prosecution of less serious drug offenders multiplied their risk of an arrest, a felony conviction, and a lengthy prison term under the new harsher sentencing laws.

In this chapter, we analyze the policies and political economic roots of this new U.S. criminal-justice regime, which we call mass incarceration. The term *mass incarceration* connotes the vast scale of the prison and criminal-justice systems, as gauged by the population under some form of correctional supervision (currently estimated to be 7.1 million people, or 3.2 percent of the total population) (Glaze and Bonczar 2006). Following David Garland (2001a), the term also signifies the disproportionate reach of the criminal-justice system into disadvantaged inner-city minority communities, where a prison experience has become more the norm than the exception among less-educated young African American and Hispanic men and, increasingly, women (Pettit and Western 2004; Raphael 2006).

Our empirical analysis focuses on the war on drugs in the state of New York from the early 1970s to the early 1990s. This case-study approach is motivated by one of our central messages: the dramatic surge in incarceration rates, especially among inner-city minority populations, depended on critical decisions made at the local level (by mayors, police commissioners, district attorneys, and judges) in implementing and strictly enforcing the sentencing policies enacted in state and federal capitols. The importance of grassroots rather than higher-order sentencing policies explains the significant time lag between the adoption of the notorious Rockefeller drug laws in 1973 and the surge in New York incarceration rates fueled by felony drug arrests, convictions, and commitments after 1980. Despite our regional focus, we also show that the New York experience follows the national trends at least until the early 1990s, because the state's and especially New York City's drug policies were forged in the same turbulent political economic crucible that shaped criminal-justice polices nationwide.

Our study draws on a variety of qualitative and quantitative sources. A systematic analysis of local newspaper reporting from the tumultuous 1970s through the early 1990s pinpoints the decisive shift in local drug enforcement policies in the early 1980s, especially after 1984. With quantitative evidence from the New York felony processing reports between 1974 and 1994, a growth accounting exercise measures the significant contribution of this local policy innovation on the flow new admissions into state prisons. Finally, with historical corrections data we can consider incarceration trends over a longer sweep of U.S. history and offer a modified version of the stability-of-punishment hypothesis. Our alternative view posits the epochal change in the incarceration rate—that is long periods of relative stability punctuated by sharp increases fueled by wars on drugs and more fundamentally structural political economic change.

MASS INCARCERATION AND THE WAR ON DRUGS

The term *regime of mass incarceration* refers to the complex of punitive criminal-justice policies that have diffused across all levels of the criminal-justice system and all levels of government. It is often characterized by the shift from discretionary to more determinate and structured sentencing to ensure that prison sentences and terms "fit" the crime and the offender.[2] The earliest examples date from the late 1970s. In 1976, both California and Maine abolished discretionary parole boards and in their place substituted simple formulas for early release based on the accumulation of "good time" and other earned credits. In the same year, California instituted a system of presumptive sentences based solely on seriousness of the offense. Four years later, Minnesota enacted a more elaborate scheme of presumptive guidelines—a matrix of sentences that also took into consideration the offender's criminal background. These policies significantly curbed the discretion of judges, who were expected to adhere to the legislated standards or justify their departure (to an appellate court).

This initial round of reforms, it should be noted, was not intrinsically punitive. Armed with actual and experimental evidence of racial and class biases or mere arbitrariness by judges and parole boards, advocates were often motivated by genuine concerns over fairness and the very legitimacy of the criminal-justice system (American Friends Service Committee 1971; Frankel 1972). Legislation in Minnesota, for example, ironed out disparities in sentencing and parole decisions, but it also imposed binding resource constraints to control the growth of prison populations.[3] Likewise, the New York Executive Advisory Committee on Sentencing (1979) proposed sentencing guidelines to replace the current "erratic and unpredictable" system of "indeterminate" sentences, but it staunchly opposed "fixed, rigid, mandatory sentencing" that imposed excessively harsh punishments (such as the New York Rockefeller drug laws) (vi).

By the mid-1990s, all states and the federal government had adopted some, if not all, of these sentencing reforms at both the front and back ends of the criminal-justice system.[4] In the more conservative political environment of the 1980s and early 1990s, however, the decisive shift to a rigid and mechanical sentencing regime systematically escalated the severity of punishments, expanding the scope of felony offenses and mandating prison and lengthier sentences and terms for felony convictions.[5] Just over half of the states (including the District of Columbia) and the federal government had opted for some type of structured sentencing, with or without a sentencing commissions to regulate or monitor judicial decisions (see table 3.1). In a more piecemeal fashion, all states and the federal government had enacted mandatory minimum sentencing laws for repeat offenders or select crimes—most often weapons possessions (76.5 percent of all jurisdictions) and drug violations (72.6 percent). Finally, nearly half of the states had adopted two- or three-strikes laws that multiplied mandated prison sentences for repeat offenders.

State governments also tightened the reigns over the terms and conditions of prisoner release and parole. Nearly two decades after California and Maine abolished discretionary parole boards, an additional thirteen states had followed suit (affecting nearly 30 percent of all jurisdictions). Even those that retained some form of discretionary release increasingly relied on formal rules for conditional release rather than the decisions of an administrative panel. Consequently, the share of discretionary parole releases fell from 54.8 percent in 1980 to only 32.3 percent in 1995, while those on mandatory release increased from 18.4 to 39 percent over the same period (Hughes, Wilson, and Beck 2001).

Truth-in-sentencing laws further curbed discretion on early-release

Table 3.1   *State Sentencing Structures as of 1996*

Front-End Reforms	Number	%
Presumptive sentencing	9	17.6
Sentencing guidelines	17	33.3
Presumptive	8	15.7
Voluntary or advisory	9	17.6
Sentencing commissions	19	37.3
Mandatory minimums	51	100.0
Drug violations	37	72.5
Weapons possession	39	76.5
Repeat or habitual	40	78.4
Two- or three-strikes	24	47.1
Back-End Reforms		
Determinate sentencing	15	29.4
Parole		
Good time	48	94.1
Supervision	50	98.0
Truth-in-sentencing	31	60.8

Source: United States Bureau of Justice Assistance (1998); Stemen, Rengifo, and Wilson (2005).
Note: The columns report the number and percentage of jurisdictions including the District of Columbia that had adopted the designated type of sentencing reform by 1996.

decisions by requiring prisoners to serve at least a minimum fraction of their sentences (most often 85 percent for serious violent offenders). The 1994 federal Crime Act spurred the diffusion of these laws (and the 85 percent standard for violent offenders) through conditional funding for prison construction. Significantly, the number of states with truth-in-sentencing laws increased sharply from five to thirty-one (or just over 60 percent) between 1994 and 1996; most qualified for the federal aid by adopting the tougher standard (Ditton and Wilson 1999). Finally, the parole system "extended the reach of [intensive] supervision" beyond prison walls and increasingly resorted to the harsher punishment of reincarceration for technical parole violations (Travis 2005, 44). In this case of "back-end sentencing," ironically, risk-averse parole officers have exercised greater discretion; this is often in response to mounting caseloads and the intensive public scrutiny and sensational reporting on heinous crimes by parolees (Peterselia 2003; Travis 2005).

These policy shifts also occurred at the local level—that is, on the front lines of the criminal-justice system. City governments, often with state and federal aid, hired additional police and deployed them in dedicated units and en masse on foot patrols to "combat" all levels of street crime.[6] Instead of simply responding to incident reports after the fact, they sought to preempt serious crime through aggressive and proactive policing strategies and sophisticated mapping technologies. Targeting "disorderly" crime-prone neighborhoods, they conducted intensive surveillance, undercover and sweep operations, stop-and-frisk searches, and minor (misdemeanor) arrests of likely suspects.

The resulting surge in arrests can overwhelm local prosecutors and courts, which in the past had typically responded to bottlenecks by dismissing less serious cases or negotiating pleas to minor charges punishable by fines, probation, or time served. Responding to political pressures, however, prosecutors and courts also adopted tougher policies. Those arrested were more likely to be indicted and ultimately convicted on more serious charges, detained while awaiting trial, and incarcerated in jail or prison for longer terms in addition to time already served during case processing (Belenko, Fagan, and Chin 1991). Complementary policies certainly strengthened prosecutors' hands by furnishing them with higher-quality, and often direct, evidence from the police officers as well as credible bargaining chips like steep minimum sentences on arrest charges. Even when prosecutors negotiated with judges for plea agreements on lesser felony offenses punished by probation or time served, these convictions could accumulate and result in harsher punishments on the second and third strikes.

Our in-depth analysis of mass incarceration focuses on the war on drugs for two reasons. First, this initiative ran the gamut of the entire criminal-justice system. It illustrates, and in many cases initiated, the pivotal "get tough" policy innovations that constituted this new regime. Second, the war on drugs is quantitatively important in accounting for the two salient features of mass incarceration: the overall surge in prison rates and the greater prevalence of prison experience among less-educated inner-city minority men.

To gauge the impact of local policies, we first chart trends in arrest rates for drug and other crimes from 1975 to 2000 (see figure 3.3). Drug arrests per 100,000 people actually fell during the late 1970s; this is perhaps because of greater police leniency, as hypothesized by Alfred Blumstein and Jacqueline Cohen (1973), or more simply it might have been due to fiscal exigencies that depleted law-enforcement resources. Beginning in 1981—several years before the turnaround in local expenditures on police protection and especially personnel—drug arrest rates began to rise and grew at average rate of 4.9 percent per year until 1997 (see the dashed trend line in figure 3.3). The sharp deviations from simple trend growth between 1986 and 1994 essentially followed the uneven course of the

Figure 3.3   *Arrest Rates for Drug, Violent, and Property Crimes (Arrests per 100,000 People)*

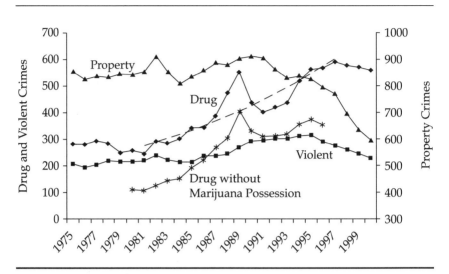

Source: U.S. Federal Bureau of Investigation (FBI), Uniform Crime Reporting Program, *Crime in the United States 2005.* Available at www.fbi.gov/ucr/05cius/index.html; historical data have been compiled by the U.S. Census Bureau, Statistical Abstract, 1977 to 2002 (available at: http://www.census.gov/compendia/statab/past_years.html), and the U.S. Bureau of Justice Statistics for drug arrests (available at www.ojp.usdoj.gov/bjs/dcf/enforce.htm).

crack epidemic and, in its wake (after 1991), a decisive shift in policing that targeted misdemeanor marijuana possession violations (Sabol 2008; King and Mauer 2006; Golub, Johnson, and Dunlap 2007; Harcourt and Ludwig 2007; Levine and Small 2008).[7]

Without incident data on drug violations, it is not possible to ascertain whether local police were simply responding to a surge in actual drug crimes over this period. We question this simple interpretation for two reasons. First, as is evident in figure 3.3, drug arrest rates grew at a much faster clip than arrests for either property or violent crimes during the pivotal decade of the 1980s. Between 1981 and 1989 the ratio between drug crime arrests and violent- or property-crime arrests doubled. Moreover, for the latter two crime types, police arrests essentially kept pace with trends in reported incidents.[8] In other words, during the 1980s, policing in these cases tended to be more reactive.

As further evidence of discretionary policing in the war on drugs, we point to the striking racial disproportionality in arrests for drug crimes versus property and violent crimes during the 1980s. Focusing on large urban centers, the graph in figure 3.4 charts the percentage of African Americans

Figure 3.4   *Percentage of Blacks Arrested for Major Crimes in U.S. Cities, 1980 to 2000*

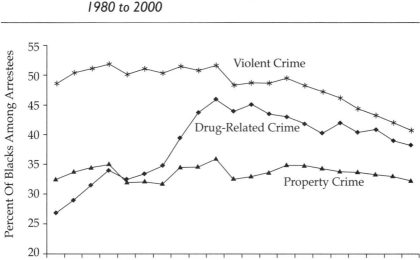

Source: Pastore and McGuire (2006) and earlier editions of the *Sourcebook of Criminal Justice Statistics* (available at: http://www.albany.edu/sourcebook/archive .html), section 4 (Arrests, Seizures).

among adults arrested for these three crime types. The African American share for drug crimes jumped from 26.9 percent in 1980 to 46.0 percent in 1989.[9] By contrast, blacks were no more likely than whites to be arrested for violent and property crimes over the same period. In comparisons between black and white adolescents, moreover, indirect evidence finds no significant differences in their use and sale of illegal drugs. Surveys of high-school seniors point to a significant and increasing white-black gap in illegal drug use during the decade. Among a representative sample of adolescents interviewed in 1980 and 2000, lower-income whites reported that they were more likely to have sold drugs than their black peers.[10]

Moving to the next stage of the criminal-justice system, table 3.2 documents the greater efficiency in the prosecution of drug arrests (or, in our terms, more aggressive prosecution). The first column shows the surge in prison commitments relative to total drug arrests between 1980 and 1996. Those arrested for drug possession and trafficking in 1990, the evidence implies, were 5.4 times more likely to serve time in prison than a decade earlier. Although the prison commitment rate fell by a quarter in 1996, it was still four times higher than at the onset of the war on drugs.[11]

The surge in prison commitment rates conflates the impacts of "get

Table 3.2   Prosecution and Sentencing of Drug Offenders in State Courts

	All		Trafficking Only							
			Convictions[2]		Sentence			Prison Sentence		
	Arrests (000s)	Prison Rates[1]	Rate (%)	% Pleas	Prison (%)	Jail (%)	Prison Rate (%)	Sentence (Months)	Term (Months)	% Served[3]
1980	471.2	1.9								
1986			41.1		36.8		15.1			
1988			38.9		40.8		15.9	66	20	30.3
1990	1008.3	10.3	53.2		49.0		26.0			
1992			54.9	93.4	48.0	27.0	26.4	72	24	33.3
1994			51.9	90.5	47.6	23.1	24.7	66	21	31.8
1996	1294.7	7.7	65.9	92.3	39.5	33.4	26.0	55	23	41.8
1998			68.0	95.0	45.0	26.0	30.6	54	22	40.7
2000			77.8	95.7	41.0	28.0	31.9	52	26	50.0

Source: Data on all drug offenses: Ditton and Wilson (1999, 4).
Data on drug trafficking only: Langan and Graziadei (1995, 2–9); Langan and Brown (1997, 2–9); Brown, Langan, and Levin (1999, 4–10); Durose, Levin, and Levin (2001, 4–11); Durose and Langan (2003, 4–11); Langan and Cohen (1996, 59–61).
[1] The prison rate equals the ratio of prison commitments to drug arrests expressed as a percentage.
[2] The conviction rate equals the ratio of court convictions to arrests; the percentage pleas equals the share of convictions on plea agreements.
[3] Percentage served is the ratio of the actual term to sentence.

tough" prosecution and sentencing laws. In states with mandatory minimum sentences for drug violations, after all, the successful prosecution of a more serious felony drug arrest will inexorably lead to a prison term. To distill the effects of these distinct policy levers over the period from 1986 to 2000, we present evidence on conviction rates per arrest as well as prison-sentence rates per conviction (only for more serious drug-trafficking offenses). In the late 1980s, both rates rose by comparable levels and together increased the risk of imprisonment on a trafficking charge by nearly three-quarters (from 15.1 to 26.0 percent). By 2000, the prison rate reached nearly one-third (over twice the rate in 1986), but this was only because aggressive prosecution more than offset the decline in prison-sentencing rates. Over the decade, felony conviction rates jumped from 53.2 percent to 77.8 percent, whereas convicted felons were more likely to receive lighter sentences to jail or even probation.

The steady growth in conviction rates attests to the greater likelihood of criminal indictments on drug-trafficking violations, as over 90 percent of the cases were settled by plea agreements and not by jury trials (this is at least true in the 1990s; see table 3.2, column 2). Still, prosecutors' hands were bolstered by higher-quality cases supported with direct police evidence. Also, tougher sentencing policies made defendants, especially first-time offenders, more likely to accept a plea agreement on lesser charges with less-harsh penalties.

The columns displaying prison sentence data offer additional evidence on the impacts of "get tough" front- and back-end sentencing policies for drug-trafficking convictions. With the diffusion of structured sentencing and mandatory minimum sentencing laws after 1980, prison sentences increased to six years, and terms increased to two years in 1992. Although average sentence lengths fell to four years over the decade, the actual time served increased by two months. The spread of truth-in-sentencing laws helps to explain these divergent trends. Their mandates contributed to the sharp increase in time served relative to sentence length (from just over one-third in 1992 to nearly one-half in 2000). The decline in average sentence length, in fact, may reflect the discretion of prosecutors and judges to compensate for tougher mandated release policies.

The greater use of back-end prison sentences by parole officers has also contributed to longer prison spells per court commitment. Between 1980 and 2000, the proportion of parole violators in new prison admissions more than doubled (from 16.1 percent to 35.0 percent). For drug offenders, this revolving door out of and back into prison has become much more common since 1980. In studies of 1983 and 1994 release cohorts, for example, the three-year reincarceration rate for drug offenders jumped from 30.3 percent to 49.2 percent over the observation period. Moreover, nearly one-quarter of the drug offenders in the 1994 cohort (that is, half of those recidivating) were returned to prison on a parole violation (Weiman, Stoll, and Bushway 2007).

Like Alfred Blumstein (1982, 1993), we also find evidence of racial disproportionality in the prosecution and sentencing of the war on drugs in the early 1990s, which reinforced the significant racial disparities in drug arrest rates. Compared to all juveniles arrested on drug violations, for example, African Americans were 37 percent more likely to be transferred to adult courts, where they faced tougher sanctions.[12] Among adults facing felony drug charges, blacks were indicted and convicted at much higher rates than whites. Although there were no significant differences in the incarceration rates of African Americans and whites convicted on drug charges, black offenders were more likely than whites to be committed to prison instead of jail, and they were more likely to receive longer sentences (Reaves and Smith 1995; Langan and Cohen 1996; Mauer and Huling 1995; Human Rights Watch 2008).[13]

To gauge the cumulative toll of the war-on-drug policies, we estimate its quantitative impact on the size and racial-ethnic composition of the prison population—that is, the two quantitative dimensions of mass incarceration. Whether measured in terms of the stock of total prisoners or the flow of new prison admissions, drug offenders contributed significantly to the expansion of the prison system, especially from 1983 to 1990 (see figure 3.5). Over this period, drug offenders accounted for just over 40 percent of the growth in state-prison population; by the end of the decade, 21.8 percent of all state prisoners had been convicted and sentenced on a drug violation (as compared to just under 7 percent at the beginning). Viewed alternatively, after this critical phase in the war on drugs, drug offenders would account for one third of all new prison admissions, whether on a new commitment or parole revocation (Raphael and Stoll, chapter 2 in this volume; Oliver and Yocom 2004).

Racial disparities in prison incarceration rates were relatively large even prior to the war on drugs (Langan 1991; Sampson and Lauritsen 1997; Weiman, Stoll, and Bushway 2007). Still, during this critical period, the cumulative risks of incarceration for blacks more than doubled from 13.4 percent in 1979 to 29.4 percent in 1991 (Bonczar and Beck 1997). In other words, if the past were a prologue, cohorts of African Americans born during this regime would face a nearly 30 percent chance of imprisonment at some point in their life. Over the same period, the lifetime risks of incarceration for whites increased by 75 percent, from a much lower base (from 2.5 percent to 4.4 percent).

The war on drugs was the proximate cause of this widening racial disparity (Mauer 1999; Tonry 1995). Focusing on new prison admission rates rather than incarceration rates, Pamela E. Oliver and James E. Yocom

Figure 3.5   *State Prisoners by Most Serious Offense*

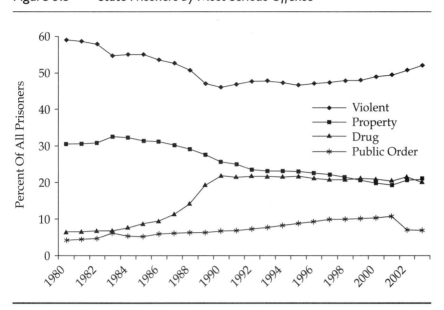

Source: Harrison and Beck (2005).

(1994) document a sharp increase in the black-white ratio: from just under seven in 1983 to around ten in 1990—an increase of more than 40 percent. When they investigate the proximate cause (that is, offense type) responsible for this abrupt change, they clearly implicate the war on drugs. Between 1983 and 1991, the racial disparity in prison-sentence rates multiplied by more than fourfold for drug offenses, but it only doubled for violent crimes. Updating their analyses of prison-admissions data, several recent reports have corroborated and refined these results (Beatty, Petteruti, and Ziedenberg 2007; Human Rights Watch 2008).

THE WAR ON DRUGS IN NEW YORK: FROM ROCKEFELLER TO KOCH

By all accounts, the state of New York was in the vanguard of the war on drugs, at least legislatively. In 1973, three years after Congress had repealed mandatory minimum sentences on drug violations dating from the 1950s, the state legislature adopted its own version of drug-law reform. What has been termed the "Rockefeller drug law" mandated steep minimum sentences on the sale and use of controlled substances (notably heroin and cocaine); significantly, like the federal statute, it also lessened the sanctions on marijuana possession.[14] At the time, the Rockefeller law was considered to be among the toughest drug sanctions in the country—a dubious distinction that still holds today.

The original Rockefeller drug law contained three key reforms. First, through a more refined system of classification, it greatly expanded the scope of felony drug offenses from an A-1 offense for the sale of one ounce of a narcotic (or possession of two ounces) to class D and E felonies for possession with intent to sell illegal drugs and drug paraphernalia. Second, it significantly stiffened the penalties on all felony drug offenses, but especially on the class A (the first through third degree) offenses. To take the most extreme case, the law elevated the sale of one ounce of co-caine and heroin from a class C to a class A-1 drug felony offense—equiv-alent to homicide, first-degree kidnapping, and arson—which carried a mandatory minimum sentence of fifteen to twenty-five years in prison. Finally, to increase the sting of these penalties, the law also sharply cur-tailed prosecutors' discretion in negotiating pleas to only those charged with class A felonies and only in exchange for material evidence.

The Rockefeller law was not passed in isolation. Immediately on its heels, the legislature also enacted a Second Felony Offender (SFO), or two-strikes, law. The law defined a new class of predicate felons, who had been convicted but not necessarily incarcerated (in any jurisdiction, not only in the state of New York) on a priory felony offense within the past ten years. If found guilty on a second offense, they either faced a steeper mandatory minimum sentence when a first offender could have received probation, or they faced an elevated charge (such as from a class C to class B offense) and associated steeper penalties (or, in some cases, both). The SFO law was largely intended for felony drug violations, and it now almost exclusively applies to these crimes because of subsequent changes to the criminal law for juvenile and violent offenders.

The politics of the Rockefeller laws illustrate the interplay of the coun-tervailing political forces shaping U.S. criminal-justice policies in the 1970s. As is evident by his seemingly contradictory drug policies during the period, Nelson Rockefeller was straddling a tenuous middle ground in an increasingly polarized polity (Barker 2006; Chartock 1974; Griset 1991). Through his budget priorities even after 1973, Governor Rocke-feller demonstrated a firm commitment to drug-rehabilitation programs and the underlying view that treatment, not incarceration, was the appro-priate cure for petty drug dealers.

His "rehabilitative ideal" was confronted with the harsh realities of the heroin and violent-crime epidemic that swept through New York City in the early 1970s, seen in the surging homicide rates just prior to the legisla-tion (see figure 3.6). However, instead of embracing the emerging conven-

Figure 3.6   *Crime Rates in New York State, 1960 to 2005 (Crimes per 100,000 People)*

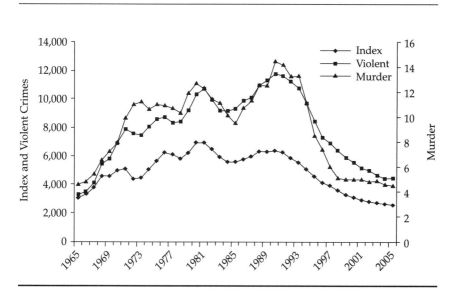

Source: U.S. Bureau of Justice, Federal Bureau of Investigation, Uniform Crime Reporting Program (2005 and earlier years).

tional wisdom that "nothing works," Rockefeller crafted a more pragmatic solution that wielded the punitive drug law against high-level drug dealers, while providing rehabilitation services for "jugglers" who sold drugs to feed their habits (Barker 2006).[15] According to this view, the two policies were complementary: the former, if successful, would disrupt the supply channels that had undermined the success of the latter by cheaply feeding the habits of drug addicts.

At the same time, Rockefeller's presidential ambitions clearly confronted and accommodated another stark reality, albeit in the political realm: the conservative drift of the Republican Party. Through his unwavering support of the drug law as well as his tough stance on the Attica prison uprising and the death penalty, Rockefeller strengthened his conservative law-and-order credentials for a likely nomination campaign against Ronald Reagan, who as California governor pioneered the conservative turn in sentencing reform. Closer to home, this political trend bolstered the ranks of the Conservative Party, which constituted the critical swing votes for the drug law (Benjamin 1974; Flanagan, McGarrel, and Lizotte 1989; Flanagan, Cohen, and Brennan 1993). The bill passed the State

Figure 3.7   *New York State and U.S. Incarceration Rates,*
                1960 to 2005

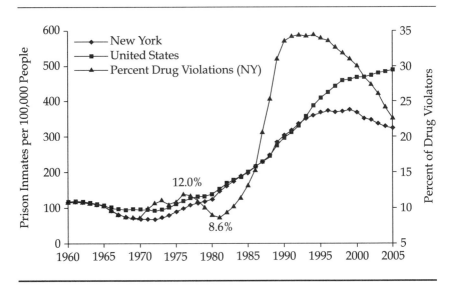

Source: Correctional Association of New York (2006).

Senate by an overwhelming forty-one to fourteen majority on April 27, but it was held up in the State Assembly by opposition from more liberal Democrats and the Conservative Party. With this choice of coalition partners, the Republican leadership pressured Rockefeller to compromise with the Conservatives on the plea-agreement provision of the bill and, particularly, on the SFO law (Griset 1991).[16]

The evidence in figure 3.7 suggests that pragmatism may have trumped politics in the immediate implementation of the Rockefeller drug and SFO laws. The trends in the overall prison population during the 1970s are certainly consistent with their expected effects. After a nearly decade-long decline, the incarceration rate reversed course in 1973 and grew steadily until 1980. Yet, the share of inmates on drug violations increased only marginally from 11 percent to 12 percent between 1972 and 1977, and then actually fell to pre-1973 levels by 1980. Moreover, there is no trend break in the annual average growth rate in this inmate population over the period from 1970 to 1977.

Resource constraints—in this case, by default and not by design—can plausibly explain the sudden shift in the state's war on drugs. Because of fiscal crisis, the New York City police department sharply cut its force size after 1974 and shifted its priorities from the drug beat to more serious violent crimes (Corman and Mocan 2000; Langan and Durose 2004; "Full Jails a Problem Throughout Region" by E. R. Shipp, *New York Times*, May 18, 1980, WC p. 1; "McGuire Appraises Police and Outlines Some Goals" by Barbara Basler, *New York Times*, June 9, 1981, p. B1). Still, other evidence—declines in drug-poisoning deaths and homicide rates beginning around 1974—points to an alternative explanation that the heroin epidemic had peaked by 1973 (see figure 3.6). Accordingly, a study conducted by the Association of the Bar of the City of New York, Joint Committee on New York Drug Law Evaluation (1977) documents a 71.9 percent drop in felony drug arrests in New York City between 1970 and 1973. Not only did this dramatic decline precede the city's fiscal crisis, but also it was due mainly to the even larger 83.3 percent fall in arrests related to heroin.

The Bar Association's careful before-after study of the immediate impact of the Rockefeller law further corroborates Vanessa Barker's (2006) hypothesis of pragmatic politics. Two years into the new legal regime, the number of inmates committed to prison on felony drug offenses had not increased significantly. The reason, the study finds, is that drug arrests, indictments, and convictions in New York City had fallen sharply over the period. Having opposed the law, which they regarded as wasteful if not counterproductive, local criminal-justice authorities from the police to judges simply refused to enforce it, at least against marginal drug offenders. Taking a more pragmatic stance, they did succeed in locking up more serious drug dealers for longer terms, although the evidence on drug markets indicates that this policy of selective incarceration had little impact on supply chains.

Obviously, conditions changed in the 1980s as convicted drug offenders fueled the rapid growth in the state's prison population and incarceration rate (see figure 3.7). Between 1980 and 1988, the share of drug offenders among prison inmates jumped from 9 percent to 25.4 percent; by this date, drug offenders accounted for 37 percent of all new prison commitments. We chose the end-date judiciously: one factor that had not changed at that point was the Rockefeller drug law, which was strengthened in 1988 in response to the raging crack epidemic in New York City (Nelson 1992; Greenstein 1989). Strikingly, the revision, which lowered the quantity thresholds to trigger the law's tough sanctions, did not significantly deflect the prior trend growth.

The escalation of the war on drugs in New York after 1980, then, depended on local policy innovations that multiplied felony drug arrests and convictions under the existing statute, rather than on legislative changes that expanded its scope. More funding from federal and state sources for additional prisons, judges, prosecutors, and police certainly

Figure 3.8   *Frequency of Reporting on Drug Enforcement-Related Topics in the* New York Times, *1980 to 1990*

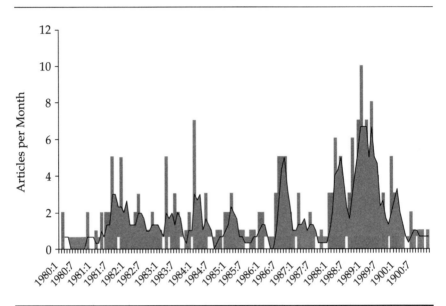

Source: Authors' calculations from ProQuest Historical Newspapers, *The New York Times* (1851–2005).

qualified as contributing to the growth in incarceration, but they too required implementation at the grassroots level (that is, complementary local policies). To identify these changes, we searched editions of the *New York Times* from the 1980s and located 222 articles related to local, state, and federal drug-law enforcement. Although the *New York Times* is an admittedly selective source on these matters, the trends in its coverage are strongly correlated with key events in the war on drugs such as recurrent drug and violent-crime epidemics as well as significant policy initiatives in response (see figure 3.8).[17]

Consistent with the turning point in the data, our search pinpointed two related developments in 1981, which Governor Hugh Carey laid out in his January budget address ("Transcript of Gov. Carey's Message at Opening of the 204th Session of Legislature," *New York Times*, January 8, 1981, p. A1; "Excerpts for Governor's Budget Statement List Some Goals for Next Decade," *New York Times*, January 20, 1981, p. 40). The first specified significant state investments in criminal-justice capacity at the state and local levels. His budget included more funding for prison construction and state prosecutors, but also more funding for local law enforcement. With state (and later federal) assistance as well as burgeoning tax coffers funded by the economic recovery and fiscal reforms, the Ed Koch administration expanded the size of the city's police force by 19 percent between 1981 and 1988 (Corman and Mocan 2000; Langan and Durose 2004).

Second, and equally important, was Governor Hugh Carey's announcement of a new joint state-local police initiative to be rolled out mid-year, which would target more serious drug trafficking offenses "in . . . cities where the[ir] incidence . . . is most severe." Significantly, at the end of July, *New York Times* ("New Police Unit to Battle Drugs in Public Places" by Leonard Buder, July 31, 1981, p. A1) reported on the formation of a "new police unit," which would conduct undercover and sweep operations "to battle drugs in public places." In striking contrast to Governor Hugh Carey's message, however, the police operation would target the "low-level drug user," who the police commissioner claimed "has not been treated seriously enough." When informed of the policy, the Manhattan district attorney pledged his cooperation, but also expressed concerns over the allocation of policing and prosecutors' resources to misdemeanor drug arrests, typically punishable by a fine or probation. Nonetheless, judging by the frequency of the reporting, the police hierarchy appeared eager to keep the press informed about the unit's activities, even though the vast majority of arrests (70 percent according to one article) "resulted in nonjail sentences" (E. R. Shipp, "City Makes Big Issue of Little Crimes," *New York Times*, August 30, 1981, p.179; see also "New Police Unit to Battle Drugs in Public Places" by Leonard Buder, *New York Times*, July 31, 1981, p. A1).

Undeterred by these outcomes, Mayor Koch affirmed his commitment to the program in late August, which he couched in terms of a broader agenda against "quality-of-life" offenses (*New York Times*, August 30, 1981, p. 179).[18] Anticipating an *Atlantic Monthly* article by James Q. Wilson and George L. Kelling in the following year ("Broken Windows," March 1982), Mayor Koch and his police commissioner articulated the foundations of this novel policing strategy to "retake the streets." They insisted that targeted operations (ranging from undercover and sweep arrests of "gamblers, prostitutes, and drug dealers" to merely disbanding loitering gangs) in neighborhoods rife with disorder and fear would restore "respect for authority and adherence to law," as well as "for other people . . . [and] other people's property." In 1984 and again in 1988, Mayor Koch and his new police commissioner, Benjamin Ward, invoked the same rationale to explain the evolution and escalation of police strategies in response to other heroin and crack epidemics (Operation Pressure Point and the Tactical Narcotics Teams, respectively).

Following the announcement of these initiatives, a series of articles in the *New York Times* recorded their short- and longer-term impacts ("Police Moving to Halt Drug Sales on Streets of Lower East Side" by David W. Dunlap, *New York Times*, January 20, 1984, p. B2; "Transfers begin at Police Unit in Queens Area" by George James, *New York Times*, March 9, 1988, p. B3). As intended, each foray immediately led to mounting arrests of low-level drug dealers and sharp drops in reported crimes—notably robberies and burglaries—in the targeted areas. Each surge in arrests translated into more felony convictions and longer prison sentences, especially for the large and increasing share of repeat offenders. Yet, the *New York Times* articles ultimately echoed the sobering conclusions about the effectiveness of the earlier crackdowns: The vast majority of arrests were either dismissed or did not result in jail sentences because of overcrowded prosecutors' offices and courts or because of the poor quality of police evidence. Moreover, with the exception of the initial Operation Pressure Point campaign on the Lower East Side, subsequent measures had, at best, transitory effects on the drug trade and more serious crime.[19] Benjamin Ward readily acknowledged that these concentrated operations would only put a dent in the drug and associated violent-crime epidemics, but still justified these costly law-enforcement initiatives on the "broken windows" grounds of reclaiming neighborhoods and calming the complaints and fears of their residents ("Police Moving to Halt Drug Sales on Streets of Lower East Side" by David W. Dunlap, *New York Times*, January 20, 1984, p. B2).

The decisive shift from the politics of pragmatism in the Rockefeller era to the politics of disorder and fear in the Koch (and Reagan) years explains why incarceration rates in New York and the United States converge over the period from 1980 to 1992 (see figure 3.7; Garland 2001b; Simon 2007). Paralleling national trends, political realignments in New York City forged a new conservative majority that coalesced around a Democratic mayoral candidate, Ed Koch (Mollenkopf 1991, 1992). John Hull Mollenkopf shows that, paralleling Ronald Reagan's electoral success, Ed Koch's coalition combined traditional Republicans, who favored his conservative economic and fiscal policies, and traditionally Democratic white working-class and middle-class voters, to whom he appealed through his racially laced antiwelfare and law-and-order rhetoric (Rieder 1985, 1989; Mahler 2005). In turn, under Ed Koch, the New York City police pioneered many of the aggressive street-level tactics that diffused across other large cities and fueled the surge in drug arrests, convictions, and prison commitments (see figure 3.3; "How Police Target Young Offenders" by Marcia Chambers, *New York Times*, September 20, 1981, p. SM29; "Police Effectiveness: The Three Views of Three Experts" by Marilyn Chambers, *New York Times*, December 15, 1982, p. B1).

A more fundamental diagnosis of Ed Koch's electoral success, in turn, identifies a common national thread: the "fall of the New Deal [Democratic] order" (Fraser and Gerstle 1989; Sugrue 1996). Like Ronald Reagan's famous reference to the "misery index," Ed Koch's politics of disorder was not mere rhetoric. After all, he could point to glaring exemplars of an earlier flawed liberal regime—notably the city's fiscal collapse in 1974, the blackout riots in Brooklyn and the South Bronx in 1977, and the raging heroin and violent-crime epidemic in minority neighborhoods (see figure 3.6; Mahler 2005; Fuchs 1992; Brecher and Horton 1991).

Like the stagflation crisis, these pivotal events were products of deeper fissures in the city's political economy during the 1970s.[20] Structural economic changes, which both magnified and were reinforced by cyclical shocks, wracked the city's traditional economic bases. Over the 1970s, it suffered sharp employment drops in industrial and other well-paid unionized sectors as well as a net out-migration of population, especially white middle-class households, to suburban and more distant locations. With a diminished tax base and retrenchment in state and federal aid, the city government also curtailed its employment and social-welfare spending. The net result of these political economic forces was a sharp increase in the levels and spatial concentration of joblessness and poverty in minority neighborhoods—precisely the conditions conducive to the spread of disorder and crime (Jargowsky 1977; Sullivan 1991).

ACCOUNTING FOR MASS INCARCERATION IN NEW YORK

To gauge the relative impacts of grassroots policing and prosecution versus higher-order sentencing initiatives on new prison admissions, we follow the methodology of Alfred Blumstein and Allen J. Beck (1999), tracking aggregate flows of individuals through the New York City and state criminal-justice systems, from arrest through indictment, conviction, and sentencing. Our data come from the felony case processing reports published by New York State Division of Criminal Justice Services for the period from 1974 to 1994 (that is, from the year immediately following the adoption of the Rockefeller laws to the year when the Koch administration's version of quality-of-life policing was dismantled) ("Police in New York Shift Drug Battle Away from Street" by Joseph B. Treaster, *New York Times*, August 3, 1992, p. A1).[21] Over these two decades, we collected data for the years 1974, 1979, 1984, and 1994; these years demarcate distinct phases of New York City's war on drugs. To see whether the selective pragmatic implementation of the Rockefeller drug laws or the resource constraints explain the relative decline in drug-related incarceration in the late 1970s, we also reexamined the original individual-level data on arrests and case processing compiled by the Association of the Bar of the City of New York, Joint Committee on New York Drug Law Evaluation (1977).

Our analysis is carried out in two steps. We first distill the rich information in the state reports into three sets of variables: total arrests, the conditional likelihood of an indictment on an arrest and of a conviction on an indictment, and the percentage distribution of convicted felons by sentence type ranging from prison to probation (see table 3.3). Including only convicted felons sentenced to prison, these variables identically determine the annual flow of new prison commitments (this is presented in the last line of table 3.3, along with an estimate of the "risk of imprisonment").[22] The data in the top and bottom panels of the table contrast trends in the policing, prosecution, and sentencing for all felony offenses and only drug felonies, respectively.

The First Five Years Under the Rockefeller Regime

Our results elaborate the anomalous findings on the initial impact of the Rockefeller drug laws on incarceration trends in the late 1970s. In 1974, the first full year of implementation of the Rockefeller laws, police statewide cleared just over 124,000 felony arrests, of which 14.1 percent were for drug violations (see table 3.3 for the levels in each year; see table 3.4 for the growth rates over each interval). Five years later, although total felony arrests increased by nearly 11 percent, the number of drug arrests under the Rockefeller laws fell by more than one-third. These statewide figures mask significant regional variation; the 5.4 percent increase in drug arrests in New York City was more than offset by a 70 percent drop in the rest of the state.

Reinforcing the trend in drug arrests, indictment rates on felony drug charges declined slightly from 35.5 percent to 30.7 percent over this five-year interval. According to the Association of the Bar of City of New York, Joint Committee on New York Drug Law Evaluation (1977), the police and prosecutors did not aggressively enforce the Rockefeller drug laws immediately after its adoption for two reasons: They regarded their earlier efforts to curb drug use through mass arrests as largely ineffective. Also, they believed that the judges would be unable to keep up with the workload generated by this policy and would either dismiss the charges or release convicted felons on probation.

Yet, despite the evident reluctance of local law-enforcement agencies, the flow of new prison commitments on felony drug charges jumped by more than 40 percent between 1974 and 1979. Put another way, the risk of imprisonment conditional on an arrest for a felony drug violation more than doubled (from 4.3 percent to 9.4 percent) over the period, and those

Table 3.3   *Flows of Felony Arrests Through the New York Criminal-Justice System*

All Felonies	1974	1979	1984	1994
Number of arrests	124,296	137,758	150,118	198,843
Indictment or arrest (%)	27.7	22.9	30.7	34.3
Convicted or indictment (%)	63.8	77.9	83.1	87.3
Sentence or conviction (%)	89.7	93.3	96.6	98.6
Prison (%)	31.7	37.8	40.1	43.9
Jail (%)	14.1	24.3	28.2	27.3
Incarceration (%)	45.7	62.2	68.3	71.3
Probation (%)	43.9	31.1	28.3	18.8
New prison commitments	6960	9286	15348	26193
Prison rate per arrest (%)	5.6	6.7	10.2	13.2

Drug Felonies	1974	1979	1984	1994
Number of arrests	17,472	11,305	23,459	55,803
(% of total)	14.1	8.2	15.6	28.1
Indictment or arrest (%)	35.5	30.7	32.7	49.8
Convicted or indictment (%)	51.0	75.7	75.4	92.9
Sentence or conviction (%)	88.4	95.2	97.9	89.2
Prison (%)	23.8	40.7	39.4	46.4
Jail (%)	10.8	26.4	34.5	29.4
Incarceration (%)	34.6	67.1	73.9	75.9
Probation (%)	53.8	28.1	24.0	13.3
New prison commitments	755	1,068	2,277	11,991
Prison rate per arrest (%)	4.3	9.4	9.7	21.5

Source: New York State Division of Criminal Justice Services (1975, 1980, 1985, 1995).

convicted on felony drug charges—especially the most serious class A offenses—received longer minimum sentences (Association of the Bar of the City of New York, Joint Committee on New York Drug Law Evaluation 1977). This greater incarceration risk derived from the 50 percent increase in the rate of conviction on drug-related indictments (from approximately 51 percent to 75.7 percent) as well as the near doubling of the share of prison sentences for convicted felons (from 23.8 percent to 40.7 percent).

This evidence further supports our view on the selective pragmatic enforcement of the Rockefeller drug laws, influenced perhaps by resource constraints. The results of the study conducted by the Association

Table 3.4   *Accounting for the Growth in New Prison Commitments*

Felonies	% Change		
	1974–1979	1979–1984	1984–1994
All			
Number of arrests	10.8	9.0	32.5
Indictment or arrest	–17.4	34.1	11.9
Convicted or indictment	22.0	6.7	5.1
Prison Sentence or conviction	19.5	6.0	9.5
New prison commitments	33.4	65.3	70.7
"Growth accounting"	34.6	64.7	69.9
Sum of factors	34.9	55.8	59.0
First-order interactions	–0.3	8.9	10.8
Local factors	12.1	55.8	55.6
Percent local	34.9	86.2	79.6
Drug			
Number of arrests	–35.3	107.5	137.9
Indictment or arrest	–13.8	6.7	52.3
Convicted or indictment	48.4	–0.4	23.2
Prison sentence or conviction	70.9	–3.3	18.0
New prison commitments	41.5	113.2	426.6
"Growth accounting"	50.8	113.5	386.0
Sum of factors	70.2	110.5	231.4
First-order interactions	–19.4	3.0	154.6
Local factors	–19.6	120.6	329.6
Percent local		106.3	85.4

Source: Authors' compilation.
Note: The figures are the percentage change of each factor over the period. The growth accounting is the sum of the percentage change of each factor and the first-order interaction effects. The local factors only sum the contributions from local factors.

of the Bar of the City of New York, Joint Committee on New York Drug Law Evaluation (1977), corroborated by our reexamination of the original data, affirm that police tended to arrest and prosecutors tended to indict those charged with more serious violations; the harshest punishments of imprisonment were reserved for older, often repeat felony offenders. Consequently, we do not see the declines in each of the steps of felony processing leading to incarceration, as predicted by the resource-constraint view.

The Rockefeller Regime After 1979

After 1979 the quantitative evidence affirms the pronouncements by Ed Koch and his police commissioner Robert McGuire of a profound shift in the city's enforcement regime, which they dubbed "quality-of-life policing," targeting less serious felony and misdemeanor drug offenders. Between 1979 and 1984, felony drug arrests in the state of New York more than doubled, from 11,300 to 23,500. Significantly, the 136 percent increase in felony drug arrests in the city accounted for virtually all of the change at the state level. This trend continued over the next decade. Drug felony arrests more than doubled by 1994, comprising 28 percent of all felony arrests statewide (up from 14 percent in 1974). Once again, leading the way was New York City, where felony drug arrests accounted for nearly 80 percent of the state totals.

Tracing these cases through the rest of the criminal-justice system, we find no evidence of tougher enforcement until 1984. During the early years of Ed Koch's administration, the incarceration rate conditional on an arrest did not change significantly, at least for those charged with drug violations. The indictment rate increased marginally, but the probabilities of a conviction and a prison sentence remained virtually unchanged. Consequently, the multiplication in drug arrests accounted for virtually the entire 113.5 percent increase in new prison commitments on drug charges and for 70 percent of the increase in new commitments to New York state prisons over the period.

After 1984, by contrast, the risk of imprisonment for the mounting numbers of individuals arrested on felony drug charges more than doubled (from 9.7 percent to 21.5 percent). As tables 3.3 and 3.4 show, this virtual noose tightened at each stage of the process. Prosecutors brought indictments against nearly half of those arrested, as opposed to indicting only a third a decade earlier. They won convictions in more than 93 percent of the cases, as compared to 75 percent in 1984, usually through a plea agreement. Finally, judges were significantly less likely to let convicted drug felons off on probation, and they were more inclined to sentence them to longer terms in prison rather than in jail. Put in context, felony drug offenders were treated more harshly than the norm under the new harsher criminal-justice regime, as measured by their significantly greater risk of imprisonment compared to the average for all felony arrests (21.5 percent versus 13.2 percent). When resolved into its constituent parts, this 63.1 percent difference in prison rates derives mainly from more aggressive prosecution of felony drug cases, which resulted in the greater frequency of indictments and negotiated convictions.

As further evidence on the timing of this regime shift, we examined

Table 3.5   *Characteristics of New Admissions to New York State Prisons (Percent of all Prison Admissions)*

	1984	1989	1994
Male	95.8	93.4	92.9
African American	67.2	51.0	77.1
High school or less	94.6	90.9	93.0
New York City	68.5	71.2	68.6
Drug crime (as any)	15.8	40.9	45.6
Trafficking	12.1	29.4	34.8
Possession	5.1	14.6	13.2

Source: National Corrections Reporting Program
Admissions Files (1984, 1989, 1999).
Note: The data on race-ethnicity are not entirely consistent because of the erratic reporting of "unknown" cases.

the individual-level data on admissions to New York state prisons as part of the National Corrections Reporting Program (see table 3.5). Our analysis confirms the staggering increase in the percentage of inmates convicted on felony drug charges after 1984. In this initial year, only 16 percent of the state's inmate population had been convicted of a drug crime. Five years later, this figure more than doubled to 41 percent, and it then increased marginally by 1994 to its current level of around 46 percent. When broken down by crime type, the evidence shows roughly comparable increases in those convicted and sentenced on trafficking and possession charges. Finally, as these data affirm, the war on drugs disproportionately targeted less-educated minority men in large urban centers such as New York City.

A Growth-Accounting Exercise

To summarize and sharpen our conclusions, we present a simple accounting analysis of the growth in new prison commitments on drug felony charges over the periods 1974 to 1979, 1979 to 1984, and 1984 to 1994 (see table 3.4). The entries under the heading "growth accounting" decompose the growth rate in prison commitments into the growth rate of the individual factors—from total arrests to the share of prison sentences among convicted felons—as well as first-order interaction terms to capture acute changes, especially after 1984.[23] Finally, to gauge the impact of local policy innovations in the war on drugs, we sum the first three factors and corresponding interaction terms.

This analysis, we caution, can only yield proximate, not definitive, results for (at least) two reasons. First, our measure clearly overstates the contribution of purely local factors to the growth in new prison commitments, as it ignores the role of state and federal spending in bolstering the ranks of local law-enforcement agencies and the role of tougher Rockefeller drug laws in bolstering the plea-bargaining power of prosecutors. Additionally, because of abrupt changes in underlying factors, the analysis clearly overstates the growth in prison commitments in the first period and understates it in the last.

The results for the period from 1974 to 1979 clearly implicates local factors in explaining why the Rockefeller laws did not have a larger immediate impact on the overall incarceration rate in the state of New York. Consistent with the findings of the Association of the Bar of the City of New York, Joint Committee on New York Drug Law Evaluation (1977) as well as our narrative account, the reluctance of local police and prosecutors to aggressively enforce the law reduced the growth in new prison commitments on drug charges by nearly 20 percentage points (by almost 30 percent). A further aggravating factor, according to the study conducted by the Association of the Bar of the City of New York, was mounting congestion in the court system. This is evidenced by the doubling of processing time for drug law cases between 1973 and 1976 (compared to a constant time to disposition for all other felony offenses).

After 1979, local factors also had a large quantitative impact; however, in this case, the impact was on the surge in drug offenders sentenced to prison. In the early years of Ed Koch's administration, the mass arrest of drug offenders was the most significant factor, which by itself accounted for virtually the entire increase. Over the period from 1984 to1994, local police and prosecutors operated in tandem (that is, almost equally) in fueling the more than fivefold multiplication in drug-related prison commitments. Put in perspective, our analysis suggests that local factors were slightly more important in explaining incarceration trends for drug relative to other felony convictions.

Through a simulation exercise, we present the drug felony results from the 1984 to 1994 period from a slightly different vantage point (see table 3.6 and figure 3.9). The first row of table 3.6 replicates the conditions for each factor and new prison commitments from the 1984 column of table 3.3. In each subsequent row, we adjust each factor from its 1984 to 1994 level, and we then estimate (or simulate) its quantitative impact on the implied level and the corresponding percent change in prison commitments. For example, if all other factors except drug arrests remained constant at their 1984 levels, then prison commitments on drug convictions would jump by 3,100, equal to 32.3 percent or almost one-third of the total growth for the decade. Tougher prosecution in the form of higher indict-

Table 3.6   *The Impact of Local and State-Level Factors in the Growth of New Prison Commitments on Felony Drug Charges: A Simulation*

Arrests	Indictment or Arrest	Convicted or Indictment	Prison Sentence or Conviction	Implied Prison Commitments	Percent of 1984–1994 Change
1984	1984	1984	1984	2279.0	0
1994	1984	1984	1984	5416.5	32.3
1994	1994	1984	1984	8249.0	61.5
1994	1994	1994	1984	10163.5	81.2
1994	1994	1994	1994	11991.0	100.0

Note: The figure in each column indicates the year of the parameter estimate. For example, the estimates in the first row all come from 1984 and yield the actual level of new drug felony commitments. "Implied Commitments" equals the simulated flow of new commitments based on the parameter estimates for the row. The "% of change" column measures the cumulative contribution of the varying parameter estimates and is simply the ratio of the change in the implied commitments relative to the original level to the change in actual commitments over the decade.

ment rates (see row 3, table 3.6) adds another 2,800 prison commitments, or nearly 30 percent of the total. If we attribute only half of the conviction rates to prosecutorial discretion, local factors would account for roughly 70 percent of the growth in prison commitments over the decade. Figure 3.9 depicts these results graphically by showing, for each step in the simulation, the quantitative impact of each factor on implied prison commitments and its contribution to total change over the decade.

EPOCHAL CHANGE AND THE RELATIVE STABILITY OF PUNISHMENT

To underscore the decisive connection between the war on drugs and mass incarceration, we track long-term trends in the U.S. incarceration rate since 1880. For the pre-1925 period, the analysis must rely on the periodic Census Bureau enumeration of the total incarcerated population, including those in jails and reformatories. Extending the Census Bureau figures to 1980, Margaret Cahalan (1979; Cahalan 1986) compiled a consistent series for the century, which matches up well with Bureau of Justice Statistics data for the modern (post-1930) period. For example, the Census Bureau series also shows the relative stability of incarceration rates, albeit at a slightly higher average level than expected (compare figure 3.10 to figure 3.1).

Figure 3.9   *The Impact of Local and State-Level Policies: A Simulation*

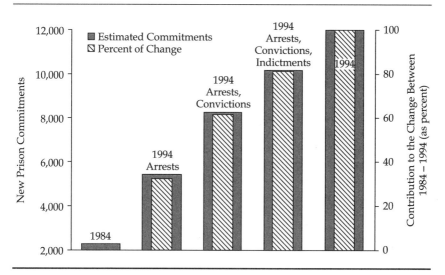

Source: Authors' calculations based on results in table 3.6.

Figure 3.10   *U.S. Incarceration Rate, 1880 to 1980 (Prison and Reformatory Inmates per 100,000 People)*

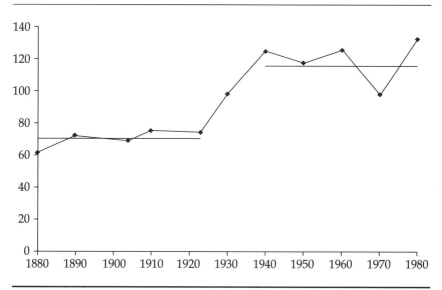

Source: Cahalan (1986, 30).

As Cahalan (1979) observes, these historical statistics call into question the very empirical foundations of Alfred Blumstein and Jacqueline Cohen's (1973) original stability-of-punishment hypothesis. According to the Census Bureau estimates, the total incarceration rate in United States hovered around 70 inmates per 100,000 until 1923, after which it increased by nearly two-thirds over the next two decades. From this perspective, the initial surge in incarceration rates before 1940 observed in the Bureau of Justice Statistics data (see figure 3.1) corresponds to an abrupt transition to a new higher plateau rather than a homeostatic adjustment from a transitory trough.

In response to Cahalan's findings, Alfred Blumstein and Soumyo Moitra (1980) qualify, not reject, the original hypothesis. They insist on the stability of punishment over extended periods of relative social order—around forty years according to these data—punctuated by sharp transitions during periods of fundamental structural economic, social, and political change. In particular, they emphasize the impact of World War I in accelerating geographical mobility and urbanization, which led to an increased reliance of formal social control in large urban centers rather than the more informal mechanisms within rural communities.

We are sympathetic to this alternative epochal view on the stability of punishment, at least for the United States as a whole (Berk et al. 1981; Schneider 2006). It would imply, for example, that the run-up in incarceration rates over the nearly two-decade period from the late 1970s to the late 1990s corresponds to yet another transition phase to an even higher plane. Of course, such a conclusion is premature until we accumulate more evidence on the relative incarceration rates after 1998, when they seem to level off again.

While skeptical of Blumstein and Moitra's (1980) explanation of the interwar transition, we can point to a common proximate cause of accelerating incarceration rates beginning in the early 1920s and in the 1980s: prohibitions against alcohol and drugs, respectively.[24] Like current corrections statistics, the historical census data enumerate the inmate population by crime type; its "moral offenses" category roughly corresponds to public-order and drug crimes in today's parlance. Between 1910 and 1923, the share of inmates incarcerated on moral offenses jumped from 5.5 percent to 17.3 percent, an almost parallel increase to the surge in imprisoned drug offenders during the 1980s (compare figure 3.11 to figure 3.5). After peaking in 1940 at 25.6 percent (or 18.4 percent using the narrower definition of prison inmates on felony charges only), the percentage of inmates incarcerated for moral offenses declined steadily until the 1970s. During the earlier episode, most of the inmates in this offense category were charged with liquor-law and drunkenness violations;

Figure 3.11   *Share of Inmates Incarcerated for "Moral" Crimes,*
                1923 to 1980

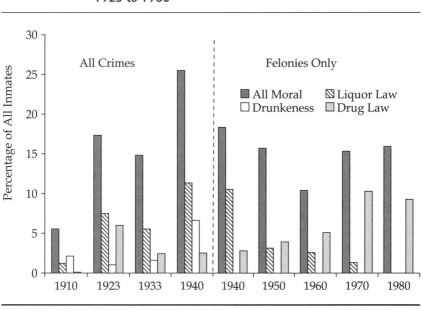

Source: Cahalan (1986, 45).

the former, more serious felony crime increased around nine-fold over the thirty-year period.

Numerous studies have found striking parallels between the earlier prohibition against alcohol and the more recent war on drugs (Musto 1999; Levine and Reinarman 1991). Despite the public-health and safety rhetoric of reformers and political allies, these policies targeted disadvantaged ethnic-racial communities, particularly in larger urban centers. Similarly, they both drew popular support from an anxious middle class, which feared the decline in traditional values and mounting social disorder, and fixed the blame on these "alien" groups (Allen 1931; Wiebe 1967; Davis 2007; Lerner 2007). Ironically, the strict enforcement of these moral codes is strongly correlated with lethal violence, seen as a dispute-resolution mechanism for turf battles within and between the illegal distribution networks that mediated the risky but potentially lucrative black markets of booze and drugs (Miron 1999, 2001).

In the end, both episodes have been aptly characterized as "moral panics" (Musto 1999; Tonry 1999). While no simple formula can account for these paroxysms in the political culture, our reading of the recent and more distant past identifies common economic and political ingredients. Both occurred in the midst of profound structural economic changes that would fuel rapid productivity and economic growth in subsequent decades (Abramowitz and David 2000; Gordon 2006; Goldin 2000; Goldin and Katz 1998; Bernstein 1989; Bresnahan 1999). More immediately, however, the economic changes caused wrenching dislocations, which derailed the relative demands for and earnings of less-skilled workers while threatening the traditional ways of life for many in the middle. At these moments, Republican politicians also scored significant electoral victories (it is unclear whether they constituted bona fide realignments) (Burnham 1986; Bartels 1998; Campbell 2006; Mayhew 2002). Through their morals and other conservative policies, these politicians bolstered the relative political economic status of their beleaguered middle-class constituents at the expense of ethnic-racial minorities in urban areas (Wilson 1976; Wacquant 2003).

NOTES

1. The incarceration rate in the U.S. case measures the number of state and federal inmates per 100,000 people. Alfred Blumstein and colleagues also present long-term evidence from Canada and Norway (Blumstein and Cohen 1973; Blumstein, Cohen, and Nagin 1976).
2. The U.S. Department of Justice, Bureau of Justice Assistance (1998) and Don Stemen, Andres Rengifo, and James Wilson (2005) systematically document these manifold policy shifts. David J. Rothman (2002), Michael H. Tonry (1996), and Jeremy Travis (2005) have studied the origins and demise of discretionary sentencing.
3. Tonry (1996) analyzes the early experience of these sentencing reforms, in particular their impact in narrowing racial-ethnic and gender disparities. The question of whether they controlled the growth in incarceration rates has sparked controversy because of potential spillovers from resource-constrained prisons to local jails. The most recent comprehensive studies statistically corroborate the effectiveness of explicit resource constraints in slowing the growth in the total, not just prison, incarceration rates (D'Alessio and Stolzenberg 1995; Marvel and Moody 1996; Nicholson-Crotty 2004; Stemen, Rengifo, and Wilson 2005; exchange between Marvel-Moody, Stolzenberg-D'Alessio, and Land-McLearly in the May 1996 issue of *Criminology* 34: 2).
4. Our terminology is inspired by Jeremy Travis (2005) and corresponds to the policies governing judges' sentencing decisions committing convicted offenders to prison versus the policies that determine a prisoner's initial release and subsequent prison spells on the initial commitment. Steven Raphael and Michael Stoll (chapter 2, this volume) analyze the frequency of multiple prison admissions on a single commitment and their impact on the length of prison terms per commitment.

5. Tonry (1996) argues that this upward bias follows from the fact that sentencing decisions are based on popular politics and abstract principles, not the concrete circumstances of the case. As evidence, Naomi Murakawa (2005) documents that federal mandatory minimum sentences on drug violations have been racheted up with each congressional election since 1983. Tonry, in turn, shows how the federal sentencing commission redrew its guidelines to ensure a mathematical consistency between each element of the sentencing grid and the new steeper minimum sentences on drug offenses.

6. This formulation conflates distinct policies of "more" versus "better" policing. Among the latter, we focus on "broken windows" and "quality of life" policing because of its relevance to New York (Wilson and Kelling 1982; Wilson 1985; Kelling and Bratton 1998). Skeptics question whether these innovations actually curbed crime (Levitt 2004; Wilson 1985). They worry that in practice the innovations amount to racial-ethnic profiling of individuals and communities (Fagan and Davies 2000; Harcourt and Ludwig 2006, 2007; Gelman, Fagan, and Kiss 2007).

7. K. Jack Riley (1997), Jeff Grogger and Micahel Willis (2000), and Roland G. Fryer and colleagues (2005) discuss the timing of the crack epidemic in the United States as a whole and by region. To underscore the relevance of the increase in misdemeanor marijuana possession violations, figure 3.3 includes an estimate of the total drug arrest rate less the arrest rate for marijuana possession over the period from 1980 to 1996. Excluding this component does not alter our subsequent analysis of the trends in drug arrests relative to violent- and property-crime arrests rates in the 1980s, but it does indicate that without this shift in policing, drug arrest rates would have leveled off in the late 1980s, rather than in the early 1990s, and at a much lower level.

8. The ratio of arrests to crimes hovered around 41.5 percent for violent crimes and 18.3 percent for property crimes. Based on a simple regression analysis, we discern no systematic trend in the arrest rate for violent crime and a slight decline (by 0.002 percent per year) in the arrest rate for property crimes. In other words, both series are basically constant.

9. The African American share of drug arrestees declined after 1991, in part because they were less likely to be arrested on misdemeanor marijuana possession charges (except in some locations such as New York City) (King 2008; Golub, Johnson, and Dunlap 2007; Levine and Small 2008; Human Rights Watch 2008).

10. Over this period, the percentage of white high-school seniors who reported using illegal drugs fell from 54.9 percent to 37.5 percent, while the percentage of blacks declined from 40.5 percent to 17 percent (Pastore and Maguire 2005; Western 2006; Fairlie 2002). Strikingly, the white-black gap in cocaine use widened in the late 1980s and again in the mid-1990s (that is, during the waves of the crack-cocaine epidemic).

11. The surge in marijuana possession arrests after 1991 partially explains the declining prison rate between 1990 and 1996. If arrest rates on these misdemeanor charges had remained constant over the period (at the average level between 1988 and 1992), then the total drug arrest rate would have been

around 20 percent lower in 1996 (461.6 arrests per 100,000, rather than 567.9); the implied prison rate would have fallen to only 9.5 percent, still five times the 1980 level.

12. Our index of racial disproportionality is a variant of the location coefficient. It compares the percentage of blacks among drug defendants transferred to adult courts (81 percent) with the percentage of black defendants adjudicated in juvenile courts (59 percent). Once in adult court, juvenile drug defendants in the early 1990s faced a 70 percent chance of conviction; if convicted, they faced a 50 percent chance of being sentenced to prison or jail (Strom, Smith, and Snyder 1998).

13. We note that the data on felony defendants come from the seventy-five largest urban counties, whereas the drug-arrest data are for all cities.

14. Ruth D. Peterson (1985), Naomi Murakawa (2005), and David T. Courtwright (2004) provide details on the federal drug-law reforms. Like the federal law, the Rockefeller drug law liberalized penalties against marijuana, which was more commonly sold and used by affluent white youth (Rosenblatt 1973). Our synopsis of the Rockefeller laws and its political history are drawn from work by Albert M. Rosenblatt (1973, 37–38), Association of the Bar of the City of New York, Joint Committee on New York Drug Law Evaluation (1977), Pamela L. Griset (1991), Vanessa Barker (2006), as well as articles from the *New York Times* ("Tough Drug Stand Urged By Both Parties at Albany" by Alfonso A. Narvaez, January 5, 1973, p. 65; "Governor's Bills to Combat Drugs Coming this Week" by Francis X. Cline, January 8, 1973, p. 109; "Legislators Seek a Compromise On Governor's Drug Penalties" by William E. Farrell, February 24, 1973. p. 60; "Mandatory Sentence Proposed For 2d-Felony Drug Offenses" by William E. Farrell, April 5, 1973, p. 49; "Governor Modifies Plan On Stiffer Drug Penalties" by William E. Farrell, April 13, 1973, p. 1; "Governor's Bill on Drug Traffic Voted by Senate" by William E. Farrell, April 28, 1973, p. 69; "Governor Urges Vote on Drug Bill" by Francis X. Cline, April 30, 1973, p 27; "G.O.P. in Assembly Delays Drug Bill" by Francis X. Cline, May 1, 1973, p. 86; "Vote on Drug Bill Is Again Delayed" by Francis X. Cline, May 2, 1973, p. 23; "Drug Bill Pressed by G.O.P. Leaders" by Francis X. Cline, May 3, 1973, p. 39; "Revised Narcotics Measure Is Voted 80-65 in Assembly" by William E. Farrell, May 4, 1973, p. 74, 77; "Governor Signs His Drug Bills And Assails the Critics Again" by William E. Farrell, May 9, 1973, p. 1).

15. For a review of the prevailing wisdoms on rehabilitation, see work by Frances T. Cullen (2005). According to Eric L. Sevigny and Jonathan P. Caulkins (2004), these "jugglers" were the modal inmate imprisoned for drug-related offenses.

16. Albert M. Rosenblatt (1973) considers this law to be particularly punitive, especially in comparison to the prior treatment of recidivists in the New York criminal code. The earlier law singled out persistent offenders—those who had been convicted and imprisoned on three felony offenses—for lengthy minimum sentences. With clear evidence of their failure to be rehabilitated in two prior prison spells, the law essentially regarded them as career criminals and opted for the treatment of incapacitation as a last, not first, resort.

17. By far, the largest share of articles was devoted to local matters, especially the policing and prosecution of drug offenses. To smooth out the trends, we also plotted a three-month (or one-quarter) moving average (shown in figure 3.7 with a solid line). We ignored the much larger number of articles focusing exclusively on the problems of rampant drug use and addiction.

18. In this and an earlier article ("Koch Takes Credit on Tougher Judges" by Barbara Basler, *New York Times*, August 25, 1981, p. B3) Mayor Koch also takes credit for pressuring judges to issue "tougher sentences" with longer jail and prison terms for less-serious misdemeanor and felony offenses.

19. Lynne Zimmer (1990) concludes that Operation Pressure Point succeeded in the Lower East Side because it operated in tandem with and reinforced the individual and collective action of pioneering settlers and developers in the gentrification of the neighborhood. In areas characterized by persistent poverty and disorder (such as Bedford-Stuyvesant and East Harlem), these targeted interventions only temporarily displaced drug traffickers to indoor or adjacent locations. The Citizens Crime Commission issued this indictment against the Tactical Narcotics Teams (TNT) initiative in late November 1988, which was affirmed by the more systematic study of a targeted Brooklyn neighborhood by the Vera Institute ("Study Faults Strategy in New York Drug Crackdown" by Selwyn Raab, *New York Times*, November 29, 1988, p. B1; Sviridoff et al. 1992). In late 1992, under the Dinkins Administration, the TNT units were gradually dismantled and replaced by a new strategy of community policing and more intensive street-level patrols (*New York Times*, August 3, 1992, p. A1).

20. Structural economic changes increasingly marginalized inner-city minority populations in New York and elsewhere (see Drennan 1991; Bailey and Waldinger 1991; Harris 1991; Mollenkopf 1992; Kasarda 1995; Wilson 1987; Sampson and Wilson 1995; Sampson and Raudenbush 1999).

21. Given the average "time to disposition" (especially for jury trials), an arrest in year 1974 may have been settled in 1975 or later. Still, the vast majority of cases were expedited through plea agreements. For this reasons, we simply link the arrest and disposition data for each year, although the growth in the latter no doubt lagged behind the growth in the former.

22. The annual flow of new prison comments is identically equal to:

$$\text{(total felony arrests)} \times \text{(indictment rate)} \times$$
$$\text{(conviction rate)} \times \text{(share of prison sentences)}$$

where the indictment rate equals the number of felony indictments per arrest; the conviction rate, the number of convictions per indictment; and the share of prison sentences, the percentage of convicted felons sentenced to prison. We define the risk of imprisonment as the ratio of new prison commitments per felony arrest; it measures the likelihood that an individual arrested on a felony charge will wind up in prison.

23. To be specific, the sum of the factors measure the growth rates in the number of arrests, the indictment-arrest rate, the conviction-indictment rate, and the share of convicted drug felons sentenced to prison. The interaction terms

measure the sum of the seven terms formed by multiplying the factors by each other.

24. Although World War I did accelerate the tide of south-north migration among whites and blacks, the observed change in incarceration rate does not occur until after 1923 (Margo 1990; Maloney 2002; Rosenbloom and Sundstrom 2004). Moreover, rural-urban migration in the northern United States grew rapidly after the Great Depression of the 1890s (Easterlin 1976). Finally, their hypothesis cannot readily explain the uneven regional trends in incarceration rates between 1910 and 1940 (for example, the sluggish growth or declining incarceration rates in receiving regions such as the Northeast and West, and the accelerating rates in sending regions such as the South).

REFERENCES

Abramovitz, Moses, and Paul A. David. 2000. "American Macroeconomic Growth in the Era of Knowledge-Based Progress: The Long-Run Perspective." In *The Long Nineteenth Century*, Vol. 2 of *The Cambridge Economic History of the United States*, edited by Stanley L. Engerman and Robert E. Gallman. New York: Cambridge University Press.

Allen, Frederick L. 1931. *Only Yesterday: An Informal History of the 1920s*. New York: Harper and Row.

American Friends Service Committee. 1971. *Struggle for Justice: A Report on Crime and Punishment in America*. New York: Hill and Wang.

Association of the Bar of the City of New York, Joint Committee on New York Drug Law Evaluation. 1977. *The Nation's Toughest Drug Law: Evaluating the New York Experience, Final Report of the Joint Committee on New York Drug Law Evaluation*. New York: Association of the Bar of New York City.

Bailey, Thomas, and Roger Waldinger. 1991. "The Changing Racial/Ethnic Division of Labor." In *Dual City: Restructuring New York*, edited by John H. Mollenkopf and Manuel Castells. New York: Russell Sage Foundation.

Barker, Vanessa. 2006. "The Politics of Punishing: Building a State Governance Theory of American Imprisonment Variation." *Punishment and Society* 8(1): 5–32.

Bartels, Larry M. 1998. "Electoral Continuity and Change, 1868–1996." *Electoral Studies* 17(3): 275–300.

Beatty, Phillip, Amanda Petteruti, and Jason Ziedenberg. 2007. "The Vortex: The Concentrated Racial Impact of Drug Imprisonment and the Characteristics of Punitive Counties." *Justice Policy Institute Report*. Washington, D.C.: Justice Policy Institute.

Beckett, Katherine, and Bruce Western. 2001. "Governing Social Marginality: Welfare, Incarceration, and the Transformation of State Policy." In *Mass Imprisonment: Social Causes and Consequences*, edited by David Garland. London: Sage.

Belenko, Steven, Jeffrey Fagan, and Ko-lin Chin. 1991. "Criminal Justice Responses to Crack." *Journal of Research in Crime and Delinquency* 28(1): 55–74.

Benjamin, Gerald. 1974. "Patterns in New York State Politics." *The Academy of Political Science* 31(3): 31–44.

Berk, Richard A., David Rauma, L. Messinger Sheldon, and Thomas F. Cooley. 1981. "A Test of the Stability of Punishment Hypothesis: The Case of California, 1851–1970." *American Sociological Review* 46(6): 805–29.

Bernstein, Michael A. 1989. "Why the Great Depression Was Great: Toward a New Understanding of the Interwar Economic Crisis in the United States." In *The Rise and Fall of the New Deal Order, 1930–1980*, edited by S. Fraser and G. Gerstle. Princeton, N.J.: Princeton University Press.

Blumstein, Alfred. 1982. "On the Racial Disproportionality of the United States' Prison Population." *The Journal of Criminal Law and Criminology* 73(3): 1259–81.

———. 1993. "Racial Disproportionality of the U.S. Prison Population Revisited." *University of Colorado Law Review* 64(3): 743–60.

Blumstein, Alfred, and Allen J. Beck. 1999. "Population Growth in U.S. Prisons, 1980–1996." *Crime and Justice: Prisons* 26: 17–61.

Blumstein, Alfred, and Jacqueline Cohen. 1973. "A Theory of the Stability of Punishment." *Journal of Criminal Law and Criminology* 64(2): 198–207.

Blumstein, Alfred, Jacqueline Cohen, and Daniel S. Nagin. 1976. "The Dynamics of a Homeostatic Punishment Process." *Journal of Criminal Law and Criminology* 67(3): 317–34.

Blumstein, Alfred, and Soumyo Moitra. 1980. "Growing or Stable Incarceration Rates: A Comment on Cahalan's 'Trends in Incarceration Rates in the United States since 1880.'" *Crime and Delinquency* 1980(1): 91–94.

Boggess, Scott, and John Bound. 1997. "Did Criminal Activity Increase during the 1980s? Comparisons across Data Sources." *Social Science Quarterly* 78(3): 725–39.

Bonczar, Thomas P., and Allen J. Beck. 1997. "Lifetime Likelihood of Going to State or Federal Prison." *Bureau of Justice Statistics Special Report*. Washington: U.S. Department of Justice.

Brecher, Charles, and Raymond Horton. 1991. "The Public Sector." In *Dual City: Restructuring New York*, edited by John H. Mollenkopf and Manuel Castells. New York: Russell Sage Foundation.

Bresnahan, Timothy F. 1999. "Computerisation and Wage Dispersion: An Analytical Reinterpretation." *Economic Journal* 109(456): F390–415.

Brown, Jodi M., Patrick A. Langan, and David J. Levin. 1999. "Felony Sentences in State Courts, 1996." *Bureau of Justice Statistics Bulletin*, NCJ 173939. Washington: U.S. Department of Justice.

Burnham, Walter Dean. 1986. "Periodization Schemes and 'Party Systems': The 'System of 1896' as a Case in Point." *Social Science History* 10(3): 263–314.

Cahalan, Margaret. 1979. "Trends in Incarceration in the United States Since 1888: A Summary of Reported Rates and the Distribution of Offenses." *Crime and Delinquency* 25(1): 9–41.

Cahalan, Margaret Werner 1986. "Historical Corrections Statistics in the United States, 1850–1984." *Bureau of Justice Statistics*. Washington: U.S. Department of Justice.

Campbell, James E. 2006. "Party Systems and Realignments in the United States, 1868–2004." *Social Science History* 30(3): 359–86.

Chartock, Alan. 1974. "Narcotics Addiction: The Politics of Frustration." *Academy of Political Science* 31(3): 239–49.

Corman, Hope, and H. Naci Mocan. 2000. "A Time-Series Analysis of Crime, Deterrence, and Drug Abuse in New York City." *American Economic Review* 90(3): 584–604.

Correctional Association of New York. 2006. "Trends in Prison Commitments." Available at: http://www.correctionalassociation.org/PPP/publications/trends_in_commitments_2006.pdf.

Courtwright, David T. 2004. "The Controlled Substances Act: How a 'Big Tent' Reform Became a Punitive Drug Law." *Drug and Alcohol Dependence* 76(1): 91–115.

Cullen, Frances T. 2005. "The Twelve People Who Saved Rehabilitation: How the Science of Criminology Made a Difference." *Criminology* 43(1): 1–42.

D'Alessio, Stewart, and Lisa Stolzenberg. 1995. "The Impact of Sentencing Guidelines on Jail Incarceration Rates in Minnesota." *Criminology* 33(2): 283–301.

Davis, Marni. 2007. "Prohibition, Anti-Semitism, and Economic Anxiety: Jewish Alcohol Entrepreneurs and Their Critics at the Turn of the Century." Unpublished manuscript, Georgia State University.

Ditton, Paula M., and Doris James Wilson. 1999. "Truth in Sentencing in State Prisons." *Bureau of Justice Statistics Bulletin*, NCJ 170032. Washington: U.S. Department of Justice.

Drennan, Matthew. 1991. "The Decline and Rise of the New York Economy." In *Dual City: Restructuring New York*, edited by John H. Mollenkopf and Manuel Castells. New York: Russell Sage Foundation.

Durose, Matthew R., and Patrick A. Langan. 2003. "Felony Sentences in State Courts, 2000." *Bureau of Justice Statistics Bulletin*, NCJ 198821. Washington: U.S. Department of Justice.

Durose, Matthew R., David J. Levin, and Patrick A. Langan. 2001. "Felony Sentences in State Courts, 1998." *Bureau of Justice Statistics Bulletin*, NCJ 190913. Washington, D.C.: U.S. Department of Justice.

Easterlin, Richard. 1976. "Population Change and Farm Settlement in the Northern United States." *Journal of Economic History* 36(1): 45–75.

Fagan, Jeffrey, and Garth Davies. 2000. "Street Stops and Broken Windows: Terry, Race and Disorder in New York City." *Fordham Urban Law Journal* 28(2): 457–504.

Fairlie, Robert W. 2002. "Drug Dealing and Legitimate SelfEmployment." *Journal of Labor Economics* 20(3): 538–67.

Flanagan, Timothy J., Debra Cohen, and Pauline Gasdow Brennan. 1993. "Crime Control Ideology among New York State Legislators." *Legislative Studies Quarterly* 18(3): 411–22.

Flanagan, Timothy J., Edmund F. McGarrel, and Alan J. Lizotte. 1989. "Ideology and Crime Control Policy Positions in a State Legislature." *Journal of Criminal Justice* 17(1): 87–101.

Frankel, Marvin. 1972. *Criminal Sentences: Law Without Order*. New York: Hill and Wang.

Fraser, Steve, and Gary Gerstle, eds. 1989. *The Rise and Fall of the New Deal Order, 1930–1980*. Princeton, N.J.: Princeton University Press.

Fryer, Roland G., Paul S. Heaton, Steven D. Levitt, and Kevin M. Murphy. 2005. "Measuring the Impact of Crack Cocaine." *NBER* working paper No. 11318. Cambridge, Mass.: National Bureau of Economic Research.

Fuchs, Ester R. 1992. *Mayors and Money: Fiscal Policy in New York and Chicago.* Chicago: University of Chicago Press.

Garland, David. 2001a. "Introduction: The Meaning of Mass Imprisonment." In *Mass Imprisonment: Social Causes and Consequences,* edited by D. Garland. London: Sage.

———. 2001b. *The Culture of Control: Crime and Social Order in Contemporary Society.* Chicago: University of Chicago Press.

Gelman, Andrew, Jeffrey Fagan, and Alex Kiss. 2007. "An Analysis of the New York City Police Department's 'Stop-and-Frisk' Policy in the Context of Claims of Racial Bias." *Journal of the American Statistical Association* 102(479): 813–23.

Glaze, Lauren E., and Thomas P. Bonczar. 2006. "Probation and Parole in the United States: 2005." *Bureau of Justices Statistics Bulletin,* no. 215091. Washington: U.S. Department of Justice.

Goldin, Claudia. 2000. "Labor Markets in the Twentieth Century." In *The Long Nineteenth Century,* Vol. 2 of *The Cambridge Economic History of the United States,* edited by Stanley L. Engerman and Robert E. Gallman. New York: Cambridge University Press.

Goldin, Claudia, and Lawrence F Katz. 1998. "The Origins of Technology-Skill Complementarity." *Quarterly Journal of Economics* 113(3): 693–732.

Golub, Andrew, Bruce D. Johnson, and Eloise Dunlap. 2007. "The Race/Ethnicity Disparity in Misdemeanor Marijuana Arrests in New York City." *Criminology and Public Policy* 6(1): 131–64.

Gordon, Robert J. 2006. "The 1920s and the 1990s in Mutual Reflection." In *The Global Economy in the 1990s: A Long-Run Perspective,* edited by Paul W. Rhode and Gianni Toniolo. New York: Cambridge University Press.

Greenberg, David F., and Valerie West. 2001. "State Prison Populations and Their Growth, 1971–1991." *Criminology* 39(3): 615–53.

Greenstein, Steven. 1989. "Arrest Rates and Post-Arrest Processing of Persons with Prior Felony Convictions." *Research Note.* Albany, N.Y.: New York State Division of Criminal Justice Services, Office of Justice Systems Analysis.

Griset, Pamala L. 1991. *Determinate Sentencing: The Promise and the Reality of Retributive Justice.* Albany, N.Y.: State University of New York Press.

Grogger, Jeff, and Michael Willis. 2000. "The Emergence of Crack Cocaine and the Rise in Urban Crime Rates." *Review of Economics and Statistics* 82(4): 519–29.

Guetzkow, Joshua. 2006. "Bars Versus Butter: The Prison-Welfare Tradeoff and its Political Underpinnings." Unpublished paper, University of California, Berkeley.

Harcourt, Bernard E., and Jens Ludwig. 2006. "Broken Windows: New Evidence from New York City and a Five-City Social Experiment." *University of Chicago Law Review* 73(1): 271–320.

———. 2007. "Reefer Madness: Broken Windows Policing and Misdemeanor Marijuana Arrests in New York City, 1989–2000." *Criminology and Public Policy* 6(1): 165–81.

Harris, Richard. 1991. "The Geography of Employment and Residence in New York Since 1950." In *Dual City: Restructuring New York,* edited by John H. Mollenkopf and Manuel Castells. New York: Russell Sage Foundation.

Harrison, Paige M. and Allen J. Beck. 2005. "Prison and Jail Inmates at Midyear 2004." *Bureau of Justice Statistics Bulletin*, no. NCJ 20880. Washington: U.S. Department of Justice.

Hughes, Timothy A., Doris James Wilson, and Allen J. Beck. 2001. "Trends in State Parole, 1990–2000." *Bureau of Justice Statistics Bulletin*, no. 184735. Washington: U.S. Department of Justice.

Human Rights Watch. 2008. *Targeting Blacks: Drug Law Enforcement and Race in the United States*. New York: Human Rights Watch.

Jargowsky, Paul A. 1997. *Poverty and Place: Ghettos, Barrios, and the American City*. New York: Russell Sage Foundation.

Kasarda, John, D. 1995. "Industrial Restructuring and the Changing Location of Jobs." In *State of the Union: America in the 1990s*, edited by Reynolds Farley. New York: Russell Sage Foundation.

Kelling, George L., and William J. Bratton. 1998. "Declining Crime Rates: Insiders' Views of the New York City Story." *Journal of Criminal Law and Criminology* 88(4): 1217–32.

King, Ryan S. 2008. *Disparity by Geography: The War on Drugs in America's Cities*. Washington, D.C.: The Sentencing Project.

King, Ryan S., and Marc Mauer. 2006. "The War on Marijuana: The Transformation of the War on Drugs in the 1990s." *Harm Reduction Journal* 3(2): 1–17.

Land, Kenneth C., and Richard McCleary. 1996. "Missing Time-Series Data and the Impact of Sentencing Guidelines in Minnesota: Can the Debate be Adjudicated." *Criminology* 34(2): 281–88.

Langan, Patrick A. 1991. "Race of Prisoners Admitted to State and Federal Institutions, 1926–86." *Bureau of Justice Statistics Special Report*. Washington: U.S. Department of Justice.

———. 1996. "Felony Sentences in the United States, 1992." *Bureau of Justice Statistics Bulletin*, NCJ 151167. Washington: U.S. Department of Justice.

Langan, Patrick A., and Jodi M. Brown. 1997. "Felony Sentences in State Courts, 1994." *Bureau of Justice Statistics Bulletin*, NCJ 163391. Washington: U.S. Department of Justice, Office of Justice Programs.

Langan, Patrick A., and Robyn L. Cohen. 1996. "State Court Sentencing of Convicted Felons in 1992." *Bureau of Justice Statistics Bulletin*, NCJ 152696. Washington: U.S. Department of Justice.

Langan, Patrick A., and Matthew R. Durose. 2004. *The Remarkable Drop in Crime in New York City*. Unpublished manuscript. Washington: U.S. Department of Justice, Bureau of Justice Statistics.

Langan, Patrick A., and Helen A. Graziadei. 1995. "Felony Sentences in State Courts, 1992." *Bureau of Justice Statistics Bulletin*, NCJ 151167. Washington: U.S. Department of Justice, Office of Justice Programs.

Lerner, Michael A. 2007. *Dry Manhattan: Prohibition in New York City*. Cambridge, Mass.: Harvard University Press.

Levine, Harry G., and Deborah Peterson Small. 2008. *Marijuana Arrest Crusade: Racial Bias and Police Policy in New York City 1997–2007*. New York: New York Civil Liberties Union.

Levine, Harry G., and Craig Reinarman. 1991. "From Prohibition to Regulation: Less from Alcohol Policy for Drug Policy." *Milbank Quarterly* 69(3): 461–94.

Levitt, Steven D. 2004. "Understanding Why Crime Fell in the 1990s: Four Factors That Explain the Decline and Six That Do Not." *Journal of Economic Perspectives* 18(1): 163–90.

Mahler, Jonathan. 2005. *Ladies and Gentlemen, The Bronx Is Burning: 1977, Baseball, Politics, and the Battle for the Soul of a City.* New York: Farrar, Straus, and Giroux.

Maloney, Thomas N. 2002. "African American Migration to the North: New Evidence for the 1910s." *Economic Inquiry* 40(1): 1–11.

Margo, Robert A. 1990. *Race and Schooling in the South, 1880–1950: An Economic History.* Chicago: University of Chicago Press.

Marvel, Thomas B., and Carlisle E. Moody. 1996. "Determinate Sentencing and Abolishing Parole: The Long-Term Impacts on Prison and Crime." *Criminology.* 34(1): 107–28.

Mauer, Marc. 1999. *Race to Incarcerate.* New York: New Press.

Mauer, Marc, and Tracy Huling. 1995. *Young Black Men and the Criminal Justice System: A Growing National Problem.* Washington, D.C.: The Sentencing Project.

Mayhew, David R. 2002. *Electoral Realignments: A Critique of an American Genre.* New Haven, Conn.: Yale University Press.

Miron, Jeffrey A. 1999. "Violence and the U.S. Prohibitions of Drugs and Alcohol." *American Law and Economics Review* 1(1/2): 78–114.

———. 2001. "Violence, Guns, and Drugs: A Cross-Country Analysis." *Journal of Law and Economics* 44(2): 615–33.

Mollenkopf, John. 1991. "Political Inequality." In *Dual City: Restructuring New York,* edited by John H. Mollenkopf and Manuel Castells. New York: Russell Sage Foundation.

———. 1992. *A Phoenix in the Ashes: The Rise and Fall of the Koch Coalition in New York City Politics.* Princeton, N.J.: Princeton University Press.

Moody, Carlisle E., and Thomas B. Marvell. 1996. "Uncertain Timing of Innovations in Time Series: Minnesota Sentencing Guidelines and Jail Sentences—A Comment." *Criminology* 34(2): 257–68

Murakawa, Naomi. 2005. "Punitive Race-to-the-Top: Elections, Race, and the Mandatory Minimum Electoral Staircase." Unpublished paper. University of Washington, Seattle.

Musto, David F. 1999. *The American Disease: Origins of Narcotic Control.* 3rd ed. New York: Oxford University Press.

Nelson, James F. 1992. "Drugs, Prosecutors, Predicate Felons, and Prison Beds: A Description of Changes in Felony Arrests and Felony Case Processing Decisions in NYS, 1981–1989." Albany, N.Y.: New York State Division of Criminal Justice Services, Office of Justice Systems Analysis, Bureau of Research and Evaluation.

New York State Division of Criminal Justice Services. 1975. *New York State Felony Processing Report.* Albany, N.Y.: New York State Division of Criminal Justice Services.

———. 1980. *New York State Felony Processing Report.* Albany, N.Y.: New York State Division of Criminal Justice Services.

———. 1985. *New York State Felony Processing Report.* Albany, N.Y.: New York State Division of Criminal Justice Services.

———. 1995. *New York State Felony Processing Report.* Albany, N.Y.: New York State Division of Criminal Justice Services.

New York Executive Advisory Committee on Sentencing. 1979. *Crime and Punishment in New York: An Inquiry into Sentencing and the Criminal Justice System.* Albany, N.Y.: New York State Division of Criminal Justice Services.

Nicholson-Crotty, Sean. 2004. "The Impact of Sentencing Guidelines on State-Level Sanctions: An Analysis over Time." *Crime and Delinquency* 50(3): 395–411.

Oliver, Pamela E., and James E. Yocom. 2004. "Explaining State Black Imprisonment Rates, 1983–1999." Unpublished paper, University of Wisconsin, Madison.

Pastore, Ann L., and Kathleen Maguire, eds. 2005. *Sourcebook of Criminal Justice Statistics.* http://www.albany.edu/sourcebook/.

Petersilia, Joan. 2003. *When Prisoners Come Home: Parole and Prisoner Reentry.* Oxford: Oxford University Press.

Peterson, Ruth D. 1985. "Discriminatory Decision Making at the Legislative Level: An Analysis of the Comprehensive Drug Abuse Prevention and Control Act of 1970." *Law and Human Behavior* 9(3): 243–69.

Pettit, Becky, and Bruce Western. 2004. "Mass Imprisonment and the Life Course: Race and Class Inequality in U.S. Incarceration." *American Sociological Review* 69(2): 151–69.

Pew Center on the States. 2008. *One in 100: Behind Bars in America 2008.* Washington, D.C.: Pew Charitable Trusts.

Raphael, Steven. 2006. "The Socioeconomic Status of Black Males: The Increasing Importance of Incarceration." In *Public Policy and the Income Distribution*, edited by Alan. J. Auerbach, David Card, and John M. Quigley. New York: Russell Sage Foundation.

Reaves, Brian A., and Pheny Z. Smith. 1995. "Felony Defendants in Large Urban Counties." *Bureau of Justice Statistics Bulletin*, no. NCJ 151167. Washington: U.S. Department of Justice, Office of Justice Programs.

Rieder, Jonathan. 1985. *Canarsie: The Jews and Italians of Brooklyn Against Liberalism.* Cambridge, Mass.: Harvard University Press.

———. 1989. "The Rise of the 'Silent Majority.'" In *The Rise and Fall of the New Deal order, 1930–1980*, edited by Steven Fraser and Gary Gerstle. Princeton, N.J.: Princeton University Press.

Riley, K. Jack. 1997. "Crack, Powder Cocaine, and Heroin: Drug Purchase and Use Patterns in Six U.S. Cities." *Office of National Drug Control Policy Research Report.* Washington, D.C.: National Institute of Justice.

Rosenblatt, Albert M. 1973. *New York's New Drug Laws and Sentencing Statutes.* New York: New York Law Journal Press.

Rosenbloom, Joshua L., and William A. Sundstrom. 2004. "The Decline and Rise of Interstate Migration in the United States: Evidence from the IPUMS, 1850–1990." *Research in Economic History* 22: 289–325.

Rothman, David J. 2002. *Conscience and Convenience: The Asylum and its Alternatives in Progressive America.* Rev. ed. *New Lines in Criminology.* New York: Aldine de Gruyter.

Sabol, William J. 2008. "Personal Communication to Authors on May 27."

Sabol, William J., Todd D. Minton, and Paige M. Harrison. 2007. "Prison and Jail Inmates at Midyear 2006." *Bureau of Justice Statistics Bulletin*, NCJ 217675. Washington: U.S. Department of Justice.

Sampson, Robert J., and Janet L. Lauritsen. 1997. "Racial and Ethnic Disparities in

Crime and Criminal Justice in the United States." In *Ethnicity, Crime, and Immigration: Comparative and Cross-National Perspectives*, edited by Michael Tonry. Chicago: University of Chicago Press.

Sampson, Robert J., and Stephen W. Raudenbush. 1999. "Systematic Social Observation of Public Spaces: A New Look at Disorder in Urban Neighborhoods." *American Journal of Sociology* 105(3): 603–51.

Sampson, Robert J., and William Julius Wilson. 1995. "Towards a Theory of Race, Crime, and Urban Inequality." In *Crime and Inequality*, edited by John Hagan and Ruth D. Peterson. Stanford, Calif.: Stanford University Press.

Schneider, Anne Larason. 2006. "Patterns of Change in the Use of Imprisonment in the American States: An Integration of Path Dependence, Punctuated Equilibrium and Policy Design Approaches." *Political Research Quarterly* 59(3): 457–70.

Sevigny, Eric L., and Jonathan P. Caulkins. 2004. "Kingpins or Mules: An Analysis of Drug Offenders Incarcerated in Federal and State Prisons." *Criminology and Public Policy* 3(3): 401–34.

Simon, Jonathan. 2007. *Governing Through Crime: How the War on Crime Transformed American Democracy and Created a Culture of Fear*. New York: Oxford University Press.

Stemen, Don, Andres Rengifo, and James Wilson. 2005. "Of Fragmentation and Ferment: The Impact of State Sentencing Policies on Incarceration Rates, 1975–2002." New York: Vera Institute of Justice.

Stolzenberg, Lisa, and Stewart J. D'Alessio. 1996. "Unintended Consequences of Linking Sentencing Guidelines to Prison Populations—A Reply to Moody and Marvell." *Criminology* 34(2): 269–80.

Strom, Kevin J., Steven K. Smith, and Howard N. Snyder. 1998. "Juvenile Felony Defendants in Criminal Courts." *Bureau of Justice Statistics Special Report*, NCJ 165815. Washington: U.S. Department of Justice.

Sugrue, Thomas J. 1996. *The Origins of the Urban Crisis: Race and Inequality in Postwar Detroit*. Princeton, N.J.: Princeton University Press.

Sullivan, Mercer. 1991. "Crime and the Social Fabric." In *Dual City: Restructuring New York*, edited by John H. Mollenkopf and Manuel Castells. New York: Russell Sage Foundation.

Sviridoff, Michele, Susan Sadd, Richard Curtis, and Randolph Grinc. 1992. "The Neighborhood Effects of Street-Level Drug Enforcement: Tactical Narcotics Teams in New York." New York: Vera Institute of Justice.

Tonry, Michael H. 1995. *Malign Neglect: Race, Crime, and Punishment in America*. New York: Oxford University Press.

———. 1996. *Sentencing Matters*. New York: Oxford University Press.

———. 1999. "Rethinking Unthinkable Punishment Policies in America." *UCLA Law Review* 46(6): 1751–91.

Travis, Jeremy. 2005. *But They All Come Back: Facing the Challenges of Prisoner Reentry*. Washington D.C.: Urban Institute Press.

U.S. Bureau of Justice, Federal Bureau of Investigation (FBI). 2005 (and earlier years). *Crime in the United States 2005*. Uniform Crime Reporting Program. Available at: www.fbi.gov/ucr/05cius/index.html and http://www.disastercenter.com/crime/nycrime.htm.

U.S. Department of Justice. Bureau of Justice Assistance. 1998. "1996 National Survey of State Sentencing Structures." *Monograph*. Washington: U.S. Department of Justice.

Wacquant, Loic. 2003. "From Slavery to Mass Incarceration: Rethinking the 'Race Question' in the United States." *New Left Review* 13(1): 40–61.

Weiman, David F., Michael A. Stoll, and Shawn Bushway. 2007. "The Regime of Mass Incarceration: A Labor Market Perspective." In *Barriers to Reentry? The Labor Market for Released Prisoners in Post-Industrial America*, edited by Shawn Bushway, Michael A. Stoll, and David F. Weiman. New York: Russell Sage Foundation.

Western, Bruce. 2006. *Punishment and Inequality*. New York: Russell Sage Foundation.

Wiebe, Robert H. 1967. *The Search for Order, 1877–1920*. New York: Hill and Wang.

Wilson, James Q. 1985. *Thinking about Crime*. Rev. ed. New York: Basic Books.

Wilson, James Q. and George F. Kelling. 1982. "Broken Windows: The Police and Neighborhood Safety." *Atlantic Monthly* 249(3):29–38.

Wilson, William J. 1976. "Class Conflict and Jim Crow Segregation in the Postbellum South." *Pacific Sociological Review* 19(4): 431–46.

———. 1987. *The Truly Disadvantaged: The Inner City, the Underclass, and Public Policy*. Chicago: University of Chicago Press.

Zimmer, Lynn. 1990. "Proactive Policing Against Street-Level Drug Trafficking." *American Journal of Police* 9(1): 43–74.

PART II

The Benefits and Costs of the Prison Boom

Shawn D.
Bushway
and Raymond
Paternoster

4 | # The Impact of Prison on Crime

Sentencing policy in the United States is guided by two general philosophies of punishment: a crime-control or instrumental philosophy, and a retributive philosophy. A crime-control philosophy is predicated on the expectation that punishing offenders is justified only because it produces some greater good—a reduction in crime that would not have occurred without punishment. Under this philosophy, the act of punishing a criminal offender involves practices by the state that involve harsh treatment or cruelty (deprivation of liberty, for example), which under normal conditions (that is, without good cause) would not be tolerated or permitted. This harsh treatment of a subject on the part of an authority can only be justified if the act of punishment is instrumental in reducing crime. Punishment, therefore, cannot be an end in itself and must serve another purpose. This other purpose is the prevention of crime.

There are several different mechanisms through which punishment can serve to reduce crime. Punishment can reduce crime by *incapacitating* the person who is being punished if the offender lacks the opportunity to commit crimes while being punished and other offenders do not substitute for the original offender. Punishment may also reduce crime by changing or reforming the offender through *rehabilitation* programs that reduce the criminal propensity of the person. Finally, punishment may reduce crime if it inhibits criminal conduct on the part of the one who was punished because she fears being punished again (*specific deterrence*) or if others for whom the punished person acts as an example refrain from committing crimes because they fear that they too would be punished (*general deterrence*). Although the precise mechanism by which punishment has its effect on subsequent crime differs, incapacitation, rehabilitation, and deterrence share the understanding that punishment is justified because it somehow produces more good (by reducing crime) than it creates evil (by punishment).

A retributive philosophy, on the other hand, does not seek to justify punishment on some instrumental or utilitarian ground. The committing of a crime is both a necessary and sufficient justification in itself to justify punishment. Punishment is demanded by the commission of a crime because in a moral sense it nullifies the harm done by the crime. As such, punishment is hardly an evil that needs any further justification; morally responsible offenders demand their punishment, and the moral wrong created by the crime is negated by the punishment. The key concept in a retributive rationale for punishment is, therefore, the notion of one's just desert. The notion of desert is that the amount of punishment an offender should receive is determined by how much she deserves. In determining what exactly is deserved by a criminal act, modern advocates of retribution are not of one mind as to whether or not desert is guided solely by the amount of harm produced by the criminal act by itself, or if desert should also consider the criminal history of the offender, with the understanding that an offender can be more culpable and blameworthy, and therefore deserving of more punishment, if they have committed criminal acts in the past (von Hirsch 1976, 1987; Singer 1979).

Another one of the important differences between an instrumental and a retributive approach to punishment is that, unlike retribution, the instrumental justifications can be examined on empirical grounds. If imprisonment, for example, is justified on the grounds that it reduces crime by rehabilitating the offender, then that claim can and should be evaluated empirically. The same is true for deterrence and incapacitation— each makes empirically testable statements about what should happen to crime when punishment occurs (or changes). Retribution, however, makes no empirical claim other than there should be some symmetry between the harm produced by criminal offenses and the punishment visited upon the offender.

Although relatively easy to distinguish conceptually, in practice instrumental and retributive justifications for punishment often become intertwined. From the inception of the penitentiary in eighteenth-century America, there has always been a concern both to inflict punishment for punishment's sake (the retributive view), as well as have punishment provide a social benefit in reducing crime. For example, the "Pennsylvania or separate system" in operation at the Eastern Penitentiary of Pennsylvania was based on a two-pronged philosophy of depriving offenders of their liberty in an amount that was grossly commensurate with the seriousness of their crime and that was also calculated to induce an internal improvement of the offender's character via the "soul searching" provided by long-term solitary confinement. Its competitor, the "Auburn or silent system," practiced in the Western Penitentiary of New York, was guided no less by a retributive philosophy, according to which the length of confinement would be partially determined by the seriousness of the offense committed. The system also employed an internal regimen that, while it permitted inmate-to-inmate contact, was disciplined and regimented (inmates could not talk to one another), as to create orderliness and control that was internally lacking in its members. It was believed by advocates of the Auburn system that the internal discipline instilled behind bars (and the benefits or lessons learned from employment permitted while in prison) would translate into less crime committed upon release. In addition, both the forced solitary confinement of the Pennsylvania separate system and the highly regimented silent system of Auburn served the dual purpose of preventing inmates from committing crimes against members of the outside society and each other, while serving as a visible lesson to all as to what could happen should one think about breaking the law.

While it is true that America's penitentiaries have been required to serve two masters—retribution and some instrumental purpose—one or the other philosophy has at different times had the upper hand. For a little more than one hundred years, from roughly 1870 when the Declaration of Principles was announced at the Cincinnati Prison Conference until the late 1970s, rehabilitation was the guiding philosophy of the American penitentiary system. During this period, sentence length was indeterminate; it was not proportionate to the harm inflicted by the crime, but open ended. The length of time the offender was to be imprisoned was (theoretically at least) to be determined by how long it would take the offender to be reformed. The length of treatment could not be determined in advance, nor could it be determined by judges at the time of sentencing. Rather, this task was left to treatment specialists or "deviant smiths" (Lofland 1969) such as psychologists, psychiatrists, and social workers who would staff parole boards. Although it was muted, the influence of a retributive philosophy did not completely disappear from the penitentiary as numerous inmates' own accounts of their life of incarceration provided testimony that they were aware of the brute fact that in addition to evidence of involvement in treatment programs, they had to bring some "time" to the parole board before they had a realistic chance of release (Irwin 1970).

A number of events began to converge in the mid- to late 1970s that created the perfect storm to wash away the prominence (but not the complete influence) of rehabilitation as the primary goal of the American penitentiary. An instrumental philosophy of punishment rehabilitation has an empirical component. If the purpose of putting people behind bars was that punishment would be the agent of self-change, then there should be some self-change ultimately manifested in lower recidivism rates. The proof of the pudding for rehabilitation, then, was evidence that correctional treatment was working and that those treated were not committing crime. The empirical evidence, however, did not appear to provide much support. Studies of correctional treatment programs did not consistently show signs that they were effective in reducing crime. This empirical failure seemed to reach a kind of critical point in 1974 when Robert Martinson (1974; Lipton, Martinson, and Wilks 1975) published his now infamous review of correctional treatment programs. Whatever else the "Martinson Report" said about the effect of correctional rehabilitation programs on recidivism and other indicators of criminal propensity, the conclusion that everyone seemed to draw, emphasize, and pass down as cultural folklore was that "nothing works."

The empirical "bad news" provided by Martinson's review, however, was not the only nail that was to be hammered into the rehabilitation coffin. There were more cultural, ideological, and political events that were conspiring against rehabilitation as the goal of the American penitentiary system. Books like Nicholas Kittrie's (1971) *The Right to Be Different* raised troubling ethical questions about forcibly changing another person's character, personality, or even behavior—practices that were at the heart of the rehabilitationist philosophy. It was argued that such forced change was a violation of a person's basic human dignity in a democratic society where presumably we all enjoy a right to be different. In addition, beginning in the early 1970s, a series of publications raised the question as to whether or not the indeterminate sentence, the sentencing platform for rehabilitation, was fair. This questioning added ideological fuel to a burgeoning prisoners' rights movement. In 1971 the American Friends Service Committee published a report, *Struggle for Justice*, which gave voice to this concern for the legal and medical rights of incarcerated prisoners and soundly denounced the rehabilitative model as "theoretically faulty, systematically discriminatory in administration, and inconsistent with some of most basic concepts of justice" (12). The report was only the most ideological and radical of other critiques against rehabilitation, and it merged seamlessly with more pragmatic calls to end rehabilitation in favor of a more retributive basis for incarceration. Books such as Andrew von Hirsch's (1976) *Doing Justice*, David Fogel's (1975) *We Are the Living Proof* and Richard Singer's *Just Deserts* (1979) collectively criticized rehabilitation as a failure and put forth a new rationale generally referred to as "the justice model," which was far more retributive, basing the amount of punishment on how much was deserved by the harm.

These critiques of rehabilitation from the left were joined at the same time by an equally pointed critique from the right. Conservative scholars such as James Q. Wilson (1975) and Ernst van den Haag (1976) were harshly critical of the empirical failure of rehabilitation to reduce crime, but they took the position that rehabilitation was essentially "soft" on crime, that efforts directed at the root causes of crime were misguided and doomed to failure, and that attempts to make criminals better citizens was wrong headed in emphasizing the offender at the expense of the victim. This conservative view joined with the liberal-radical attack on rehabilitation in urging for an end to indeterminate sentencing as well as parole. The preferred alternative was determinate sentences. Liberals hoped these would be more fair by being proportionate to the harm done, and conservatives hoped they would have more of a deterrent impact by being more certain and severe.

Today's sentencing regimes are still motivated by a mixture of retributive and instrumental rationales for imprisonment. While rehabilitation has faded in importance (but not disappeared entirely), it has been eclipsed by deterrence and incapacitation. What has not changed is that deterrence and incapacitation as instrumental justifications for punishment are no less subject to empirical review and judgment than rehabilitation. The question remains an empirical one. If rehabilitation was criticized because prison did not seem to be the agent through which criminal propensity could be reduced, does imprisonment serve any better as a general or specific deterrent? Does it serve the ends of incapacitation? The purpose of this chapter is to critically review the literature with respect to the instrumental justifications for punishment: deterrence, incapacitation, and rehabilitation. In the process, we will address the fact that it is extraordinarily difficult to empirically disentangle these various effects and partition them into separate components.

INCAPACITATION

At the aggregate level, incapacitation is just the number of crimes saved by having someone in prison, net of any replacement effects. Replacement occurs when people who would not have otherwise participated in criminal activity commit crimes due to the incarceration of another individual. Incarceration will also necessarily limit or restrict the lifetime offending of an individual offender in a causal, if mechanistic, way.

Two key studies in criminology make this point in an indirect way. Both are concerned with estimates of trajectories of offending over the life course. Criminologist Alex Piquero and colleagues (2001) were the first to suggest that it is important to control for periods of incarceration. In this context, incarceration is a control for exposure time. They demonstrate that the picture of offending from age eighteen to thirty-two (measured as arrests) changes dramatically for serious offenders once controls for incarceration are included in the model. Two key differences are observed.

First, and least surprising, the arrest rate while free goes up after controlling for incarceration because the same number of arrests are now spread out over a smaller amount of time. Without incarceration, it is reasonable to conclude that the incarcerated offender would have committed more crimes. The second finding of Piquero and colleagues (2001) was that the models without controls for incarceration predicted declines in offending for all offenders after a peak in the mid-twenties, while models with controls for offending showed more people on nondeclining trajectories of offending. In other words, some people were only showing a decline because they were in prison. From this perspective, prison is a life event that can help explain the age-crime curve. A second study by criminologists Elaine Eggleston, John Laub, and Robert Sampson (2004) found much the same result. Controls for incarceration led to higher estimates of offending per time free. Without prison, these individuals would have had more lifetime offending.

Most individual-level incapacitation research is not based on statistical inference; rather, it is based on estimates of offending while free for incarcerated offenders based on self-reports of offending before incarceration—so-called inmate surveys (Spelman 1994). These estimates have a long and somewhat complicated history revolving around the highly skewed nature of the distribution. Estimates based on the mean number of crimes committed range as high as one hundred Part I crimes averted for every year in prison.[1] Estimates that focus on the median, essentially ignoring the skewed tail of the distribution tend to center on consensus estimates of around sixteen to twenty Part I crimes averted for every additional year of prison (Spelman 1994, 2000; Donohue and Siegelman 1998).

There is no reason that statistical models cannot be used to generate individual estimates of the incapacitative effect to supplement the estimates that have been generated from inmate surveys. A 2007 special issue of the *Journal of Quantitative Criminology* focused new attention on the issue of incapacitation, and three studies present new estimates of the incapacitative effect at the individual level. Each of the three studies uses a different dataset and a different approach to generate estimates of incapacitation. Sociologists Arjan Blokland and Paul Nieuwbeerta (2007) use a major national data set on offenders in the Netherlands, tracking a 4 percent sample (4,615 individuals) of all those convicted in 1977 over the following twenty-five years. They simply count the number of offenses committed during an imaginary incarceration spell that would have accompanied any given arrest. This approach can be justified in this sample given the very low levels of incarceration during this time period in the Netherlands. The authors explicitly assume that there is no deterrence or any other change in behavior. While this is a stark assumption, it does generate a lower bound on the potential benefits of incarceration.

Empirically, they find that much more severe punitive policies would have only very modest effects on crime in the Netherlands. Somewhat incredibly, they predict that reducing crime by 25 percent through selective incapacitation would require a prison population forty-five times the current level.

Criminologists Gary Sweeten and Robert Apel (2007) take a different approach and study the self-reported offending of a group of individuals in a contemporary U.S. sample who have been incarcerated. In contrast to most prior research, they do not generate estimates by relying on the reports of offending before incarceration by the same respondents. Rather, they rely on self-reported data from other people who are otherwise similar but not incarcerated. That is, they use an altogether new counterfactual—the offending rates of a matched control group. This is the first time that a matched sample approach has been used to generate estimates of incapacitation. They estimate that an additional year of prison prevents ten Part I crimes—about half the consensus estimate from the inmate surveys. Since it is likely that those who are incarcerated are different from those who are not, in unobservable ways, it is reasonable to assume that Sweeten and Apel's estimates also underestimate the incapacitative benefits. However, this cost comes with the benefit of avoiding the many well-documented problems raised by short-term fluctuations in offending that usually accompany a spell of incarceration. Researchers are typically worried that inmate surveys overestimate the incapacitative benefit because they focus on offending immediately before incarceration, when offenders are experiencing a crime spurt. Sweeten and Apel's approach also has the merit of being tied to a specific change in imprisonment policy, namely increasing the numbers of those who are given prison as a punishment, as opposed to extending the sentence lengths of those currently incarcerated.

In a third study, economist Avinash Bhati (2007) takes the most complicated approach by relying on individual trajectories of offending generated from information about all of the individuals in the sample. He takes advantage of a large Bureau of Justice Statistics database on thirty-eight thousand offenders in fifteen states who were released in 1994 and followed in official records for three years. Bhati estimates what would have happened if the person had not been in prison based on information both from the individual himself and the other people in the sample. This counterfactual is somewhat less obvious than the counterfactual used by Sweeten and Apel, but it has the advantage of using information from the individual's own offending as in Arjan Blokland and Paul Nieuwbeerta's study, in which the individual serves as his own counterfactual. Because of the size of his database, Bhati is able to offer separate estimates of incapacitation effects for each of thirteen states for specific crime types and specific sex-race groups. He finds substantial variation in the state-specific estimates by crime type, although on average his estimates tend to agree with those of Sweeten and Apel (ten Part I crimes per year of prison). Bhati's approach, or some variant of it, can be easily adapted for policymakers seeking to estimate the impact of some given policy on real state-level data.

It is noteworthy that estimates of incapacitation obtained by Bhati and by Sweeten and Apel on fairly broad U.S. samples of around ten Part I crimes per year are lower than estimates usually found in the literature based on inmate surveys (which are on the order of sixteen or twenty Part I crimes prevented). Bhati's estimates as well as Sweeten and Apel's estimates might be capturing the new equilibrium caused by higher incarceration rates in the past. The larger estimates were based on data from the 1970s, before the huge increase in incarceration. It is reasonable that the average incapacitative benefit should decline as more people get incarcerated, and those left behind at any given time have a lower overall offending rate.

A study by economist Emily Owens (forthcoming) adds to these contributions with a different approach that has a tighter identification strategy which should control for both unobserved and observed differences between those who are incarcerated and those who are not. She takes advantage of a technical change in Maryland sentencing guidelines that was not driven by changes in crime rates but nonetheless had a substantial effect on a subset of sentenced offenders: males ages twenty-three to twenty-five years old with juvenile records.[2] The change involved the use of juvenile records in sentencing decisions. Until 2001, these records were included in the criminal history of all individuals up to the age of twenty-five; after 2001, the age for which juvenile histories counted was lowered to twenty-two. Thus, some of those ages twenty-three to twenty-five received shorter sentences than they would have received in the earlier years. Owens estimates that this change reduced the average sentence under the Maryland guideline system by between one-eighth to one-quarter (about nine to eighteen months). During the time period that the offenders were at liberty compared to their unlucky pre-2001 counterparts, they were arrested an average of 2.5 times per annum. Taking account of the specific offenses for which they were arrested and the ratio of recorded arrests to recorded offenses of the same type, she estimates that they were responsible for 1.5 Part I crimes per annum. This provides a relatively precise estimate of their recorded criminal activity during a period when they would have been incarcerated under the previous rules. This estimate is unique because it uses information from other offenders to generate a counterfactual incarceration spell rather than a counterfactual offending rate. Then, the individual's own offending during this time period after the initial period of incarceration is used to estimate the incapacitation effect.

Owens' estimate of crimes averted is smaller by an order of magnitude than the consensus estimate of sixteen to twenty index crimes previously cited in the literature. It is also smaller than any of the estimates generated by the other three studies. The most important reasons for the lower estimates are first that Owens is the first researcher who exclusively uses post-incarceration behavior, and second that she has in all likelihood captured the lower tail of the distribution. One of the main contributions of Bhati (2007), Sweeten and Apel (2007), and Blokland and Nieuwbeerta (2007) is that they all generate estimates that reflect the heterogeneity of offending in the population using fairly broad distributions of offenders. Owens' study focuses on a small group of offenders: twenty-three- to twenty-five-year-old offenders in Maryland who served less than three years. As a result, it is likely she captured fairly low-risk offenders. She has also explicitly captured the cost, in crimes, of the change in policy by the sentencing commission—in other words, one element of the cost of treatment on the treated.

The takeaway from any discussion of incapacitation is fairly straightforward. There will always be some benefit to incarcerating an active offender. The exact size of the benefit depends on where the offender fits in the overall offending distribution, where that offender is located on their own "career" path, and the degree to which other offenders replace that offender. Recent estimates of incapacitation that are roughly half the size of estimates based on older data at least raise the possibility that the policy of mass incarceration has resulted in the incarceration of less active offenders and therefore has created fewer benefits. Incapacitation, of course, will always be more concrete and less ephemeral than deterrence, but it is also less efficient. One prison bed can only incapacitate one person, but it can potentially deter many. The key to incapacitation as a crime-control strategy is to make sure that prison beds are being used to incapacitate the most active and serious offenders. This goal is usually called *selective incapacitation*.

Selective incapacitation as a strategy for crime control almost begs for sentencing and parole decisions to be made using risk-assessment tools that attempt to identify the most serious and potentially still-active offenders. These tools incorporate information like criminal history, contact with the criminal-justice system, and dynamic characterizations of the individual's current state of mind to predict the individual's potential for future offending. The use of such risk-assessment tools has proliferated at an almost dizzying rate over the last ten years. For example, the majority of states now use risk-assessment tools as part of their parole process (Harcourt 2006). There is some consensus in the literature that these techniques are particularly good at identifying low-risk offenders, but serious questions exist about how good they are at identifying high-risk offenders (Gottfredson and Gottfredson 1994; Auerhahn 1999).

In keeping with this consensus, the state of Virginia used risk-assessment tools at sentencing in response to a legislative mandate to reduce its prison population by 25 percent (Ostrom et al. 2002; Kleiman, Ostrom, and Cheesman 2007). This apparently successful utilitarian exercise in selective incapacitation—prison populations declined with no increase in crime—was met with blistering opposition by proponents of limited retributivism (Tonry 1999). Bernard Harcourt (2006) also raises some questions about whether these incapacitation-based policies might have negative implications from a deterrence perspective, particularly if low-risk offenders are more responsive to threats from the criminal-justice system than are high-risk offenders.

These types of selective incapacitation schemes do not take replacement effects into account. High-risk offenders might be more easily replaced than low-risk offenders, leading to lower than expected aggregate crime-control benefits. A narrow focus on the crime-control effects of prison for the individual threatens to overestimate the impact on crime for society as a whole, if other people step in to take advantage of the opportunities not seized by the incarcerated offender. However, the threat of replacement may be relatively small. Related research on crime in places suggests that crimes suppressed by criminal-justice efforts are in large part not displaced to other places (Di Tella and Schargrodsky 2004), even for drug offenses (Weisburd et al. 2006). Research on temporal displacement also suggests that most "lost" crime is not replaced (Jacob, Lefgren, and Moretti 2007).

Ironically, it may not be strictly necessary to adopt a strong selective incapacitation policy to selectively incapacitate the minority of criminals who are responsible for the majority of crime. According to Alex Piquero and Alfred Blumstein (2007) and Jose Canelo-Cacho, Alfred Blumstein, and Jacqueline Cohen (1997), policies that incarcerate repeat offenders for serious crime will inevitably incapacitate the most active offenders, even if that is not the explicit goal. The further irony there is that a strictly retributive punishment regime will incapacitate offenders simply through its use of incarceration. The main conceptual difference between a strictly retributive punishment scheme and one based on selective incapacitation is the use of criminal history to assign punishment, a key feature of selective incapacitation but a controversial component of retributive designs (Bushway and Piehl 2007). It would be interesting and worthwhile to generate estimates of the incapacitative benefits generated by the current allocation of incarcerative sentences in given jurisdictions and to compare that with other estimates based on different allocation mechanisms. Since most reasonable sentencing regimes will incarcerate the most serious and frequent offenders responsible for the vast majority of crime, we predict that there will be little difference in the total incapacitative benefit associated with different methods of assigning a given number of prison beds and that increased incarceration will necessarily be correlated with reductions in the marginal incapacitative benefit of the one more additional prison cell.

REHABILITATION

Since the publication of Martinson's "Nothing Works" report (1974), a small group of criminal-justice scholars (for a list, see Cullen 2005) have built a literature trying to rebut this conclusion, starting with a detailed rebuttal of Martinson's original review by Ted Palmer (1975). This literature essentially looks at the same literature that Martinson used and points out that the results are more ambiguous than what one would guess from the label "Nothing Works." They interpret this ambiguity to mean that some programs work for some people (from "nothing works" to "some things work on some people sometimes"). The key, in this view, is to identify the right program for the right person (see also Andrews and Bonta 2003), an approach that is consistent with the psychological background of many of the researchers in this literature. This group is also responsible for focusing attention on the need for higher quality evaluations—preferably experiments—and the need for systematic reviews or other mechanisms so that what is learned in evaluations can be brought to the field and policymakers.

This literature now consists of a large number of program evaluations of various correctional programs including work, education, and drug treatment programs; as well as a growing body of systematic reviews, which include a number of meta-analyses and compiled lists of programs that work (Sherman et al. 2002). The overwhelming consensus of this literature is that there are at least some programs that appear to decrease recidivism among some people in prison (for a definitive review of adult correctional programs, see Gaes et al. 1999). The basic belief is that the success of these programs depends critically on matching specific inmate needs to programs as well as having programs with treatment integrity—a challenging task in prison. Effect sizes of these programs can be moderately large; for example, David Wilson, Catherine Gallagher, and Doris MacKenzie (2000) found that prison vocational programs reduced recidivism by about 20 percent. Gerald Gaes and colleagues (1999) found that multi-modal programs addressing multiple criminogenic needs (for example, drug treatment as well as vocational and occupational training) tended to do better than single-need programs such as job training. There was also evidence in support of correctional drug treatment programs (especially when linked with treatment outside the institution) and for cognitive behavioral training. This latter type of treatment focuses on helping offenders understand and avoid patterns of thoughts and behaviors that lead to antisocial behavior. In this literature there is a strong belief that these types of programs have a stronger impact than job-skill or job-training programs that focus on helping ex-offenders get employment. This strong belief sets up an interesting and unresolved conflict with the criminological literature on desistance, which tends to emphasize the importance of social control (that is, employment and marriage) and deemphasizes the need for change in identity or thought processes (Laub and Sampson 2001). This conflict is clearly evident in the recent National Research Council (2007) review of parole and recidivism.

For this chapter, the finding that in-prison programs can help reduce recidivism has limited value. The focus is instead on what happens to the offenses committed by people sentenced to prison rather than probation or some other type of alternative sanction. However, rehabilitation analyses focus on the impact of prison programs on prisoners who take part in the program compared with prisoners who do not. Probation-versus-prison comparisons usually treat prisons as a black box, making it difficult if not impossible to distinguish between specific-deterrence explanations and rehabilitation. It is also difficult to find comparisons of people who are receiving a prison sentence with treatment versus those are in a parole or probation setting. One rare example of such a program is a recent evaluation by Megan Kurlychek and Cynthis Kempinen (2006) that compares the outcomes for youth enrolled in a three-month aftercare program involving a halfway house with those who are released directly into the community from a boot camp. Although a halfway house is not a prison, it is a more structured and controlled environment relative to parole in the community. They found a 33 percent reduction in recidivism for the juveniles who were given the ninety-day aftercare treatment. We take this evaluation as evidence that more supervision can potentially lead to better rehabilitative outcomes.

A recent study by Ilyana Kuziemko (2006) has raised the possibility that rehabilitation in prison depends in large part on how the incarceration is structured. She used Georgia prison data to compare a control group subject to parole supervision with a chance of release conditional on parole-board approval with a group of offenders who were mandated to serve 90 percent of their time. The average time served of the two groups is similar, but we see changes in both program participation and recidivism. Those individuals who were under determinate sentences reduced their program participation by 18 percent, and their recidivism increased by 13 percent. This effect is at least consistent with the claim that rehabilitation programs work. Policies meant to reduce discretion may inadvertently have a negative effect on other outcomes.

A related insight about the power of incentives can be gained from criminologists Denise Gottfredson, Stacy Najaka, and Brook Kearley's (2003) experimental evaluation of a drug-court program in Baltimore for low-level offenders. The drug-court participants were given probation, subject to the constraints of participating in the drug court (including mandatory drug treatment). The drug court had the power to assign jail time for noncompliance. The control group was given jail sentences of about seventy-five days. The treatment group had an 18 percent lower re-arrest rate after two years than the control group, yet the number of jail days used by the two groups was not significantly different (the drug-court group spent fifty-five days in jail for noncompliance). The overall effect of prison could be viewed as some type of specific deterrence where people learn to comply based on short jail spells, or as a general deterrent effect where a short jail spell was threatened with great certainty (if you failed a drug test) and celerity (immediately after the drug test). The evidence appears to suggest that jail time can be used to coerce good behavior (participation in drug treatment) that then leads to declines in crime over time. Rehabilitation is apparently possible, and prison or jail might potentially play a role in that rehabilitation as part of a carrot-and-stick approach.

More research that considers program participation and outcomes between prisons and probation departments is needed if we want to document the rehabilitative capacity of prison versus options that do not involve incarceration. But these examples clearly highlight the fact that maintaining distinct boundaries between deterrence and rehabilitation may not be appropriate. Rehabilitation, or desistance, involves real and fundamental change in how a person interacts with her environment (Maruna 2001; Giordano, Cernkovich, and Rudolph 2002). People need incentives to make these kinds of deep structural changes, and prison, or the threat of prison, can provide that incentive. But that incentive by itself may not be effective if people do not have resources available to make these kinds of structural changes. As a result, policymakers may want to think about deterrence and rehabilitation as goals that can work together rather than as separate and distinct goals of the criminal-justice system.

DETERRENCE

The idea of deterrence is relatively simple. It is defined as the omission or inhibition of a criminal act because of the fear of legal punishment. Since the time of Bentham and Beccaria, the notion of deterring offenders though the penalties provided by the criminal law has been the foundation of all Western legal systems. The properties of punishment that have been central to deterrence theory have been its certainty, severity, and celerity (swiftness). Presuming that human beings are self-interested and at least minimally rational, deterrence theorists hypothesize that would-be offenders will refrain from committing crimes if legal punishment is certain enough to be credible, severe enough to be costly, and swift enough so that the offender clearly forms an association between the criminal act and its punishment.

Deterrence theorists have always differentiated between two different kinds of deterrence, although both are based on the threat of legal punishment. General deterrence refers to the inhibition of criminal conduct by a would-be offender who fears being punished if she were to commit an offense. For example, the state of Maryland has a number of possible punishments it can impose on those who would commit armed robbery (for example, probation or a term of some length in the state penitentiary). It is thought by those who believe in deterrence that one of the things that keeps Marylanders from committing armed robbery is that they fear the possible legal penalty that would be visited upon them if they were to commit the crime and get apprehended. Specific deterrence refers to the inhibition of further criminal conduct on the part of the punished offender because the offender fears being punished again. In punishing armed robbers with prison terms, the state of Maryland hopes to convince previously punished armed robbers that if they commit another crime they will be punished again. If a punished offender contemplates crime but refrains from doing so because they fear being punished again, they have been specifically deterred. In establishing punishments for the breaking of laws, both general and specific deterrence is enhanced and crime is theoretically reduced. Specific deterrence works though the small number of offenders actually punished, while general deterrence is manifested by a much larger group—the would-be offenders who react to those who are punished. Although they are conceptually intertwined in practice, it is possible to separately evaluate the predictions made by general and specific deterrence, although as we will see it may not be so easy to distinguish specific deterrence from rehabilitation or general deterrence from incapacitation.

Specific Deterrence

The idea behind specific deterrence is that the experience of a punishment will increase the fear of punishment in the punished offender's mind such that they will refrain from subsequent criminal conduct. If in fact specific deterrence occurs, two things should be true: first, penalties that are imposed on an offender should increase the certainty and severity of punishment that the offender expects (that is, there should be an updating of one's perceptions in response to actual punishment); second, the offender will refrain from criminal behavior as a result. There is not a great deal of research with respect to the first of these hypotheses, but substantially more devoted to the latter. Further, the research on perceptions of punishment that does exist generally concerns the certainty and severity of arrest, with virtually no research to date on how perceptions of imprisonment are formed or changed and what the effect is on behavior.

The first part of the deterrence question is whether punishing someone increases their estimate of the threat of sanctions. There is some evidence that the experience of punishment does in fact make sanction threats more credible while the experience of escaping punishment after committing crimes decreases its credibility. For example, sociologists Ross Matsueda, Derek Kreager, and David Huizinga (2006) used a sample of youth (with a mean age of fifteen) to measure the actual certainty of punishment (that is, arrest) experienced. They did so by taking the ratio of the number of times they were arrested or questioned by the police to the number of self-reported crimes. In support of the ideas behind specific deterrence, they found that there was a monotonically increasing relationship between the probability of getting arrested for past criminal acts and the perceived certainty of arrest. The higher the ratio of arrests to crimes committed in the past, the higher the perceived certainty of punishment. They also found that those who committed criminal acts in the past and got away with it had the lowest estimates of the probability of arrest. This updating of the perceived certainty of punishment with respect to new information (that is, getting arrested) is precisely the process described by specific-deterrence theory. Interestingly, the group with the highest estimates of the certainty of punishment was the group of youth who had no prior offending experience at all. These naïve offenders who perceive the probability of arrest with the greatest certainty provide evidence for what sociologist Charles Tittle (1980, 67) has referred to as the "shell of illusion"—those with no personal experience in offending grossly overestimate the probability of punishment.

There is additional information that the experience of punishment and punishment avoidance is related to perceptions of punishment in the way predicted by specific deterrence. In an earlier study with a sample of incarcerated felons, Julie Horney and Ineke Marshall (1992) found that those who evaded detection for crimes committed had lower estimates of the certainty of arrest. Criminologists Greg Pogarsky, Alex Piquero, and Raymond Paternoster (2004) found, in a sample of high-school students, that those who were arrested for past crimes had higher estimates of the certainty of punishment. Similarly, economist Lane Lochner (2007) found in two nationally representative samples of youth (the National Longitudinal Survey of Youth [NLSY97] and the National Youth Survey [NYS]) that those who were arrested in the previous year increased their estimate of the risk of arrest (this is the case in the NYS but only marginally true in the NLSY97), while those who committed crimes without apprehension substantially lowered their estimates. In addition, there is research in the criminological literature about the experiential effect—the fact that those who commit criminal acts (usually minor crimes among adolescents) with impunity (and those who know others who have committed crimes without apprehension) lower their estimate of the risks involved as predicted from deterrence theory (Paternoster 1987; Paternoster and Piquero 1995; Piquero and Paternoster 1998; Pratt et al. 2006). Consistent with the process of specific deterrence, perceptions about punishment do appear to be generally responsive to experiences that people have with punishment and punishment avoidance. Note, however, that the updating of perceptions in this literature concerns the probability of arrest, and there is no available research on updating with respect to the probability or severity of imprisonment.

Not all of the evidence, however, is clearly supportive of specific-deterrence predictions. Pogarsky and Piquero (2003) have found that offenders who had been apprehended in the past actually lowered their estimates of the certainty of arrest. They attributed this downward updating of perceptions in response to punishment to a process akin to the gambler's fallacy, where offenders think that now that they have been caught they should experience a series of "free crimes" that they can expect to get away with. Finally, we note that what is particularly interesting about all of this work to date on perceptions of sanction threats is that, although there is evidence that punishment experienced in the past is related to perceptions of future punishment, these effects are very modest in magnitude and punishment perceptions are not very well predicted. In virtually all regression-based models where variance explained estimates have been reported, they are in the range of 0.05 to 0.10. Because the theoretical model for specific deterrence seems to require a fairly robust correlation between punishment experienced and perceptions about punishment, this cannot be good news for the theory.

The second question raised by specific deterrence is whether those who have been incarcerated in the past refrain from offending in the future because of the fear of more punishment. There have been no studies to date that we are aware of which link both prongs of the specific-deterrence process—showing that those who were punished and increase their estimates of the risk of sanction threats are then inhibited from offending—but there are legions that look at the association between experienced punishment and subsequent crime. The leimotif of these studies is a comparison on postpunishment behavior between those imprisoned for different lengths of time (time incarcerated is the measure of punishment severity); others compare those receiving different forms of punishment (such as probation versus imprisonment). There is a very small body of work that directly tests the impact of prison relative to probation on future offending. Graduate student Charles Loeffler (2006) catalogs eight papers that have tested for the impact of prison versus probation in the literature. Paul Gendreau, Claire Goggin, and Francis Cullen (1999) do a separate review in which they include any evaluation of prison (versus probation) as a control variable. Loeffler's list focuses on studies whose primary aim was a comparison of prison versus probation. In every case except for a study by criminologists Cassia Spohn and David Holleran (2002), the effect of prison on recidivism, however measured, is zero. Even at the bivariate level, the criminogenic effects of prison are fairly mild, in the 10 to 15 percent range, and the effects disappear in the face of fairly standard regression controls for selection. The selection controls are intended to control for the fact that people who are sentenced to prison are likely to be more serious offenders than those who are sentenced to probation; without random assignment to prison, we need some way to control for who goes to prison. Researchers usually conclude that prison has no negative effect on behavior relative to probation, and therefore does not work. In the framework of this chapter, this is not strictly true. A null effect of prison after release would imply that the net effect of prison on the offending career of the individual is negative, since the long-term response after prison does not counterbalance the short-term incapacitation effect.[3]

Spohn and Holleran's 2002 study stands out because of its huge effect sizes. The study was conducted for drug offenses in a court system that generally preferred probation to prison for drug offenders. The authors attempted to control for selection using a Heckman two-step model, but they find no evidence of selection once simple controls for offense type, gender, race, unemployment, age, and the number of prior felony convictions are included. This is somewhat surprising, given that it implies that any of the other variables that predict prison are uncorrelated with recidivism. One potential confounder that might explain these results is the different supervision regimes for prisoners and probationers. It seems reasonable to think that parole supervision would be stricter than probation supervision. Jack Gibbs (1975) has argued this point, noting that differences in punitive surveillance after prison might be responsible for differences in offending afterward.

Another recent study by Paul Nieuwbeerta, Arjan Blokland, and Daniel Nagin (2007) uses Dutch data on first-time prisoners to estimate the effect of prison on recidivism. They use a propensity-score model to predict incarceration. Individuals with similar probabilities of incarceration between ages twenty-six and twenty-eight were compared from age twenty-nine to thirty-one with those who were not convicted as well as to those who were convicted but not incarcerated. The imprisoned offenders had a three-year conviction rate that was five times higher than those who were not convicted and three times higher than those who were convicted and not imprisoned. Notice that using someone who was not assigned to probation as a counterfactual dramatically overstates the result. Nonetheless, these effects are huge, although the magnitude can be explained in part by the small base rate of convictions. If one believes the selection controls, this study says that the first experience of prison leads to a rather dramatic increase in offending. This result is supported by criminologist Christina DeJong's (1997) hazard analysis, which found that the biggest impact of prison on recidivism occurred for first-time offenders. This result is also consistent with labeling theory, which suggests that the first experience of a new label should have the largest deleterious effect on behavior. This might be especially relevant in a country like the Netherlands, where prison is a rare punishment.

Two other studies make explicit use of sentencing guidelines to find the opposite effect. Economist Randi Hjalmarsson (forthcoming b) used the juvenile-sentencing guidelines in Washington to conduct a regression discontinuity test of juvenile detention versus probation. She found that incarceration reduced future offending by 35 percent. Criminologists Jeffrey Ulmer and Christine Van Kasten (2004) looked at the use of restrictive intermediate punishments (that is, intensive supervision probation) in Pennsylvania, which was mandated in the sentencing guidelines. They found that recidivism appeared to increase as a result of the use of these restrictive intermediate punishments rather than prison. Both studies suffer from the lack of information on time served, which could bias the results toward finding that prison reduces crime. This is because those assigned to prison may still be in prison during the follow-up period, while those assigned to probation are at risk for crime.

An empirical study on juvenile incarceration by Denise Gottfredson and William Barton (1993) is not often included in reviews of the treatment effect of prison. The authors looked at what happened to individual offending after the closure of one of two correctional facilities for serious delinquents in Maryland (Montrose Training School). The idea here is simple: they compared youth who they believed would have gone to Montrose with kids who had been sentenced to Montrose earlier in the process. Gottfredson and Barton found that the juveniles who they predicted would have gone to Montrose were nearly 50 percent more likely to be rearrested within one year of release and 25 percent more likely to be rearrested within two and half years of release than those who were sentenced to Montrose. The key problem with this study is that it is not clear what exactly the non-Montrose sample was doing—many still experienced an incarceration, although they were more likely to experience probation than the control groups. The strength of this study is that it examines an actual policy decision.

The final study of the effect of incarceration on future crime is probably the least cited but, in our view, the most important. The study by Charles Manski and Danial S. Nagin (1998) hopes to generate an empirical estimate of the treatment effect of a juvenile residential placement in Utah. Other studies of this type rely on the assumption that treatment is random after controlling for the observables in the model. That means that none of the unobserved variables in the model can be related to treatment. Here the issue is not selection bias but the fact that treatment might actually have an impact on behavior. Suppose that the system believes that alcohol abuse is correlated with behavior, and it uses signs of alcohol abuse to assign a person to a short-term prison stay rather than probation. Suppose further that there is a prison-based treatment program that helps to reduce drinking and crime. If the model does not control for alcohol abuse, the treatment variable will be endogenously correlated with the error term, and the coefficient on incarceration will be biased towards zero. Individuals with alcohol-abuse problems are more likely to get treated and therefore have lower alcohol-abuse levels than they would have otherwise. Yet, we do not get to observe what their behavior would have been if they had been given probation. Without controls for alcohol abuse, we are likely to conclude that prison and probation lead to the same result.

Manski and Nagin (1998) make this point more formally with two different treatment rules: skimming and crime control. They model the selection process under each treatment rule and use an instrumental variable to estimate the effect of incarceration on subsequent behavior under both treatment rules. Using one set of assumptions, incarceration accelerates crime; under the other, it lowers offending. Plausible arguments can be made for either strategy or for any number of other mixed strategies. The crucial lessons are that great care should be taken in any conclusion based on strong assumptions, and much more needs to be learned about decision making in the criminal-justice system if we are to understand the impact of that decision making on individual behavior. The power of the studies by economist Randi Hjalmarrson (2008a) and Jeffrey Ulmer and Christine Van Kasten (2004), concerns about data aside, comes from their ability to map formal decision making to recidivism.

Any fair conclusion about specific deterrence at this point must start from the current consensus that prison seems to have no long term effect on crime. However this conclusion is based on a fairly weak empirical base. There appears to be some renewed interest in this topic in criminology, but the empirical and conceptual hurdles are substantial. Without information that directly links a change in perceived sanction threats to the result of punishment, it is not clear that a reduction in recidivism upon release from prison can clearly be credited to specific deterrence. Some treatment programs in prison such as rational-cognitive therapy take as their goal increasing the person's consideration of the consequences of their actions. If, as a result of this cognitive therapy, released offenders restrain from committing crimes because they are newly aware of its long-term costs, then such an effect is not entirely due to the fear of sanction threats. In this case and in others, rehabilitation is at work. This point calls attention to the analytically troubling issue that the impact of punishment at the society level (imprisonment generating specific deterrence) might not be the same as the impact of the same punishment at the individual level (imprisonment being the agent of rehabilitation). It is often not easy to disentangle the different effects of punishment.

General Deterrence

The core premise of general deterrence is that the existence of punishment serves to remind people that the commission of criminal offenses comes at a cost—for example, arrest, conviction, and imprisonment. To the extent that persons contemplating committing a crime refrain from doing so because they fear punishment, then general deterrence is at work. When stated with respect to the specific case of imprisonment, the deterrence hypothesis would be that a state uses the penitentiary to strike fear into the hearts of would-be offenders; if that fear encourages them to comply with the law, they have been generally deterred. General deterrence relies on the objective properties of punishment: how certain, severe, and swift authorities actually impose sanctions. However, the precise causal mechanism linking the objective properties of punishment to the inhibition of crime requires a conceptual dimension. In order to be deterred by the threat of sanctions that are actually imposed by the state, would-be offenders must be aware of such sanctions and must be aware of changes in these sanctions when that occurs. Therefore, much like specific deterrence, general deterrence consists of both a perceptual component and a behavioral component.

The behavioral component of general deterrence claims that there is an inverse relationship between the objective properties of punishment and crime. For example, if state A punishes armed robbery with an average prison sentence of five years, and state B punishes armed robbery with an average prison sentence of three years, general deterrence would predict that there will be less armed robbery in state A than state B. This is because the objective severity of punishment in state A is higher (five years) than in state B (three years). The reduced level of armed robbery in state A, however, can only be due to general deterrence if those in states A and B are aware of the punishment in their respective jurisdiction. If persons in state B actually thought that the average length of imprisonment for armed robbery in their state is ten years, then the higher armed robbery rate in state B cannot be due to general deterrence. In fact, it would seem that general deterrence requires that the objective properties of punishment are related to the crime rate only if these objective properties are directly related to the perceptual properties. A central consideration of general deterrence and any system of punishment based upon it, then, is that crime itself is driven by perceptions of sanction threats, and perceptions of sanctions are based upon actual punishment.

Although it is a central premise of general deterrence, there is not a great deal of research that has examined whether actual punishment or punishment policies are related to perceptions of punishment. What exists is not entirely supportive of a deterrence mechanism. While it is obvious that everyone has perhaps some inchoate understanding that those who commit crimes at least sometimes get punished, it would seem that general deterrence would require more specific knowledge. It would seem that to make general deterrence work, it would require some non-trivial association between the actual punishment practices and policies, and people's perceptions and understanding of those policies.

In telephone interviews with more than one thousand residents of fifty-four large urban counties, criminologist Gary Kleck and colleagues (2005) examined the relationship between the actual certainty (of arrest and conviction), severity (that is, the probability of imprisonment and the length of sentence), and celerity of punishment (that is, the time from arrest to sentencing) for four offense types in these counties; they then examined the perceptions of these punishment properties among a sample of residents in those counties. They found negligible bivariate correlations between the actual punishment and the perceived punishment. No correlation was higher than 0.13, only two of sixty were above 0.05, and the average correlation was 0.02. When the sample was split into those who had been previously arrested at least one time and all nonarrestees, there was again no difference between the groups in the correlation between actual and perceived punishment. These null findings were corroborated in a multivariate analysis that also showed, contrary to general deterrence, that there was no correlation between actual punishment practices and perceptions.

Lochner (2007), using NLSY97 data, found two interesting things: first, there is no significant relationship between the county arrest rate for car theft and the perceived probability of car theft among respondents; second, with actual punishment and other expected correlates of perceptions considered, only three percent of the variance in perceptions of arrest certainty for auto theft could be explained. When he examined perception updating, the author found that changes in county arrest rates were unrelated to changes in perceptions of the probability of arrests. Using the NYS, there was also no evidence that perceptions of the certainty of arrest for four minor crimes were related to how much crime respondents thought existed in their neighborhood. Economist Hjalmarsson (forthcoming a), using the NLSY97, found that youths' perceptions of the probability of going to jail for car theft significantly increased when they transitioned from the jurisdiction of juvenile court to adult court, where the penalties for car theft would be higher. Interestingly, the author found that the effect of entering adulthood was more substantial for the actual probability of punishment than for its perception, and the perceptional change had no deterrent effect on behavior. Other work in criminology generally corroborates these null findings. Among studies that use hypothetical scenarios in which crime situations are described in some detail and query subjects about their perceptions and intentions to commit a crime, there are no consistent factors that are related to perceptions of punishment (for example, the presence of police check points, or the distance one would have to drive after drinking alcohol; Klepper and Nagin 1989; Nagin and Paternoster 1993). Differences in the situation of crime related to deterrence were also not consistently related to the person's self-reported intention to commit the offense.

In sum, the link between actual punishment and perceptions is a critical part of general-deterrence theory, yet little has changed since 1998 when Daniel Nagin wrote that "the literature on the formation of sanction risk perception is small and narrow in scope" (1998, 17). It may be that this is of only minor importance; if a punishment policy is effective in lowering crime, it may matter little if the crime reduction occurs through the effect of actual punishment on perceptions of punishment or whether it occurs through some nondeterrent mechanism (such as incapacitation).

The behavioral component of general deterrence can be indirectly examined by investigating the relationship between actual sanctions (the objective certainty, severity, and celerity of punishment) and crime rates. There is a substantial body of research that exists concerning the relationship between the objective properties of law-enforcement practices (such as police contact and arrest, or the presence and numbers of police and crime) that we cannot review (for more details, see Levitt 1998; Marvell and Moody 1996; Nagin 1978, 1998). Nor can we review the innumerable studies conducted by both economists and criminologists on the deterrent effect of the death penalty relative to life imprisonment (Donohue and Wolfers 2005; Berk 2005). Although this has been a highly contentious area of research, the safest conclusion seems to be that there is no consistent evidence that capital punishment is a more effective deterrent to murder than life in prison (Becker 2006; Posner 2006; Rubin 2006). With this in mind, we limit our attention here to studies that have examined the certainty and severity of imprisonment and crime rates.

Some of the earliest deterrence research in criminology focused on the relationship between the certainty and severity of imprisonment and crime (Gibbs 1975). For example, sociologists Theodore Chiricos and Gordon Waldo (1970) measured the objective certainty of imprisonment across states by examining the ratio of the number of prison admissions for a given crime during a particular year to the number of crimes of that type reported during the year (sometimes these measures were lagged to account for temporal ordering). Objective severity was measured as the median length of prison sentence for a type of crime. Using such measures, they found consistent and strong inverse relationships between the objective certainty of imprisonment and crime, but there was no consistent effect for perceived severity (Gibbs 1968; Tittle 1969; Logan 1972). This and other more recent research on the deterrent effect of imprisonment seems to suggest that incarceration does act as a general deterrent (Nagin 1998); places that used imprisonment more frequently and with longer sentences generally had lower crime rates than those jurisdictions that did not.

There are two obvious problems with much of this research, however. One problem is that states that imprison their inmates for longer periods of time might have lower rates of crime for reasons other than the general-deterrent effect of imprisonment. More than thirty years ago, Jack Gibbs (1975) cautioned that there are alternative consequences of punishment that may easily be confounded with deterrence in empirical research. For example, long prison terms may generate lower crime rates not through deterring would-be offenders but instead by effectively incapacitating high-rate offenders, or rehabilitating offenders with high criminal propensity. It is also conceivable that the relationship between long prison terms and low crime rates is spurious, due to the normative or cultural climate of some places. A high moral condemnation of criminal conduct may incline citizens both to enshrine those moral beliefs in the criminal law and penal practices as well as disincline them to commit criminal offenses. The general point is that although we can conceptually separate the various causal mechanisms linking high imprisonment to low crime, it may be difficult or impossible to distinguish them in practice; some researchers have given up trying (Miles and Ludwig 2007).

A second problem with much of this line of research is the stubborn empirical fact of the simultaneity between prison and crime (Nagin 1998; Spelman 2008). Places with high crime tend to make more use of prison as a crime-control strategy, and the presence of high crime in a jurisdiction may lead to increased attempts to address it via greater imprisonment. As a result, a simple correlation between crime and prison rates in aggregate data would show a positive correlation. Research that hopes to study a general-deterrence effect needs to separate the causal impact of crime on prison from the causal impact of prison on crime rates, because studies that do not take the mutual determination of crime rates and imprisonment run the risk of underestimating any preventive effect of prison on crime.

Although the awareness among researchers of these two problems in imprisonment research is now greater than it was thirty years ago, strategies that can deal with them are not simple nor without pitfalls of their own. Still, efforts are underway to deal with them. With respect to the confusion of general deterrence with the other consequences of imprisonment, researchers have attempted to make use of the unique features of any given policy to disentangle the different effects. For example, Daniel Kessler and Steven Levitt (1999) argue that California's Proposition 8, which was passed in 1982 and called for enhanced sentences for certain crimes, did not have any immediate incapacitative effect because most of the effected crimes would carry some prison penalty in the absence of a third-strike policy. The sentence enhancement simply made the sentence longer. They then argue that any immediate effect, which was on the order of a 4 to 8 percent decline in effected crime, and longer-term effects on the order of about 20 percent (which continued even eight years after the onset of Proposition 8), were due to general deterrence. Of course, the reliability of these estimates depends on the existence of relevant control groups—places and crimes that were not affected by Proposition 8. Even with creative research efforts, all the bugs are not out of the basement: a recent study by Cheryl Webster, Anthony Doob, and Franklin Zimring (2006) raised some questions about these estimated deterrent effects, and the ensuing discussion by Steven Raphael (2006) made it clear that there are limits to the causal inference that can be drawn from this kind of time-series analysis. Nonetheless, these estimates represent reasonable upper bounds on the deterrent impact of increased sentence lengths.

These estimates are also roughly consistent with the recent individual estimates by economists Eric Helland and Alexander Tabarrok (2007) of the marginal impact of the third strike. In that study, the authors avoided the issue of confounding general deterrence with incapacitation by studying the impact of the threatened third strike on eligible offenders relative to similar offenders who had similar criminal histories but only faced a second strike. They find that recidivism was 15 percent lower among those facing a third strike. While instructive, this line of research underlines the practical difficulty of separating the different instrumental consequences of punishment into unique components. Economists Thomas Miles and Jens Ludwig (2007) suggest that such efforts are likely to be unproductive; they argue that estimates of elasticities of –0.2 to –0.4, which represent the combination of both deterrence and incapacitation, provide the necessary information for policy decisions about the relative merit of increased incarceration.

With respect to the simultaneity problem, empirical work has advanced far beyond the initial efforts of David Greenberg, Ronald Kessler, and Charles Logan (1979) to estimate the reciprocal effects between punishment and crime. For example, work by Steven Levitt (1996) on incarceration was unique in its ability to present new and innovative solutions to this identification problem. Levitt used court-ordered reductions in prison size to estimate the impact of prison on crime, making use of changes in policy that affected some crimes but not others. He found that incarcerating one additional prisoner per year resulted in the prevention of fifteen Part I U.C.R. crimes—a substantial preventive effective effect whether due to general deterrence or incapacitation. This is consistent with Thomas Marvell and Carlisle Moody's (1994) earlier estimate of seventeen index crimes prevented for each additional prisoner, although they attributed the reduction to incapacitation rather than general deterrence. From these studies, it is clear that disentangling the different consequences of punishment is not an easy task and will require creative efforts on the part of researchers.

CONCLUSION

The American penal system is guided by two distinct philosophies. On the one hand, practice is guided by the need for retribution: punishment should be apportioned solely in accordance with what is deserved by the harm produced by the act and the culpability of the offender. Under this regime, punishment serves no other purpose than to correct some moral harm produced by the crime, and the punishment inflicted should be proportionate to that harm. The proof that such a system is working would be found when the most serious offenses are punished more severely than less serious offenses. Any ancillary benefits (or costs) from incapacitation or deterrence are irrelevant.

However, at various times in our history, penal practice has been directed by a set of more instrumental philosophies. Under this instrumental regime, punishment is viewed as a harm whose only justification is that it reduces harm by preventing crimes. The precise mechanism of

crime prevention would include the incapacitation, deterrence, and rehabilitation of the offender.

The retributive and instrumental philosophies can sometimes directly
conflict with one another. A offender who commits a string of minor
crimes but has no job skills, is addicted to drugs and alcohol, is poorly educated, and has psychological problems would be punished lightly under
a retributive scheme; however, the prisoner may need longer confinement
in either a prison or community setting under a rehabilitation or incapacitation perspective. A first-time offender who accidentally kills his grand-
mother in a fit of rage would require severe punishment from a retributive point of view, but not necessarily from an instrumental perspective
(few crimes are likely to be prevented by incapacitating such a person, for
example). A retributive and instrumental regime need not lead to contrary punishments in practice, however, as it is possible to set retributive
limits to punishment that could accommodate punishments which are
consistent with instrumental goals.

Therefore, the persistent problem with American corrections is not primarily philosophical, but practical. The practical problem is that, with
existing knowledge, it is extremely difficult to determine whether instrumental goals are being met and, if met, through what mechanism. Economists have provided us with evidence from crude natural experiments
that suggest that there are crime-prevention benefits from incarceration
policies with elasticities in the neighborhood of –0.2 to –0.4. But even after
years of research, we simply do not have knowledge with respect to key
questions such as whether or not there is a connection between punishment policies intended to deter and perceptions of sanctions.

We also have evidence of countless criminal-justice polices (such as
laws that provide for enhance punishment for gun crimes), with no evidence that such laws effectively prevent crime (McDowall, Loftin, and
Wiersema 1995). They may fail to reduce crime because they fail to alter
perceptions among would-be and actual offenders, or they may fail because they are practically corrupted by the wide amount of discretion
available to actors in the system. These policies may only appear to fail
because crime-suppression effects are cancelled out by the possibly criminogenic (labeling) effects of the policy; such policies may only affect a
small group of marginal offenders who have not yet been identified and
are irrelevant to most of us. And if this is not discouraging enough, consider the fact that in order to generate compliance, it is not enough that
authorities enact policies; others must also see the policies to be enacted
in a procedurally fair way (Tyler 2006). Finally, most of the research on the
instrumental consequences of punishment has either explicitly or implicitly presumed a classical expected utility model of offender decision making. In other areas, expected utility models have been found to be good

normative models but poor descriptive models of decision making. It is possible that the research has produced murky results because offenders and would-be offenders think in terms of gains or losses rather than utility (Kahneman and Tversky 1979). A valuable point of departure from this might be the examination of alternative models of offender decision making.

NOTES

1. Part I or Index I crimes are the eight major crime categories in the uniform crime report. The eight crimes are murder-nonnegligent manslaughter (1 category), forcible rape, robbery, aggravated assault, burglary, larceny theft, auto theft, and arson.
2. The Maryland Sentencing Commission made the change because it felt that the difference between Maryland and surrounding states was unfair; in other states the juvenile record did not count after age twenty-two.
3. The only way that this would not be true is if ex-prisoners somehow put off desistance to compensate for lost time. If this is true, it should show up in the recidivism studies, especially those with longer follow-ups.

REFERENCES

American Friends Service Committee. 1971. *Struggle for Justice: A Report on Crime and Justice in America*. New York: Hill and Wang.

Andrews, D. A., and James Bonta. 2003. *The Psychology of Criminal Conduct*. 3rd ed. Cincinnati, Ohio: Anderson.

Auerhahn, Kathleen. 1999. "Selective Incapacitation and the Problem of Prediction." *Criminology* 37(4): 703–34.

Beccaria, Cesare. 1764. *Essay on Crimes and Punishments*, translated by Henry Paolucci. Indianapolis, Ind.: Bobbs-Merrill, 1964.

Becker, Gary S. 2006. "On the Economics of Capital Punishment." *The Economists' Voice* 3(3): article 4. http://www.bepress.com/ev/vol3/iss3/art4.

Beirne, Piers. 1993. *Inventing Criminology: Essays on the Rise of Homo Criminalis*. Albany, N.Y.: SUNY Press.

Bentham, Jeremy. 1789. *An Introduction to the Principles of Morals and Legislation*. London: Pickering.

Berk, Richard A. 2005. "New Claims About Executions and General Deterrence: Déjà Vu All Over Again." *Journal of Empirical Legal Studies* 2(2): 303–30.

Bhati, Avinash. 2007. "Estimating the Number of Crimes Averted by Incapacitation: An Information Theoretic Approach." *Journal of Quantitative Criminology*. 23(4): 355–75.

Blokland, Arjan, and Paul Nieuwbeerta. 2007. "Selectively Incapacitating Frequent Offenders: Costs and Benefits of Various Penal Scenarios." *Journal of Quantitative Criminology* 23(4): 327–53.

Bushway, Shawn, and Anne M. Piehl. 2007. "The Inextricable Link Between Age and Criminal History in Sentencing." *Crime and Delinquency* 53(1): 156–183.

Canela-Cacho, Jose A., Alfred Blumstein, and Jacqueline Cohen. 1997. "Relationship Between the Offending Frequency (λ) of Imprisoned and Free Offenders." *Criminology* 35(1): 133–76.

Chiricos, Theodore G., and Gordon P. Waldo. 1970. "Punishment and Crime: An Examination of Some Empirical Evidence." *Social Problems* 18(2): 200–17.

Cullen, Francis. 2005. "The Twelve People Who Saved Rehabilitation." *Criminology* 43(1): 1–42.

DeJong, Christina. 1997. "Survival Analysis and Specific Deterrence: Integrating Theoretical and Empirical Models of Recidivism." *Criminology* 35(4): 561–75.

Di Tella, Rafael, and Ernesto Schargrodsky. 2004. "Do Police Reduce Crime? Estimates Using the Allocation of Police Forces After a Terrorist Attack." *American Economic Review* 94(1): 115–33.

Donohue, John J., III, and Peter Siegelman. 1998. "Allocating Resources Among Prisons and Social Programs in the Battle Against Crime." *Journal of Legal Studies* 27(1): 1–43.

Donohue, John J., III and Justin Wolfers. 2005. "Uses and Abuses of Empirical Evidence in the Death Penalty Debate." *Stanford Law Review* 58: 791–845.

Einstadter, Werner J., and Stuart Henry. 2006. *Criminological Theory: An Analysis of Its Underlying Assumptions, 2d.* Lanham, Md.: Rowman and Littlefield.

Eggleston, Elaine, John Laub, and Robert Sampson. 2004. "Methodological Sensitivities to Latent Class Analysis of Long-Term Criminal Trajectories." *Journal of Quantitative Criminology* 20(1): 1–26.

Fogel, David. 1975. *We Are the Living Proof.* Cincinnati, Ohio: Anderson.

Gaes, Gerald, Timothy Flanagan, Lawrence Motiuk, and Lynn Stewart. 1999. "Adult Correctional Treatment." In Vol. 26 of *Crime and Justice: An Annual Review of Research,* edited by Michael Tonry. Chicago: University of Chicago Press.

Gendreau, Paul, Claire Goggin, and Francis Cullen. 1999. "The Effects of Prison Sentences on Recidivism. A Report to the Corrections Research and Development and Aboriginal Policy Branch, Solicitor General of Canada." Ottawa, Ontario: Public Works and Government Services Canada.

Gibbs, Jack P. 1968. "Crime, Punishment and Deterrence." *Southwestern Social Science Quarterly* 48: 515–30.

———. 1975. *Crime, Punishment, and Deterrence.* New York: Elsevier.

Giordano, Peggy C., Stephen A. Cernkovich, and Jennifer L. Rudolph. 2002. "Gender, Crime, and Desistance: Toward a Theory of Cognitive Transformation." *American Journal of Sociology* 107: 990–1064.

Gottfredson, Don, and William Barton. 1993. "Deinstitutionalization of Juvenile Offenders." *Criminology* 31: 591–611.

Gottfredson, Don, Stacy Najaka, and Brook Kearley. 2003. "Effectiveness of Drug Treatment Courts: Evidence from a Randomized Trial." *Criminology and Public Policy* 2: 171–96.

Gottfredson, Stephen D., and Don Gottfredson. 1994. "Behavioral Prediction and the Problem of Incapacitation." *Criminology* 32(3): 441–74.

Greenberg, David F., Ronald C. Kessler, and Charles H. Logan. 1979. "A Panel Model of Crime Rates and Arrest Rates." *American Sociological Review* 44(October): 843–50.

Harcourt, Bernard. 2006. *Against Prediction: Profiling, Policing and Punishing in an Actuarial Age.* Chicago: University of Chicago Press.

Helland, Eric, and Alexander Tabarrok. 2007. "Does Three Strikes Deter? A Nonparametric Estimation." *Journal of Human Resources* 42(2): 309–30.

Hjalmarsson, Randi. Forthcoming a. "Crime and Expected Punishment: Changes in Perception at the Age of Criminal Majority." *American Law and Economics Review.*

Hjalmarsson, Randi. Forthcoming b. "Juvenile Jails: A Path to the Straight and Narrow or Hardened Criminality?" *Journal of Law and Economics.*

Horney, Julie, and Ineke H. Marshall. 1992. "Risk Perceptions Among Serious Offenders: The Role of Crime and Punishment." *Criminology* 30(4): 575–94.

Irwin, John. 1970. *The Felon.* Englewood Cliffs, N.J.: Prentice Hall.

Jacob, Brian, Lars Lefgren, and Enrico Moretti. 2007. "The Dynamics of Criminal Behavior: Evidence from Weather Shocks." *Journal of Human Resources* 42(3): 489–527.

Kahneman, Daniel, and Amos. Tversky. 1979. "Prospect Theory: An Analysis of Decision Under Risk." *Econometrica* 47(2): 263–92.

Kessler, Daniel, and Steven D. Levitt. 1999. "Using Sentence Enhancements to Distinguish Between Deterrence and Incapacitation." *Journal of Law and Economics* 42(1): 343–63.

Kittrie, Nicholas. 1971. *The Right to be Different: Deviance and Enforced Therapy.* Baltimore, Md.: Johns Hopkins University Press.

Kleck, Gary, Brion Sever, Spencer Li, and Marc Gertz. 2005. "The Missing Link in General Deterrence Research." *Criminology* 43(3): 623–60.

Kleiman, Matthew, Brian Ostrom, and Fred Cheesman. 2007. "Using Risk Assessment to Inform Sentencing Decisions for Nonviolent Offenders in Virginia." *Crime and Delinquency* 53(1): 106–32.

Klepper, Steven, and Daniel S. Nagin. 1989. "The Deterrent Effect of Perceived Certainty and Severity of Punishment Revisited." *Criminology* 27(4): 721–46.

Kurlychek, Megan, and Cynthia Kempinen. 2006. "Beyond Boot Camp: The Impact of Aftercare on Offender Reentry." *Criminology and Public Policy* 5(2): 363–88.

Kuziemko, Ilyana. 2006. "Going Off Parole: How the Elimination of Discretionary Prison Release Affects the Social Cost of Crime." Unpublished manuscript. Cambridge, Mass.: Harvard University.

Laub, John H., and Robert J. Sampson. 2001. "Understanding Desistance from Crime." In Vol. 28 of *Crime and Justice: An Annual Review,* edited by Michael Tonry. Chicago: University of Chicago Press.

Levitt, Steven D. 1996. "The Effect of Prison Population Size on Crime Rates: Evidence from Prison Overcrowding Litigation." *Quarterly Journal of Economics* 111(2): 319–51.

———. 1998. "Why Do Increased Arrest Rates Appear to Reduce Crime: Deterrence, Incapacitation, or Measurement Error?" *Economic Inquiry* 36(3): 353–72.

Lipton, Douglas, Robert Martinson, and Judith Wilks. 1975. *The Effectiveness of Correctional Treatment: A Survey of Treatment Evaluation Studies.* New York: Praeger.

Lochner, Lance. 2007. "Individual Perceptions of the Criminal Justice System." *American Economic Review* 97(1): 444–60.

Loeffler, Charles. 2006. "Using Inter-Judge Sentencing Disparity to Estimate the Effect of Imprisonment on Criminal Recidivism." Working paper. Cambridge, Mass.: Harvard University.

Lofland, John. 1969. *Deviance and Identity.* Englewood Cliffs, N.J.: Prentice-Hall.

Logan, Charles H. 1972. "General Deterrent Effects of Imprisonment." *Social Forces* 51(3): 64–73.

Luken, Karol, and Thomas Blomberg. 2000. *American Penology: A History of Control.* New York: Aldine.

Manski, Charles, and Daniel S. Nagin. 1998. "Bounding Disagreements About Treatment Effects: A Case Study of Sentencing and Recidivism." *Sociological Methodology* 28: 99–137.

Martinson, Robert. 1974. "What Works? Question and Answers About Prison Reform." *The Public Interest* 35(1): 22–54.

Maruna, Shadd. 2001. *Making Good: How Ex-Offenders Reform and Reclaim Their Lives.* Washington, D.C.: American Psychological Association.

Marvell, Thomas A., and Carlisle E. Moody. 1994. "Prison Population Growth and Crime Reduction." *Journal of Quantitative Criminology* 10: 109–40.

———. 1996. "Specification Problems, Police Levels, and Crime Rates." *Criminology* 34(4): 609–46.

Matsueda, Ross, Derek Kreager, and David Huizinga. 2006. "Deterring Delinquents: A Rational Choice Model of Theft and Violence." *American Sociological Review* 71(1): 95–122.

McDowall, David, Colin Loftin, and Brian Wiersema. 1995. "Easing Concealed Firearm Laws: Effects on Homicide in Three States." *Journal of Criminal Law and Criminology* 86: 193–206.

Miles, Thomas, and Jens Ludwig. 2007. "Silence of the Lambdas: Deterring Incapacitation Research." *Journal of Quantitative Criminology* 23(4): 287–301.

Morris, Norval, and David J. Rothman. 1997. *The Oxford History of the Prison: The Practice of Punishment in Western Society.* New York: Oxford University Press.

Nagin, Daniel S. 1978. "General Deterrence: A Review and Critique of the Empirical Evidence." In *Deterrence and Incapacitation: Estimating the Effects of Criminal Sanctions on Crime Rates,* edited by Alfred Blumstein, Jacquelin Cohn, and Daniel Nagin. Washington, D.C.: National Academy of Sciences.

———. 1998. "Criminal Deterrence Research: A Review of the Evidence and a Research Agenda for the Outset of the 21st Century." In Vol. 23 of *Crime and Justice: An Annual Review of Research,* edited by Michael Tonry. Chicago: University of Chicago Press.

Nagin, Daniel S., and Raymond Paternoster. 1993. "Enduring Individual Differences and Rational Choice Theories of Crime." *Law and Society Review* 27(3): 467–96.

National Research Council. Committee on Law and Justice. 2007. *Parole, Desistance from Crime and Community Integration.* Washington, D.C.: National Academies Press.

Nieuwbeerta, Paul, Arjan Blokland, and Daniel S. Nagin. 2007. "The Relationship

Between First Imprisonment and Criminal Career Development: A Matched Samples Comparison." Working paper. Leiden, The Netherlands: Netherlands Institute for the Study of Crime and Law Enforcement.

Ostrom, Brian, Matthew Kleiman, Fred Cheesman, Randall Hansen, and Neal Kauder. 2002. *Offender Risk Assessment in Virginia: A Three-Stage Evaluation.* Williamsburg, V.A.: National Center for State Courts.

Owens, Emily. Forthcoming. "More Time, Less Crime? Estimating the Incapacitative Effect of Sentence Enhancements." *Journal of Law & Economics.*

Palmer, Ted. 1975. "Martinson Revisited." *Journal of Research in Crime and Delinquency* 12: 133–52.

Paternoster, Raymond. 1987. "The Deterrent of the Perceived Certainty and Severity of Punishment: A Review of the Evidence and Issues." *Justice Quarterly* 4(2): 173–217.

Paternoster, Raymond, and Alex Piquero. 1995. "Reconceptualizing Deterrence: An Empirical Test of Personal and Vicarious Experiences." *Journal of Research in Crime and Delinquency* 32(3): 251–86.

Piquero, Alex, and Alfred Blumstein. 2007. "Does Incapacitation Reduce Crime?" *Journal of Quantitative Criminology* 23(4): 267–85.

Piquero, Alex, Alfred Blumstein, Robert Brame, Rudy Haapanen, Edward Mulvey, and Daniel S. Nagin. 2001. "Assessing the Impact of Exposure Time and Incapacitation on Longitudinal Trajectories of Criminal Offending." *Journal of Adolescent Research* 16: 54–74.

Piquero, Alex, and Raymond Paternoster. 1998. "An Application of Stafford and Warr's Reconceptualization of Deterrence to Drinking and Driving." *Journal of Research in Crime and Delinquency* 35(1): 3–39.

Pogarsky, Greg, and Alex Piquero. 2003. "Why May Punishment Encourage Offending and Lower Perceived Sanction Threats? Investigating the Resetting and Selection Explanations." *Journal of Research in Crime and Delinquency* 40: 95–120.

Pogarsky, Greg, Alex R. Piquero, and Raymond Paternoster. 2004. "Modeling Change in Perceptions About Sanction Threats: The Neglected Linkage in Deterrence Theory." *Journal of Quantitative Criminology* 20: 344–39.

Posner, Richard A. 2006. "The Economics of Capital Punishment." *The Economists' Voice* 3(3): article 3. http://www.bepress.com/ev/vol3/iss3/art3.

Pratt, Travis C., Francis T. Cullen, Kristie R. Blevins, Leah E. Daigle, and Tamara D. Madensen. 2006. "The Empirical Status of Deterrence Theory." In *Taking Stock: The Status of Criminological Theory*, edited by Francis T. Cullen, John Paul Wright, and Kristie R. Blevins. New Brunswick, N.J.: Transaction Books.

Raphael, Steven. 2006. "The Deterrent Effects of California's Proposition 8: Weighing the Evidence." *Criminology and Public Policy* 5(3): 471–78.

Rubin, Paul H. 2006. "Reply to Donohue and Wolfers on the Death Penalty and Deterrence." *The Economists' Voice* 3(5): article 4. http://www.bepress.com/ev/vol3/iss5/art4.

Sherman, Lawrence W., David P. Farrington, Brandon Welsh, and Doris MacKenzie. 2002. *Evidence-Based Crime Prevention.* New York: Rutledge Press.

Singer, Richard G. 1979. *Just Deserts: Sentencing Based On Equality and Desert.* Cambridge, Mass.: Ballinger Publishing.

Spelman, William. 1994. *Criminal Incapacitation.* New York: Plenum Press.

———. 2000. "What Recent Studies Do (And Don't) Tell Us About Imprisonment and Crime." In Vol. 27 of *Crime and Justice: An Annual Review of Research*, edited by Michael Tonry. Chicago: University of Chicago Press.

———. 2008. "Specifying the Relationship Between Crime and Prisons." *Journal of Quantitative Criminology* 24(2): 149–78.

Spohn, Cassia, and David Holleran. 2002. "The Effect of Imprisonment on Recidivism Rates of Felony Offenders: A Focus on Drug Offenders." *Criminology* 40(2): 329–57.

Sweeten, Gary, and Robert Apel. 2007. "Incapacitation: Revisiting an Old Question With a New Method and New Data." *Journal of Quantitative Criminology* 23(4): 303–26.

Tittle, Charles R. 1969. "Crime Rates and Legal Sanctions." *Social Problems* 16(4): 408–28.

———. 1980. *Sanctions and Social Deviance: The Question of Deterrence*. New York: Praeger.

Tonry, Michael. 1999. "Rethinking Unthinkable Punishment Policies in America." *UCLA Law Review* 46: 1781–91.

Tyler, Tom R. 2006. *Why People Obey the Law*. Princeton, N.J.: Princeton University Press.

Ulmer, Jeffrey T., and Christine Van Asten. 2004. "Restrictive Intermediate Punishments and Recidivism in Pennsylvania." *Federal Sentencing Reporter* 16(3): 182–87.

van den Haag, Ernest. 1975. *Punishing Criminals: Concerning a Very Old and Painful Question*. New York: Basic Books.

von Hirsch, Andrew. 1976. *Doing Justice: The Choice of Punishments*. New York: Hill and Wang.

von Hirsch, Andrew. 1987. *Past or Future Crimes: Deservedness and Dangerousness in the Sentencing of Criminals*. New Brunswick, N.J.: Rutgers University Press.

Webster, Cheryl M., Anthony Doob, and Franklin Zimring. 2006. "Proposition 8 and Crime Rates in California: The Case of the Disappearing Deterrent." *Criminology and Public Policy* 5(3): 417–48.

Weisburd, David, Laura Wyckoff, Justin Ready, John Eck, Joshua Hinkle, and Frank Gajewski. 2006. "Does Crime Just Move Around the Corner? A Controlled Study of Spatial Displacement and Diffusion of Crime Control Benefits." *Criminology* 44(3): 549–92.

Wilson, David B., Catherine A. Gallagher, and Doris L. MacKenzie. 2000. "A Meta-Analysis of Corrections-Based Education, Vocation, and Work Programs for Adult Offenders." *Journal of Research in Crime and Delinquency* 37(4): 347–68.

Wilson, James Q. 1975. *Thinking About Crime*. New York: Basic Books.

Amy E. Lerman

The People Prisons Make: Effects of Incarceration on
5 | Criminal Psychology

The rise of the drug war and the move to get "tough on crime" that began in the 1980s marked an unmitigated shift in the policy paradigm of the criminal justice system. Nowhere did this ideological change play out as clearly as it did in America's prisons. Not only did incarceration rates surge, but what was once a system predicated on a rehabilitation ethic transitioned into one largely dominated by models of deterrence and incapacitation (Garland 2001). These dramatic changes in the practice of penology underscore the need to measure variation across prisons and to understand the effects of different types of prisons on individual outcomes. What are the implications of harsher prisons for the experience of incarceration? Can variation in the culture of prisons affect inmate outcomes?

This chapter utilizes survey data from the California Department of Corrections and Rehabilitation (CDCR) to address the question of whether incarceration in different types of prisons can have criminogenic consequences. The CDCR oversees the third largest prison system in the world, second in size only to the federal Bureau of Prisons and the Chinese national correctional system. Like American national incarceration rates, the population of California inmates has steadily increased over the past few decades, with the number of prison inmates growing from 22,632 in 1979 to 168,350 as of 2006. There are now about 446 inmates for every 100,000 Californians. If the current trend continues, the state prison population is projected to reach 190,000 by 2015 (Petersilia 2006). Likewise, California was—and arguably continues to be—on the forefront of the move toward a more punitive approach to corrections. In her comprehensive study, "Understanding California Corrections," Joan Petersilia points out that California enrolls a significantly lower percentage of inmates in vocational and educational programs than the national average: nationwide, 31 percent of inmates participate in vocational programs and 38 percent in educational programs, while California inmates participate at a rate of only 13.8 percent for the two types of programs combined (2006).

The analyses in this chapter employ a regression discontinuity design to assess the effects of prison culture on inmate criminal psychology. The findings suggest that there is a significant and criminogenic effect of placement in a higher-security prison. However, the effect does not appear significant in the sample as a whole. Rather, security placement appears only to affect those with little or no prior criminal involvement—inmatese who have the fewest prior jail commitments, arrests, convictions, or probations. For this group, the effects of security placement are focused predominantly in attitudes related to anger and violence; it is these dimensions of criminal thinking that differ between those in higher and lower custody. On other psychological dimensions of criminality, such as the tendency to manipulate others or to self-isolate socially, security placement appears to have only a weak effect.

It is possible that effects on criminal attitudes represent only posturing by inmates, a pretension taken on by individuals looking to assimilate to an environment where heightened criminality is the norm. If this is the case, behavioral differences need not necessarily follow. That is, the criminal attitudes described in this chapter may not lead to criminal behavior. However, previous research has presented substantial evidence tying these types of criminal attitudes to criminal behavior. Meta-analyses have consistently identified criminal psychology as one of the strongest predictors of prison misconduct (Gendreau, Goggin, and Law 1997) as well as of criminal conduct and recidivism (Gendreau et al. 1992; Gendreau, Little, and Goggin 1995).

THE CAUSAL PATHWAYS OF INCARCERATION EFFECTS

A significant amount of research has been conducted examining the effects of incarceration on individual criminality. Theories stressing the deterrent function of incarceration suggest that prisons can diminish levels of crime by providing a strong disincentive. Emerging from an economic theory of rationality, deterrence theory argues that when deciding whether or not to commit a crime, individuals will weigh the possibility of being caught and sentenced to a term of incarceration. The more unappealing the threat of this punishment, and the higher the perceived probability of receiving it, the less motivated individuals will be to engage in criminal activity (Andenaus 1968; Nagin 1998; Von Hirsch et al. 1999).

Those who have direct experience with the discomfort of prison life should be particularly loath to repeated punishment. By contrast, if inmates find that serving prison time is comfortable or easy, the threat of incarceration should less successfully deter subsequent offending.

Others argue that prisons may actually have a criminogenic effect. Theories of "institutionalization" or "prisonization" posit that the prison environment socializes inmates toward heightened criminality. Either through peer learning in "schools for crime," or through the "hardening" required to survive in a prison environment that is often violent and unpredictable, a harsh prison environment can make inmates less social, more violent, and more likely to internalize the stigma associated with being a criminal (Jaman, Dickover, and Bennett 1972; Bukstel and Kilmann 1980; Walker 1987).

While theories concerning the deterrent or criminogenic effects of prisons have been much debated, empirical studies comparing the effects of incarceration relative to other types of sanctions reveal mixed results (Song and Lieb 1993; Smith, Goggin, and Gendreau 2002; Villettaz, Killias, and Zoder 2006). In their meta-analysis, Patrice Villettaz, Martin Killias, and Isabel Zoder report on a number of studies that assess the effects of custodial versus noncustodial punishment. The authors define custodial sanctions as "any sanction where offenders are placed in a residential setting, i.e. deprived of their freedom of movement, no matter whether or not they are allowed to leave the facility during the day or at certain occasions" (2006, 6). By contrast, noncustodial sanctions include any nonresidential or "open" sanction, such as community work, electronic monitoring, or probation.

Of the three hundred relevant studies initially reviewed by Villettaz, Killias, and Zoder, the authors were able to find only four randomized experimental studies, one natural experiment, and an additional twenty-three nonrandomized quasi-experimental studies that contained a sufficiently large number of control variables. Of the results reported in these studies, two revealed lower reoffending rates among those with custodial sanctions, while eleven were more favorable to noncustodial sanctions. An additional four results were favorable to noncustodial sanctions but were not statistically significant. The remaining ten results detailed in the meta-analysis found no difference between custodial and noncustodial sentences.

Other review articles find similarly inconclusive results. A meta-analysis by Paula Smith, Claire Goggin, and Paul Gendreau (2002) analyzes thirty-one studies comparing incarceration with community sanctions. Overall, incarceration appeared to yield a slight increase in recidivism. However, the effect was insignificant when weighted by sample size. Likewise, of four studies described by Lin Song and Roxanne Lieb (1993), two found incarceration to be less effective in reducing recidivism than probation, one found incarceration to be more effective than probation for first-time offenders, and one found no significant difference between incarceration and probation.

There is even less available evidence concerning the effects of different types of prisons on inmate outcomes. In part, this is due to the difficulties of measuring variation across prison facilities. In his classic book, "Governing Prisons," John DiIulio (1987) tackles the difficult proposition of measuring the culture of a prison. He identifies two separate but interrelated dimensions that constitute the culture of a prison: the informal society of prison inmates and the formal organization of the prison. Inmate culture organizes life among inmates, providing "rules" around such things as trading property, interracial relationships, and what constitutes respectful behavior. It also governs the rules of an internal inmate hierarchy. It is this informal culture that has traditionally dominated prison memoirs (Bunker 1981; Thompson 1988; Shakur 1993; Braly 2002) and sociological studies of prisons (Sykes 1958; Irwin 1985; Kruttschnitt 2005).

Social interactions can have a significant effect on rates of crime across time and place (Glaeser, Sacerdote, and Scheinkman 1996; Zenou 2003), and previous research has found a strong and consistent correlation between individual criminal behavior and peer delinquency (Glueck and Glueck 1950; Elliott, Huizinga, and Ageton 1985; Matsueda and Heimer 1987; Warr and Stafford 1991). Incarcerating people who are convicted of criminal behavior places them in sustained contact with a group of peers who have a history and propensity for criminal behavior. This can have significant effects on their likelihood of recidivism. In their study of more than eight thousand juvenile offenders serving time in one hundred sixty-nine different youth correctional facilities, Patrick Bayer, Randi Hjalmarsson, and David Pozen (2007) find a significant effect of peers on criminal behavior. The authors find that peer influence can reinforce an individual's prior criminality; individuals who have committed a particular crime, when exposed to peers who have also committed that type of crime, will be more likely to recidivate with that crime.

Peer effects in prisons can operate through a variety of different, and not mutually exclusive, mechanisms. Prisons may provide for the transmission of information and skills that make individuals "better" criminals. They can likewise serve as sites of contact between potential co-offenders, building social networks that can be called upon for future co-offending. The most serious of these social networks are formed through prison gangs or "threat groups." Prisons may also socialize offenders toward the entrenchment or adoption of antisocial norms, which reinforce attitudes that undermine compliance. Similarly, it may build an "us against them mentality" that leads individuals to feel isolated from correctional workers, law-abiding citizens, or society as a whole. This may be compounded by being grouped within a category of people characterized by society as "inmates" or "offenders," leading individuals to internalize a strong social stigma.

By comparison to the informal regime defined by social norms and structure, the formal prison regime includes a wide variety of institutional factors, ranging from the programs offered to inmates to the security design of the physical structure in which inmates are housed (DiIulio 1987; Logan 1993). John DiIulio (1987) focuses his attention on classifying the formal prison regime, identifying different models of correctional management that are predicated on different correctional philosophies. Through extensive site visits and interviews with correctional staff and management, DiIulio compares three different state prison systems: Texas, Michigan, and California. He argues that these three systems represent three distinct "keeper philosophies," typifying a *control model*, a *responsibility model*, and a *consensual* or *mixed model*, respectively.

The control model is marked by a highly regulated, restrictive environment that mandates clearly communicated punishments for poor behavior and rewards for good behavior. All rules are strictly enforced, movement is tightly controlled, and inmates are exhorted to "do their own time" and stay out of trouble. The responsibility model, by comparison, focuses its attention on inmates' accountability for their own conduct. "Whereas the control model involved policies and procedures intended to maximize the paramilitary content of prison life, the responsibility model involved measures that minimized the symbols and substance of formal administrative authority over inmates" (DiIulio 1987, 118). The responsibility system has an elaborate classification system and grievance process, as well as an inmate self-government body and a wide variety of rehabilitation programs.

The California system is in turn described by DiIulio as a mixed model, focused neither completely on control nor responsibility, but rather stressing a less-restrictive inmate environment that is simultaneously organized by a strong formal hierarchy and a paramilitary-style officer force. The central tenet of this model "is the notion that prison government rests ultimately on the consent of the governed—that is, the inmates" (129). DiIulio notes as significant that the state's powerful correctional officer's union sought and won such concessions as the right for correctional officers to carry concealed weapons while off-duty, and for the right of on-duty officers to wear military-style uniforms. At the same time, many officers in the California system reported to DiIulio that they prided themselves on an informal relationship with inmates and the ability to speak to inmates in their own language.

More recently, the Bureau of Justice Statistics' Study Group on Criminal Justice Performance Measures put together a series of reports measuring various areas of criminal justice administration (DiIulio 1993). Writing in the series, Charles Logan expands on DiIulio's tripartite measurement, identifying eight dimensions on which prisons can be measured and evaluated: security, safety, order, care, activity, justice, conditions, and management (Logan 1993). Each dimension is described by a wide variety of indicators that can be used to make comparisons across different facilities. For example, Logan uses these dimensions to compare three women's prisons—one private, one state, and one federal—to argue that the quality of confinement is higher in the private prison than in either public facility (Logan 1992).

The analyses in this chapter do not allow for adjudication between the formal and informal dimensions of prison life. Indeed, it is arguably impossible to separate out the myriad, highly correlated attributes of prison culture that likely shape the experience of incarceration and account for psychological effects. Likewise, this chapter does not address the question of whether incarceration has a criminogenic effect relative to other types of punishment, such as probation. Rather, the focus here is on the effects of placement into a higher relative to a lower security level. However, to the extent that higher-security prisons serve as a proxy for a set of important prison characteristics—namely, that higher-security prisons are more violent, have higher rates of gang participation and activity, are more restrictive, and are more punitive facilities (Lerman 2008)—the findings presented in this chapter illuminate how these differences across prisons can lead to different outcomes among inmates.

REGRESSION DISCONTINUITY AND CAUSAL INFERENCE

In order to estimate the effects of prison culture on inmate outcomes, this chapter relies on a regression discontinuity design. Regression discontinuity was introduced by Donald Thistlethwaite and Donald Campbell in the Journal of Educational Psychology (1960), and has since been applied to a wide variety of issues in education research (Ross and Lacey 1983; Van der Klaauw 2002; Jacob and Lefgren 2004). A number of recent studies have also made use of these methods in criminal justice research (Berk and Rauma 1983; Berk and De Leeuw 1998; Chen and Shapiro 2007; Pintoff 2004; Lee and McCrary 2005; Kuziemko 2006). Most notably, Keith Chen and Jesse Shapiro (2007) use a regression discontinuity design similar to the one employed here, and find a significant and positive effect of harsher prison conditions on postrelease recidivism rates.

The regression discontinuity design takes advantage of situations in which the probability of getting some type of treatment changes discontinuously as a function of some continuous factor. So, for example, those who earn below a certain income threshold would be eligible for enrollment in a job training program, while those above that threshold would not. The decision rule for assignment is known and can be observed; no unobservable variables affect assignment to treatment. In addition, the conditional expectation functions for each of the two groups must be linear in parameters and parallel (Rubin 1977), making it possible to estimate an unbiased value for the treatment effect.

The classic regression discontinuity relies on a pre- and post-test model. The effect of a program or treatment is estimated with a model, such that

$$Y_i = b_0 + b_1 X_i + b_2 Z_i + e_i \tag{5.1}$$

where Y_i is the outcome of interest for a given individual, and X_i is that individual's score on a continuous variable determining eligibility for placement into the treatment group. In addition, the error sum of squares can be reduced by including additional regressors in the estimated model (Berk and Rauma 1983). The variable Z_i is a binary indicator denoting whether an individual has received the treatment, such that

$$Z_i = 1 \text{ if } X_i \geq x_{Tr}, \text{ and} \tag{5.2}$$

$$Z_i = 0 \text{ if } X_i \leq x_{Tr}, \tag{5.3}$$

where x_{Tr} is a predetermined and stable value of X. Assuming that there is some randomness in the continuous score X_i, comparing those who fall just below the cutoff for treatment with those just above allows for a reasonable simulation of randomization.

In a sharp regression discontinuity, where treatment is deterministic given the eligibility score, $Z_i = f$ if (X_i), the effect of receiving treatment can be estimated directly. The slope of interest, b_2, indicates the strength and direction of the treatment effect. In some cases, however, the classification score is not a perfect predictor of whether an individual is in the treatment group or the control group. In this case, the regression discontinuity design is considered "fuzzy" rather than "sharp," and estimating a discontinuity at the classification score cutoff value, x_{Tr} depends on the probability of being placed in a higher-security prison, given the classification score,

$$E[Z_i \mid X_i = x] = \Pr[Z_i = 1 \mid X_i = x] \tag{5.4}$$

The California Department of Corrections and Rehabilitation (CDCR) uses a unidimensional classification score to determine the security level at which an inmate will be housed. Cutoff points in the classification score determine assignment to a particular security level: an inmate with a classification score of zero through eighteen is designated for placement in a Level I facility. A score of nineteen through twenty-seven designates an inmate for placement in a Level II facility; twenty-eight through fifty-one for a Level III facility; and fifty-two and greater for a Level IV facility. Inmates are assigned to an institution that corresponds to their custody status: minimum (Level I), medium (Level II), close (Level III), or maximum (Level IV).[1] As specified in section 3377 of the Rules and Regulations of the Director of Corrections:

- Level I facilities and camps consist primarily of open dormitories with a low security perimeter.

- Level II facilities consist primarily of open dormitories with a secure perimeter, which may include armed coverage.

- Level III facilities primarily have a secure perimeter with armed coverage and housing units with cells adjacent to exterior walls.

- Level IV facilities have a secure perimeter with internal and external armed coverage and housing units . . . or cell block housing with cells non-adjacent to exterior walls.

The classification instrument employed by the CDCR has been in use since 2003, when it was modified according to recommendations made by sociologist Richard Berk (2004). The new classification system relies less on the length of an inmate's sentence and instead places emphasis on a wider variety of background characteristics and security and custody needs. This change in the classification system led to a somewhat higher proportion of inmates classified as medium security (Level II), and a somewhat lower proportion placed in other categories (Petersilia 2006). The sample analyzed in this study includes only those inmates who were classified after these procedural changes took effect.

The classification score takes into account a series of items related to background and prior incarceration behavior. Background factors taken into consideration include age at first arrest; age at reception; term in years; gang involvement, type of gang, and method of verification (for example, self-admission, tattoos, and symbols); prior jail or county juvenile sentence of more than thirty-one days; and prior incarcerations. Factors related to prior incarceration behavior include any serious disciplinary history; battery or attempted battery on a nonprisoner; battery or attempted battery on an inmate; distribution of drugs; possession of a deadly weapon (double weighted if within the last five years); inciting a disturbance; and battery causing serious injury.

The background factor score is then combined with the prior incarceration behavior score to obtain the preliminary score. The preliminary score is equal to the final placement score unless there is a factor in the inmate's record requiring the addition of a mandatory minimum. As defined in section 61010.11.5 of the Director's Rules, "A Mandatory Minimum Score is a numerical value identifying the least restrictive security level for an inmate who has a case factor that requires he/she be housed no lower than a specific security level." If the mandatory minimum is applied, the final placement score is either the mandatory minimum or the preliminary score (whichever is greater).[2]

To verify that there is no selection on observables, table 5.1 describes the demographic attributes of individuals who fall just above and just below the cutoff points for assignment to Level III. On most relevant predictors of criminal thinking, the groups do not significantly differ. In terms of their level of education, type of controlling offense, number of current charges, score on a Current Violence Scale (measuring the degree of violence in the present offense), and term in years, inmates above and below the cutoff are on average indistinguishable. This suggests that these dependent variables are smooth around the cutoff point; these characteristics do not appear to jump discontinuously at the cutoff for assignment into a higher-security prison, and so would not explain a gap in criminal attitudes.

There is a slight difference in the mean age between the two groups. However, the difference occurs only within the two upper-age groups: those between thirty-one and forty years old, and those older than forty-one. This is significant, in that it is between the younger and older cohorts where a difference in propensity for crime, particularly violent crime, would be expected (Hirschi and Gottfredson 1983; Farrington 1986; Laub and Sampson 2003). Moreover, a larger percentage of those in the oldest cohort are actually likely to be in the higher rather than the lower custody group. There is also a slight difference in the percentage of inmates incarcerated for robbery. Again, while this should be noted, it does not easily account for the effects described in this chapter, which are predominantly focused in the areas of anger and violence.

There is likewise no apparent difference between those just above and just below the cutoff for assignment to Level III on measures of past criminality. The two groups are comparable in the frequency of past failures at community-based corrections, such as violations of parole and failure to appear for court.[3] They are likewise similar in terms of their past violent behavior, such as the number of past arrests and convictions for violent

Table 5.1   *Individual Demographics Above and Below Classification Cutoff Points*

	Low Criminal History			Total Sample		
	Below Cutoff	Above Cutoff	T/KS p-val	Below Cutoff	Above Cutoff	T/KS p-val
Mean age (years)	24.18	22.95	.01	25.93	25.28	.00
Mean education (years)	10.6	10.84	.70	10.70	10.69	.76
Current charge (%)						
Homicide	0.0	1.4	.16	0.3	0.7	.16
Sex offense	0.7	1.4	.60	0.0	1.2	.05
Assault	21.6	17.4	.48	15.7	15.3	.32
Robbery	16.4	9.0	.06	9.0	7.5	.41
Property	29.9	29.2	.85	36.2	36.8	.84
Domestic violence	5.2	2.8	.27	5.9	5.8	.45
Drugs	10.4	14.6	.15	12.9	11.4	.86
Weapons	28.4	32.6	.63	18.5	25.2	.03
Number current charges or offenses	1.60	1.40	.06	1.79	1.59	.00
Violence of charge (decile)	5.15	4.66	.45	4.07	4.37	.38
Term (years)	5.17	5.18	.55	4.98	5.28	.07
Number previous arrests	2.60	2.65	.64	3.55	3.40	.11
Number previous convictions	1.34	1.50	.10	2.90	2.67	.07
Criminal history (decile)						
History of noncompliance	3.65	3.75	.41	6.19	5.70	.16
History of violence	4.66	4.83	.43	6.31	5.87	.02
History of family criminality	3.74	4.23	.25	4.21	4.40	.35
Early socialization failure	4.83	6.28	.00	6.02	6.53	.05
History of substance abuse	3.23	3.89	.20	4.05	4.17	.86
History of poverty	4.50	5.01	.45	5.10	5.14	.30
History of educational failure	6.07	6.67	.24	6.43	6.63	.33

Source: Author's compilation.
Note: Data are for all offenders in the COMPAS database with an 839 placement score less than 2 points from the cutoff for classification: 26 or 27 below the classification cutoff and 28 or 29 above the classification cutoff.
Individuals placed through administrative determinants or classified prior to 2003 are omitted.
Total Sample: N = 1264 (677 below the cutoff and 587 above)
Low Criminal History: N = 278 (134 below the cutoff and 144 above)
T test p-values are given for Current Charge categories. All other p-values are for bootstrapped Kolmogorov-Smirnov tests, Nboots = 1000.

crimes, as well as documented incidents of violent activity against other inmates.[4] On measures of past family criminality, which describe the criminal history of an individual's close relatives, including parents, siblings, and spouse or partner, average scores are also indistinguishable between the two groups.[5]

Finally, measures of inmates' own criminal history and background are again comparable. Those with classification scores just below and just above the cutoff are equally likely to have been charged with a violent felony as a juvenile and have an equivalent number of juvenile felony charges. There is a slight difference between the two in the probability of having been incarcerated while a juvenile. However, the size of the difference is small and only marginally statistically significant, and there is no statistically significant difference in criminal-cognition or criminal-personality scores for those with different histories of juvenile incarceration.[6] Finally, there is also little difference on measures of personal history. On measures of past substance abuse, past financial problems, and previous vocational or educational problems, the two groups are statistically equivalent.[7] The absence of any significant differences between those inmates with classification scores just above and just below the cutoff provides an excellent setup with which to estimate the effect of prison culture on several psychological outcomes.

MEASURING CRIMINAL PSYCHOLOGY

The regression discontinuity design allows for a causal estimate of the effects of security level assignment on several measures of criminal psychology. Psychometrics of criminality are taken from the Correctional Offender Management Profiling for Alternative Sanctions (COMPAS) system, which was purchased by the California Department of Corrections and Rehabilitation to augment the state's Parole Automation Tracking System (PATS). COMPAS was designed by Northpointe Institute for Public Management, Inc., a private correctional research and consulting firm, and is a risk and needs assessment tool for use in the supervision and case management of individuals in the correctional system. COMPAS gathers information on 141 separate items, combining official records, a self-report survey, and a semistructured interview. Surveys are conducted with inmates roughly 120 days before release from prison (Brennan, Dieterich, and Oliver 2006).

In its first phase of implementation, COMPAS was deployed by the CDCR in such a way that those included in the database do not constitute a representative sample of the total inmate population. Assessments were done first on a limited group of offenders—those being released for the first time rather than those who had returned on a parole violation, and those without extensive mental-health and substance-abuse problems. Clearly this does not describe the average offender and thus limits the generalizability of this chapter's findings. However, the subset of inmates represented in the data is arguably the group of offenders who could be most easily diverted from criminal behavior: those without personal characteristics and criminal histories that strongly predict future criminality. Thus, it is not unreasonable to be especially concerned with criminogenic effects of incarceration on this particular subset of offenders.

COMPAS includes two psychometrics of criminality: a Criminal Personality Scale and a Criminal Cognitions Scale. In answering questions related to these scales, respondents are instructed that items "are about what you are like as a person, what your thoughts are, and how other people see you," and that "there are no right or wrong answers" (Brenan, Dieterich, and Oliver 2006). A statement is then posed, and the respondent is asked to rate the extent to which he or she agrees. Responses are coded one through five, with a five indicating a high degree of criminal thinking. Scores on individual items are then automatically added together to create descriptive scales.[8]

Raw scores on each of the scales are then converted to decile scores, ranking individual scores relative to the appropriate gender-specific norm group: male incarcerated, female incarcerated, male community, or female community. A decile score of one indicates a scale score in the lowest 10 percent of the normative comparison group; a decile score of two means that an individual has a score above 10 percent but below 20 percent of the norm group; and so on up to a decile score of 10. These scores are then used to place an offender in a high-, medium-, or low-risk category. This risk category is intended to guide both the level of oversight and types of services that an individual will receive once paroled.[9]

The Criminal Personality Scale includes thirteen items describing "impulsivity, absence of guilt, selfishness/narcissism, a tendency to dominate others, risk-taking, and violence and aggression" (Brenan, Dieterich, and Oliver 2006, 137). Table 5.2 details the individual items that make up this scale. The Cronbach's alpha for the scale items is 0.725, suggesting a reasonable degree of internal consistency and confirming that it is not inappropriate to combine the items into a single scale. A principal components factor analysis with varimax rotation, however, suggests that these thirteen items are better described as multidimensional rather than unidimensional. The variables load on four distinct dimensions: a high criminal personality is defined as being prone to anger and violence, having a propensity for boredom and "get[ting] into trouble," having a talent for manipulating others, and a tendency to self-isolate from other people.

The second criminal psychology scale measures criminal cognitions. The Criminal Cognitions Scale is constructed from ten separate items measuring "moral justification, refusal to accept responsibility, blaming

Table 5.2   *Individual Items in the Criminal Personality Scale*

Question Wording	Mean	Standard Deviation	Factor	Factor Description
1. I have gotten involved in things I later wished I could have gotten out of.	2.63	1.11	2	Trouble-maker
2. I get into trouble because I do things without thinking.	2.32	1.05	2	Trouble-maker
3. I am often restless and bored.	2.60	1.16	2 [4]	Trouble-maker; Socially Isolated
4. I am seen by others as cold and unfeeling.	2.13	.98	1 4	Anger/Violence; Socially Isolated
5. I feel bad if I break a promise I have made to someone.	1.87	.82	[1] 2	Anger/Violence; Trouble-maker
6. The trouble with getting close to people is that they start making demands on you.	2.61	1.07	4	Socially Isolated
7. To get ahead in life you must always put yourself first.	3.04	1.23	4	Socially Isolated
8. I have the ability to "sweet talk" people to get what I want.	2.67	1.09	3	Manipulative
9. I'm really good at talking my way out of things.	2.74	1.09	3	Manipulative
10. If people make me angry or I lose my temper, I can be dangerous.	2.22	1.03	1	Anger/Violence
11. Some people see me as a violent person.	2.11	1.02	1	Anger/Violence
12. I almost never lose my temper.	2.88	1.15	1	Anger/Violence
13. I have a short temper and can get angry quickly.	2.38	1.11	1	Anger/Violence
Scale (Possible Criminal Personality Scale Range 13–65)	32.21	6.74	—	—

Source: Author's calculations.
Data are for all completed offender assessments in the COMPAS database through October 2006.
N = 16,045
Note: A variable is considered part of a particular dimension if it loads greater than 0.40. A factor is in brackets if the loading for that variable is higher than 0.30 but lower than 0.40.

the victim, and rationalizations (excuses) that minimize the seriousness and consequences of criminal activity" (Brenan, Dieterich, and Oliver 2006, 130). Table 5.3 describes the individual items that compose this scale. The internal consistency of this index is high, with a Cronbach's alpha of 0.795.[10] A factor analysis suggests that this set of items is also described by more than one dimension. The first dimension describes justifications for hurting others. Five variables load high on this factor, and one loads weakly.[11] The second dimension describes justifications for breaking the law. Six variables load high on this dimension.

RESULTS

As a starting point for assessing the effects of custody placement on criminal psychology, this study compares the average criminal personality and criminal cognitions scores of those with classification scores that fall just below the cutoff between Levels II and III (a score of either twenty-six or twenty-seven) to those just above the cutoff (a score of either twenty-eight or twenty-nine). In the sample as a whole, there appears to be no significant difference between the two groups (see table 5.4).

However, a clear effect appears when the sample is divided into subgroups by criminal history. COMPAS includes a Criminal Involvement Scale, detailing "extent of involvement in the criminal justice system . . . and extensiveness of the criminal history" (Brennan, Dieterich, and Oliver 2006). The scale is constructed from four items measuring the number of times an individual has been previously jailed, convicted, arrested, or on probation. Table 5.4 details scores on both the Criminal Cognitions and Criminal Personality Scales for those in the bottom three deciles of the Criminal Involvement Scale, who have classification scores just above and just below the cutoff. As table 5.4 shows, among those with a relatively limited criminal past—with little experience in the criminal justice system and few past offenses—placement in a higher-security prison appears to have a criminogenic effect on both cognitions and personality. Placement in a higher-security prison predicts an increase of 1.8 points on the Criminal Involvement Scale and a jump of 2.33 points on the Criminal Personality Scale.

To get a sense of the substantive import of these differences, it is helpful to compare the decile scores corresponding to each group's criminal psychology scores. Recall that the decile scores compare individual scores to the total population of male incarcerated offenders. On this measure, there are clear differences between the two groups. The mean criminal involvement decile score is 5.98 for those below the cutoff and 6.7 for those above ($F = 5.142$, $p = 0.024$). Those with classification scores that fall just below the cutoff have a median at the sixth decile. By comparison, those with classification scores that fall just above the cutoff have a significantly higher median,

Table 5.3   *Individual Items in the Criminal Cognitions Scale*

Question Wording	Mean	Standard Deviation	Factor	Factor Description
1. A hungry person has a right to steal.	2.12	0.934	1	Justifies Harm to Others
			[2]	Justifies Law Breaking
2. The law doesn't help average people.	2.38	1.03	2	Justifies Law Breaking
3. When people get into trouble with the law it's because they have no chance to get a decent job.	2.15	0.99	2	Justifies Law Breaking
4. Some people get into trouble or use drugs because society has given them no education, jobs, or future.	2.37	1.08	2	Justifies Law Breaking
5. Some people just don't deserve any respect and should be treated like animals.	1.77	0.08	1	Justifies Law Breaking
6. Some people must be treated roughly or beaten up just to send them a clear message.	1.96	0.87	1	Justifies Harm to Others
7. If someone insults my friends, family, or group they are asking for trouble.	2.67	1.09	1	Justifies Harm to Others
8. I won't hesitate to hit or threaten people if they have done something to hurt my friends or family.	2.32	1.06	1	Justifies Harm to Others
9. When people do minor offenses or use drugs they don't hurt anyone except themselves.	2.51	1.22	2	Justifies Law Breaking
10. When things are stolen from rich people they won't miss the stuff because insurance will cover the loss.	1.97	0.85	1	Justifies Harm to Others
			2	Justifies Law Breaking
Criminal Cognitions Scale (Possible Range 10–50)	22.23	5.92	—	—

Source: Author's compilation.
Data are for all completed offender assessments in the COMPAS database through October 2006.
N = 16,043
Note: A variable is considered part of a particular dimension if it loads greater than 0.40. A factor is in brackets if the loading for that variable is higher than 0.30 but lower than 0.40.

Table 5.4   *Criminal-Thinking Scale Scores for Offenders Just Above and Below Classification Cutoff, by Extensiveness of Criminal History*

| | Above and Below the Cutoff for Placement in Level II/Level III Custody | | | |
	Mean Below	Mean Above	Difference	F
Criminal cognitions				
Low criminal involvement (deciles 1 to 3)	22.9	24.7	1.8	6.487 (p = 0.011)
Medium criminal involvement (deciles 4 to 7)	23.5	23.5	0	.000
High Criminal Involvement (deciles 8 to 10)	23.7	23.4	−0.3	.101
Total (All deciles)	23.4	23.8	0.4	1.227
Criminal personality				
Low criminal involvement (deciles 1 to 3)	31.7	34.03	2.33	7.059 (p = 0.008)
Medium criminal involvement (deciles 4 to 7)	34.0	33.3	−0.7	0.922
High criminal involvement (deciles 8 to 10)	34.1	33.2	−0.9	0.837
Total (All deciles)	33.4	33.5	0.1	0.089

Source: Author's calculations.
Note: Sample includes those with a classification score of 26 or 27 (below the cutoff), and 28 and 29 (above the cutoff). Those placed with an administrative determinant are excluded. Low criminal involvement N = 278 (134 cases below cutoff and 144 above); Medium criminal involvement N = 375 (206 cases below cutoff and 169 above); High criminal involvement N = 229 (122 cases below cutoff and 107 above).

at the eighth decile. The same disparity can be observed in criminal personality decile scores. Compared to a median decile score of 4.5 for those with classification scores below the cutoff, those with classification scores above the cutoff have a median decile score of 6. The mean criminal personality decile score is 5.07 below the cutoff and 5.81 above ($F = 4.252, p = 0.040$).

These between-group differences appear to be driven primarily by differences in dimensions of criminal attitudes related to anger and violence. The Criminal Cognition Scale is composed of two distinct dimensions: one identifying justifications for doing harm to others, and the other identifying justifications for breaking the law. There is no significant difference between the two groups in endorsement of justifications for breaking the law. Rather, it is in the degree to which people espouse justifications for harming others—measured by sentiments such as "I won't hesitate to hit or threaten people if they have done something to hurt my friends or family," and "Some people must be treated roughly or beaten up just to send them a clear message"—that a statistically significant effect appears. Those with a classification score just above the cutoff are more likely to agree with this type of statement than are those just below the cutoff.[12]

The same is true of group differences on the Criminal Personality Scale. The scale has four dimensions, described by a propensity for getting into trouble, a tendency to self-isolate, a talent for manipulating others, and a predisposition toward violence and anger. While there is no significant difference between the two groups along three of these dimensions, those above the cutoff have higher scores on the variables describing anger and violence. Those above the cutoff are more likely on average to agree with statements such as "If people make me angry or lose my temper, I can be dangerous," and "Some people see me as a violent person." Conversly, they are more likely to disagree with statements like "I almost never lose my temper."[13]

To examine the robustness of these findings, treatment effects were also estimated by regressing criminal cognition and criminal personality scores on a third-order polynomial of classification score, a dummy for scores above and below the cutoff (coded "zero" for scores between nineteen and twenty-seven and "one" for scores between twenty-eight and fifty-one); an interaction term; and the full set of demographic, criminal-history, socialization, and personal-history controls. Slopes for the classification score appear to differ between the two groups, but not significantly. In fact, for those with classification scores both below and above the cutoff, there is no significant relationship between classification score and criminal thinking, *ceteris paribus*. As the interaction term proved insignificant, it was trimmed from the final specification.

As figure 5.1 shows, the results from this model reveal a clear discontinuity at the cutoff point between Level II and Level III. The estimated equation includes 1,207 cases, and the slope coefficient for the assignment variable is 1.85 ($p = 0.001$). This suggests that having a classification score above the cutoff point between Level II and Level III predicts a jump of 1.85 points on the Criminal Cognitions Scale. To provide a sense of the substantive meaning of this discontinuity, I estimate the same equation on criminal cognition decile scores. At the cutoff point for classification between Level II and Level III facilities, there is a jump of more than two-thirds of a decile (0.72, $p = 0.005$). There does not, however, appear to be a similar discontinuity in scores on the Criminal Personality Scale. There is a gap of 0.77 in predicted criminal personality scores at the cutoff, but the difference is not statistically significant ($p = 0.2$).[14]

Figure 5.1   *Discontinuity in Criminal Cognitions, with SubGroup Loess Fit*

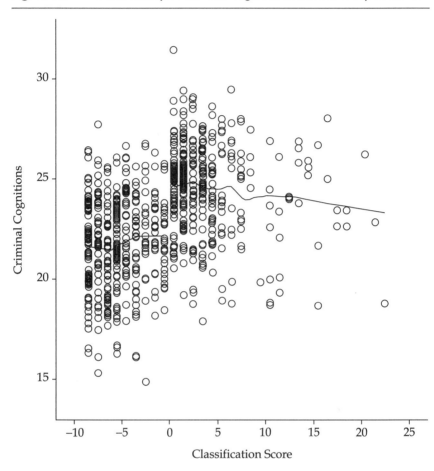

Source: Author's calculations.
Note: Sample includes only those in the lowest three deciles of the Criminal History Scale.
Inmates placed with an administrative determinant are excluded.
N = 1,207

CONCLUSION

This chapter has presented evidence that placement in a higher-security prison increases psychological criminality among those inmates with minimal criminal history—those less likely to have been arrested or convicted in the past. Among this group, being placed in a higher-security facility predicts an increase of about 1.85 points on the Criminal Cognitions Scale. This represents a predicted gap of about two-thirds of a decile over those placed in a lower-security facility. These effects are driven largely by changes in psychological dimensions related to anger and violence. Inmates assigned to Level III rather than Level II prisons are more likely to agree with statements such as "I won't hesitate to hit or threaten people if they have done something to hurt my friends or family," and "Some people must be treated roughly or beaten up just to send them a clear message."

Understanding the dynamics of security classification, which is a specific bureaucratic procedure that can be controlled by correctional practitioners and policymakers, has clear value for those concerned with community corrections and crime control. The finding that incarceration in a higher-security prison may lead to increased psychological criminality has direct policy implications. The decision to place an offender in a lower-security prison has certain associated risks. In a custody setting that offers more lenient oversight and fewer impediments to physical movement, individuals face a smaller number of obstacles to attempted escape or the perpetration of violence. This may lead risk-averse correctional practitioners to take a conservative position towards security assignment, choosing to default offenders into higher custody. However, for those with little prior history of criminality, a higher-custody placement may ultimately have criminogenic consequences. Incarcerating these individuals in higher-security prisons might successfully contain them during the period of incarceration, but may lead to increased criminal thinking by the time they exit.

These findings may also have consequences for the practice of community corrections. Understanding the effects of incarceration on inmate outcomes can help guide the negotiation of risk in community corrections and the provision of appropriate postparole reintegration services. More than 90 percent of offenders who enter prison will eventually be released back into the community (Petersilia 2003). In 1975, the state of California alone released about 21,000 parolees. By 2001, this had increased to roughly 125,000 annually. The growing size of the reentry population has dramatically increased the scope of the correctional bureaucracy and the need for more systematic parolee monitoring and oversight of postrelease service delivery.

Community corrections are defined as any program or service that puts monitoring restrictions on an individual who has commit a crime, either before, following, or in lieu of incarceration. Examples include probation and parole, home confinement and electronic monitoring, check-in programs, curfews, and community-based drug and alcohol programs. Like custody placement, community corrections also present a calculation of risk. Different levels of oversight, offered by different types of programs, put more or less trust in a person released from incarceration. For example, electronic monitoring places little trust in the individual, as it allows for constant scrutiny of his location. If the individual goes somewhere he is not supposed to—close to a school or to his victim's house or place of work—police can be made aware immediately. By comparison, day check-in programs place a lot of trust in the individual, allowing him relative freedom during most of the day and night. Yet in offering less oversight, they arguably offer more risk.

The fundamental problem associated with such policies is how to find the right balance between trust and risk. Traditionally, formal risk assessments have been used to help practitioners contend with this issue. While the clinical assessment tools that dominated the early practice of risk evaluation came under attack as being too subjective, new highly quantitative risk assessments have made a recent resurgence in popularity. A number of such modern actuarial tools have been developed for correctional risk assessment, including the VRAG, the SIR scale, Static 99, and the SONAR.[15] These instruments bear little resemblance to the older "holistic but subjective" model that fell from favor in the 1970s and 1980s (Simon 2005).

Despite their return to favor and the improvements that have been made in the science of risk prediction, many of even the most sophisticated modern risk assessment instruments ignore the possibility that the experience of incarceration has itself become a factor in shaping an individual's likelihood to reoffend.[16] As Jonathan Simon writes, "the [subjects of risk assessments] were mostly persons who had been institutionalized for a long period prior to the moment of risk assessment, which meant that prior history and other available risk factors might have become less relevant to the individual case" (2005, 404). A better understanding of institutional effects will assist policymakers in providing the necessary safeguards and supports that offenders need to successfully reintegrate back into society. Addressing the ways in which institutionalization shapes attitudes related to crime and criminality may ultimately help decrease risk factors among those leaving prison and helps practitioners to more effectively manage community-based monitoring and treatment.

Finally, these results suggest that the move towards more punitive prisons that has dominated the past few decades may have undesirable consequences. If incarcerating individuals in more punitive prisons and with more "criminal" peers leads them to adopt antisocial attitudes, this may result in detachment from prosocial networks, a further deterioration of adherence to social and legal norms, and ultimately a greater likelihood of recidivism following release. Greater understanding of the criminogenic effects of these prison conditions should help guide the future trajectory of correctional policy.

NOTES

1. The state correctional system includes over one hundred facilities. California inmates are held in thirty-three state prisons, as well as about forty custody camps, twelve community correctional facilities, and five prisoner mother facilities (California Department of Corrections 2008). While the phrase "a higher- or lower-security prison" is used throughout this chapter, it is worth noting that most prisons in California house more than one security level. Inmates are kept separate, but are assigned to the same physical institution.

2. In addition, a caseworker can apply an administrative determinant to a case or otherwise suggest an irregular placement. An irregular placement is the assignment of an inmate to an institution that does not correspond to the security level of his or her final placement score. An administrative determinant can include, among other things, youthfulness or immaturity, enemies, escape potential, family ties, gang involvement, need for medical attention, need to be housed close to a court jurisdiction, mental-health condition, academic program involvement, sexual orientation, or work skills. Systemwide, about 25 percent of inmates are placed according to administrative determinants (California State Senate Assembly 1997; Berk 2004). The most common reason for an administrative override occurs when there is a lack of available bed space in the security level to which an inmate is designated (Petersilia 2006).

3. The History of Noncompliance Scale combines the number of times probation has been suspended or revoked, the number of arrests or charges for a crime while on pretrial release, the number of failures to appear for court, and the number of arrests or charges while on probation or parole.

4. The History of Violence Scale includes total prior arrests and convictions for juvenile and adult felony assault, assault (not murder), sex offenses with force, homicide and manslaughter, robbery, weapons, and family violence. It also includes the number of prior times a victim had physical injuries and number of write-ups for fighting or threatening inmates.

5. The Family Criminality Scale includes indicators of whether a father, mother, siblings, or spouse or partner were ever arrested; whether a parent or parent figure had drug or alcohol problems; and whether a parent was ever sent to jail or prison.

6. The Socialization Failure Scale includes a set of items repeated from the Family Criminality and Educational/Vocational Problem Scales. The two groups do differ somewhat in scores on the total Socialization Failure Scale. Those just above the cutoff have somewhat higher scores on this scale than those just below the cutoff. This scale and individual items from this scale are included as predictors in the regression models.

7. The Substance Abuse Scale includes indicators of whether the current charge includes drunk driving; whether the individual would benefit from treatment for drugs or alcohol; whether the offender thinks legal problems are due to alcohol; juvenile use of heroin, cocaine, or crack; past treatment for alcohol or drugs; and using alcohol or drugs when arrested for current offense. The Financial Problems and Poverty Scale includes questions on family conflicts over money, recent fears about financial survival, a recent job paying

under minimum wage, recent trouble paying bills, and the feeling of having barely enough money to get by. The Vocational/Educational Problems Scale includes indicators for high school graduation, suspensions or expulsions from school, usual grades in high school, current employment, usable skill or trade, extent of recent work or school experience, fail or repeating a grade level, feeling that one needs training in a new job or skill, sense of difficulty finding a job above minimum wage, rating of chances for successfully locating work, and currently verifiable local employer or school.

8. The Criminal Psychology Scales are two of the twenty-two scales automatically generated by COMPAS from individual items in the inmate survey assessments. The majority of the scales are descriptive: seven describe dimensions of criminal and antisocial behavior, including history of violence and early socialization failure; eight describe aspects of inmates' social and personal stability and adjustment, including substance abuse, financial problems, and residential instability; and three describe psychological dimensions related to criminal thinking, criminal personality, and social isolation. In addition, four COMPAS scales are predictive, assessing the likelihood of future criminal activity in the areas of violence, recidivism, failure to appear, and community noncompliance.

9. As with any survey that touches on sensitive topics, there is some concern about the veracity of responses. This is particularly true when the survey is administered under some level of duress, as might be expected with a correctional risk assessment conducted on individuals about to parole from prison. While it is impossible to ever definitively confirm the honesty of subjective responses, the COMPAS system does include two separate validity tests, a "lie test" that checks for "defensiveness in responding," and a test for randomness and inconsistency.

10. There are several straightforward items in the scale, such as "Some people just don't deserve any respect and should be treated like animals," and "Some people must be treated roughly or beaten up just to send them a clear message." These seem to clearly indicate a type of psychological cognition that would be expected to predict criminality. Several of the other items, however, seem more difficult to place as purely psycho-criminal. One can imagine a reasonable percentage of liberal-minded individuals with no criminal tendencies who would agree with such statements as "Some people get into trouble with the law because society has given them no education, jobs, or future," and "The law doesn't help average people."

11. The sixth variable loading high on the first dimension loads weakly on the second dimension. This variable, "A hungry person has a right to steal," does not appear to fit the pattern, in that it seems substantively more similar to the second set of variables.

12. Combined into an additive linear index, the F statistic for group differences on these items is 9.123, significant at $p = 0.003$.

13. Combined into an additive linear index, the F statistic for group differences on these items is 7.569, significant at $p = 0.006$.

14. As an additional robustness check, I estimate a two-stage least squares model to account for the fuzziness of the regression discontinuity. I employ a

linear probability model as equation 5.1, estimating the likelihood of placement in a higher-security prison (level III) as a function of whether the score
falls above (coded as one) or below (coded as zero) the cutoff, and a set of
controls. Equation 5.2 looks similar to the reduced-form equation, but instruments for the placement dummy with the dummy variable for security
score. The sample is limited to those with scores right around the cutoff
(twenty-six to twenty-nine). The coefficient on the criminal cognitions scale
is similar to that obtained in the reduced form, and the effect remains significant in the direction of increased criminality. This and other robustness
checks are further detailed in a technical working paper.

15. There is still a great deal of debate over how accurate these newer actuarial
assessments are in predicting reoffending. In particular, many argue that the
indicators on which risk evaluations are based have not been sufficiently
standardized. There is also some discussion over whether many actuarial instruments focus too heavily on static factors.

16. The static risk factor with the most significant predictive power is prior contact with the criminal justice system or the mental health system (Gottfredson and Gottfredson 1994; Shaffer, Waters, and Adams 1994). Likewise, incidents of prior violence, as well as mental illness and substance abuse, are the
best predictors of future violent offenses (Limandri and Sheridan 1995). Dynamic factors have likewise been shown to predict recidivism, arguably
more consistently than static factors (Offender Risk Assessment 2000). Significant dynamic predictors include antisocial personality, poor social support, and substance abuse. Some new instruments are attempting to build in
these dynamic factors, taking into account institutional effects rather than relying solely on preincarceration behavior.

REFERENCES

Bayer, Patrick, Randi Hjalmarsson, and David Pozen. 2007. "Building Criminal
Capital Behind Bars: Peer Effects in Juvenile Corrections." NBER working paper 12932. Cambridge, Mass.: National Bureau of Economic Research.

Berk, Richard. 2004. "Conducting a Randomized Field Experiment for the California Department of Corrections: The Experience of the Inmate Classification Experiment." Working paper CCPR-005-04. Los Angeles, Calif.: California Center
for Population Research.

Berk, Richard, and Jan D. de Leeuw. 1998. "An Evaluation of California' s Inmate
Classification System Using a Generalized Regression Discontinuity Design."
Journal of the American Statistical Association 94(448): 1045–52.

Berk, Richard A., and David Rauma. 1983. "Capitalizing on Nonrandom Assignment to Treatments: A Regression-Discontinuity Evaluation of a Crime Control
Program." *Journal of the American Statistical Association* 78(381): 21–27.

Blondell, Richard D., Stephen W. Looney, Alan P. Northington, Mary Ellen Lasch,
Sandra B. Rhodes, and Regina L. McDaniels. 2001. "Can Recovering Alcoholics
Help Hospitalized Patients with Alcohol Problems?" *Journal of Family Practice*
50(5): 447.

Braly, Malcolm. 2002. *On the Yard*. New York: New York Review of Books, Classics.

Brennan, Tim, William Dieterich, and William Oliver. 2006. "California Department of Corrections, Parole, and Community Services Division: COMPAS Pilot Psychometric Report." Traverse City, Mich.: Northpointe Institute for Public Management.

Bukstel, Lee H., and Peter R. Kilmann. 1980. "Psychological Effects of Imprisonment on Confined Individuals." *Psychological Bulletin* 88: 469–93.

Bunker, Edward. 1981. *Little Boy Blue*. New York: St. Martin's Press.

California Department of Corrections and Rehabilitation. 2008. "Second Quarter Facts and Figures." *Adult Operations Quarterly Report*.

California State Senate Assembly. Committee on Public Safety. 1997. SB 491 Senate Bill—Bill Analysis.

Chen, M. Keith, and Jesse M. Shapiro. 2007. "Do Harsher Prison Conditions Reduce Recidivism? A Discontinuity-Based Approach." *American Law and Economic Review* 9(1): 1–29.

DiIulio, John J. 1987. *Governing Prisons: A Comparative Study of Correctional Management*. New York: Free Press.

———. 1993. "Returning to the Criminal Justice System: Toward a New Paradigm in Performance Measures for the Criminal Justice System." In *Study Group on Criminal Justice Performance Measures*, edited by John J. DiIulio. Bureau of Justice Statistics—Princeton Project.

Elliott, Delbert S., David Huizinga, and Suzanne S. Ageton. 1985. *Explaining Delinquency and Drug Use*. Beverly Hills, Calif.: Sage.

Farrington, David P. 1986. "Age and Crime." In *Crime and Justice: An Annual Review of Research*, edited by Norval Morris. Chicago: University of Chicago Press.

Ferri, Marcia, Laura Amato, and Marina Davoli. 2006. "Alcoholics Anonymous and Other 12-step Programmes for Alcohol Dependence." *Cochrane Database of Systematic Reviews* 3. New York: John Wiley & Sons, Ltd.

Garland, David. 2001. *The Culture of Control: Crime and Social Order in Contemporary Society*. Chicago: University of Chicago Press.

Gendreau, Paul, Claire Goggin, F. Chanteloupe, and Donald A. Andrews. 1992. "The Development of Clinical and Policy Guidelines for the Prediction of Criminal Behaviour in Criminal Justice Settings." Ottawa, Ontario: Ministry of the Solicitor General of Canada.

Gendreau, Paul, Claire E. Goggin, and Moira A. Law. 1997. "Predicting Prison Misconduct." *Criminal Justice and Behavior* 24(4): 414–31.

Gendreau, Paul, Tracy Little, and Claire Goggin. 1995. "A Meta-Analysis of the Predictors of Adult Offender Recidivism: Assessment Guidelines for Classification and Treatment." Ottawa, Ontario: Ministry of the Solicitor General of Canada.

Glaeser, Edward L., Bruce Sacerdote, and Jose A. Scheinkman. 1996. "Crime and Social Interactions." *Quarterly Journal of Economics* 111(2): 507–48.

Glueck, Sheldon, and Eleanor Glueck. 1950. *Unraveling Juvenile Delinquency*. Cambridge, Mass.: Harvard University Press.

Gottfredson, Stephen, and Don Gottfredson. 1994. "Behavioral Prediction and the Problem of Incapacitation." *Criminology* 32(3): 441–74.

Hirschi, Travis, and Michael Gottfredson. 1983. "Age and the Explanation of Crime." *American Journal of Sociology* 89: 552–84.

Irwin, John. 1985. *Jail: Managing the Underclass in American Society.* Berkeley, Calif.: University of California Press.

Jacob, Brian, and Lars Lefgren. 2004. "Remedial Education and Student Achievement: A Regression-Discontinuity Analysis." *Review of Economics and Statistics* 86: 226–44.

Jaman, Dorothy R., Robert M. Dickover, and Lawrence A. Bennett. 1972. "Parole Outcomes as a Function of Time Served." *British Journal of Crimonology* 12: 5–34.

Kruttschnitt, Candace R. G. 2005. *Marking Time in the Golden State.* New York: Cambridge University Press.

Kuziemko, Ilyana. 2006. "Going Off Parole: How the Elimination of Discretionary Prison Release Affects the Social Cost of Crime." *Mimeo.*

Laub, John H., and Robert Sampson. 2003. *Shared Beginnings, Divergent Lives: Delinquent Boys to Age 70.* Cambridge, Mass.: Harvard University Press.

Lee, David, and Justin McCrary. 2005. "Crime, Punishment, and Myopia." NBER working paper 11491. Cambridge, Mass.: National Bureau of Economic Research.

Lerman, Amy. 2008. *The Citizens Prisons Produce: How Criminal Justice Policies Shape American Communities and Civic Life.* Phd. diss. Berkeley, Calif.: University of California, Berkeley.

Limandri, Barbara J., and Daniel J. Sheridan. 1995. "Assessing Dangerousness: Violence by Sexual Offenders, Batterers, and Child Abusers." In *Predication of Intentional Interpersonal Violence: An Introduction,* edited by J. C. Campbell. Thousand Oaks, Calif.: Sage.

Logan, Charles H. 1992. "Well Kept: Comparing Quality of Confinement in Private and Public Prisons." *The Journal of Criminal Law and Criminology* 83(3).

———. 1993. "Criminal Justice Performance Measures for Prisons." In *Study Group on Criminal Justice Performance Measures,* edited by John J. DiIulio. Bureau of Justice Statistics—Princeton Project.

Matsueda, Ross L., and Karen Heimer. 1987. "Race, Family Structure, and Delinquency." *American Sociological Review* 7(2): 319–49.

Nagin, Daniel S. 1998. "Criminal Deterrence Research at the Outset of the Twenty-First Century." In *Crime and Justice: A Review of Research,* edited by Michael Tonry. Chicago: University of Chicago Press.

Offender Risk Assessment. 2000. Alberta, Canada: John Howard Society of Alberta.

Petersilia, Joan. 2000. "Challenges of Prisoner Reentry and Parole in California." *California Policy Research Center Brief Series.*

———. 2006. "Understanding California Corrections." University of California, Irvine Center for Evidence Based Corrections.

Pintoff, Randi. 2004. "The Impact of Incarceration on Juvenile Crime: A Regression Discontinuity Approach." Working paper. New Haven, Conn: Yale University.

Ross, Abraham, and Beth Lacey. 1983. "A Regression Discontinuity Analysis of a Remedial Education Programme." *Canadian Journal of Higher Education* 13(1): 1–15.

Rowe, Michael, Chyrell Bellamy, Madelon Baranoski, Melissa Wieland, Maria J. O'Connell, Patricia Benedict, Larry Davidson, Josephine Buchanan, and Dave Sells. 2007. "A Peer-Support, Group Intervention to Reduce Substance Use and

Criminality Among Persons with Severe Mental Illness." *Psychiatric Services* 58: 955–61.

Rubin, Donald. 1977. "Assignment to Treatment Group on the Basis of a Covariate." *Journal of Educational Statistics* 2: 1–26.

Shaffer, C. Edward, William Waters, and Serrbel Adams. 1994. "Dangerousness: Assessing the Risk of Violent Behavior." *Journal of Consulting and Clinical Psychology* 62(5): 1064–68.

Shakur, Sanyika. 1993. *Monster: The Autobiography of an L.A. Gang Member.* New York: Grove Press.

Simon, Jonathan. 2005. "Reversal of Fortune: The Resurgence of Individual Risk Assessment in Criminal Justice." *Annual Review of Law and Social Science* 1: 397–421.

Smith, Paula, Claire Goggin, and Paul Gendreau. 2002. "The Effects of Prison Sentences and Intermediate Sanctions on Recidivism: General Effects and Individual Differences." Saint John, Center for Criminal Justice Studies, University of New Brunswick.

Song, Lin and Roxanne Lieb. 1993. "Recidivism: The Effect of Incarceration and Length of Time Served." Olympia, Wash.: Washington State Institute for Public Policy.

State of California, California Code of Regulations. 2004. "Rules and Regulations of the Director of Corrections." Title 15. *Crime Prevention and Corrections*. Sacramento, Calif.: State of California.

Sykes, Gresham M. 1958. *The Society of Captives: A Study of a Maximum Security Prison*. Princeton, N.J.: Princeton University Press.

Thistlethwaite, Donald, and Donald Campbell. 1960. "Regression-Discontinuity Analysis: An Alternative to the Ex Post Facto Experiment." *Journal of Educational Psychology* 51: 309–17.

Thompson, Leon "Whitey." 1988. *Last Train to Alcatraz*. Fiddletown, Calif.: Winter Book Publisher.

Van der Klaauw, Wibert. 2002. "Estimating the Effect of Financial Aid Offers on College Enrollment: A Regression-Discontinuity Approach." *International Economic Review* 43(4): 1249–87.

Villettaz, Patricia, Martin Killias, and Isabel Zoder. 2006. "The Effects of Custodial Vs. Non-custodial Sentences on Reoffending: A Systematic Review of the State of Knowledge." Report to the Campbell Collaboration Crime and Justice Group. Lausanne, Switzerland: University of Lausanne.

Von Hirsch, Andrew, Anthony Bottoms, Elizabeth Burney, and Per-Olot Wikstrom. 1999. *Criminal Deterrence and Sentence Severity: An Analysis of Recent Research*. Oxford, U.K.: Hart Publishing.

Walker, Nigel. 1987. "The Unwanted Effects of Long-Term Imprisonment." In *Problems of Long-term Imprisonment*, edited by R. Light. Aldershot, UK: Gower.

Warr, Mark, and Mark Stafford. 1991. "The Influence of Delinquent Peers: What They Think or What They Do." *Criminology* 29: 851–65.

Zenou, Yves. 2003. "The Spatial Aspects of Crime." *Journal of the European Economic Association* 1: 459–67.

Rucker C. Johnson

Ever-Increasing Levels of Parental Incarceration the Consequences and for Children

6

The enormous increase in incarceration led to a parallel, but far less documented, increase in the proportion of children who grew up with a parent incarcerated at some point during their childhood. Moreover, the concentration of these incarceration trends among less-educated African Americans has resulted in a larger gulf between the early-life experiences of white and black children, which may have profound effects on their later-life socioeconomic attainments. The implications for child well-being of policy-induced increases in the incidence of parental incarceration are not well understood.

The consequences of incarceration on children have received little attention in academic research, prison statistics, public policy, and media coverage. If we fail to consider potential impacts of incarceration on children, we risk neglecting at-risk youth; this may contribute to crime problems in the next generation. This is an important potential negative externality and unintended consequence of criminal-justice policy, with parental incarceration imposing larger social costs than merely the prison cost.

This chapter aims to produce nationally representative estimates of the prevalence of parental incarceration for children born between 1985 and 2002, by race and socioeconomic status. It also aims to investigate the effects of parental incarceration on child outcomes, including early antecedents of youth crime, using intergenerational correlations in the likelihood of criminal involvement (arrest, conviction, incarceration).

The empirical analyses use nationally representative longitudinal data covering a nearly forty-year period in the United States to produce evidence that concern each of these issues. I exploit unique features of the Panel Study of Income Dynamics (PSID) and its Child Development Supplement (CDS) to tackle these interrelated research questions. This is the first such study of the full U.S. population.

Using the PSID-CDS, I provide evidence on a series of important descriptive questions regarding how often white, black, and Hispanic children experience paternal incarceration; how the risk has changed over the past twenty-five years (recent birth cohorts versus older birth cohorts from other data sources); and how this risk varies within racial and ethnic groups.

The focus of the regression analysis section investigates the consequences for children of parental incarceration. The results highlight changes in the child's family income and poverty status before, during, and following a father's incarceration. It is shown that children from families with an incarceration history have worse behavioral outcomes. This chapter presents evidence on intergenerational correlations in deviant behavior. Several different empirical strategies are employed to distinguish whether this correlation emanates primarily from observed and unobserved disadvantaged childhood-environment characteristics (proximate causes) versus the causal effects of parental incarceration.

PREVIOUS RESEARCH ON PARENTAL
INCARCERATION AND CHILD WELL-BEING

Children of prisoners have been referred to as the "orphans of justice" and "innocent victims of punishment." The limited extant evidence on prisoners' children is drawn from small-scale, mostly qualitative research studies, and have rarely included longitudinal follow-up. The consequences of ever-increasing levels of incarceration for children are perhaps the least understood aspect of the potential positive or deleterious impacts of incarceration policy on families and communities.

Over the decade of the 1990s, the number of children with a parent in state or federal prison in the United States rose from 1 million to 1.5 million (Mumola 2000). Ninety-two percent had a father in prison, which disproportionately affects black children. The number of parents in prison doubled over this period, with nearly 3.6 million parents placed under some form of correctional supervision, including parole, by 2000. On any given day, 7 percent of black children have an incarcerated parent, compared with 2.6 percent of Hispanic children and 0.8 percent of white children. Before entering prison, 64 percent of imprisoned mothers lived with their children, compared to 44 percent of imprisoned fathers in the United States (Mumola 2000). Current prison statistics contain only point-in-time prevalence rates, which mask the extent of childhood experiences of incarceration that could be gleaned from incidence rates. Snapshot cross-sectional estimates significantly understate cumulative risk of exposure to parental incarceration during childhood.

Parental separation that results from incarceration may pose unique risks in its effect on children and the family, relative to parental separations due to divorce, which has a voluminous research literature. A prison sentence may be a death sentence of a father's relationship with his child; conversely, it may liberate a child from an oppressive, abusive, or negligent environment growing up. Alternatively, it may have negligible effects because of limited father involvement in the child's life prior to imprisonment.

The small research literature on children of incarcerated parents suggests that parental incarceration is associated with increased aggressive behavior and withdrawal (Baunach 1985), criminal involvement (Johnston 1995), and depression (Kampfner 1995). Existing studies, however, have not been able to separately identify the causal effects of incarceration from the effects of preincarceration risk factors such as parental substance abuse, mental-health problems, and abuse histories that may have already put the child at risk before the parent was imprisoned (Johnson and Waldfogel 2002). Although previous research on children with an incarcerated parent has been methodologically weak in assessing causality, these studies consistently document significantly more behavior problems among these children, including aggressive behavior, depression, hyperactivity, withdrawal, running away, sleep and eating disorders, poor school grades, and delinquency (Johnston 1995). Potential explanations for the association between parental incarceration and child behavior problems include the following:

- Trauma of separation

- Parental role-modeling effects (poor parenting, substance abuse, domestic violence)

- Potential beneficial effects from removing abusive parent from household

- Shared childhood socioeconomic deprivation prior to imprisonment

- Depleted parental resources following parental incarceration—reduction in family income and reduced quality of care (disruptions in children's care arrangements accompanied by school and residential moves)

- Genetic predisposition or inherited traits (temperament, parental criminality)

The direction of the predicted impacts on children is not clear theoretically. The incarceration of an abusive or negligent parent may benefit children and contribute to a more nurturing environment. On the other hand, the incarceration of a parent may be a traumatic event in the life of a child that has deleterious impacts on subsequent emotional and behavioral outcomes. Assessing the relative importance of these potential explanations and evaluating whether parental incarceration is merely a risk marker as opposed to a causal risk mechanism has implications for policy. For example, if shared childhood socioeconomic deprivation is the most salient factor underlying the relationship, then policies aimed at reducing poverty also reduce crime. Alternatively, if inherited traits or genetic predispositions are driving factors, then the efficacy of interventions targeted directly at the children of incarcerated parents may be very limited (without significant nature-nurture interaction effects).

There are myriad ways in which parental incarceration may compound disadvantage. It may increase the probabilities of growing up poor or with a single parent, or it may elevate the risk of criminal involvement and incarceration later in life for children of the incarcerated prison-boom generation. There are a variety of potential mechanisms through which parental incarceration may affect child outcomes, including economic instability, living-arrangement instability, parental-attachment issues, and role-model effects, to name a few. A primary goal of this research is to identify the reduced-form effects—not to separately identify the pathways.

The evidence presented in this chapter will bear on the question of the likelihood and extent that parental incarceration has exacerbated racial disparities in childhood and early adulthood. Given extant evidence that children who begin early formation of deviant behaviors in childhood are more likely to develop persistent, serious criminal involvement in adulthood, as well as the greater economic efficiency of policies aimed at prevention versus remediation, it is important to target intervention in early childhood.

Using data from Sweden, economists Randi Hjalmarsson and Matthew Lindquist (2007) report significant father-son correlations in criminal activity that begin to appear between ages seven and twelve, and that are fully established between ages thirteen and nineteen. The implication of this finding is that expectations during childhood about future adulthood opportunities shape deviant behavior over the life course and can explain a significant part of the father-son correlation. Identifying early antecedents for deviant behavior has the potential to reduce risks of criminal involvement in adulthood, and thereby break the cycle of the victimization-to-offending behavior pattern.

Because most incarcerated parents are fathers (with whom boys might identify more), and because boys appear to be more negatively impacted than girls by other types of family disruption such as parental divorce (McLanahan 2002), we expect the consequences for boys to be larger. Previous research has shown that the absence of the father leads to "acting-out" behavior (externalizing behavior problems), and the absence of the mother is associated with "acting-in" behavior (internalizing behavior problems) (Fritsch and Burkhead 1981). It is important to bear in mind that not all children respond similarly to parental criminal involvement, incarceration risk, or neighborhood disadvantage. For some, these experiences cause permanent developmental disruptions; others experience latent effects and appear to respond well in the face of difficult challenges early on, followed by behavior problems later in adolescence and the transition to adulthood. Still others exhibit resilience in the face of adversity and appear to be strengthened by these early-life traumatic events (Rutter 1987, 1993).

Cross-sectional evidence provides an incomplete and perhaps misleading portrait of the proportion of children who experience parental incarceration during childhood, as well as how parental incarceration may affect the developmental trajectories of children. It is important to consider dynamic issues by analyzing separately the short-run effects of the imprisonment and separation of the child from the parent, the impact of the parent's unavailability during the incarceration spell, and the effects of reunion after prison release. As well, one must consider whether the child is living with the parent at the time of incarceration; whether a two-parent or single-parent family is involved; and if it is a two-parent family, which parent is incarcerated. The most recent estimates (Mumola 2000) indicate that 36 percent of state-inmate mothers and 16 percent of federal-inmate mothers were not living with their children at the time of their incarceration; meanwhile, 56 percent of state-inmate fathers and 45 percent of federal-inmate fathers were not living with their children at the time of admission. Investigations of the patterns of visitation show that about half of incarcerated parents do not receive any visits from their children, and the frequency of visits is typically not often (Snell 1993).

DATA

The PSID began interviewing a national probability sample of families in 1968. These families were reinterviewed each year through 1997, when interviewing became biennial. All persons in PSID families in 1968 have the PSID "gene," which means that they are followed in subsequent waves. In addition, anyone born to or adopted by PSID sample members acquires the PSID "gene" and therefore is followed. When children with the "gene" become adults and leave their parents' homes, they become their own PSID "family unit" and are interviewed in each wave. Studies have concluded that the PSID sample of heads and wives remains representative of the national sample of adults (Fitzgerald, Gottschalk, and Moffitt

1998a; Becketti et al. 1988), and that the sample of "split offs" is representative (Fitzgerald, Gottschalk, and Moffitt 1998b). The 95 to 98 percent wave-to-wave response rate of the PSID makes this possible. Moreover, the genealogical design implies that the PSID sample today includes numerous adult parent-child groupings that have been members of PSID-interviewed families for nearly four decades.

Two samples are examined in the study. The adult sample in this chapter consists of PSID sample members who were children when the study began and who have been followed into adulthood. Specifically, I choose PSID sample members born between 1951 and 1975, which consists of children up to seventeen years old in the first wave of interviewing in 1968, plus children born into the PSID sample between 1968 and 1975. We then obtain all available information on these individuals for each wave, from 1968 to 2005. Therefore, by 2005 the oldest person in the adult sample is fifty-five years old, and the youngest is thirty years old.

For the deviant behavior, crime outcomes, and incarceration outcomes, the adult sample consists of original sample PSID males born between 1951 and 1975 who answered the criminal-history questions in the 1995 wave of the PSID or were positively identified as incarcerated in any wave of the survey between 1968 and 2005 (total $N = 2,944$; whites $N = 1,612$; blacks $N = 1,207$; Hispanics $N = 103$; other $N = 22$).

Spells of incarceration can be recovered from each survey, which includes whether a respondent was incarcerated at the time of the interview. This data alone on incarceration has limitations. Among the most important is that this will only identify incarceration in a given year if it was ongoing at the time of the survey interview. As a result, we are likely to miss individuals serving shorter sentences that did not coincide with the time of the interview.

The 1995 wave added a criminal-history module to the PSID including several key questions that this chapter uses to augment and obtain more precise information about the timing and duration of incarceration and minimize measurement error. In particular, information was collected for all adults in the 1995 wave on whether respondents had ever been expelled or suspended from school; whether they had ever been booked or charged with a crime; whether they had ever been placed in a juvenile correctional facility; and whether they had ever served time in jail or prison, the number of times, and the month and year of release.

Using the PSID information, I identify whether an incarcerated individual was a parent, and then I compare the dates of these incarceration spells to children's birth dates in order to identify which parents were incarcerated while they had children at home and how old the children were. It is important to note that I will not be able to identify parents who were incarcerated but never lived with the child at any time during their childhood. Thus, these analyses will systematically miss parents who have not been involved in their children's lives, which will likely result in a positive selection bias of families with an incarceration experience relative to the entire universe of parents with an incarceration history. In many ways, however, this is precisely the set of children for which parental incarceration may have consequences (either positive or negative) because of greater contact with children prior to the incarceration spell. Incarceration among parents who would not have been involved in their children's lives even without incarceration is less interesting for assessing child well-being and implications for criminal-justice policy.

Child Sample

In 1997, children up to twelve years old in PSID families and their caregivers were administrated a series of instruments as part of the Child Development Supplement (CDS). Up to two children within the same family were interviewed, resulting in a sample of 3,540 children in 2,348 different families in 1997 (1,132 families included two interviewed children). Interviews for these children were completed again in 2002 and 2003 when they were five to eighteen years old. In total there are 6,447 child-year observations (for more details about CDS, see Mainieri 2005; Mainieri and Grodsky 2006).

This chapter examines the effects of parental incarceration on children's educational and behavioral outcomes using data from the PSID-CDS, allowing for differential impacts for father's and mother's incarceration. Using this data, this study finds that the prevalence rates of parental incarceration at some point during childhood are significantly larger than point-in-time estimates. In this study, the consequences for children are considered by using information on the timing of parental criminal and incarceration history; changes in multiple dimensions of children's development and lives before and after the parental incarceration occurrence are then compared. These dimensions include child behavioral outcomes, family economic resources (such as income), family noneconomic resources (such as family structure and parenting behavior), and neighborhood conditions.

These data include a rich set of variables related to the mother, father, and the child, including parental criminal history, a set of child behavioral problem indices, standardized child cognitive assessments, and whether the child has ever been suspended or expelled from school. Armed with this array of information, the PSID-CDS is uniquely suited to consider the impacts of parental criminal and incarceration history on adolescent outcomes and to analyze the intergenerational transmission of risks of imprisonment. The child behavior problems index that is analyzed as an outcome has been shown to be a predictor of juvenile crime. This study utilizes information about these child outcomes as reported by the primary caregiver (the mother in most cases); where data permits, it also utilizes multiple informants of child behavior (including teacher reports).

CUMULATIVE RISKS OF DEVIANT BEHAVIOR, CRIMINAL INVOLVEMENT, AND INCARCERATION

Table 6.1 reports nationally representative estimates of the cumulative risks of deviant behavior, criminal record, and incarceration or death by ages thirty-five to forty for the PSID birth cohort born between 1951 and 1975. These estimates are presented for men separately by race-ethnicity and educational attainment. Deviant behavior is defined here as individuals who had ever been either expelled or suspended from school, charged or booked for a crime, or incarcerated. Incarceration includes individuals sentenced to jail or prison sometime during adulthood.

We find alarmingly high rates of these lifetime risks, especially for black high-school dropouts. Roughly two-thirds of black high-school dropouts have either died or been incarcerated before reaching the age of forty. For black high-school dropouts, the lifetime risk of deviant behavior is 63 percent, 55 percent have a criminal record, and one-half have served time in prison or jail. These rates are staggering and unique to this prison-boom generation.

The rates for African Americans are roughly two times the rates of non-Hispanic whites, and, not surprisingly, lifetime risks are substantially lower for college-educated men. However, we also see that there are dramatic racial disparities in lifetime risks of incarceration among non-college-educated men. In fact, black men with some college education had similar lifetime risks of incarceration as white non-college-educated (high-school graduate) men (a lifetime risk of 10 percent).

These estimates are broadly consistent with those from the Bureau of Justice Statistics (BJS) (Bonczar and Beck 1997), the NLSY (Pettit and Western 2004), and census data using a synthetic cohort approach and life table calculations (Raphael 2005).[1] The BJS estimates that lifetime incarceration risks have more than doubled for black men for more recent cohorts. Examining the birth-cohort differences in the risks of incarceration in the PSID sample, I find that the younger cohorts born in the 1960s and early 1970s have roughly 70 percent (7 percentage points) higher lifetime risks of incarceration relative to those born in the 1950s.

One key aspect of the PSID is the information on parental histories of criminal involvement and risky behaviors that might influence children's early formation of these behaviors. There is a paucity of nationally repre-

Table 6.1   *Cumulative Risk of Criminal History, Incarceration, or Death by Age Thirty-Five to Forty, by Race and Education*

	All	High School Dropout	High School Grad/GED	All Noncollege	Some College+
Cumulative risk of death or incarceration (%)					
Black men	30.25	65.71	27.98	39.89	10.44
White men	11.60	42.19	11.58	18.89	4.37
Cumulative risk of incarceration					
Black men	25.28	50.81	26.38	33.69	8.65
White men	8.57	29.03	9.53	13.97	3.34
Cumulative risk of criminal history**					
Black men	34.44	55.27	31.20	38.39	25.01
White men	18.15	41.77	20.64	25.42	11.35
Cumulative risk of deviant behavior***					
Black men	47.61	62.96	45.90	50.84	39.33
White men	24.13	53.31	27.29	33.08	15.91

Source: The sample consists of original-sample PSID males born between 1951 and 1975 who answered the criminal-history questions in the 1995 wave of the survey or were positively identified as incarcerated in any wave of the survey between 1968 and 2005. (blacks N = 1,207; whites N = 1,612). Incarceration includes individuals sentenced to jail or prison sometime during adulthood. All descriptive statistics are sample weighted to account for the oversampling of blacks and low-income families, to generate nationally representative estimates.
** "Criminal history" is defined as ever having been charged with a crime or incarcerated for a crime.
*** "History of deviant behavior" is defined as ever having been charged with a crime, incarcerated for a crime, or suspended or expelled from school.

sentative longitudinal data sets with information on both children and their parents that are large enough to have reasonable sized subsets of children with parents with a criminal history—the PSID is a rare exception.

For the PSID original sample of males born between 1951 and 1975, I first document, among their offspring (born sometime over the subsequent period from 1968 to 2005), the proportion that had a father with an incarceration history. Among the 1951 to 1975 birth cohort who became fathers, I calculate the proportion with an incarceration history, criminal record, and deviant-behavior history, separately by race-ethnicity and educational attainment. Table 6.2 presents these descriptive results for their children. As shown in table 6.2, I find that 20 percent of black children had a father with an incarceration history; among black children with fathers who did not graduate from high school, an alarmingly 33 percent of their fathers had an incarceration history. The differences in the risk of paternal incarceration are more closely linked to racial differences than parental-education differences. For example, black children whose fathers attended college were only slightly less likely to experience paternal incarceration than white children whose fathers were high-school graduates but did not attend college. It is important to note that these are likely lower-bound estimates because we identify only those parents who lived with the child at some point during childhood.

The use of the PSID-CDS data paints a similar picture regarding how often black and white children experience parental incarceration, and how this risk varies within racial-ethnic groups. Comparing these statistics for these recent birth cohorts to older cohorts from other data sources demonstrates how significantly the risk has changed over the past twenty-five years. For example, sociologist Christopher Wilderman (2006) uses criminal-justice data and vital-statistics data to estimate the risk of paternal incarceration during early childhood for the 1978 and 1990 U.S. birth cohorts. He reports that roughly one in nine black children born in 1978 could expect to have their father incarcerated before their ninth birthday, and nearly one in five black children from the 1990 birth cohort could expect the same—an increase of nearly 60 percent over only a twelve-year period.

Using the PSID-CDS, I also examine the proportion of children who have a parent or other 1968 descendent family member with an incarceration history, criminal-involvement history, or deviant-behavior history. These results show that black children, on average, have one person in their immediate or extended family with an incarceration history and roughly three family members with a deviant-behavior history (that is, either expelled from school, criminal record, or incarceration history).

Table 6.3 presents the average change in the child's family income as well as the change in the probability that the child is living in poverty between the years immediately before, during, and after the release of a father from prison or jail. Family poverty status is assessed by matching a child's total family income with corresponding poverty thresholds (based on income and family size). I find that the proportion of children growing up poor increases by 8.5 percentage points (from 22.3 to 30.9) in the years during the father's incarceration spell as compared with the years immediately before the incarceration spell. This significant increase only mod-

Table 6.2   *Children with Paternal Criminal History, Incarceration, or Death, by Race and Fathers' Education*

	All	High School Dropout	High School Grad/ GED	All Non-college	Some College+
Cumulative risk of paternal death or incarceration (%)					
Black children	20.74	34.82	22.22	25.59	10.72
White children	10.71	23.69	12.77	15.38	5.35
Cumulative risk of paternal incarceration					
Black children	18.66	32.20	19.51	22.91	9.89
White children	10.10	23.06	11.57	14.33	5.26
Cumulative risk of paternal criminal history**					
Black children	23.21	36.25	23.51	26.93	15.53
White children	16.67	30.51	19.10	21.84	10.74
Cumulative risk of paternal deviant behavior***					
Black children	38.41	46.15	43.54	44.24	26.35
White children	25.69	50.76	28.72	34.01	16.15

Source: The sample consists of the next-generation children whose fathers were original-sample PSID members born between 1951 and 1975, lived with them in at least one year between 1968 and 2005, and who answered the criminal-history questions in the 1995 wave of the survey or were positively identified as incarcerated in any wave of the survey between 1968 and 2005. (black children N = 1,708; white children N = 2,626). All descriptive statistics are sample weighted to account for the oversampling of blacks and low-income families, to generate nationally representative estimates.
** "Criminal history" is defined as ever having been charged with a crime or incarcerated for a crime.
*** "History of deviant behavior" is defined as ever having been charged with a crime, incarcerated for a crime, or suspended or expelled from school.

Table 6.3 *Child Family Income Immediately Before, During, and After Father's Prison Release*

Child family income (1997 dollar)	
Year before father's incarceration	$38,960
Average during incarceration	$30,234
Year after release	$33,100
Difference*** (during—before)	–$8,726
Income-to-needs ratio	
Year before father's incarceration	2.41
Average during incarceration	2.08
Year after release	2.43
Difference* (during—before)	–0.33
In poverty (%)	
Year before father's incarceration	22.34
Average during incarceration	30.87
Year after release	24.40
Difference*** (during—before)	8.53***

Source: The sample consists of children born between 1985 and 2000 (from the PSID-CDS). Results use sample weights to generate nationally representative estimates.
***$p < .01$; **$p < .05$; *$p < .10$

estly declines in the first several years following the father's release. Similarly, we see family income decline by an average of $8,726 (from $38,960 to $30,234) in the years during the incarceration spell (relative to the year prior to the incarceration spell), and the child's family income does not resume or regain its preincarceration level in the years following the fathers' release. The lack of data on fathers with an incarceration history who never lived with the child at anytime during childhood likely leads these estimates to be upwardly biased.

EMPIRICAL APPROACH

I examine the effects of parental incarceration on children's educational and behavioral outcomes using PSID-CDS, allowing for differential impacts for incarceration of the father and the mother. These data include a rich set of variables related to both the mother and the child, including parental criminal history and a set of standardized child cognitive assessments.

The dependent variables capture aspects of children's emotional wellbeing with three measures of child behavior: behavior problems index, externalizing behavior problems, and internalizing behavior problems. Each of these scales relies on maternal reports of children's behavior. In addition, I assess the incidence of the child ever being expelled or suspended from school, disruptive behavior problems in school, school absenteeism, being placed in special education, and grade repetition. The child behavioral outcomes examined are important in part because early manifestations of problem behavior in children have been shown to often be a precursor to more serious involvement in deviant behavior in adolescence and criminal involvement in adulthood.

In both surveys, primary caregivers were asked to provide information on their children's behavior (for those ages three to seventeen years old), and how often they exhibited a particular problem. Particular behaviors were grouped together to create scales of internalizing (withdrawn or sad) and externalizing (aggressive or angry) behaviors.[2] While I do not devote substantial attention to age variation in the behavior problems index, it is recognized that a high score may mean something different for a six-year-old child than for a seventeen-year-old child.

I first document a simple correlation between parental incarceration history and child behavior problem indices. I then attempt to identify whether this simple relationship is causal. To this end, various empirical approaches are used to address potential omitted variables bias, including the estimation of hierarchical random-effects models with an extensive set of controls.

Table 6.4 presents simple descriptive statistics for the child behavior problems index by the parents' most severe offense (incarceration, booked or charged with a crime, expelled or suspended from school, or none of these). The estimates indicate a substantial positive relationship between parental incarceration history and child behavioral problems. For example, the average child who has a parent with an incarceration history scores 0.55 to 0.83 standard deviations above the average behavior problems score of a child without any parental or family incarceration history (BPI = 7.7 among children with no family history of deviant behavior versus BPI scores between 10 and 11 among children with a parental incarceration history). Among children who have a father with an incarceration history, the proportion of children who have ever been expelled or suspended is 22.8 percent, compared to 4 percent among children without a family history of deviant behavior. We see similarly large differences when comparing children who have a mother with an incarceration history to children without any parental incarceration history.

Of course, children who experience parental incarceration are different from other children in a multitude of ways that may also contribute to the raw differences in child behavioral outcomes that we observe. Table 6.5 highlights this point by presenting a series of family and neighborhood characteristics for children who have parents with an incarceration history and those who do not. We see children from families with an incar-

Table 6.4   *Children's Outcomes Classified by Parents' Most Severe Deviant Behavior Offense*

	No Family History of Deviant Behavior	Father's Most Severe Offense			Mother's Most Severe Offense		
Child Outcome		Incarceration	Criminal History	Expelled	Incarceration	Criminal History	Expelled
BPI—Total Score	7.7087	10.0641	9.7221	9.4128	11.2655	10.5723	9.7247
BPI—Internalizing	2.8595	3.3683	3.3756	3.4490	4.2251	3.9445	3.4002
BPI—Externalizing	4.9828	6.9143	6.5391	6.1467	7.3797	6.9755	6.5590
Expelled or Suspended (%)	4.19	22.83	6.87	7.31	14.33	9.29	22.96

Source: The sample consists of all CDS children who were interviewed in 1997 or 2002 and 2003. Family members include all descendent PSID extended family members; using PSID incarceration-history info through 2005. All descriptive statistics are sample weighted to account for the oversampling of blacks and low-income families, to generate nationally representative estimates.

Table 6.5 Other Characteristics of Childhood Families Classified by Parents' Most Severe Deviant Behavior Offense

	No Family History of Deviant Behavior	Father's Most Severe Offense			Mother's Most Severe Offense		
		Incarceration	Criminal History	Expelled	Incarceration	Criminal History	Expelled
Family background							
Family income (1997 dollar)	$75,406	$52,500	$74,237	$48,571	$58,389	$58,021	$53,976
Income-to-needs ratio	4.55	3.19	4.45	2.96	3.76	3.96	3.26
In poverty (%)	4.98	19.33	5.83	10.77	11.10	7.12	8.31
Mother's background							
Currently married	86.52	68.56	89.87	82.54	71.82	72.11	75.83
Mother's education (if mother is present)	14.01	13.02	13.66	12.65	13.78	12.78	12.69
Father's education (if father is present)	14.09	12.51	13.32	12.51	13.77	13.55	12.67
Religious							
Very	23.95	8.55	7.14	23.02	50.82	0.85	1.44
Moderately	26.69	20.79	35.94	14.71	8.60	18.11	38.77
Not at all	49.36	54.10	40.54	51.33	27.21	55.94	45.19
Family member with alcohol problem	8.96	16.56	16.38	10.94	13.37	25.10	14.60

Table 6.5   (Continued)

	Father's Most Severe Offense				Mother's Most Severe Offense		
	No Family History of Deviant Behavior	Incarceration	Criminal History	Expelled	Incarceration	Criminal History	Expelled
Neighborhood characteristics							
Neighborhood quality (self-rated)							
Excellent	43.49	22.46	40.41	40.58	58.29	37.1	29.42
Very good	36.44	45.10	33.41	38.80	16.82	42.79	34.50
Good	14.38	22.85	19.32	13.50	23.52	10.82	20.40
Fair	4.12	8.20	6.80	6.22	0.95	6.56	8.48
Poor	1.57	1.39	0.06	0.90	0.42	2.73	7.20
Neighbor policing of drugs							
Very high	33.17	33.99	27.94	29.69	22.68	28.65	22.57
High	8.38	10.95	14.24	10.10	0.42	8.17	9.81
Moderate	13.95	13.39	19.70	13.82	24.64	14.83	8.91
Low	44.50	41.67	38.12	46.39	52.26	48.35	58.71

Source: The sample consists of all CDS children who were born between 1985 and 2000, and who were interviewed in 1997 or 2002 and 2003. Family members include all descendent PSID extended family members; using PSID incarceration history info through 2005. All descriptive statistics are sample weighted to account for the oversampling of blacks and low-income families, to generate nationally representative estimates.

ceration history are disadvantaged along many other dimensions. For example, compared with children who do not experience parental incarceration, children with a family incarceration history come from significantly poorer families, are more likely to be raised in single-parent families, more likely to grow up in worse-quality neighborhoods (particularly, neighborhoods with crime and drug-use problems), and have less-educated parents.

Perhaps the most important difference is that their family income was considerably lower. Poverty rates are 5 percent among children who had no family history of deviant behavior, compared to 19 percent for those children exposed to paternal incarceration. Based on the relationship between family income and child outcomes shown elsewhere (Duncan and Brooks-Gunn 1997), it may come as no surprise that children who have parents with an incarceration history have more behavioral problems.

The remainder of this analysis attempts to identify whether it is the parental incarceration itself that leads to greater child behavioral problems, or whether these other differences in family characteristics, including family income, are the main causal factors and mechanisms that link parental incarceration and child well-being.

Although the descriptive analyses in table 6.4 make a compelling prima facie case that there is a relationship between parental incarceration and child behavioral problems, children who experience parental incarceration differ from children who do not in both observable and unobservable ways. As well, an example of a potential source of omitted variable bias is that a drop in family income could lead both to a child experiencing lower levels of development investment and to a parent engaging in crime. In this chapter, I investigate whether parental incarceration precipitated the problematic behavior or merely aggravated and caused preexisting problems to become worse; another explanation is that parental incarceration merely represents a risk marker with no causal relationship links. Incarceration is often preceded by poverty, multiple mental-health problems, marital instability, absent fathers, child abuse and neglect, and substance abuse. The empirical design utilized in this study aims to distinguish selection effects preceding parental incarceration (preexisting risk factors) from direct, mediating, and moderating effects following the incarceration.

The empirical strategy relies on Ordinary Least Squares (OLS) estimation of a series of sequential specifications, with each specification including a unique and extensive array of family- and neighborhood-background variables. The empirical model specifications test for differential effects of parental incarceration by childhood life stage—early childhood (up to age five); middle years (ages six to ten); adolescence (ages eleven to seventeen)—and by length of parental incarceration exposure. The child-development literature conceptualizes these ages as distinct stages of rapid growth in which parental resources may differentially matter. The hierarchical random-effects models highlight the significant heterogeneity in the effects of parental incarceration on child well-being.

This study employs several alternative model specifications to gauge the role of potential biases due to unobservable heterogeneity. First, parental incarceration experiences prior to birth are added to the regression model to test for bias due to unobserved parental factors.[3] I compare children who experienced parental incarceration exposure sometime during childhood with children whose parents were only imprisoned before their birth. If the association between parental incarceration and child behavior problems was due mostly to genetic risk factors, then the timing of parental imprisonment would be of little importance for child outcomes.

If we assume that both the magnitudes of omitted variables and their effects are time invariant, then their influence on child behavior outcomes will be captured in part by controlling for the childhood stage-specific incarceration exposure. It is difficult to identify omitted variables correlated strongly with our child behavior outcomes and with incarceration in adolescent years that would not also correlate with incarceration at other stages. The usual suspects, such as genetic influences, are as likely to affect later and early childhood incarceration risks, and thus be controlled, in some degree, by the inclusion of incarceration in other childhood stages. Incarceration prior to the child's birth is included as a specification check to test for a spurious correlation; incarceration prior to birth obviously should not directly causally influence these outcomes in a well-specified model.

Some of our childhood conditions and socioeconomic factors were not measured prior to the parental imprisonment; as a result, we cannot determine whether they were present prior to the initial incarceration or were themselves the product of the subsequent incarceration experience. To the extent that parental incarceration actually caused these factors, the total impact of parental incarceration is underestimated by controlling for these childhood conditions in models shown in tables 6.6, 6.7, and 6.8.

REGRESSION RESULTS

The first column of table 6.6 presents the results of estimating a simple OLS model of the intergenerational relationships between parental deviant-behavior history and child behavior problem indices. These models include controls for self-rated neighborhood quality, extent of neighborhood policing of drugs (which may serve to proxy for neighborhood social cohesion), indicator variables for whether there is a family member residing in household with an alcohol problem, parental religiosity, parental education, marital status, child gender, race-ethnicity, and age.

As shown in table 6.6, the results indicate that parental deviant-behavior history, including school expulsion, criminal record, or incarceration, is significantly associated with greater child behavioral problems, and the magnitudes are substantive. The patterns of results are similar across the child behavior problem outcomes. Paternal incarceration history and maternal deviant-behavior history are each associated with an increased likelihood that their children are expelled or suspended from school. The effects of other family members' incarceration or criminal history are not significantly related to child outcomes when the parents do not have such a history.

The results in table 6.6 also show that neighborhood quality, the extent of neighborhood policing of drugs, whether there is a family member residing in household with an alcohol problem, parental religiosity, parental education, and marital status are all independently significantly related to these child behavioral outcomes.

There is variation in the overall incidence and timing of parental incarceration exposure among children, including a significant portion that have parents with an incarceration history that occurred prior to the child's birth and not during their childhood years. If the association between parental incarceration exposure and child behavioral outcomes reflects a causal influence, then we should expect to see effects only when it occurs during the child's life. Exploiting this fact, these analyses test for the presence of unobserved heterogeneity bias by including parental incarceration that occurred prior to the child's birth as a model specification check.

Table 6.7 presents these model results. The results for the effects of parental incarceration pass this falsification test. In particular, the estimated effects of parental incarceration on child well-being are only significant when it occurs during childhood—the estimated effects of parental incarceration prior to birth are small and statistically insignificant. This pattern of results holds for all the behavior problem indices.

Up to this point, these analyses have considered the impact of exposure to parental incarceration at some point during childhood, yet recent research emphasizes the importance of the early childhood environment on subsequent outcomes (Johnson and Schoeni 2007). In table 6.8, I investigate whether the timing of parental incarceration exposure makes a difference for children's behavioral outcomes. The models estimated allow parental incarceration up to age five (preschool), between six and ten years old (middle years), and between eleven and seventeen (adolescence), to have differential effects on children. One might expect larger effects in the early childhood years, and during adolescence when role-modeling influences may be particularly salient.

Table 6.6 *Intergenerational Relationship of Parental Deviant-Behavior History on Child Behavior Problems*

	Dependent Variable			
	BPI: Total Score	BPI: Internal-izing	BPI: External-izing	Probability (Expelled) Marginal Effects (Probit)
	(1)	(2)	(3)	(4)
Father's most severe offense (reference category: none)				
Expelled from school	0.6865*	0.2289+	0.4477*	–0.0035
	(0.3819)	(0.1747)	(0.2590)	(0.0168)
Criminal history	1.4157**	0.3753+	1.0788***	0.0355
	(0.5705)	(0.2603)	(0.3775)	(0.0293)
Incarceration history	1.0782**	0.3930*	0.7094**	0.0804***
	(0.4215)	(0.2022)	(0.2764)	(0.0257)
Mother's most severe offense (reference category: none)				
Expelled from school	0.5340+	0.2063	0.3559+	0.0556***
	(0.3657)	(0.1716)	(0.2344)	(0.0171)
Criminal history	1.8190**	0.7572*	1.2141**	0.0441
	(0.9069)	(0.4383)	(0.5750)	(0.0392)
Incarceration history	1.9130**	0.8193**	1.2157**	0.0429+
	(0.7890)	(0.3902)	(0.4841)	(0.0311)
Other family members' most severe offense (reference category: none)				
Expelled from school	–0.2912	–0.1347	–0.1824	0.0024
	(0.3544)	(0.1710)	(0.2295)	(0.0142)
Criminal history	–0.1528	–0.1524	–0.0230	0.0549+
	(0.5959)	(0.2680)	(0.4256)	(0.0337)
Incarceration history	0.1736	0.1254	0.0336	0.0043
	(0.2825)	(0.1327)	(0.1840)	(0.0104)
Neighborhood quality (self-rated) (reference category: excellent)				
Very good	0.6077***	0.1856*	0.4510***	0.0067
	(0.2325)	(0.1123)	(0.1516)	(0.0112)
Good	1.2953***	0.4868***	0.8433***	0.0202+
	(0.2695)	(0.1286)	(0.1754)	(0.0128)
Fair	1.8134***	0.6238***	1.2485***	0.0176
	(0.3394)	(0.1676)	(0.2171)	(0.0140)
Poor	2.1535***	0.8429***	1.4180***	0.0267
	(0.6044)	(0.2885)	(0.3923)	(0.0245)

Table 6.6 (*Continued*)

	Dependent Variable			
	BPI: Total Score	BPI: Internal-izing	BPI: External-izing	Probability (Expelled) Marginal Effects (Probit)
	(1)	(2)	(3)	(4)
Neighbor policing for drugs (reference category: very likely)				
Likely	0.4301+	0.2906**	0.1191	−0.0110
	(0.3017)	(0.1450)	(0.1963)	(0.0125)
Unlikely	0.0593	0.0572	0.0180	−0.0144+
	(0.3039)	(0.1482)	(0.1974)	(0.0111)
Very unlikely	0.1897	0.0923	0.0960	−0.0104
	(0.2387)	(0.1162)	(0.1550)	(0.0105)
Parental background factors				
Family member with	1.6100***	0.7448***	0.9120***	0.0239+
alcohol problem	(0.3511)	(0.1751)	(0.2256)	(0.0152)
Religiosity (reference category: very)				
Somewhat	0.3299	0.1994+	0.1223	0.0090
	(0.2698)	(0.1300)	(0.1793)	(0.0140)
Not at all	0.5145**	0.2205*	0.2742*	0.0027
	(0.2347)	(0.1150)	(0.1526)	(0.0111)
Mother's education	−0.1788***	−0.0614**	−0.1233***	−0.0064***
	(0.0583)	(0.0271)	(0.0387)	(0.0023)
Father's education (if present)	−0.1311**	−0.0391+	−0.0953**	−0.0018
	(0.0598)	(0.0275)	(0.0402)	(0.0024)
Mother married	−1.0474***	−0.4349***	−0.6480***	−0.0232**
	(0.2263)	(0.1090)	(0.1474)	(0.0090)
Male	0.8805***	0.1014	0.8023***	0.0639***
	(0.1875)	(0.0885)	(0.1225)	(0.0078)
Child age	0.0386+	0.0829***	−0.0451***	0.0180***
	(0.0248)	(0.0118)	(0.0164)	(0.0012)
Black (reference category: white)	−1.4361***	−0.7982***	−0.7018***	0.1072***
	(0.2372)	(0.1130)	(0.1547)	(0.0119)
Constant	11.0090***	3.0873***	8.2235***	
	(0.9581)	(0.4400)	(0.6364)	
Child-year observations	5542	5542	5542	4766

Source: Author's calculations.
Note: Robust standard errors in parentheses
***$p < 0.01$, **$p < 0.05$, *$p < 0.10$, +$p < 0.20$.

Table 6.7   *OLS Estimates of Impact of Parental Incarceration on Child Behavior Problems*

	Dependent Variable		
	BPI: Total Score	BPI: Internalizing	BPI: Externalizing
	(1)	(2)	(3)
Parental incarceration prior to birth	0.4201 (0.5179)	0.0837 (0.2463)	0.3630 (0.3365)
Parental incarceration sometime during childhood	2.3433*** (0.6229)	1.0604*** (0.3093)	1.3864*** (0.3887)
Neighborhood quality (self-rated) (reference category: excellent)			
Very good	0.5786** (0.2314)	0.1781+ (0.1115)	0.4259*** (0.1512)
Good	1.2369*** (0.2695)	0.4627*** (0.1286)	0.8049*** (0.1756)
Fair	1.8097*** (0.3373)	0.6160*** (0.1668)	1.2510*** (0.2159)
Poor	2.1817*** (0.6123)	0.8505*** (0.2922)	1.4409*** (0.3963)
Neighbor policing for drugs (reference category: very likely)			
Likely	0.4619+ (0.3019)	0.3073** (0.1448)	0.1350 (0.1968)
Unlikely	0.1446 (0.3036)	0.0916 (0.1479)	0.0730 (0.1975)
Very unlikely	0.2466 (0.2401)	0.1189 (0.1164)	0.1279 (0.1561)
Parental background factors			
Family member with alcohol problem	1.7205*** (0.3525)	0.7910*** (0.1752)	0.9809*** (0.2266)
Religiosity (reference category: very)			
Somewhat	0.2667 (0.2714)	0.1673 (0.1306)	0.0880 (0.1804)
Not at all	0.4830** (0.2360)	0.2048* (0.1150)	0.2554* (0.1537)

Table 6.7   (*Continued*)

	Dependent Variable		
	BPI: Total Score	BPI: Internalizing	BPI: Externalizing
	(1)	(2)	(3)
Mother's education	−0.2083***	−0.0734***	−0.1422***
	(0.0578)	(0.0269)	(0.0385)
Father's education (if present)	−0.1370**	−0.0404+	−0.0988**
	(0.0594)	(0.0274)	(0.0397)
Mother married	−1.3012***	−0.5093***	−0.8417***
	(0.2174)	(0.1054)	(0.1405)
Male	0.8832***	0.1010	0.8049***
	(0.1881)	(0.0886)	(0.1229)
Child age	0.0286	0.0788***	−0.0511***
	(0.0249)	(0.0118)	(0.0165)
Black (reference category: white)	−1.4489***	−0.8107***	−0.7006***
	(0.2330)	(0.1105)	(0.1524)
Constant	12.0184***	3.4504***	8.8909***
	(0.9166)	(0.4230)	(0.6088)
Child-year observations	5542	5542	5542

Source: Author's calculations.
Note: Robust standard errors in parentheses
***$p < 0.01$, **$p < 0.05$, *$p < 0.10$, +$p < 0.20$

The OLS results shown in the first column of table 6.8 reveal precisely this pattern. The results indicate that parental incarceration is associated with significantly greater behavioral problems at all stages of childhood, with the largest impacts found when incarceration exposure occurs during the adolescent and early-childhood years.

These results show that a child with a parent who is incarcerated during their childhood years exhibits significantly more behavioral problems. This result holds when we control for a wide range of observable family- and neighborhood-background characteristics, and it is not present when the incarceration exposure only occurred prior to the child's birth and not during their childhood years.

Table 6.8   *Impacts of Parental Incarceration by Childhood Life Stage on Child Behavior Problems*

	BPI: Total Score	BPI: Internalizing	BPI: Externalizing
	Dependent Variable		
	(1)	(2)	(3)
Parental incarceration exposure			
Parental incarceration prior	0.4128	0.0467	0.3929
to birth	(0.5217)	(0.2475)	(0.3384)
Parental incarceration between	2.0423**	0.9604**	1.1650**
Age 0 and 5	(0.8782)	(0.4503)	(0.5396)
Parental incarceration between	1.1947+	0.5774+	0.6896
Age 6 and 10	(0.8846)	(0.4252)	(0.5592)
Parental incarceration between	3.9885***	1.5753**	2.5866***
Age 11 and 16	(1.4554)	(0.7334)	(0.9484)
Neighborhood quality (self-rated) (reference category: excellent)			
Very good	0.5771**	0.1817+	0.4203***
	(0.2313)	(0.1111)	(0.1511)
Good	1.2560***	0.4904***	0.7963***
	(0.2692)	(0.1283)	(0.1754)
Fair	1.8186***	0.6286***	1.2470***
	(0.3367)	(0.1664)	(0.2154)
Poor	2.2003***	0.8683***	1.4421***
	(0.6105)	(0.2915)	(0.3954)
Neighbor policing for drugs (reference category: very likely)			
Likely	0.4719+	0.3139**	0.1390
	(0.3016)	(0.1439)	(0.1965)
Unlikely	0.1574	0.0948	0.0831
	(0.3031)	(0.1473)	(0.1975)
Very unlikely	0.2324	0.1006	0.1319
	(0.2390)	(0.1152)	(0.1558)

Table 6.8   (*Continued*)

	BPI: Total Score	BPI: Internalizing	BPI: Externalizing
	Dependent Variable		
	(1)	(2)	(3)
Parental background factors			
Family member with alcohol	1.7194***	0.8011***	0.9690***
problem	(0.3515)	(0.1741)	(0.2256)
Religiosity (reference category: very)			
Somewhat	0.2899	0.1753+	0.1041
	(0.2700)	(0.1294)	(0.1797)
Not at all	0.5102**	0.2150*	0.2739*
	(0.2354)	(0.1139)	(0.1538)
Mother's education	−0.2092***	−0.0724***	−0.1442***
	(0.0577)	(0.0268)	(0.0384)
Father's education (if present)	−0.1325**	−0.0385+	−0.0959**
	(0.0593)	(0.0273)	(0.0396)
Mother married	−1.2921***	−0.5099***	−0.8311***
	(0.2170)	(0.1050)	(0.1403)
Male	0.8911***	0.1128	0.8008***
	(0.1884)	(0.0886)	(0.1233)
Child age	0.0784	0.1082***	−0.0315
	(0.0667)	(0.0327)	(0.0430)
Black (reference category: white)	−1.4283***	−0.8042***	−0.6861***
	(0.2324)	(0.1102)	(0.1521)
Constant	10.7154***	2.5439***	8.4921***
	(1.4620)	(0.7035)	(0.9497)
Child-year observations	5,542	5,542	5,542

Source: Author's calculations.
Note: Robust standard errors in parentheses.
***$p < 0.01$, **$p < 0.05$, *$p < 0.10$, + $p < 0.20$.

CONCLUSION

This study examines the intergenerational consequences of incarceration by examining the children of the next generation. It finds, using the PSID-CDS data, that the prevalence rates of parental incarceration at some point during childhood are significantly larger than point-in-time estimates. I find that 20 percent of black children had a father with an incarceration history; among black children with fathers who did not graduate from high school, an alarming 33 percent of their fathers had an incarceration history.

This study finds linkages between exposure to parental incarceration and child behavioral outcomes. These results suggest that parental incarceration exposure leads children to develop greater behavioral problem trajectories. The pattern of results is remarkably similar across all of the empirical model specifications utilized, including hierarchical random-effects models with an unusually extensive set of controls. This evidence bears on the question of the extent to which parental incarceration has exacerbated racial disparities in childhood and in early adulthood. Understanding if and how parental absence due to incarceration differs from separation (due to parental divorce or death) may prove instrumental in designing interventions with families that have an incarcerated parent (Johnson and Waldfogel 2002).

This study identifies some potential unintended negative consequences for children of incarceration policies designed to "get tough" on crime. A key goal of social-welfare policy in the United States should be to break the cycle of poverty and unemployment from one generation to the next. It is only by following the children of at-risk parents that we can know whether their developmental trajectories point toward a brighter economic future than the one their own parents once faced.

Imprisoning parents may cause greater deviant behavior and crime in the next generation, thereby contributing to the intergenerational transmission of criminal involvement. The extent to which parental incarceration causes deviant behavior problems and crime in the next generation is an important question for criminal-justice policy and sentencing policy to consider as a potential negative externality. If parental incarceration does lead to greater child behavior problems as the evidence in this chapter suggests, parenthood could be treated as an extenuating factor in sentencing, given concerns about the child's well-being. As well, there should be a more extensive range of family- and child-support services offered when parental incarceration does occur. Future work is needed to improve our understanding of how social-welfare policies can protect children from some of the potential adverse effects of parental incarceration. Policymakers may need to consider the merits of provision of some form of community-based sentencing as an alternative to noncustodial prison sentencing.

Future research should examine pathways through which parental incarceration may affect child well-being. It should examine whether the effects depend on the length of the parent's sentence and type of crime, paternal versus maternal incarceration, child developmental stage, differential effects for boys versus girls, internalizing versus externalizing behavioral problems, the amount of parent-child contact before imprisonment, and the amount of contact maintained during the incarceration spell. Other key issues include the explanations given to children about their parent's absence, children's experiences of stigma, levels of social support, socioeconomic status, race, and neighborhood disadvantage.

Criminologists Joseph Murray, Carl-Gunnar Janson, and David Farrington (2007) identify significant effects of parent imprisonment on boys' delinquency and behavior problems in England but not in Sweden. They speculate that the reasons for this cross-national difference may be the combined result of shorter prison sentences in Sweden, more family-friendly prison policies, a welfare-oriented juvenile justice system, and more sympathetic public attitudes toward crime and punishment. In Sweden, child welfare rather than punishment is the paramount concern in cases of child delinquency. There is more to learn from cross-national comparisons as well as variation within the United States due to differences in state social and prison policies. For example, the effects of parental incarceration could be compared between states with different policies on prisoner-family contact, average length of sentence, and social support provided to prisoners' families. Given the significant rise in parental incarceration in the United States (and disproportionate incidence among African American children), the coordinated efforts of courts, prisons, community and social-service agencies, schools, and policymakers informed by research evidence are requisite to develop and implement effective programs that will support children, families, and kin of incarcerated parents. There are currently no policies and programs targeting this subset of at-risk children. The societal-welfare implications warrant a major research agenda to further study these issues.

NOTES

1. The incarceration estimates contained in this chapter include individuals sentenced to jail or prison. The PSID survey data do not allow one to distinguish between jail and prison sentences. Thus, these estimates are not directly comparable to BJS estimates of the proportion of males who have ever served time in a state or federal prison, or the estimates by Steven Raphael (2005) using administrative records from the California prison system during the 1990s.

2. The internalizing behavior index includes the following behaviors, which are combined to create a continuous count of behaviors: child has felt loved, has been fearful or anxious, has been easily confused, has felt worthless, is disliked by other children, has been obsessed with thoughts, has been sad or depressed, has been withdrawn, has been clinging to adults, has cried too much, has felt others were out to get him or her.
3. This approach draws on the method used by Peter Gottschalk (1996) for examining the intergenerational correlation in welfare participation and used by Christopher Ruhm (2004) for analyzing the effects of parental employment and child cognitive development.

REFERENCES

Baunach, Phyllis J. 1985. *Mothers in Prison*. New Brunswick, N.J.: Transaction Books.

Becketti, Sean, William Gould, Lee Lillard, and Finis Welch. 1988. "The PSID After Fourteen Years: An Evaluation." *Journal of Labor Economics* 6(4): 472–92.

Bonczar, Thomas P., and Allen J. Beck. 1997. "Lifetime Likelihood of Going to State or Federal Prison." *Bureau of Justics Statistics Bulletin*, NCJ 160092. Washington: U.S. Department of Justice.

Cho, Rosa M. 2007. "The Impact of Maternal Imprisonment on Children's Educational Achievement—Results from Children in Chicago Public Schools." Unpublished manuscript. Chicago: University of Chicago.

Duncan, Greg J., and Jeanne Brooks-Gunn. 1997. *Consequences of Growing Up Poor*. New York: Russell Sage Foundation.

Fitzgerald, John, Peter Gottschalk, and Robert Moffitt. 1998a. "An Analysis of Sample Attrition in Panel Data." *Journal of Human Resources* 33(2): 251–99.

———. 1998b. "An Analysis of the Impact of Sample Attrition on the Second Generation of respondents in the Michigan Panel Study of Income Dynamics." *Journal of Human Resources* 33(2): 300–44.

Freeman, Richard. 1992. "Crime and the Employment of Disadvantaged Youth." In *Urban Labor Markets and Job Opportunity*, edited by George Peterson and Wayne Vroman. Washington, D.C.: Urban Institute.

Fritsch, Travis A., and John D. Burkhead. 1981. "Behavioral Reactions of Children to Parental Absence Due to Imprisonment." *Family Relations* 30(1): 83–88.

Gaviria, Alejandro, and Steven Raphael. 2001. "School-Based Peer Effects and Juvenile Behavior." *Review of Economics and Statistics* 83(2): 257–68.

Gottschalk, Peter. 1996. "Is the Correlation in Welfare participation Across Generations Spuious?" *Journal of Public Economics* 61(1): 1–25.

Hagan, John, and Ronit Dinovitzer. 1999. "Collateral Consequences of Imprisonment for Children Communities, and Prisoners." *Crime and Justice* 26: 121–62.

Hjalmarrson, Randi, and Matthew Lindquist. 2007. "Like Godfather Like Son: Explaining the Intergenerational Nature of Crime." Unpublished manuscript. College Park, Md.: University of Maryland.

Johnson, Elizabeth Inez, and Jane Waldfogel. 2002. "Children of Incarcerated Parents: Cumulative Risk and Children's Living Arrangement." *Joint Center for*

Poverty Research working Paper 306. Chicago: Northwestern University/University of Chicago.

Johnson, Rucker, and Robert Schoeni. 2007. "The Influence of Early Life Events on Health, Human Capital Accumulation, and Labor Market Outcomes Over the Life Course." Working paper. Ann Arbor, Mich.: National Poverty Center.

Johnston, Denise. 1995. "Effects of Parental Incarcerations." In *Children of Incarcerated Parents*, edited by Katherine Gabel and Denise Johnston. Lanham, Md.: Lexington Books.

Kampfner, Christina J. 1995. "Post-Traumatic Stress Reactions in Children of Imprisoned Mothers." In *Children of Incarcerated Parents*, edited by Katherine Gabel and Denise Johnston. Lanham, Md.: Lexington Books.

LaLonde, Robert J., and Susan M. George. 2002. *Incarcerated Mothers: The Chicago Project on Female Prisoners and Their Children*. Irving B. Harris Graduate School of Public Policy Studies, University of Chicago.

Mainieri, Tina. 2005. *The Panel Study of Income Dynamics Child Development Supplement: User Guide for CDS-II*. University of Michigan. Available at: http://psidonline.isr.umich.edu/CDS/cdsii_userGd.pdf.

Mainieri, Tina, and Malgorzata Grodsky. 2006. *The Panel Study of Income Dynamics Child Development Supplement: User Guide Supplement for CDS-II*. University of Michigan. Available at: http://psidonline.isr.umich.edu/CDS/CDS1_UGSupp.pdf.

McLanahan, Sara. 2002. "Life Without Father: What Happens to Children?" *Contexts* 1(1): 35–44.

Mednick, Sarnoff A., William F. Gabrielli, and Barry Hutchings. 1984. "Genetic Influences on Criminal Convictions: Evidence from an Adoption Cohort." *Science* 224(4651): 891–94.

Moore, Quinn, and Heidi Shierholz. "Externalities of Imprisonment: Does Maternal Incarceration Affect Child Outcomes?" Unpublished manuscript. Ann Arbor, Mich.: University of Michigan.

Mumola, C.J. 2000. *Incarerated Parents and Their Children*. Washington, D.C.: Bureau of Justice Statistics.

Murray, Joseph. 2005. "The Effects of Imprisonment on Families and Children of Prisoners." In *The Effects of Imprisonment*, edited by Alison Liebling and Shadd Maurna. Devon, U.K.: Willan.

Murray, Joseph, and David P. Farrington. 2005. "Parental Imprisonment: Effects on Boys' Antisocial Behaviour and Delinquency through the Life-Course." *Journal of Child Psychology and Psychiatry* 46(12): 1269–78.

Murray, Joseph, Carl-Gunnar Janson, and David P. Farrington. 2007. "Crime in Adult Offspring of Prisoners: A Cross-National Comparison of Two Longitudinal Samples." *Criminal Justice and Behavior* 34(1): 133–49.

Pettit, Becky, and Bruce Western. 2004. "Mass Imprisonment and the Life Course: Race and Class Inequality in U.S. Incarceration." *American Sociological Review* 69(2): 151–69.

Raphael, Steven. 2005. "The Socioeconomic Status of Black Males: The Increasing Importance of Incarceration." In *Poverty, the Distribution of Income, and Public Policy*, edited by Alan Auerbach, David Card, and John Quigley. New York: Russell Sage Foundation.

Rowe, David C., and David P. Farrington. 1997. "The Familial Transmission of Criminal Convictions." *Criminology* 35(1): 177–201.

Ruhm, Christopher. 2004. "Parental Employment and Child Cognitive Development." *Journal of Human Resources* 39(1): 156–92.

Rutter, Michael. 1987. "Psychosocial Resilience and Protective Mechanisms." *American Journal of Orthopsychiatry* 57: 316–31.

Snell, Tracy. 1993. *Correctional Populations in the United States, 1991.* Washington: U.S. Department of Justice.

Western, Bruce. 2002. "The Impact of Incarceration on Wage Mobility and Inequality." *American Sociological Review* 67: 526–46.

Wildeman, Christopher. 2006. "Paternal Incarceration, the Prison Boom, and the Concentration of Disadvantage." Unpublished manuscript, Princeton, N.J.: Princeton University.

John W. Ellwood
and
Joshua Guetzkow

7 | Footing the Bill: Causes and Budgetary Consequences of State Spending on Corrections

This chapter provides an overview of state budgeting for corrections. As such it addresses the following questions: How much do states spend on corrections? To what degree has state corrections spending grown over time? How does that spending vary across the states and over time? What factors account for this variation? Finally, does rising spending on corrections affect the amount of money spent on other state activities?

In examining these questions, we find that the amount that states spend on corrections has significantly risen over time. This is true whether one focuses on current dollars, constant dollars, or the percentage of state budgetary expenditures allocated to corrections. It is also the case, however, that some states spend much more on corrections than others. This is true even when the figures are adjusted for a state's population.

The most significant factors in differences in state spending are a state's incarceration rate and its violent crime rate. States that have more people in prisons spend more on corrections, and states vary widely in their incarceration rates. Others have analyzed what drives these rates (chapter 2 this volume); part of the answer is that the incarceration rates are affected by factors that directly affect crime rates, and part of the answer is that the rates are affected by state policies adopted to deal with crime. However, even when one statistically controls for state incarceration and crime rates, we find that some states spend more on corrections than others. These are states with higher real per capita income levels and higher percentages of African Americans in their population. We also find that states with a direct initiative process that allows voters to directly enact legislation spend less on corrections after many other factors are taken into account.

This study also seeks to explain the relative growth in state spending on corrections between 1977 and 1998. Once again, a state's incarceration rate and its violent crime rate are positively associated with the growth of state corrections spending, even when many other variables are taken into account. Growth in state spending on corrections is associated with its level of personal income and the rise in its price level (the level of the state consumer price index).

Once the incarceration rate and the crime rate are taken into account, it is interesting to note that political variables—the degree to which a state's population is liberal or conservative, which political party controls the state executive branch and its governorship, and whether one political party controls one branch of government while the other party controls the other branch—are not statistically significantly associated with the level of or growth of state corrections spending.

However, even when other factors are taken into account some budgetary procedures affect the level of state spending on corrections. Thus a budgetary process that sets funding targets is associated with lower levels of corrections spending, as is a process that requires the use of measures of performance. The presence of requirements for performance measurement is associated with a lower rate of growth of state corrections spending between 1988 and 2000, but the presence of a performance management system and a budget that set out these performance measures is associated with increased spending on corrections over this period.

Given the rise in state spending on corrections over the past several decades, many commentators have hypothesized that this increase would lead to the crowding out other types of state spending—in particular, spending on education, health, transportation, and welfare. Our analysis found a crowding-out effect only in one policy area: welfare. But we did not find a crowding-out effect in education, health, or transportation.

TRENDS AND VARIATION IN STATE SPENDING ON CORRECTIONS

The explosive growth in the prison population over the past several decades has led to an enormous increase in the amount of money spent by states on their corrections systems. In 1980, states spent an average of approximately $280 million on corrections, or about $60 per person.[1] By the end of the millennium, they spent $1 billion dollars on average annually, or about $164 per capita.

How does the growth of state corrections spending compare to the growth of other types of state spending? Figure 7.1 presents state expenditures between 1977 and 2002 in six areas: corrections, elementary and secondary education, higher education, welfare, health, and transportation. The top panel of figure 7.1 presents the growth in per capita expenditures. Although much has been made of the growth of state corrections spending at the state level, per capita state spending on elementary and secondary education and on healthcare (including Medicaid) was greater and grew by much more in absolute terms over the period. Per capita spending on welfare programs actually grew slightly during this period, growing from about $226 to $295 per person.

The bottom panel of figure 7.1 presents the trends in the average share of the state budget devoted to each of those areas from 1977 to 2002. This comparison is useful, because state spending as a whole increased substantially over this period, so examining changes in the portion of all expenditures devoted to corrections provides a better indication of the priority that states placed on corrections compared to other areas. This graph paints a slightly different picture, showing that average state spending on corrections doubled from approximately 1.25 percent to 2.5 percent of total expenditures; meanwhile spending on primary and secondary education declined from just over 5 percent to just over 4 percent, and spending on welfare programs declined from 24.3 percent to 21.5 percent. The driver of state expenditures during this period was spending on health, which grew from 11 percent of state budget outlays in 1977 to nearly 17 percent by 2002. This increase was driven entirely by increased Medicaid expenditures; non-Medicaid spending on health remained flat as a percentage of total state spending.

The overall pattern of state spending on corrections masks a great deal of variation across the states. There is a wide variation is in the amount of dollars spent on corrections across the states. In 2000, for example, the five states that spent the most on corrections (Delaware, Nevada, Florida, Maryland, and Arizona) spent 2.6 times more on a per capita basis than the five states that spent the least on their corrections systems (North Dakota, Alabama, Maine, Minnesota, and Iowa). This wide variation is also reflected in incarceration rates. Thus, in 2000 the five states with the highest incarceration rates (Delaware, Louisiana, Texas, Mississippi, and Oklahoma) had 3.4 times more prisoners per capita than the five states with the lowest incarceration rates (North Dakota, New Hampshire, Minnesota, Massachusetts, and Maine).

Figures 7.2 and 7.3 illustrate the variation across individual states. Figure 7.2 plots the variation in state incarceration rates in 2000 on the x-axis and the changes in state incarceration rates between 1978 and 2000 on the y-axis. States with high incarceration rates in 2000 tend also be those states with the highest growth in their incarceration rates between 1978 and 2000, although the association is not perfect. With one glaring exception—Delaware—the states with the highest incarceration rates in 2000 were located in the South and Southwest, while those with the lowest incarceration rates in 2000 were located in New England and the upper

Figure 7.1   *Trends in Average State Spending by Area, 1977 to 2002*

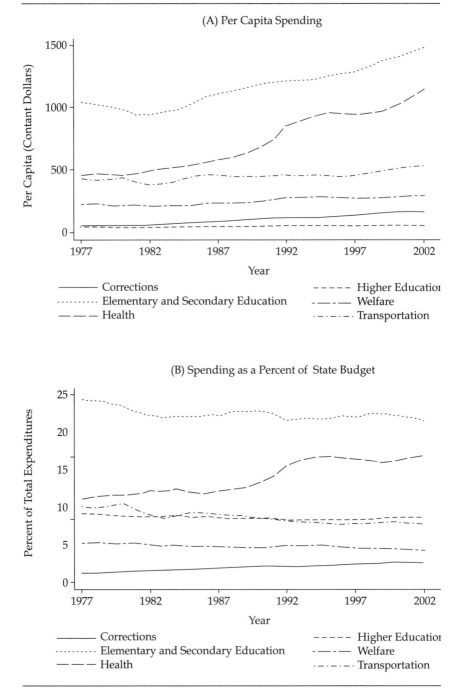

Source: Public Policy Institute of California: Annual State and Local Government Finance Data.

Figure 7.2   *State Incarceration Rates in 2000 and Changes in State Incarceration Rates from 1978 to 2000*

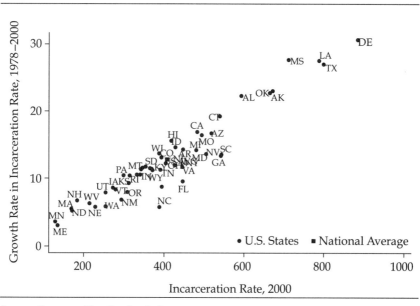

Source: Bureau of Justice Statistics.

Midwest. The differences in the 2000 incarceration rates of these states is quite dramatic: the eight states with the highest rates have an average incarceration rate that is more than four times the average incarceration rate of the eight states with the lowest rates in 2000. As also indicated in figure 7.2, the states with the highest incarceration rates in 2000 also tend to have had the highest rates of growth in incarceration rates between 1978 and 2000. Delaware, Mississippi, Louisiana, Texas, Oklahoma, Arkansas, and Alabama are in the top eight states in terms of incarceration rate growth. Maine, Minnesota, Massachusetts, North Dakota, and Nebraska are among the states with the slowest incarceration rate growth.

In figure 7.3, the level of spending in 2000 is presented on the *x*-axis, while the growth rate in state and local spending per capita is presented on the *y*-axis. Compared to the distributions of the states in figure 7.2, the picture in figure 7.3 is not as clear. A number of northern states (New York, Oregon, and California) are among the highest spending states on a per capita basis, but so are a number of southern states (Arkansas and Florida). Although a number of southern states are at the bottom of the per capita spending distribution (Alabama, Tennessee, and Mississippi),

Figure 7.3   *Real (2000 Dollars) Per Capita State and Local Spending on Corrections in 2000 and Growth in Real Per Capita State and Local Spending on Corrections Between 1978 and 2000*

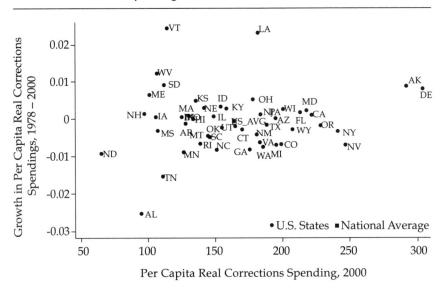

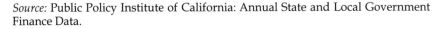

Source: Public Policy Institute of California: Annual State and Local Government Finance Data.

so are a number of northern states (North Dakota, Minnesota, New Hampshire, and Iowa). Moreover, the association between the level of spending in 2000 and the growth rate of spending between 1978 and 2000 is not as strong as the association between the level of incarceration in 2000 and the growth rate of incarceration between 1978 and 2000.[2]

Because states vary in the total size of their budgets, they also vary in the percentage of their budgets devoted to corrections. Figure 7.4 presents the distribution of the states in terms of the percentage of their budgets devoted to corrections spending in 2000 (on the *x*-axis); the growth in the distribution of their budgets devoted to corrections spending between 1978 and 2000 is presented on the *y*-axis.

Again, a mixed picture emerges. In general, the states with lower incarceration rates spend a lower percentage of their budgets on corrections (North Dakota, Minnesota, Vermont, Massachusetts, Maine, and New Hampshire). However, there are some interesting exceptions. Several southern states with high incarceration rates (Alabama, Tennessee, South Carolina, and North Carolina) are also at the lower end of the distribution.

Figure 7.4   *Percentage of State Budget Spent on Corrections in 2000 and Growth in the Percentage of the State Budget Spent on Corrections Between 1978 and 2000*

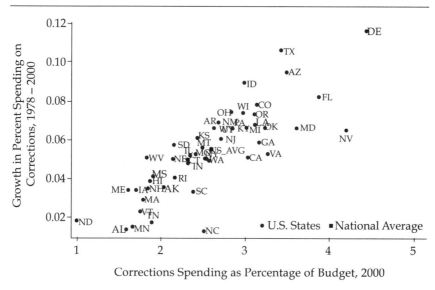

Corrections Spending as Percentage of Budget, 2000

Source: Public Policy Institute of California: Annual State and Local Government Finance Data.

This wide variation across the states leads to several questions: Why do some states spend more on their corrections systems than others? Is it simply a question of the size of their prison populations? Holding incarceration rates constant, do some states spend more on their correction systems? Do some states run more efficient systems than do others? Is the cost of doing business in some states simply higher than in others?

DATA AND METHODS

In this chapter we employ a series of multivariate cross-section time-series regressions to analyze how a range of state-level factors are associated with spending on corrections. We also examine whether increased spending on corrections has affected spending in other areas. We seek to explain the variation in two types of variables: the level of spending in a given year, and the growth in spending over time measured as the change in spending from the previous year. Unless noted, our data is measured in per capita real (inflation adjusted) dollars. All models are in first differences and use robust, clustered standard errors. In most cases, independent variables are lagged one year.

All analyses in this chapter are based on annual cross-section time-series data on 49 U.S. states from 1977 to 2002, though for some analyses we use a subset of years due to data limitations.[3] The unit of analysis is state-year. Variable descriptions and sources are listed in table 7.1.[4] Expenditure data on state corrections data were provided by the Public Policy Institute of California (PPIC). Descriptive statistics for most variables that appear in these and subsequent analyses are reported in table 7.2.

EXPLAINING THE VARIATION OF CORRECTIONS SPENDING ACROSS THE STATES

Why do some states spend so much more than others on their corrections systems? Evidence shows that states vary in their incarceration rates, and states certainly vary in their crime rates, but incarceration rates vary across states even when one holds crime rates constant. We know that policy clearly matters. Some states choose to apply longer sentences than others. Some states have tighter parole systems than others. Some states choose to spend more per inmate than others; even when variation in the cost of living across the states is taken into account. This variation could also be caused by different political and policy beliefs across states. Different political institutions, such as supermajority voting requirements to raise taxes or enact budgets, could also cause the variation. Finally, states vary in their budgetary systems, and this variation could lead to greater or lesser amounts of spending on corrections.[5]

In explaining why some states spend more on corrections, we focus on four categories or classes of variables: socioeconomic variables, state political institutions (including measures of governmental and citizen ideology), state budgetary practices, and measures of crime.

Levels of State Spending Over Time

We begin by seeking to explain the level of three categories of state budgetary spending: total state expenditures, total state expenditures on corrections, and total state noncorrections expenditures. These analyses are based on data from 1977 through 1998. The dependent variables (total spending, total corrections spending, and total noncorrections spending) are measured in per capita real 2002 dollars. The full models (with all variables) are found in tables 7.2 and 7.3.

Table 7.1 *Variables Used in OLS Multiple Regressions to Explain the Level and Growth of State Expenditures*

Variable Name	Definition	Unit	Year	Data Source
Dependent variables				
Total per capita real spending	Total per capita real spending (2002 dollars)	$1	1970–2002	PPIC 2006
Corrections per capita real spending	Corrections per capita real spending (2002 dollars)	$1	1948–1998	PPIC 2006
Total noncorrections per capita real spending	Total per capita real spending (2002 dollars)— Corrections per capita real spending (2002 dollars)	$1	1970–2002	PPIC 2006
(1) Socioeconomic				
Personal income	Personal income	$1	1950–2000	Besley and Case 2003
State CPI	State CPI index		1948–1998	Berry et al, 2000
Kids	% of population under 18	Percentage(%)	1950–2000	Besley and Case 2003
Aged	% of population over 64	Percentage(%)	1950–2000	Besley and Case 2003
Black	% of population black	Percentage(%)	1977–2000	Census
Metro	% of population in metropolitan areas	Percentage(%)	1977–2000	Census
Unemployment rate	Unemployment rate	Percentage(%)	1950–2000	Besley and Case 2003

(continued on page 219)

Table 7.1 (*Continued*)

Variable Name	Definition	Unit	Year	Data Source
(2) Institutions				
Government ideology	Government ideology (liberal) index	1–100	1948–1998	Besley and Case 2003
Citizen ideology	Citizen ideology (liberal) index	1–100	1948–1998	Besley and Case 2003
Divided government	Divided government (1 if yes)	Dummy (1,0)	1950–2000	Besley and Case 2003
Tax/expenditure limit	Tax/expenditure limit (1 if yes)	Dummy (1,0)	1950–2000	Besley and Case 2003
Supermajority	Supermajority required for tax increases (1 if yes)	Dummy (1,0)	1950–2000	Besley and Case 2003
Direct initiative	Existence of direct initiative (1 if yes)	Dummy (1,0)	1950–2000	Besley and Case 2003
Term limit	Term limit (1 if yes)	Dummy (1,0)	1950–2000	Besley and Case 2003
(3) Budgetary practices				
Funding targets	Funding targets (1 if yes)	Dummy (1,0)	1988–2000	Alderete 2007
Legislative access	Legislative access (1 if yes)	Dummy (1,0)	1988–2000	Alderete 2007
Performance measurement	Performance measurement in at least one government area (1 if yes)	Dummy (1,0)	1988–2000	Alderete 2007
Performance management	Performance management in at least one government area (1 if yes)	Dummy (1,0)	1988–2000	Alderete 2007
Performance budget	Performance budgeting in at least one government area (1 if yes)	Dummy (1,0)	1988–2000	Alderete 2007
Midsession revision	Mid-session revision (1 if yes)	Dummy (1,0)	19882000	Alderete 2007
(4) Crime				
Incarceration rate	Incarceration rate	Percentage(%)	19772004	BJS
Crime rate (violent)	Violent crime rate	Percentage(%)	19692002	FBI
Crime rate (property)	Property crime rate	Percentage(%)	19692002	FBI

Table 7.2   Descriptive Statistics of Dependent and Independent Variables

Variable	Mean	Standard Deviation	Within-State Standard Deviation
Dependent variables			
Δ Per capita corrections spending	4.637	12.114	12.033
Δ Per capita elementary and secondary ed spending	17.580	54.888	54.440
Δ Per capita higher education spending	0.522	7.145	7.120
Δ Per capita welfare spending	2.777	27.070	26.864
Δ Per capita health spending	27.508	56.443	55.557
Δ Per capita transportation spending	4.164	49.277	49.083
Δ Percent spending on elementary and secondary ed	−0.111	0.889	0.883
Δ Percent spending on higher education	−0.019	0.514	0.511
Δ Percent spending on welfare	−0.038	0.461	0.457
Δ Percent spending on health	−0.229	0.900	0.891
Δ Percent spending on transportation	−0.091	0.823	0.819
Independent variables			
Δ Percent spending on corrections	0.049	0.201	0.200
Democratic governor	0.530	0.499	0.446
Δ Percent legislature democratic	−0.006	0.039	0.039
Δ Interparty competition	−1.063	7.896	7.865
Δ Unemployment rate	−0.005	1.039	1.038
Δ Poverty rate	0.000	0.018	0.018
Δ Proportion Africa American population	0.001	0.011	0.011
Δ Gross income per thousand	0.895	0.424	0.400
Δ Revenue-to-debt ratio (logged)	−0.019	0.180	0.177
Δ Violent crimes per ten thousand	0.196	4.093	4.069
Δ Property crimes per ten thousand	−2.828	26.916	26.578
Δ Population 0 to 17	−0.190	0.341	0.336
Δ Population 18 to 24	−0.141	0.251	0.250
Δ Population 25 to 44	0.052	0.507	0.504
Δ Population 45 to 64	0.197	0.364	0.358
Δ School enrollments	0.003	0.380	0.358

Source: Authors' compilation.

Table 7.3   *OLS Regressions of Different Levels of State Spending, 1977 to 1998*

	Total Spending	Corrections Spending	Noncorrections Spending
Independent variables—socioeconomic			
State income	0.001*	0.000*	0.001*
	(0.000)	(0.000)	(0.000)
State CPI	6.553.087**	105.58	6,448.030**
	(1,191.449)	(101.309)	(1,153,694)
Children (% under 18)	−26.185	−0.989	−25.195
	(16.997)	(0.921)	(16.680)
Aged (% over 64)	−15.751	−1.329	−14.422
	(31.918)	(2.477)	(30.436)
Black (%)	62.688	9.817*	52.871
	(99.210)	(4.281)	(95.856)
Metropolitan (%)	2.788	0.202	2.586
	(11.771)	(0.927)	(11.226)
Unemployment rate	49.220**	0.691	48.529**
	(9.976)	(0.852)	(10.196)
Independent variables—institutions			
Government ideology	0.729	−0.095	0.824
	(0.929)	(0.073)	(0.909)
Citizen ideology	−1.823	0.190	−2.013
	(2.948)	(0.222)	(2.865)
Divided government	−38.482	2.017	−40.498
	(46.323)	(4.667)	(44.077)
Tax expenditure limit	2.925	5.418	−2.493
	(79.285)	(5.316)	(76.914)
Supermajority required	−170.221	0.077	−170.298
for tax increase	(137.694)	(9.872)	(129.741)
Direct initiative	252.756**	−21.216**	273.973**
	(85.910)	(8.401)	(100.718)
Term limits	−297.575***	−7.861	−289.714***
	(100.508)	(8.401)	(100.718)
Independent variables—measures of crime			
Incarceration rate	−0.174	0.118**	−0.292
	(0.272)	(0.027)	(0.270)
Crime rate (violent)	−566.273*	50.819^	−617.092*
	(269.808)	(27.630)	(258.548)
Crime rate (property)	135.570**	−0.658	136.228**
	(39.450)	(4.015)	(36.785)
Constant	−248.478	−26.088	−222.390
	(1,287.719)	(130.458)	(1,242,028)
Observations	1101	1101	1101
R–squared	0.97	0.94	0.97

Source: Authors' compilation.
Note: Robust, clustered socioeconomics are shown under coefficients. All models control for state and year fixed effects and are weighted by state population.
$^\wedge p < 0.1$; $*p < 0.5$; $**p < 0.01$.

Total State Spending

The results for the levels of total state spending follow the general pattern found in the literature (Besley and Case 2003; Alderete 2007). That is, in this multivariate analysis, the level of total state expenditures in the 1977–1998 period is positively associated with the level of personal income and the state price level. Richer states spend more through their state budgets. Where the cost of doing business is higher, states spend more money. The unemployment rate is statistically significant and positively associated with total state spending: on average, a one percentage point increase in the unemployment rate is associated with $49.20 increase in total state spending per capita, holding everything else constant. Total state spending is also associated with higher property crime rates and lower violent crime. The incarceration rate is not statistically significant.

A series of institutional and process variables are also significantly associated with the level of total state spending. Specifically, the presence of a direct initiative is positively associated with the level of total state spending while the presence of a term-limit provision is negatively associated. On average, a state that adopted a citizen directive initiative will spend $252.76 more per capita than when it does not have a directive initiative.

Total Corrections Spending

As with total spending, state spending on corrections is positively associated with state personal income. As one would expect, total state corrections spending is significantly positively associated with the state's incarceration rate. It is also significantly associated with the violent-crime rate, but it is inversely (and not significantly) associated with the state property-crime rate.

State spending on corrections is significantly associated with the percentage of the state population that is African American. It is also negatively associated with an index of the degree to which the state's elected officials are from the Democratic Party.

When it comes to state political institutions, spending on corrections is inversely associated with the presence of the direct initiative (unlike total spending, which is higher in the presence of a direct initiative). But the presence of term limits is not significantly associated with corrections spending. Nor is the presence of a supermajority voting requirement to enact tax increases.

Total Noncorrections Spending

In general, the pattern for noncorrections spending follows that of total spending. That is, the level of noncorrections spending is significantly associated with the level of personal income, the state price level, the unemployment rate, and the presence of a direct initiative. The level is negatively associated with term limits and the violent-crime rate. Interestingly, the level of noncorrections spending is negatively associated with the violent-crime rate. Neither the ideology of government officials nor of the citizenry is significantly associated with either total state spending or total noncorrections state spending.

GROWTH IN STATE SPENDING OVER TIME

When measured in terms of changes, total state spending is positively associated with changes in the price level, the unemployment rate, and the incarceration rate. It is negatively associated with growth in the percentage of a state's population residing in metropolitan areas. The adoption of a direct initiative is statistically significant and positively associated with the change in total state spending, as it is with the levels of total state spending. Compared to the explanation of the levels of total state spending, changes in personal income ceases to be statistically significant.

Changes in Total Corrections Spending

When explaining the growth in state corrections spending, some of the results from the regressions that explain the levels of spending reappear. Changes in the price index and the incarceration rate are statistically significant and positively associated with change in total corrections spending. Changes in personal income, however, are negatively associated with changes in total corrections spending. The supermajority required for a tax increase is associated with a decrease in total corrections spending.

Changes in Total Noncorrections Spending

The pattern for changes in noncorrections spending follows that of total spending. The state price level, the unemployment rate and the adoption of the direct initiative are positively associated with changes in noncorrections spending, while the growth in a state's metropolitan population is negatively associated with changes in noncorrections spending. Of interest is the fact that changes in the incarceration rate and changes in our two measures of the crime rate are not significantly associated with changes in noncorrections spending (although they are significantly associated with the levels of total noncorrections spending).

THE EFFECTS OF BUDGETARY PROCEDURES

Holding constant all the variables in table 7.1, one might ask if policy-makers can affect the level and growth rate of state corrections spending through the adoption of new budgetary procedures. In a recent study, Jaime Calleja Alderete (2007) of the Public Policy Institute of California examined the effect of six budgetary practices on the levels of state expenditures:

- Funding targets: Executive branch agencies are told they must adhere to bottom-line budget numbers when developing their budgets before the official budget is finalized and presented.

- Legislative access: Members of the state legislature are informed about executive-agency budget requests before the annual budget is officially presented to them for debate and adoption.

- Midsession revision: The budget submitted to the legislature is updated midway through the process to reflect more recent, and presumably more accurate, economic and financial data.

- Performance measurement: Government agencies use benchmarks of their success in carrying out their missions. These include such measures as test scores for education agencies or recidivism rates for corrections departments.

- Performance management: Performance measures are used more explicitly to guide and manage internal agency budgetary decisions and implementation of programs.

- Performance budgeting: Performance measures become the justification for most, if not all, funding decisions.

Jaime Calleja Alderete found that a significant number of states had adopted these budgetary practices in recent years (see table 7.4). To see whether these budgetary procedures are associated with the levels or changes in the state spending on corrections, we merged Alderete's data with our data (as described in table 7.1). As Alderete's data only cover the years 1988 to 2000, our analysis is limited by a much smaller sample size (N = 573). Tables 7.5 and 7.6 present the OLS regressions coefficients for the presence or absence of these budget reforms when they are included in the complete models (with all the independent variables set out in table 7.1).

In terms of the levels of total state spending on corrections, the regression coefficients in table 7.5 indicate that the existence of funding targets

Table 7.4   *The Number of States Following Each Budget Practice,*
             1988 and 2002

	1988	2002
Funding targets	22	34
Legislative access to requests	42	30
Performance measurement	8	38
Performance management	8	19
Performance budgeting	8	19
Midsession revisions	19	14

Source: Alderete 2007, viii.

and performance measurement are associated with statistically significant lower levels of total state corrections spending. The other budgetary procedures—legislative access, performance management, and midsession revision—are not statistically associated with levels of state corrections spending.

From the regression coefficients in table 7.6, it appears that the adop-

Table 7.5   *OLS Regression Coefficients for the Presence of Budgetary*
             Practices on the Level of State Spending, 1988 to 2002

	Total Spending	Corrections Spending	Noncorrections Spending
Funding targets	−51.225^	−12.225**	−38.999
	(29.742)	(4.096)	(28.999)
Legislative access	−36.348	1.352	−37.700
	(57.372)	(3.536)	(56.711)
Performance measurement	−47.149	−7.776*	−39.373
	(36.284)	(3.361)	(35.592)
Performance management	12.830	5.244	7.585
	(38.271)	(3.728)	(39.121)
Performance budget	−28.291	4.451	−32.743
	(0.860))	(0.071)	(0.832)
Midsession revision	−93.190*	−2.335	−90.854^
	(45.522)	(5.506)	(45.661)

Source: Authors' compilation.
Note: Robust, clustered socioeconomics are shown under coefficients. All models control for state and year fixed effects and are weighted by state population. Data are in 2002 per capita dollars.
^$p < 0.1$; *$p < 0.5$; **$p < 0.01$.

Table 7.6   *OLS Regression Coefficients for the Presence of Budgetary Practices on Year-Over-Year Changes in State Spending, 1988 to 2002*

	Total Spending	Corrections Spending	Noncorrections Spending
Funding targets	−9.284	−4.460	13.744
	(35.786)	(3.535)	(34.579)
Legislative access	−50.784	0.234	−51.017
	(47.961)	(2.777)	(48.323)
Performance measurement	−22.858	−11.856**	−11.002
	(28.368)	(2.777)	(28.256)
Performance management	6.311	6.519**	−0.208
	(30.656)	(2.005)	(31.206)
Performance budget	−10.939	7.247**	−18.186
	(22.582)	(2.048)	(23.449)
Midsession revision	5.729	−5.938^	11.667
	(47.953)	(3.317)	(48.036)

Source: Authors' compilation.
Note: Robust, clustered socioeconomics are shown under coefficients. All models control for state and year fixed effects and are weighted by state population. Data are in 2002 per capita dollars.
$^p < 0.1$; $^*p < 0.5$; $^{**}p < 0.01$.

tion of a performance management system and a performance budgeting system are significantly associated with the growth of state corrections spending. The adoption of performance measurement and midsession review are associated with lower levels of state corrections spending. Funding targets and legislative access are not statistically significantly associated with changes in the level of state corrections spending.

The bottom line of this analysis is that there are budgetary procedures that can affect the level of state spending on corrections.

DOES CORRECTIONS SPENDING CROWD OUT OTHER TYPES OF SPENDING?

We now turn to the question of whether states' spending on corrections has come at the expense of spending in other areas. As indicated in figure 7.1, even though states spend a lot on corrections in absolute terms, and corrections expenditures witnessed substantial growth during this period, by 2002 corrections spending comprised a relatively small share of all state and local spending. Still, state budgets are finite and competition for state appropriations is fierce. Each additional dollar spent on prisons usually means one less dollar spent on something else. In this chapter, we examine the budgetary consequences of the growth in corrections spending. Specifically, we examine spending trade-offs by modeling whether increases in corrections expenditures are associated with decreases in spending on any of the other five areas of spending in figure 7.1 (elementary and secondary education, higher education, welfare, health, and transportation). While many observers regard state prison spending as the cause of spending constraints on areas like higher education and highways, there is very little systematic empirical evidence of this.

For this analysis, we employ the same cross-section time-series data to analyze the effect of corrections spending on other areas, using a technique—two-stage least squares (2SLS) regression with instrumental variables—that allows us to control for the reciprocal effect that spending on other areas will have on prison spending. Data sources and definitions for the dependent and independent variables are listed in the appendix. Table 7.2 presents descriptive statistics for variables used in these models.

Our main analysis of spending trade-offs is comprised of five regression models. Each model corresponds to one of the five spending areas listed above: primary and secondary education, higher education, welfare, health, and transportation. We model the relationship between changes in each of these spending areas and changes in corrections spending in a given state and year, controlling for factors that might otherwise affect state spending.[6] Standard OLS estimates are likely to be biased, however, because of the endogeneity between state-spending categories—while decisions about corrections spending may affect decisions about spending on other areas, it is also the case that spending on those other areas will influence decisions about corrections spending, either sequentially or simultaneously.

This could lead to two possible outcomes. If the relationship between spending in other areas and spending on corrections is bidirectional and negative, as in a zero-sum situation, then the endogeneity would likely bias the absolute magnitude of the coefficients upwards, producing larger negative coefficients than actually warranted. Alternatively, there is the closely related problem of omitted variables bias. A spurious correlation between spending categories could be produced by unobserved factors that affect different categories of spending in a similar direction. For example, exogenous budgetary shocks (such as a recession, inflation in healthcare provision, new laws mandating or capping certain expenditures, or new bond issues) might affect spending on one or more budget categories in either the same or different directions. Political scientists William Jacoby and Saundra Schneider (2001) examined state spending in 1992 and attempted to classify state spending patterns. They found states clustered among those that spent on general social provisions, such as highways, parks, and primary and secondary education; another cluster of states tended to also invest in programs that affected the state's neediest populations, spending more on hospitals, transportation, employment security, and welfare. Notably, states in this cluster also spent relatively more on corrections. As the authors note, states with the neediest populations may tend to spend more on welfare while at the same time incarcerating a larger share of their population. The models attempt to control for the extent of poverty and crime, but there are important aspects of both that are not adequately captured, such as the concentration of poverty and drug crimes. Thus, we use 2SLS to help identify the exogenous effect of corrections spending on other categories of state spending.

Our identification strategy employs the instrument developed by economists Rucker Johnson and Steven Raphael (2006), which uses annual changes in the prison population to estimate the "disparity between the actual incarceration rate and the equilibrium incarceration rate implied by the current period transition probabilities describing movements into and out of prison" (2). Because this predicted change, or "implied equilibrium rate," is highly predictive of future incarceration rates but determined exogenously from them, it can be used to instrument for subsequent changes in actual incarceration rates. We thus use this "theoretically predicted dynamic adjustment path of future incarceration rates" (2) to instrument for changes in spending on corrections.

The use of this instrument rests on the assumption that annual shifts in corrections budgets are responsive in the short term to annual changes in incarceration rates. The idea is that we are identifying some aspect of corrections spending that is essentially nondiscretionary, in that it is the part that responds to changes in incarceration rates and hence can be considered a source of change in corrections spending that is exogenous to spending in other areas. In addition to its face validity, this assumption is supported by regression results showing a strong positive relationship between changes in the incarceration rate and changes in corrections spending. It is further supported by the first-stage regression results (see table 7.7), where we regress prison spending on the instrument developed by Johnson and Raphael (2006). Those results indicate a strong, robust relationship between the instrument and corrections spending—in bivariate models, multivariate models, and in models that include state and year fixed effects. Although the coefficient for the instrument—the predicted change in incarceration—diminishes as the specification includes more covariates, and the standard error increases, the instrument is highly significant in all models (with F-statistics ranging from thirteen to fifty). Thus, the first-stage relationship is strong and survives inclusion of control variables as well as state and year fixed effects.

Table 7.7 First-Stage Effect of the Predicted Change in Incarceration Rates on the Current Change in Corrections Spending

	Change in Per Capita Corrections Spending			Change in Percent Spending on Corrections		
	(1a)	(1b)	(1c)	(2a)	(2b)	(2c)
Predicted Δ in Incarceration	0.099**	0.102**	0.079**	0.002**	0.002**	0.001**
	(0.015)	(0.015)	(0.021)	(0.000)	(0.000)	(0.000)
Democratic government		0.922	1.417		0.008	0.012
		(0.738)	(0.972)		(0.011)	(0.014)
Δ Percentage democratic legislature		8.687	-7.179		-0.141	-0.199
		(9.817)	(12.950)		(0.206)	(0.272)
Δ Interparty competition		0.077	0.018		0.001	-0.001
		(0.110)	(0.116)		(0.002)	(0.002)
Δ Unemployment rate		-0.518	-0.249		-0.024**	-0.017^
		(0.325)	(0.440)		(0.006)	(0.009)
Δ Poverty rate		-29.081	-0.094		-0.223	0.094
		(37.063)	(28.237)		(0.569)	(0.463)
Δ Percent black		-44.048**	-41.634**		-0.868**	-0.864**
		(7.024)	(6.802)		(0.125)	(0.134)
Δ Per capita income		-0.401	-0.437		-0.021	-0.040
		(1.047)	(1.628)		(0.015)	(0.025)
Δ Revenue-to-debt ratio		3.771	3.749		0.079^	0.070
		(2.429)	(2.541)		(0.041)	(0.045)

	(1)	(2)	(3)	(4)	(5)	(6)
Δ Violent-crime rate		0.056	0.187		-0.002	0.001
		(0.140)	(0.145)		(0.002)	(0.002)
Δ Property–crime rate		-0.007	-0.018		-0.000	-0.000
		(0.018)	(0.028)		(0.000)	(0.001)
Δ Population 0 to 17		6.347**	4.875**		0.048*	0.031^
		(2.228)	(1.292)		(0.023)	(0.018)
Δ Population 18 to 24		5.313*	7.989**		0.066^	0.108**
		(2.277)	(2.209)		(0.033)	(0.037)
Δ Population 25 to 44		2.892	1.553		0.057^	-0.001
		(2.388)	(2.490)		(0.029)	(0.037)
Δ Population 45 to 64		-1.494	-1.552		-0.080*	-0.060
		(2.214)	(2.386)		(0.035)	(0.039)
Constant	4.183**	5.872**	2.699	0.027**	0.067**	-0.060^
	(0.298)	(1.251)	(1.776)	(0.004)	(0.016)	(0.030)
Year effects	No	No	Yes	No	No	Yes
State effects	No	No	Yes	No	No	Yes
N	1175	1175	1175	1175	1175	1175
R-squared	0.02	0.07	0.17	0.03	0.10	0.17
F-statistic†	42.25	49.43	14.54	28.75	50.22	13.26†
P-value†	(<0.00001)	(<0.00001)	(<0.0004)	(<0.0008)	(<0.00001)	(<0.0007)

Source: Authors' compilation.
Note: Robust, clustered socioeconomics are shown under coefficients. All models are weighted by state population.
†Reported from F-test of the instrumental variable.
^$p < 0.1$; *$p < 0.05$; **$p < 0.01$).

We use the first-stage estimates to identify the effect of changes in corrections spending on changes in spending on other areas. Tables 7.8 and 7.9 present the full results for per capita spending and spending expressed as budget share. These tables present the instrumental variable results alongside coefficients from an OLS regression.

Our results indicate that increases in corrections spending are only associated with decreases in welfare spending and not decreases in any of the other spending areas. An increase of $1 in corrections spending is associated with a decline of an average of about $1.40 in spending on welfare. Note that in the OLS regression for welfare spending (table 7.8, model 3a), the corrections spending coefficient is positive and statistically significant, but it then reverses sign in the instrumental variable regression. One way to interpret this pattern is that there is no trade-off between welfare spending and "discretionary" corrections spending—that is, funding that is not a function of changes (or projected changes) in the incarceration rate. Only when the spending is driven by changes in the incarceration rate do we see a trade-off occur. Our confidence in the usefulness of the instrument in this case is enhanced by the observation that a similar pattern holds for most of the other areas of spending, where the corrections coefficient switches signs from positive to negative moving from the OLS to the instrumental variable specifications. This suggests that a spurious positive correlation exists between corrections spending and other categories until an exogenous source of variation in corrections spending can be identified.

The results of the analysis for budget shares provide even stronger evidence that increases in corrections spending are associated with declines in welfare spending. They indicate that a 1 percentage point increase in the share of the budget devoted to corrections spending is associated with a decline of about 1.7 percentage points in welfare on average. One puzzle is why the magnitude of the coefficient is greater than 1. If only a budgetary trade-off is taking place, then we would expect a coefficient of 1. This would indicate that for every additional dollar spent on corrections, a dollar is taken out of welfare spending. First, it is worth pointing out that the confidence intervals for the coefficients span 1, meaning that the true value of the trade-off could be closer to 1. Another possibility is that, if changes in corrections spending bring about reductions in welfare spending, legislators may use that legislative moment as an opportunity or excuse to make further cuts in welfare spending, either to spend on something else or to reduce taxes.

What implications do our results have for broader patterns of spending on corrections and welfare? As indicated in figure 7.1, average per capita spending on corrections tripled from $54 to $170 on average, climbing from 1.25 to 2.5 percent of all expenditures. At the same time, welfare spending increased from $226 to $295 per person, dropping from about 5.2 to 4.2 of all state expenditures. The coefficients in table 7.8 indicate that if per capita growth in corrections had matched the growth rate of total per capita expenditures, which increased by just over 60 percent from $4,300 per capita to nearly $7,000, spending on corrections would have only increased to about 87 dollars per capita.[7] Meanwhile spending on welfare would have grown by an additional $40 to $335, nearly matching the 60 percent growth rate enjoyed by total expenditures.[8] In terms of the budget share, welfare spending would have remained at a constant 5.2 percent of state budgets if corrections spending had grown more modestly to encompass only 1.9 percent of all expenditures.[9]

CONCLUSION

After reviewing trends in state spending on corrections, this chapter sought to examine two questions: What state-level factors are associated with higher corrections spending levels and changes in corrections spending, with particular interest in political institutions and budgetary procedures? Has increased spending on corrections come at the cost of spending on other significant areas of state expenditures?

Our analyses showed that although state spending on corrections was strongly associated with the state's incarceration rate and crime rate, other factors played an important role. Significantly, per capita spending on corrections is higher in states where the black population is larger. Political institutions also matter: corrections spending is lower in states that have a direct initiative. Thus, when voters are given greater direct control over decision making, states tend to spend less on corrections. Emerging budgetary procedures also exert an influence on corrections spending. Funding targets and performance measurement are associated with lower corrections spending levels. The presence of a supermajority voting requirement for spending bills and the use of performance measurement are associated with an average decline in corrections spending. The use of performance management and performance budgeting are associated with an increase in corrections spending.

With regard to budgetary trade-offs, our analysis showed that an increase of 1 percentage point in the share of the budget devoted to corrections is associated with an approximate decrease of 1.7 percentage points in spending on welfare. Although spending on prisons has increased dramatically, it still does not garner a large enough share of the budget to make a big dent in programs other than welfare.

Table 7.8   Per Capita Spending Trade-Offs, 1977 to 2002

	(1a) Elementary and Secondary OLS	(1b) Elementary and Secondary I.V.	(2a) Higher Ed OLS
Δ Corrections spending	0.081	−0.577	−0.026
	(0.138)	(0.799)	(0.035)
Democratic government	1.787	2.226	0.705**
	(4.547)	(5.032)	(0.259)
Δ Percentage democratic legislature	−3.758	−20.424	9.922
	(57.787)	(57.140)	(6.397)
Δ Interparty competition	−0.758	−0.823	0.074
	(0.603)	(0.622)	(0.062)
Δ Unemployment rate	1.560	0.648	0.143
	(2.806)	(2.856)	(0.215)
Δ Poverty rate	−22.937	−5.802	−26.364^
	(75.466)	(78.775)	(14.979)
Δ Percent black	199.907**	178.091 **	−4.671
	(34.113)	(52.026)	(5.416)
Δ Per capita income	19.331*'	16.801**	0.819
	(4.495)	(4.251)	(0.744)
Δ Revenue-to-debt ratio	12.274	15.120	0.017
	(10.145)	(11.958)	(1.145)
Δ Violent-crime rate	−0.208	−0.112	0.099
	(0.531)	(0.614)	(0.071)
Δ Property-crime rate	0.188*	0.170^	0.008
	(0.074)	(0.096)	(0.013)
Δ Population 0 to 17	40.863**	42.006**	0.997
	(8.004)	(9.050)	(1.519)
Δ Population 18 to 24	33.186**	36.728*	0.686
	(10.562)	(13.813)	(1.608)
Δ Population 25 to 44	40.798**	38.848**	−0.023
	(11.307)	(11.632)	(2.581)
Δ Population 45 to 64	29.107**	28.589**	−0.372
	(10.502)	(10.172)	(2.123)
Δ School enrollments	11.987**	13.058**	−0.019
	(1.179)	(1.648)	(0.177)
Constant	5.688	63.781 **	1.255
	(9.613)	(12.490)	(0.963)
N	1225	1175	1225
R–squared	0.38	0.37	0.11

OLS and IV Estimates

(2b) Higher Ed I.V.	(3a) Welfare OLS	(3b) Welfare I.V.	(4a) Health OLS	(4b) Health I.V.	(5a) Transportation OLS	(5b) Transportation I.V.
−0.029	0.336*	−1.422^	0.306	−1.467	0.054	−0.191
(0.080)	(0.127)	(0.860)	(0.210)	(1.468)	(0.117)	(0.881)
0.725*	3.202*	5.893*	2.883	6.129	1.279	1.176
(0.274)	(1.406)	(2.285)	(3.710)	(5.615)	(2.579)	(3.402)
9.776	16.291	5.568	150.159*	124.138^	39.829	44.796
(6.660)	(18.046)	(30.250)	(68.605)	(69.681)	(27.019)	(28.150)
0.073	−0.039	0.022	0.818	0.874	0.789^	0.940^
(0.066)	(0.252)	(0.330)	(0.725)	(0.785)	(0.470)	(0.474)
0.190	−0.458	−0.764	2.515	1.962	1.083	2.013
(0.228)	(0.931)	(1.057)	(2.495)	(2.905)	(1.512)	(1.395)
−25.991 ^	93.580*	94.793	19.975	27.685	−48.046	−49.891
(15.076)	(44.657)	(79.971)	(101.339)	(111.970)	(101.844)	(102.333)
−5.056	18.150	−50.313	−26.411	−98.495	−47.769^	−59.772
(6.022)	(13.718)	(32.368)	(28.780)	(60.067)	(26.411)	(45.015)
0.816	0.532	0.124	13.962*	12.596^	3.225	4.221
(0.747)	(2.485)	(2.832)	(6.199)	(7.139)	(4.705)	(4.796)
−0.109	−0.653	6.711	5.826	13.796	4.550	2.949
(1.160)	(5.005)	(4.784)	(7.952)	(12.833)	(6.071)	(8.020)
0.100	0.487*	0.892**	0.667	0.862	0.746**	0.694*
(0.071)	(0.229)	(0.311)	(0.520)	(0.670)	(0.226)	(0.314)
0.009	−0.045	−0.106	−0.072	−0.088	−0.029	−0.014
(0.014)	(0.040)	(0.067)	(0.088)	(0.141)	(0.051)	(0.065)
0.914	5.147	14.484**	4.043	10.286	11.409^	12.621
(1.709)	(4.139)	(4.950)	(6.864)	(8.793)	(6.445)	(8.146)
0.730	−0.176	15.680*	2.410	14.709	12.461	15.818
(1.894)	(6.003)	(7.636)	(9.200)	(11.369)	(9.583)	(11.569)
−0.149	1.488	5.442	10.131	9.094	14.127*	14.818*
(2.744)	(6.828)	(6.681)	(10.866)	(11.419)	(6.525)	(7.168)
−0.419	2.489	0.430	−0.967	−3.626	6.249	5.655
(2.146)	(4.681)	(6.401)	(8.872)	(10.074)	(11.219)	(11.061)
−0.010	—	—	—	—	—	—
(0.188)						
2.356^	3.788	27.203	10.687	52.300*	4.388	20.188
(1.201)	(6.493)	(17.169)	(9.203)	(20.567)	(9.124)	(16.372)
1175	1225	1175	1225	1175	1225	1175
0.11	0.17	0.008	0.35	0.24	0.13	0.13

Source: Authors' compilation.
Note: Robust, clustered socioeconomincs are shown under coefficients. All models include state and year fixed effects and are weighted by state population.
^p < .1; *p < 0.05; **p < 0.01.

Table 7.9   *Budget Share Spending Trade-Offs, 1977 to 2002*

	(1a) Elementary and Secondary OLS	(1b) Elementary and Secondary I.V.	(2a) Higher Ed OLS
Δ Corrections spending	−0.117	−0.021	0.020
	(0.184)	(0.874)	(0.086)
Democratic government	−0.053	−0.079	−0.021
	(0.068)	(0.080)	(0.044)
Δ Percentage democratic legislature	−0.897	−0.958	0.187
	(1.237)	(1.260)	(0.511)
Δ Interparty competition	−0.023	−0.028^	−0.004
	(0.014)	(0.014)	(0.006)
Δ Unemployment rate	−0.075	−0.092^	−0.013
	(0.052)	(0.051)	(0.025
Δ Poverty rate	−0.268	0.007	−1.698^
	(1.397)	(1.431)	(0.920)
Δ Percent black	3.429**	3.687**	1.913**
	(0.586)	(0.905)	(0.344)
Δ Per capita income	0.089	0.058	0.086
	(0.075)	(0.076)	(0.074)
Δ Revenue–to–debt ratio	0.161	0.134	0.024
	(0.137)	(0.124)	(0.101)
Δ Violent-crime rate	−0.016^	−0.016^	−0.002
	(0.008)	(0.008)	(0.004)
Δ Property–crime rate	0.003**	0.003^	−0.002
	(0.001)	(0.001)	(0.001)
Δ Population 0 to 17	0.299^	0.276^	−0.165^
	(0.156)	(0.146)	(0.088)
Δ Population 18 to 24	0.269	0.228	0.069
	(0.241)	(0.261)	(0.128)
Δ Population 25 to 44	0.369	0.333	−0.148
	(0.222)	(0.210)	(0.139)
Δ Population 45 to 64	0.374*	0.369*	−0.210^
	(0.171)	(0.180)	(0.123)
Δ School enrollments	0.077*	0.074*	0.000
	(0.030)	(0.030)	(0.013)
Constant	−0.357**	0.037	−0.033
	(0.120)	(0.154)	(0.106)
N	1225	1175	1225
R–squared	0.25	0.26	0.11

Budget Shares						
(2b) Higher Ed I.V.	(3a) Welfare OLS	(3b) Welfare I.V.	(4a) Health OLS	(4b) Health I.V.	(5a) Trans- portation OLS	(5b) Trans- portation I.V.
−0.041	0.123	−1.719*	−0.207	−1.656	−0.245^	0.158
(0.747)	(0.083)	(0.843)	(0.133)	(1.181)	(0.127)	(0.986)
−0.016	0.040^	0.066^	−0.027	0.009	0.016	−0.000
(0.045)	(0.023)	(0.034)	(0.049)	(0.067)	(0.048)	(0.054)
0.161	0.014	−0.260	1.986^	1.467	0.272	0.483
(0.617)	(0.375)	(0.650)	(1.116)	(1.133)	(0.455)	(0.476)
−0.002	−0.003	−0.004	0.011	0.010	0.013	0.016^
(0.007)	(0.005)	(0.007)	(0.010)	(0.011)	(0.009)	(0.008)
−0.014	−0.048**	−0.075**	−0.048	−0.075	−0.030	−0.006
(0.023)	(0.014)	(0.024)	(0.038)	(0.046)	(0.027)	(0.031)
−1.740^	1.859**	1.987	0.343	0.536	−0.372	−0.439
(0.934)	(0.693)	(1.288)	(1.887)	(2.076)	(1.966)	(2.038)
1.811 **	0.062	−1.452*	−1.121*	−2.354*	−1.273**	−0.984
(0.523)	(0.252)	(0.644)	(0.507)	(1.098)	(0.471)	(0.964)
0.091	−0.035	−0.094	0.137	0.078	−0.034	0.006
(0.059)	(0.042)	(0.067)	(0.085)	(0.108)	(0.065)	(0.088)
0.033	0.017	0.160	0.130	0.249	0.090	0.003
(0.088)	(0.103)	(0.104)	(0.128)	(0.189)	(0.103)	(0.147)
−0.001	0.005	0.009^	0.006	0.005	0.013**	0.010*
(0.003)	(0.004)	(0.005)	(0.009)	(0.010)	(0.004)	(0.004)
−0.002	−0.001	−0.002^	−0.002	−0.003	−0.001	0.000
(0.001)	(0.001)	(0.001)	(0.002)	(0.002)	(0.001)	(0.001)
−0.122	−0.068	0.019	−0.193	−0.177	0.050	0.039
(0.091)	(0.067)	(0.063)	(0.123)	(0.125)	(0.110)	(0.120)
0.118	−0.143	0.106	0.050	0.187	0.131	0.117
(0.178)	(0.105)	(0.123)	(0.150)	(0.165)	(0.157)	(0.182)
−0.088	−0.106	−0.062	−0.160	−0.203	0.047	0.054
(0.134)	(0.111)	(0.100)	(0.185)	(0.176)	(0.136)	(0.161)
−0.192	−0.061	−0.161	−0.256	−0.349*	−0.037	−0.028
(0.124)	(0.078)	(0.117)	(0.157)	(0.167)	(0.182)	(0.205)
0.005	—	—	—	—	—	—
(0.014)						
0.032	0.031	0.256	0.143	0.373	0.112	0.090
(0.104)	(0.090)	(0.157)	(0.185)	(0.240)	(0.155)	(0.200)
1175	1225	1175	1225	1175	1225	1175
0.11	0.10		0.28	0.20	0.14	0.13

Source: Authors' compilation.
Note: Robust, clustered socioeconomics are shown under coefficients. All models include state and year fixed effects and are weighted by state population.
^p < 0.1; *p < 0.05; **p < 0.0l.

APPENDIX: SPENDING
VARIABLES DEFINITIONS

All spending data come from the U.S. Department of the Census Annual Survey of State Government Finances and were provided to the authors by the Public Policy Institute of California. We use data that combine state- and local-government spending.

Corrections Spending

Corrections spending includes census codes 4 and 5.

- Code 4: "Residential institutions or facilities for the confinement, correction, and rehabilitation of convicted adults or juveniles adjudicated delinquent or in need of supervision, and for the detention of adults and juveniles charged with a crime and awaiting trial."

- Code 5: "Correctional activities other than . . . facilities described under Correctional Institutions, local government correctional activities (residential or other), and intergovernmental expenditure for corrections."

Elementary and Secondary Education

Elementary and secondary education includes census codes 12 and 21.

- Code 12: "Operation, maintenance, and construction of public schools and facilities for elementary and secondary education (kindergarten through high school), vocational-technical education, and other educational institutions except those for higher education, whether operated by independent governments (school districts) or as integral agencies of state, county, municipal, or township governments; and financial support of public elementary and secondary schools."

- Code 21: "State government special programs and institutions primarily for training and education (rather than care) of the blind, deaf, or other handicapped; programs for adult, vocational, or special education that operate outside school systems; and educational activities not assignable to other education functions."

Higher Education

Higher Education includes census codes 16 and 18.

- Code 16: "Activities and facilities connected with a state institution of higher education providing supplementary services to students, faculty or staff, and which are self-supported (wholly or largely through charges for services) and operated on a commercial basis."

- Code 18: "Degree-granting institutions (associate, bachelor, master, or doctorate) operated by state or local governments which provide academic training beyond the high school (grade 12) level, other than for state-operated auxiliary enterprises."

Welfare

Welfare includes census codes 67, 68, 75, 77, and 79.

- Code 67: Federal "Direct payments to beneficiaries under the Federal categorical public assistance programs, Supplemental Security Income (SSI) and Temporary Assistance for Needy Families (TANF); and intergovernmental aid under the Federal Medicaid program."

- Code 68: Other "Cash payments made directly to individuals contingent upon their need, other than those under Federal categorical assistance programs."

- Code 75: "Payments under public welfare programs made directly to private vendors (i.e., individuals or nongovernmental organizations furnishing goods and services) for services and commodities, other than medical, hospital, and health care, on behalf of low-income or other needy persons unable to purchase such goods and services."

- Code 77: "Provision, construction, and maintenance of nursing homes and welfare institutions owned and operated by a government for the benefit of veterans or needy persons (contingent upon their financial or medical need)."

- Code 79: "Public employment for all public welfare activities and expenditures for welfare activities not classified elsewhere."

Health

Health includes census codes 32, 36, 38, and 74.

- Code 32: "Provision of services for the conservation and improvement of public health, other than hospital care, and financial support of other governments' health programs."

- Code 36: "Hospital facilities providing in-patient medical care and institutions primarily for care and treatment of handicapped (rather than education) which are directly administered by a government, including those operated by public universities. Also covers direct payments for acquisition or construction of hospitals whether or not the government will operate the completed facility."

- Code 38: "Provision of hospital care in other hospitals (public or private) and support of other public and private hospitals."

- Code 74: "Payments under public welfare programs made directly to private vendors (i.e., individuals or nongovernmental organizations furnishing goods and services) for medical assistance and hospital or health care, including Medicaid (Title XIX), on behalf of low-income or other medically-needy persons unable to purchase such care."

Transportation

Transportation includes census codes 01, 44, 45 and 47.

- Code 01: " Provision, operation, construction, and support of airport facilities serving the public-at-large on a scheduled or unscheduled basis; and the regulation of the airline industry."

- Code 44: "Maintenance, operation, repair, and construction of nontoll highways, streets, roads, alleys, sidewalks, bridges, tunnels, ferry boats, viaducts, and related structures."

- Code 45: "Maintenance, operation, repair, and construction of highways, roads, bridges, ferries, and tunnels operated on a fee or toll basis."

- Code 47: "Payments in support of privately-owned and operated transit utility operations, including railroads."

This chapter was completed with the assistance of Jeongsoo Kim of the Goldman School of Public Policy, University of California, Berkeley.

NOTES

1. Unless otherwise noted, all state spending figures referred to in this chapter combine expenditures at the state and local levels. All dollar figures are expressed in constant 2002 dollars.
2. The correlation between the level of incarceration in 2000 and the growth rate of incarceration between 1978 and 2000 is 0.28. The correlation between real per capita spending on corrections in 2000 and the growth rate in real per capita spending on corrections between 1978 and 2000 is 0.12.
3. Nebraska is excluded in the data because the political party of state legislator—one of our control variables—is not identified (Klarner 2003).

4. Additional details about the corrections spending variable are available in the appendix.
5. In recent years, economists and political scientists have made significant strides in developing and testing models that explain the patterns of budgetary expenditures and revenues in the United States. We extend existing work in this area by focusing on patterns of corrections expenditures, relying particularly on the work of Timothy Besley and Anne Case (2003) and Jaime Calleja Alderete (2007). In addition to these articles, we have relied on five other articles that have sought to model corrections spending (Marlow and Shires 1999; Nicholson-Crotty, Theobald, and Wood 2006; Stucky, Heimer, and Lang 2007; Lowery, Konda, and Garand 1984; Gordon et al. 2006).
6. Measuring spending variables in first differences renders them stationary. All models are weighted by state population, use clustered standard errors, and include both year and state fixed effects.
7. Average total state and local expenditures also more than doubled over this period, from nearly $20 billion (in constant dollars) to just over $40 billion.
8. If per capita corrections spending was only $87 in 2002, this is $29 less than the observed average. Taking the coefficient for corrections spending implies that an additional $40 (that is, 29 times 1.4) per capita would have been spent on welfare.
9. An increase of corrections spending to 1.9 percent of all expenditures implies a difference of 0.6 percentage points from observed spending, which equals 1 additional percentage point for welfare when multiplied by the coefficient of 1.7 in model 3b of table 7.9.

REFERENCES

Alderete, Jaime C. 2007. *Budget Practices and State Expenditures: Lessons for California.* San Francisco: Public Policy Institute of California.

Berry, William D., Richard C. Fording, and Russell L. Hanson. 2000. "An Annual Cost of Living Index for the American States, 1960–95." *Journal of Politics* 60(2): 550–67.

Besley, Timothy and Anne Case. 2003. "Political Institutions and Policy Choices: Evidence from the United States." *Journal of Economic Literature* 41(1): 7–73.

Gordon, Tracy, Jaime Calleja Alderete, Patrick J. Murphy, Jon Sonstelie, and Ping Zhang. 2006. *Fiscal Realities: Budgetary Tradeoffs in California Government.* San Francisco: Public Policy Institute of California.

Jacoby, William G., and Saundra K. Schneider. 2001. "Variability in State Policy Priorities: An Empirical Analysis." *The Journal of Politics* 63(2): 544–68.

Johnson, Rucker, and Steven Raphael. 2006. "How Much Crime Reduction Does the Marginal Prisoner Buy?" *Goldman School of Public Policy* working paper. University of California, Berkeley.

Klarner, Carl. 2003. "The Measurement of the Partisan Balance of State Government." *State Politics and Policy* Quarterly 3(3): 309–19.

Lowery, David, Thomas Konda, and James Garand. 1984. "Spending in the States: A Test of Six Models." *Western Political Quarterly* 37(1): 48–66.

Marlow, Michael L., and Alden F. Shires. 1999. "So Law Enforcement Expenditures Crowd-Out Public Education Expenditures?" *Applied Economics* 31(1999): 255–66.

Nicholson-Crotty, Sean, Nick A. Theobald, and B. Dan Wood. 2006. "Fiscal Federalism and Budgetary Tradeoffs in the American States." *Political Research Quarterly* 59(2): 313–21.

Public Policy Institute of California. 2008. *Pirot Tables of Annual State and Local Government Data*. Available at http://www.ppic.org/main/datadept.asp. San Francisco, Calif.: Public Policy Institute of California.

Stucky, Thomas D., Karen Heimer, and Joseph B. Lang. 2007. "A Bigger Piece of the Pie? State Corrections Spending and the Politics of Social Order." *Journal of Research in Crime and Delinquency* 44(1): 91–123.

U.S. Bureau of the Census. Multiple years. *Annual Survey of State and Local Government Finances*. Last accessed October 2006. Washington: U.S. Bureau or the Census.

Harry J. Holzer

Collateral Costs: Effects of Incarceration on Employment and Earnings
8 | Among Young Workers

The enormous increases in incarceration that have occurred in the United States over the past few decades have no doubt generated major benefits and costs to society. On the one hand, they have likely reduced crime, at least to some extent, which generates a large benefit to society. On the other hand, it has cost enormous public sums to build and operate prisons in the United States (Donohue, chapter 9, this volume).

In addition, there are a range of "collateral" benefits and costs to the individuals who are incarcerated, their families and communities, and others that need to be considered as well. For instance, the experience of incarceration could potentially have either positive or negative effects on the employment and earnings of offenders after their release. Incarceration might have a range of other effects on individuals as well, including their civic participation, voting behavior, access to public benefits, and the like. These, too, could have implications for their families and communities as well as themselves.

This chapter reviews what we know about the collateral costs and benefits of incarceration on earnings and employment. It does so partly because these benefits and costs have been the subject of much more research to date than the collateral effects along other dimensions. But another reason to focus on employment is that these effects are extremely important. For one thing, the employment of ex-offenders is quite negatively correlated with their tendency to reoffend and recidivate; at least to some extent, this effect appears to be causal (Raphael and Weiman, 2007). Indeed, of the roughly 650,000 inmates who are released from jail or prison each year, a majority recidivate within three to five years (Travis 2004); for those who do not "reenter" successfully, the costs to the individuals, their families, and society are very large.[1]

Even among those who do not recidivate, employment outcomes are correlated with (and perhaps causally related to) health and other measures of their own well-being. Employment prospects and outcomes after incarceration thus appear to be major determinants of whether or not ex-prisoners "reenter" civil society successfully and of the myriad costs to the individual and to society when reentry is unsuccessful.

This chapter presents the potential effects of incarceration on both the demand for labor (by employers) and its supply (among potential workers). These effects can, in theory, be either positive or negative. Exploring the different studies on this topic, this chapter focuses on the data sources and empirical methods used, and on the magnitudes of the effects generated. In doing so, it seeks to reconcile conflicting results and generate a useful summary of what is known. The studies based on workers include those using individual data, either from surveys or from administrative sources, as well as more aggregated data.

While the credible empirical evidence is quite mixed, the preponderance of it points to negative effects of incarceration on the subsequent employment and earnings of offenders. By reducing their employment prospects, these effects likely raise recidivism rates of released offenders, which imposes further costs on society (in the form of both crime and incarceration expenditures). Policies designed to reduce these collateral costs, either through direct reductions in incarceration rates or in their negative effects on subsequent earnings, might therefore generate positive benefits to the individuals in question and to society more broadly.

EFFECTS OF INCARCERATION ON SUBSEQUENT EARNINGS: THEORETICAL CONSIDERATIONS

When individuals are incarcerated and subsequently released, why should we expect their incarceration to potentially impact their employment and earnings? (For further discussion, see Sampson and Laub 1993; Western 2006.) Table 8.1 presents a range of possible effects, both positive and negative. These effects could operate through the employment and earnings of the incarcerated individuals themselves—whether before, during, or especially after incarceration—and also on the employment outcomes of certain nonprisoners as well. Furthermore, they could operate through the attitudes and hiring behaviors of employers, on the demand side of the labor market, as well as through those of potential job applicants and workers on the supply side of that market.

A number of important considerations appear in table 8.1. Any positive effects that incarceration might have on employment would operate primarily through their deterrence effects on criminal behavior, primarily

Table 8.1   *Potential Impacts of Incarceration on Labor-Market Outcomes*

	Potential Impacts on Offenders		
	Positive	Negative	
	Workers	Workers	Employers
When			
Preincarceration	—	—	—
During Incarceration	Education	Incapacity	—
Post-Incarceration	Deterrence	Skill Depreciation	Legal Prohibitions
	—	Networks/Information Depreciation	Employer Fears of Liability
	—	Reduced Work Incentives (Child Support)	Negative Signals
	Potential Impacts on Nonoffenders		
	Positive	Negative	
	Workers	Workers	Employers
	Deterrence	—	Statistical Discrimination

Source: Author's compilation.

after incarceration for those who engage in crime and more generally for those who do not (but who, in the absence of potential incarceration, might choose to do so).[2] To the extent that incarceration might actually help previous offenders organize their lives (Nagin and Waldfogel 1995) and even enhance their educational credentials, perhaps by obtaining a GED (Tyler and Kling 2007), these positive effects would be enhanced. The evidence presented by Jeffrey Kling (2006) of positive short-term effects of length of incarceration on postprison employment outcomes is certainly consistent with this view.

But there are a number of reasons to believe that incarceration might have negative effects on employment as well. Clearly, incarceration will directly reduce employment during the period of imprisonment (by incapacitating the offender), assuming that the offenders might have engaged in at least some positive work experience in the absence of their incarceration. As most survey and administrative evidence show significant work activity for individuals in the periods directly prior to their incarceration (Travis 2004), it seems likely that some would have been at least partly employed had they not been imprisoned.

Once released, the tendency of ex-prisoners to work might be reduced for a variety of supply-based reasons, such as the fact that their skills (or human capital) depreciate over time, their information about the job market weakens, and their work networks atrophy.[3] As these individuals withdraw from the labor market (and perhaps recidivate), their behavior can also reduce the opportunities for and interest in employment among young men in poor neighborhoods who otherwise might not engage in crime (Wilson 1996). This may happen by thinning out their informal employment networks as well or by generating more negative peer effects.

A potentially important effect of prior incarceration on incentives to work might also operate through the child-support system. According to Harry J. Holzer, Steven Raphael, and Michael Stoll (2004), the vast majority (roughly 70 percent) of men released from prison are noncustodial fathers. These men are now subject to much more rigorous child-support enforcement policies that were implemented throughout the 1980s and 1990s (Mincy and Sorensen 1998; Garfinkel 2001).

Even without incarceration, these policies could have either positive or negative effects on work incentives (Edelman, Holzer, and Offner 2006; Holzer, Offner, and Sorensen 2005). On the one hand, the pressure to generate payments, and the risk of punishment for those who do not do so, creates positive incentives to work. But, on the other hand, the tax rates on earnings generated by the child-support system reduce these incentives, especially in states where punishments for nonpayment are not rigorously enforced. According to standard labor-supply theory in economics (Ehrenberg and Smith 2000), one's willingness to work depends on the wages available, net of taxes, and also on one's "elasticity of labor supply," which measures the responsiveness of work effort to these net wages. Much available evidence (Juhn, Murphy, and Topel 1991; Grogger 1998; Katz 1998) suggests that, for low-wage men, labor supply is indeed responsive to these net wages. Furthermore, the tendency of some states to withhold payments from families and children who have been on public assistance further limits the incentives of noncustodial fathers to make these payments, as their own children do not necessarily benefit from their doing so; this makes the analogy of the child-support order to a tax on earnings even stronger.[4]

The likely effect of incarceration is to raise the tax rates on noncustodial fathers associated with child support. Maureen Pirog, Marilyn Klotz, and Katharine Byers (1998) estimate that the tax rates on earnings are generally in the 20 to 35 percent range for low-income fathers. However, for those in "arrears"—or in debt to the child-support system—tax rates are generally as high as 65 percent (Edelman, Holzer, and Offner 2006). These tax rates will then be supplemented by payroll, sales, and other taxes on earnings (Primus 2002). Furthermore, any noncustodial father who has been incarcerated will automatically be in arrears, as the child-support orders remain in effect during their periods of incarceration.

Of course, the effects of the child-support collection system and how it interacts with imprisonment reflect specific policy choices, which could be changed or offset by other policies. Thus, if states were to engage in "arrears management" to create better incentives for payment on current orders, or if the Earned Income Tax Credit (EITC) were more fully extended (by the federal or state governments) to this population to improve their work incentives in low-wage jobs, then the negative effects of arrears on work incentives of those previously incarcerated might be modified.[5] Neither the federal government nor most states have implemented such policies. Thus, the vast majority of ex-offenders face very high tax rates on their meager earnings, which likely reduces their legitimate work activity if they can go undetected by the formal system of child-support enforcement.

While the net effects of incarceration on incentives to and rewards from work are thus somewhat mixed on the supply side of the labor market, their effects on employer demand for labor are unambiguously negative. Ceteris parabis, employers might be unwilling to hire those with criminal records for many reasons, including the risk of legal liability if a previous offender harms a customer or coworker, the risk of financial liability if the offender engages in theft, fears of personal violence, and the negative signals that a period of incarceration sends about their general skills or trustworthiness. Given various legal rulings by courts about employer liability for physical or property damage generated by previous offenders whom they have hired (Holzer, Raphael, and Stoll 2004), and given the correlation between offender status and a range of health and educational characteristics (Travis 2004), it might be perfectly rational for employers to engage in such behavior. However, some fears might also be exaggerated and based on stereotypes. It is also likely that these fears will be stronger for some types of jobs—such as those involving direct contact with customers or the handling of cash—than for others. The many state and federal laws that prohibit the hiring or licensing of those with criminal records into various occupations clearly reinforce these tendencies (Legal Action Center 2004).

Clearly, these factors imply that a period of incarceration for any individual directly reduces employability above and beyond the effects of poor skills and work experience prior to incarceration. In other words, incarceration causes lower employer demand, controlling for other characteristics and behaviors of the individual that might have already reduced their employment. Once again, there are policy options (such as tax credits for employers who hire ex-offenders and bonding to protect them from legal and financial liabilities) that might potentially offset these negative effects. Without greater use of these policy offsets however, the effects of previous incarceration on employer demand are likely negative.

Will this reduction in labor demand for ex-offenders definitely reduce employment outcomes for this group? While the reduction in potential opportunities is clear, its impact on actual employment outcomes depends on the magnitudes of the reductions in job offers for the offender population, and the size of the offender relative to nonoffender labor forces (Becker 1975; Heckman 1998). If the number of offenders seeking employment is small relative to the number of employers still willing to hire them, and if they have sufficient information about and access to these jobs, then it might be possible for offenders to find such employment and avoid being hurt by their offender status. On the other hand, if a large number of men carry this stigma relative to the number of available jobs, and if these men have limited information about where these other opportunities exist or face additional barriers to being offered these jobs (because of skill deficiencies, "spatial mismatch" between locations of jobs and their own residences, or weak informal networks), then the reduction in potential job offers might well translate into reduced employment and earnings outcomes for this population (Holzer 2001).

Furthermore, the negative effects of incarceration on labor demand are not necessarily limited to those who have actually been incarcerated. Because job applicants have little incentive to directly inform prospective employers about their criminal histories, and because many employers do not check criminal background (the checks are at least somewhat costly and potentially inaccurate), employers generally do not have perfect information about which applicants have or do not have criminal records. In such a situation, employers might well engage in a form of statistical discrimination; in such cases, employers use personal characteristics that are statistically correlated with offender status—such as being a less-educated black male—to predict criminal history in the absence of direct individual information. They might tend to avoid hiring from some broader demographic groups (such as black men) simply to avoid hiring ex-offenders inadvertently.[6]

In sum, an episode of incarceration could have either positive or negative effects on the subsequent employment of the offenders themselves, by virtue of its impacts on their incentives to work, their skills, and their information or networks. Impacts on nonoffenders might be positive or negative as well. Incarceration almost certainly limits the interests of employers in hiring previous offenders (or those whom they think might be), though there remain questions about its relative magnitude and impact. Overall, the net impacts of these factors on the employment outcomes of workers who either have or have not been incarcerated remain unclear a priori. The net effects of incarceration on employment, then, can only be ascertained by a careful review of the empirical evidence.

EMPIRICAL EVIDENCE ON INCARCERATION AND EMPLOYMENT OUTCOMES

A set of relevant studies on incarceration and employment outcomes are summarized in table 8.2. Broadly, the studies fit into three categories: those focusing on the demand side of the labor market, or employer hiring behavior; those on the supply side, focusing on employment outcomes for individuals with and without criminal records; and those that use more aggregate state-level data to explore these effects. The studies focusing on the demand side of the market can be further subdivided into those using employer survey data versus those based on experimental "audits" of actual hiring behavior. The studies on the supply side of the market can also be subdivided into those primarily using survey data versus those using administrative data.

Demand-Side Studies

One subset of studies in this section (Holzer, Raphael, and Stoll 2004, 2006, 2007) use employer survey data to analyze the demand for ex-offender labor. These studies are based on a set of employer surveys first administered by Harry J. Holzer (1996) and later by Harry J. Holzer, Steven Raphael, and Michael Stoll (2007). The original survey was administered to about three thousand employers in four large metropolitan areas (Atlanta, Boston, Detroit, and Los Angeles) between 1992 and 1994 as part of the Multi-City Study of Urban Inequality (sponsored by the Ford and Russell Sage Foundations). The follow-up survey was administered to about six hundred employers in Los Angeles in 2001.

Both surveys were based on size-weighted samples of firms in which the distributions of firms across size categories were chosen to replicate the actual distribution of workers across firms in the labor force. The questions gauged employers' willingness to hire a variety of workers with various stigmas (such as having a criminal record, being a welfare recipient, or having an unstable work history) into the job filled by the last worker hired at the firm. With considerable data on the characteristics of the firms as well as the jobs they were filling, the authors were able to consider the effects of both on their stated willingness to hire offenders.

Table 8.2   *Empirical Studies of Incarceration Impacts on Subsequent Earnings: Less-Educated U.S. Prisoners*

Author	Data Source	Comparison Group?	Finding: Negative Impact?
Labor demand			
Holzer, Raphael and Stoll (2004, 2006, 2007)	Employer Surveys	Yes	Yes
Pager (2003)	Hiring Audits	Yes	Yes
Pager and Western (2003)	Hiring Audits	Yes	Yes
Labor supply			
Freeman (1992)	NLSY	Yes	Yes
Grogger (1992)	NLSY	Yes	Yes
Raphael (2007b)	NLSY	Yes	Yes
Western (2002)	NLSY	Yes	Yes
Cho and Lalonde (2005)	Administrative: IL	Yes	No
Grogger (1996)	Administrative: CA (1980s)	Yes	Yes
Kling (2006)	Administrative: FL (1990s)	Yes	No
Pettit and Lyons (2007)	Administrative: WA (1990s)	No	Yes[1]
Sabol (2007)	Administative: OH (1990s)	No	Yes[2]
Aggregate			
Holzer, Offner and Sorensen (2005)	CPS-ORG, 1979–2000	Yes	Yes

Source: Author's compilation.
[1] Negative impacts were observed on average earnings and on employment rates ten quarters after release.
[2] Negative impacts were observed on employment six quarters after release.

The survey also gauged whether or not employers perform criminal-background checks when filling these jobs. The follow-up survey asked about actual hiring of ex-offenders, as well as self-reported willingness to do so; it also asked a more detailed set of questions about employer perceptions of offenders and their willingness to hire them.

The audit studies of employers use a methodology that has been widely used to measure employer discrimination at the hiring stage (Fix and Struyk 1993; Neumark 1996). In this method, matched applicant pairs that varied on race-ethnicity or gender but had otherwise equivalent credentials are sent out to apply for jobs; the relative tendency of applicants to receive callbacks, interviews, or offers by race-ethnicity or gender is then used to measure discrimination against minorities or women whose credentials appear identical to those of white male applicants.

Devah Pager (2003) was the first to apply this methodology to the issue of offenders and nonoffenders applying for jobs. She sent out roughly 200 matched pairs of black applicants (that is, similar applicants where one purports to have a criminal record and one does not) and 150 pairs of white applicants to employers in Milwaukee. Devah Pager and Bruce Western (2005) then applied a similar methodology to a larger sample of employers in New York City, with Hispanic offenders and nonoffenders also included among the matched applicant groups.

There are some clear advantages and disadvantages to each type of employer study. The employer survey paints a broader portrait of how offenders are viewed in the labor market and how they are treated relative to other disadvantaged groups. The detailed characteristics of firms and jobs also enable us to disaggregate how offenders are treated across various sectors of the labor market. In contrast, the audit studies more successfully control for unobserved characteristics of applicants and can more clearly test causal claims about employer aversion to hiring offenders and minorities. They also measure actual employer behavior—not merely what is reported.

But, as with any experiment, there are questions about the extent to which the particular findings from these small samples of employers and applicants generalize to the broader population of offenders and the broader labor market, and whether any employer behavior measured really affects labor-market outcomes (for a range of critiques of audit studies, see Heckman 1998). The studies conducted by Pager, in particular, raise a number of questions, such as whether the employers audited and the characteristics of applicants with criminal records are truly representative of the relevant actors in the labor market, and whether self-reported criminal records by auditors have the same impacts on employment as real records that show up in the employer background checks that have become quite prevalent (Holzer, Raphael, and Stoll 2007).[7]

Yet, despite the relative strengths and weaknesses of each approach, the results are quite clear: both show strong employer aversion to hiring men with criminal records. In the employer surveys, roughly 40 percent of employers would "definitely" or "probably" hire applicants with criminal records, whereas much higher percentages (80 to 90 percent) would hire former welfare recipients, workers with little recent work experience or lengthy unemployment, and those with other stigmatizing characteristics. In the audit studies, the fraction of applicants receiving callbacks or job offers falls by roughly half among whites with criminal records, and it falls as much or more among blacks.[8]

In the employer survey data, there is wide variation across firms and jobs in willingness to hire offenders. Jobs requiring reading or writing, contact with customers, and handling cash are less open to offenders than jobs without these required tasks. More broadly, employers who need to "trust" the honesty and dependability of their applicants will likely be more averse to hiring from this population. Also, the nature of the offense and the recent experiences of the offenders affect employers' reported willingness to hire. For example, if employers are told that the offender has only one nonviolent drug offense and has participated successfully in recent work assignments, reported employer willingness to hire rises. Apparently, the kind of information provided to employers about the offenders can strongly affect their demand for these workers.

And, if applicants can self-select and apply for jobs predominantly with employers that are not averse to offenders, their employment prospects might not be greatly diminished by having criminal records. This would, of course, require them to have sufficient information about employer preferences and hiring practices, both across and within sectors, to make such choices. Even if they have such information, would there be sufficient numbers of jobs for all to be hired at wages comparable to what they would have earned without a criminal record? The fraction of jobs available to offenders with limited other barriers (such as very poor skills, little work experience, substance-abuse or mental-health problems, lack of labor-market information and contacts, or spatial disconnection from jobs) might be sufficient for most to gain some kind of employment with some moderate job-search effort. However the combination of additional barriers and their offender status might well limit job availability or earnings for this group.

There is also important variation in hiring behavior according to the race of the job applicant. The audit studies find that black offenders and nonoffenders both receive many fewer offers than their white counterparts in each category; indeed, white offenders generally receive as many offers as black nonoffenders. The authors of these studies interpret this as evidence that racial discrimination is at least as large a barrier to hiring as is offender status.

Holzer, Raphael, and Stoll (2006) also show that black nonoffenders appear to be hurt by a form of statistical discrimination in which employers might suspect that they really are offenders. Their data show that, among employers who prefer not to hire offenders, the use of criminal-background checks actually raises the likelihood that employers will hire black men, as they eliminate uncertainty about who really is or is not an offender (for other evidence, see Autor and Scarborough 2004).

This reinforces the notion that information is a critical part of the hiring process for minorities with or without criminal backgrounds and that labor-market intermediaries who help link offenders to jobs and provide appropriate information to employers can improve these employment prospects.

Overall, the two sets of studies leave little doubt that men with criminal records—and in particular black men—face much weaker demand for their labor than do comparable men without these records. They also imply that there is spillover of this stigma in the form of statistical discrimination against black male nonoffenders as well. Whether this limited demand translates into worse employment outcomes, or instead can be offset through vigorous job search or other third-party interventions (like job-placement assistance), remains unclear from these studies. To address these issues, we address studies using data from the supply side of the labor market.

Supply-Side Studies

This section focuses on studies that measure the impact of ex-offender status on subsequent employment and earnings in the United States, omitting studies that focus primarily on highly educated or white-collar offenders (for example, Lott 1992a, 1992b; Waldfogel 1994) and those that deal with offenders in other countries (for example, Nagin and Waldfogel 1995). Others, including Richard Freeman (1999) and Bruce Western, Jeffrey Kling, and David Weiman (2001), have also reviewed these studies, but they lack some of the most recent papers.

The supply-side studies listed in table 8.2 differ from one another along several critical dimensions. For instance, some are based on administrative data from state penal institutions that are merged with earnings data from state Unemployment Insurance (UI) earnings records; others are based on survey data with self-reported measures of incarceration, employment, and earnings. Of the studies using administrative data, some do not contain a comparison or control group, relying instead on comparisons of earnings pre- and postincarceration. The samples vary in terms of the ages of offenders considered, the time period and locations in which the studies are conducted, and the length of time before and after incarceration during which individuals are observed. The studies also use a variety of methods to deal with various likely statistical biases. These include unobserved heterogeneity (or omitted variables) across workers (which could lead researchers to overstate the negative impacts of a criminal record on earnings if those with records are weaker job applicants than apparently comparable workers without them) as well as measurement error in earnings or offender status (which might lead estimated impacts to be biased toward zero, especially if the measurement error in offender status is "classical").[9]

Survey data   In general, the studies using survey data (based almost completely on the National Longitudinal Survey of Youth [NLSY] 1979 cohort) uniformly find substantial negative effects of incarceration on earnings and employment of individuals. The first generation of these studies, notably those by Richard Freeman (1992) and Jeffrey Grogger (1992), find quite large negative effects of arrests or imprisonment on the likelihood of employment for young men with records.[10] These studies compare such men directly to comparable nonoffenders, controlling for observable characteristics such as education and previous work experience.

The second generation of NLSY studies, notably those by Bruce Western (2002, 2006) and Steven Raphael (2007b), follow offenders and nonoffenders over much longer time periods and use more sophisticated statistical techniques to deal with unobserved characteristics of offenders and nonoffenders as well as measurement error. For instance, both studies use individual-specific dummy variables within the longitudinal data to control for fixed effects; this eliminates the effects of permanent personal characteristics for which they cannot control. Both also construct alternative samples of nonoffenders who are at risk of offending, particularly because many were arrested or incarcerated after the periods during which they are used as comparison observations. The studies also attempt to deal with measurement error on self-reported incarceration by looking at whether any interview took place in prison to measure incarceration.[11]

All of these second-generation studies also find substantial negative effects of incarceration on reported employment and earnings. Western focuses primarily on wage levels and wage growth, finding both are significantly lower among those with criminal records than those without them, regardless of which specification he uses.[12] Raphael considers both the number of weeks worked and wage levels in his analysis, along with other measures of the "transition to adulthood" such as the tendency to live at home with parents or the tendency to marry. He finds all of these outcomes significantly lower among offenders than nonoffenders as well, though his estimated negative impact on wages is smaller and less significant in some specifications than those estimated by Western with similar data.[13]

Administrative data   The studies based on administrative data paint a somewhat more mixed picture of the impacts of incarceration on subsequent earnings. Of these studies, one by Grogger (1995) stands apart from the rest. He uses data from the adult criminal-justice system in California merged with UI earnings data from the period 1980 to 1984. As a comparison sample, he also uses a group that was incarcerated subsequently to 1984, as did Raphael (and, to an extent, Western). He estimates the impact of being arrested, convicted, or going to jail (or state prison) on both quarterly earnings and the likelihood of employment, with or without fixed effects, for up to six quarters after the original justice "event."

Generally, Grogger finds somewhat modest negative effects on employment and earnings of all of these outcomes, which are weaker after controlling for fixed effects, and which generally fade away for most outcomes. However, negative impacts persist for those who have been jailed. The negative impacts of state imprisonment are even larger but also less reliable, as more of these men might still be incarcerated six quarters after the original observation.[14] Even among those jailed, some might be incarcerated (either in jail or in state prison) for the entire period subsequent to incarceration (six quarters) that he studies.

The other studies using administrative data differ somewhat from those of Grogger. In particular, Jeffrey Kling (2006) uses data from California and Florida; Becky Pettit and Christopher Lyons (2007) use data from the state of Washington; William Sabol (2007) uses data from Ohio; and Rosa Cho and Robert Lalonde (2005) use data on women offenders from Illinois. In all of these cases, 1990s data from the state penal institutions are linked to UI earnings data.[15]

The primary purposes of these studies are not necessarily to focus on the impacts of incarceration on employment, though these impacts are often inferred from these studies. Kling's (2006) study focuses primarily on the impact of the duration of incarceration (rather than its incidence) on the subsequent earnings for those incarcerated. In other words, he analyzes the effects of shorter or longer spells of imprisonment within the sample of the incarcerated, rather than the effect of being incarcerated per se. Sabol's (2007) study focuses mostly on how local labor-market conditions affect labor-market reentry. Still, inferences about the effects of incarceration on earnings have been drawn from both studies. By focusing on women rather than men, the study by Cho and Lalonde is also somewhat different (and much less representative of the incarcerated population) than the rest.

These studies (excluding that conducted by Grogger) also have some common findings. For one thing, they all show very low levels of employment and earnings among ex-offenders, with only 30 to 40 percent generally showing any employment per quarter; quarterly earnings often average $2,000 among those working.[16] However, this seems to be true before as well as after incarceration for most individuals. Surprisingly, all three studies show significant increases in employment and earnings during the period immediately after incarceration relative to the period immediately before, though these gains then fade away over time.

After the initial gains fade, how do the offenders' employment and earnings compare to the period before incarceration? Here the studies present more mixed evidence. Pettit and Lyons (2007) find lower earnings (by 4 to 5 percent), and lower employment ten quarters after release. Sabol (2007) also finds that, six to seven quarters beyond release, employment rates are lower than before release. However he does not find this for earnings conditional on employment. Kling (2006) finds both employment and earnings to be comparable or slightly higher two to six years after release than before incarceration, regardless of the duration of incarceration.[17] Cho and Lalonde find that initially positive postprison effects (of about 5 percentage points in quarterly employment) fade by the third full quarter after release.

The initial rise in employment and earnings after release does not appear in the studies using the NLSY, perhaps because these studies focus mostly on current hourly wages or weeks worked in the prior year; it also did not appear in Grogger's study (1995) using administrative data. Maybe the discrepancies across these studies represents a timing issue—more stringent postrelease supervision of parolees and stricter enforcement of child-support orders in the 1990s leads to a temporary spurt of formal employment activity that did not occur earlier.[18]

A number of problems plague all of the studies based on administrative data, at least insofar as we try to infer from them the impacts of incarceration on employment and earnings. For one thing, the UI records only capture earnings in formal jobs, especially those covered by UI in any state. That would automatically exclude public-sector jobs, any employment that occurs in another state, any self-employment, and, most importantly, any casual and informal work for cash. In many contexts, these limitations would not be terribly severe; but part-time and casual employment likely characterize much work among offenders and ex-offenders, both pre- and postincarceration. Indeed, the very low quarterly employment rates measured here are dramatically lower than those found in any of the NLSY studies or any other surveys of those incarcerated.[19] The self-reported earnings in the NLSY might also be measured with some error, though any bias toward underreporting is less clear in those data. Indeed, studies that compare earnings measures among the disadvantaged using survey versus administrative data generally (though not always) find lower earnings among the latter (Kornfeld and Bloom 1999; Hotz and Scholz 2001; and Piliavin, Dworsky, and Courtney 2004).[20]

The exact directions of any resulting biases in estimated effects of incarceration from these different data sources also remain somewhat unclear. If measurement error in the survey data are more random than in the administrative data, that might create some greater inefficiency in estimates using the former (where earnings are the dependent variable) but no clear bias. For the administrative data, any biases in estimates of incarceration on earnings or employment would depend on whether the incidence of unreported employment is greater before or after incarceration. But the tendency to be casually employed is probably greater for younger than older workers, with the latter more represented in preincarceration samples. Furthermore, the tendency to underreport such work is probably somewhat lower immediately after incarceration, when attempts to meet parole and child-support obligations through formal employment are likely to be most serious; if this is the case, the initial surge in employment right after incarceration might well be overstated relative to what existed before incarceration (or somewhat later), in which case the estimated impact of incarceration on these subsequent outcomes will be upwardly biased.

Another problem arises from the absence of a clear control or comparison group of nonoffenders in at least some of these studies. Simple pre-post incarceration comparisons of employment and earnings outcomes may tell us little about the counterfactual situation that would have existed in the absence of incarceration. Assuming at least some growth in earnings due to labor-market experience would have occurred without incarceration, the simple pre-post test likely biases downwards any measured loss of earnings after incarceration.

To deal with this problem, Cho and Lalonde (2005) as well as Kling (2006) use preincarceration earnings of those ultimately incarcerated as a comparison group (as did Grogger 1996, Raphael 2007b, and Western 2002).[21] In both of these cases, we find little evidence of strong earnings growth before incarceration; if anything, we find some strong downward trends in the year or two before incarceration. But any such study must be careful to make sure that individuals have not been incarcerated at all in the period before administrative data on incarceration are available. Though Cho and Lalonde (2005) are careful to focus on first-time experiences of imprisonment, they note that women might have been incarcerated in local jails in the year or two preceding their first-time imprisonment in a state facility, thus reducing their measured earnings before incarceration.

Furthermore, these studies sometimes observe these individuals for fairly short time periods before incarceration; for instance, Kling's (2006) data from Florida provide just four quarters of preincarceration employment data. They may not capture offenders early in the life cycle when earnings growth is likely greatest. Indeed, Cho and Lalonde (2005) focus on women who are over thirty years old (on average) at the time of first incarceration—a sample whose employment experiences may not be representative of the earnings potential of younger (and mostly male) offenders in the absence of incarceration.

For the comparison groups to be valid, they should involve similar age groups and be observed in the same time periods (or at least under similar labor-market conditions) as those incarcerated earlier. These conditions are not always met in the administrative data studies. For instance, the data used by Cho and Lalonde (2005) compare preincarceration employment for women right before or during the implementation of welfare reform (that is, between 1995 and 1997) to postincarceration employment in the period right afterward (between 1998 and 2000), though the former might well be downward biased compared to the latter.

While not perfect, the NLSY data on comparison groups do not so clearly suffer from these biases.[22] Western's data (2002) clearly show earnings growth before incarceration among young men in the NLSY (after controlling for year effects). Other studies of low earners (Gladden and Taber 2000) show earnings growth among the least educated workers that is at least comparable to that of the more educated per unit of actual labor-market experience.

These considerations suggest that the studies based on administrative data might well understate the negative impacts of incarceration on subsequent earnings or employment. It is quite noteworthy that at least some of these studies (except for those conducted by Cho and Lalonde [2005] and Kling [2006]) still find such effects at some point after release from prison.

Studies Using Aggregate Data

At least one other problem arises in all of the supply-side studies. The demand-side studies (especially those by Holzer, Raphael, and Stoll 2004, 2006, 2007) clearly suggest that, at least among young black men, the stigma associated with previous incarceration spills over onto those not incarcerated because of statistical discrimination when offender status is uncertain. This implies yet more support that measured gaps between the incarcerated and nonincarcerated may be biased downwards and that incarceration might reduce employment and earnings among young unskilled men, and especially black men.

This notion is tested in a study by Harry J. Holzer, Paul Offner, and Elaine Sorensen (2005). Pooling data from the Outgoing Rotation Groups of the Current Population Surveys (CPS-ORG) between 1979 and 2000, they analyze the effects of incarceration rates of black men (as well as child-support enforcement activities) by state and year on the employment and labor-force activity of all young black men (ages sixteen to twenty-four and twenty-five to thirty-four) with high-school education or less. The incarceration rates are lagged by three years to estimate the flows of offenders back into the noninstitutional population.[23] Equations

for employment and labor-force participation of individuals were estimated as functions of these state-level variables as well as controls for
personal characteristics (such as age and education); metropolitan-area
labor-force characteristics (such as local unemployment rates, industrial
composition of employment, and percent female or Hispanic in the local
workforce); and year and state dummies.

The results clearly showed that previous incarceration was associated
with large declines in employment and labor-force participation among
young black men. Indeed, for every percentage point rise in the overall
incarceration rate of black men, employment and labor-force participation in the noninstitutional population declined by a percentage point or
more.[24] Of course, it is possible that these results pick up some endogeneity of incarceration with respect to employment rates or some unobserved
state-level characteristics negatively correlated with employment and
positively with incarceration. But the presence of state and time fixed effects and substantial controls for local labor markets render this interpretation somewhat unlikely. Estimates using difference-in-difference (DD)
techniques—in which any effects found for whites are attributed to omitted variables, and only the differences between blacks and whites are considered true causal effects—are similar to those generated by ordinary
least squares (OLS) regressions. A variety of Hausman tests are also consistent with the notion that these results capture real causal effects of previous incarceration on employment.[25]

Directions and Magnitudes of Impacts

The existing literature indicates that the high rates of imprisonment in the
United States reduce employment opportunities (that is, employer demand for labor) for those who have been incarcerated and even for some
of those who have not been. Whether these reduced opportunities actually translate into reduced employment and earnings outcomes is less
clear, though the preponderance of the evidence considered suggests that
it does. Studies using either self-reported survey data or more aggregated
state-level findings from the CPS clearly imply reduced employment or
earnings, and at least some (though not all) of the studies using administrative data on imprisonment and earnings suggest this as well. Other
studies of more highly educated prisoners in the United States (Lott
1992a; Waldfogel 1994) also have similar findings.

How large are these negative effects? Holzer, Offner, and Sorensen
(2005) find that each additional percentage point of imprisonment of
black men overall is associated with a decline in employment or labor-
force participation of 1 to 1.5 percentage points among younger black
men.[26] Since each percentage point of current incarceration of black men

translates into 5 to 6 percentage points of previous incarceration for young black men, the estimates imply that each additional percentage point of previous offender status reduces employment by about 0.17 to 0.30 percentage points for black men, and the overall levels of earlier incarceration inferred for this population reduce employment activity by 4 to 9 percentage points.[27] These estimates are roughly consistent with those by Western (2002), Raphael (2007b), and Freeman (1992) using data from the NLSY. They also imply that the increases in incarceration since 1980 have reduced young black male labor-force activity by 3 to 5 percentage points.

Whether these effects are as large for white and Latino men (or for women) is not as clear, though most studies show effects for these groups as large or larger than those for black men. Any effects on wages—which, according to Raphael (2007b) and Western (2002), are reduced by 3 to 16 percent for this population—further add to the collateral costs of incarceration.

CONCLUSION

This chapter reviews the empirical evidence on one of the primary collateral consequences of mass imprisonment: the effects of incarceration on subsequent employment and earnings. At least theoretically, these impacts could be positive or negative. By deterring crime and even by spurring some additional educational attainment among prisoners, it is possible that incarceration could have positive effects. But, by reducing work experience, labor-market contacts, and incentives to work (especially among those with child-support arrearages), incarceration might well have negative effects on labor-force activity. The likely negative effects of incarceration on employer demand compound this likelihood, though it is unclear whether or not these effects are large enough to actually translate into lost earnings.

Our review of the empirical evidence suggests that, despite the mixed nature of the findings reviewed, the net effects of incarceration on employment and earnings are likely negative. Studies of employer behavior—either from general surveys or from audits with matched pairs of applicants with and without criminal records—all strongly show that a criminal record reduces labor demand. Among less-educated black men, the data suggest that the effects of incarceration also spill over onto the nonincarcerated, reducing their job opportunities as well.

Studies of individual workers using survey data (primarily from the NLSY) imply reduced earnings and employment for those who have been incarcerated. The most recent of these studies use more sophisticated statistical techniques to control for omitted variables and for measurement error in incarceration, and they still generate these findings. Studies using micro-level administrative data are more mixed in terms of results. However, these studies are less useful for inferring the impacts of incarceration, mostly because they miss so many informal jobs (and, more generally, even formal jobs not covered by Unemployment Insurance). Also, they often lack appropriate comparison groups with which to infer the counterfactual experiences of nonincarceration for those who have been jailed. Still, at least some of these studies find negative effects of incarceration on postrelease employment or earnings relative to their prerelease level. More aggregated data at the state level show that incarceration reduces subsequent employment among young black men broadly, including those who have not been incarcerated themselves. This type of study avoids the bias towards zero in cross-sectional estimates based on individual comparisons; this is because of the likely spillovers of employer attitudes towards the incarcerated onto the nonincarcerated.

Of course, the effects of collateral costs in employment go beyond the formerly incarcerated individuals themselves. For instance, reduced employment and earnings of fathers certainly reduce the family incomes of their children and may have important intergenerational effects well beyond those measured here. The lost employment in neighborhoods and communities likely weakens employment networks and, more broadly, norms about work that suggest wider negative impacts.

Further research is clearly needed to quantify these many costs and to compare them with the crime-reduction benefits associated with incarceration. But the estimates described here suggest that current levels of incarceration have substantial costs that policymakers should try to limit. One way or doing so might be to reduce rates of incarceration if we judge that these currently go beyond some social optimum (as John Donahue suggests in chapter 9 of this volume).

Alternatively, we might try to reduce the negative effects on employment associated with incarceration. Programs to support prisoner reentry, both before and especially after release, seek to do so. Virtually all of these programs rely on labor-market intermediaries to improve the access of offenders to employers, to improve offenders' basic skills and work readiness, and to provide employers with more accurate information about offenders' recent work-related activities. Some, like the Center for Employment Opportunities (CEO) in New York also provide the ex-offenders with paid transitional jobs for several months (MDRC 2006). While our knowledge of the cost-effectiveness of such programs remains somewhat limited (Bushway 2003), we should continue to explore and rigorously evaluate the various programs that exist.

Other state and federal policies might also be useful in this regard. For instance, states can be encouraged to reconsider the many barriers that limit the access of ex-offenders to employment or occupational licensing in a variety of sectors. Also, state-level child-support policies might also be reconsidered—particularly in regard to readjusting or even forgiving arrearages for men meeting their current orders, and in regard to "passing through" collected payments to families that have been on public assistance. An extension of the EITC to low-income men and women without custody of children would likely help offset at least some of the negative incentive effects of incarceration, though its impacts would likely depend on exactly how such a policy is administered.[28]

Much further research and evaluation thus remains to be done. But the large employment costs associated with current levels of incarceration need to be acknowledged and addressed through some remedial policy and programmatic activity.

NOTES

1. Jens Ludwig (U.S. Congress 2006) argued in a U.S. Senate testimony that the aggregate costs of crime and incarceration to the United States might be as high as $2 trillion per year, and a large fraction of this cost appears to be associated with repeat offenders.

2. The most widely accepted economic models of crime (Becker 1968; Freeman 1999) suggest that individuals choose between legal and illegal employment, depending on the relative costs and returns associated with each type of activity. Since incarceration raises the costs of participating in crime, it should reduce the percentage of individuals making this choice and thereby raise the percentage choosing legitimate work. The notion that there is a trade-off between employment and crime is quite clearly supported by the evidence, as Richard Freeman (1999) shows. Even among those who engage in crime and ultimately become incarcerated, it is possible that the perceived risks of incarceration reduce the frequency or severity of the crimes they commit.

3. The importance of informal networks in generating employment has long been emphasized by both economists and sociologists (Rees 1966; Granovetter 1974). Harry J. Holzer (1987) emphasized the particular importance of these weakened informal networks for the employment opportunities of young black men. The empirical evidence on the role of these networks more broadly is summarized by Yannis Ioannides and Linda Datcher Loury (2004).

4. The Personal Responsibility and Work Opportunity Act (PRWOA) of 1996, which constituted the federal government's effort to reform welfare, contained a number of child-support provisions that strengthened enforcement but also increased the discretion of states over whether or not to "pass through" payments to families on public assistance (Garfinkel 2001). Recent evaluation evidence of a child-support pilot project in Wisconsin also indicates that "pass through" affects the tendency of noncustodial fathers to pay support (Cancian, Meyer, and Roff 2006).

5. For example, the high tax rates on arrears might be foregone if poor noncus-

todial fathers agree to pay their full current orders and perhaps small percentages each year on what they owe from the past.

6. In other contexts, such discrimination might also be called racial profiling. For further evidence on statistical discrimination or racial profiling in the criminal-justice system, see work by Ambrose Leung and colleagues (2004) and Billy Close and Patrick Mason (2002).

7. For instance, the employers in Devah Pager's study are primarily from help-wanted ads in newspapers, which draw more from the middle than the bottom of the skill distribution of workers and include more sales jobs than do other recruitment methods (Holzer 1996). Her applicants all report high-school diplomas and significant work experience, including some in a managerial capacity, which goes beyond what most real ex-offenders can report. "Offenders" in her study also report just one nonviolent felony drug offense.

    Offender status might be either more or less harmful to job applicants in a fuller sample of employers or with a sample of workers whose other characteristics more closely approximate those of actual offenders. If employers take self-reported criminal history less seriously than that generated by background checks (because of the incentive of applicants with records to hide their history in the former), the negative effects of these self-reports might be biased downwards; whether this is more true for white or minority applicants is also unclear.

8. For instance, in Milwaukee the presence of a criminal record reduced the fraction of whites receiving callbacks from 34 to 17 percent, while the comparable fractions for blacks were 14 and 5 percent. In New York, the comparable fractions for whites are 31 and 17 percent.

9. "Classical," or purely random, measurement error in a dependent variable generates inefficient but unbiased estimates, while it leads to biases towards zero in estimated coefficients in an independent variable. If the measurement error in either variable is correlated with other observational characteristics, it might generate biased estimates (though the directions of the biases are not clear a priori). Self-reported offender status is well known to be frequently understated, especially among minorities (Hindelang, Hirschi, and Weis 1981).

10. Freeman (1992) finds that having been in prison reduces subsequent employment activity by 15 to 30 percentage points (or by roughly 20 to 40 percent). Grogger estimates that previous arrests account for roughly one-third of the black-white employment gap among youth in the NLSY and significantly more than that in a sample of California arrestees also analyzed in the study.

11. By relying only on the location at the time of the interview to determine incarceration, they still might have missed shorter episodes of incarceration.

12. Western (2002) finds that his estimates of whether offenders experience any wage growth after incarceration are very sensitive to his inclusion of year dummies. But the gap in rates of wage growth between offenders and nonoffenders is not sensitive to specification. Overall, he finds wage levels of offenders reduced by at least 16 percent, and wage growth reduced by approximately half of a percentage point per year. However, the estimated impacts for blacks are smaller than for whites.

13. Raphael estimates that weeks worked are reduced by at least six weeks per year, or about 15 percent, and by as much as ten weeks (or 25 percent) in some specifications. His findings on wages are only weaker than Western's when he uses both fixed effects and a restricted sample of nonoffenders who themselves ultimately become incarcerated. In this case, he finds an average reduction in wages of only 3 percent instead of 15 percent or more. Raphael speculates that his comparison sample is stricter than that of Western, who uses those at risk of incarceration (including those who report any contact with the criminal-justice system) rather than those actually incarcerated. It is also possible that the combination of fixed effects and measurement error leads to downward biased estimates in both studies (Freeman 1984).

14. Grogger finds that employment rates per quarter for those jailed are reduced by roughly 4 percentage points, or about 8 percent overall, as much as six quarters after the initial period of incarceration. Earnings are reduced by $170 per quarter (in 1980 dollars), or by about 14 percent.

15. Needels (1996) also conducted a study on the impacts of the duration of incarceration on a much smaller sample of prisoners released in Georgia.

16. Among the female offenders studied by Cho and Lalonde, employment and earnings are even lower. Average employment rates are about 25 percent per quarter before incarceration, while mean and median earnings are about $1,800 and $1,200 per quarter respectively. Most of these women have two to three children and are single mothers.

17. Kling analyzes data for twenty-eight quarters (or seven years) after the spells of incarceration begin, and he considers men with anywhere from one to four years of incarceration. The maximum spell of incarceration he considers is fifty-three months long, which leaves about thirty months of postincarceration observations for these individuals and much more for those incarcerated for shorter spells.

18. Pettit and Lyons (2007) speculate that special employment efforts undertaken for those released in the state of Washington might generate these results, but it is less clear that these could also account for the results observed by Kling (2006) and Sabol (2007) in Florida and Ohio respectively.

19. Surveys of offenders often indicate that up to two-thirds of respondents report some sort of employment activity at the time of arrest (Travis 2004). Young men in the NLSY usually report employment rates of about 60 percent, or about thirty weeks worked per year, after incarceration (Freeman 1992; Raphael 2007b).

20. See Kornfeld and Bloom (1999), Hotz and Scholz (2001), and Piliavin et al. (2004). These studies tend to compare administrative and survey reports of earnings for workers in welfare or job training programs, mostly for the purposes of evaluating program impacts; none has focused on the incarcerated or on low-income young men more broadly.

21. Kling (2006) uses a difference-in-difference (DD) strategy to estimate the impact of imprisonment duration on earnings, comparing those whose prison spells occur before employment relative to those whose spells occur afterwards. But this is not the same as comparing earnings or employment levels overall for those who are incarcerated earlier versus later. Kling also uses an

instrumental variables (IV) strategy here, using the identity of judges who tend to impose different sentence lengths as the instrument; however, these estimates tell us nothing about the effect of incarceration incidence.

22. For instance, the NLSY data begin observing most people in their teens, capturing critical periods of early labor-market activity; they also record all spells of incarceration (except for very short ones) that occur from that point on.

23. The average length of a spell of incarceration for those released in the 1990s was roughly three years, but the estimated results were not very sensitive to the length of this lag. It is also important to remember that while the individuals are actually incarcerated they do not show up in the CPS data on those not institutionalized. Even after release, those incarcerated likely contribute to the well-known undercount of black men in CPS data (Baker and Schmitt 2006). This implies again that estimated effects of previous incarceration on employment using these data might be downwardly biased.

24. Estimated impacts of child-support enforcement on employment for this group were more mixed, though the impacts were more clearly negative for men ages twenty-five to thirty-four. Any impacts of child-support enforcement on the outcomes of men in states with high levels of incarceration are likely captured by those variables.

25. The Hausman tests use two instrumental variables: one was created by Levitt (1996) to capture prison overcrowding litigation as an exogenous determinant of incarceration, and the other was generated by Reitz (2004) to capture state-level sentencing laws. For more detail on Hausman tests, see work by Wooldridge (2005).

26. This represents the range of estimates generated by DD techniques. Those using OLS were a bit smaller for employment and comparable for labor-force participation.

27. Overall incarceration rates for black men were roughly 5 percent in 2000, while the percentages of young black men with criminal records were estimated to be 25 to 30 percent by Raphael (2007b), Western (2002), Bonczar (2003), and others. Thus, the 1 to 1.5 percentage point drop translates into a range of 0.17 to 0.30 percentage points of lost employment for those with records. As 25 to 30 percent of young black men have these records, this implies reduced employment activity of 4 to 9 percentage points.

28. For two possible proposals, see work by Berlin (2007) and Edelman, Holzer, and Offner (2006). These proposals are reviewed and analyzed by Raphael (2007a).

REFERENCES

Autor, David, and David Scarborough. 2004. "Will Job Testing Harm Minority Workers?" NBER working paper 10763. Cambridge, Mass: National Bureau of Economic Research.

Baker, Dean, and John Schmitt. 2006. "The Impact of Undercounting in the Current Population Survey." Working paper. Washington, D.C.: Center for Economic Policy Research.

Becker, Gary. 1968. "Crime and Punishment: An Economic Approach." *Journal of Political Economy* 76(2): 169–217.

———. 1975. *The Economics of Discrimination*. 2nd ed. Chicago: University of Chicago Press.

Berlin, Gordon. 2007. "Rewarding the Work of Individuals: A Counterintuitive Approach to Reducing Poverty and Strengthening Families." *The Future of Children* 17(2): 17–42.

Bonczar, Thomas. 2003. *Prevalence of Imprisonment in the U.S. Population, 1974–2001*. Washington, D.C.: Bureau of Justice Statistics.

Burtless, Gary. 1985. "Are Targeted Wage Subsidies Harmful? Evidence from a Wage Voucher Experiment." *Industrial and Labor Relations Review* 39(1): 105–14.

Bushway, Shawn. 2003. "Reentry and Prison Work Programs." Paper presented at the Urban Institute Reentry Roundtable, New York University. New York City (May 21, 2003).

Cancian, Maria, Daniel Meyer, and Jen Roff. 2006."The Effect of Child Support Pass-Through and Disregard Policies." Unpublished paper, Madison, Wisc.: Institute for Research on Poverty.

Cho, Rosa, and Robert Lalonde. 2005. "The Impact of Incarceration in State Prison on the Employment Prospects of Women." IZA discussion paper 1792. Bonn, Germany: IZA.

Close, Billy, and Patrick Mason. 2002. *Traffic Stop Data Analysis: The Florida Highway Patrol and Racial Differences in Traffic Stops and Driver Treatment*. Florida Department of Transportation.

Edelman, Peter, Harry J. Holzer, and Paul Offner. 2006. *Reconnecting Disadvantaged Young Men*. Washington, D.C.: Urban Institute Press.

Ehrenberg, Ronald, and Robert Smith. 2000. *Modern Labor Economics*. New York: Addison Wesley and Longman.

Fix, Michael, and Raymond Struyk. 1993. *Clear and Convincing Evidence*. Washington, D.C.: Urban Institute Press.

Freeman, Richard. 1984. "Longitudinal Analyses of Trade Unionism." *Journal of Labor Economics* 2(1): 1–18.

———. 1992. "Crime and the Employment of Disadvantaged Youths." In *Urban Labor Markets and Job Opportunity*, edited by George Peterson and Wayne Vroman. Washington, D.C.: Urban Institute Press.

———. 1999. "The Economics of Crime." In Vol. 3 of *The Handbook of Labor Economics*, edited by Orley Ashenfelter and David Card. Amsterdam: North Holland.

Garfinkel, Irwin. 2001. "Child Support in the New World of Welfare." In *The New World of Welfare*, edited by Rebecca M. Blank and Ron Haskins. Washington, D.C.: Brookings Institution.

Gladden, Tricia, and Christopher Taber. 2000. In *Finding Jobs: Work and Welfare Reform*, edited by David Card and Rebecca M. Blank. New York: Russell Sage Foundation.

Granovetter, Mark. 1974. *Getting a Job: A Study of Careers and Contacts*. Cambridge, Mass.: Harvard University Press.

Grogger, Jeffrey. 1992. "Arrests, Persistent Youth Joblessness, and Black/White Employment Differences." *Review of Economics and Statistics* 74(1): 100–06.

————. 1995. "The Effects of Arrests on the Employment and Earnings of Young Men." *Quarterly Journal of Economics* 110(1): 51–72.

————. 1998. "Market Wages and Youth Crime." *Journal of Labor Economics* 16(4): 756–91.

Heckman, James. 1998. "Detecting Discrimination." *Journal of Economic Perspectives* 12(2): 101–16.

Hindelang, Michael, Travis Hirschi, and Joseph Weis. 1981. *Measuring Delinquency*. Beverly Hills, Calif.: Sage.

Holzer, Harry J. 1996. *What Employers Want: Job Prospects for Less-Educated Workers*. New York: Russell Sage Foundation.

————. 2001. "Racial Differences in Labor Market Outcomes Among Men." In *America Becoming: Racial Trends and their Consequences*, edited by Neil Smelser, William Julius Wilson, and FaithMitchell. Washington, D.C.: National Academy Press.

————.1987. "Informal Job Search and Black Youth Unemployment." *American Economic Review* 77(2): 446–52.

Holzer, Harry J., Paul Offner, and Elaine Sorensen. 2005. "Declining Employment among Young Black Men: The Role of Incarceration and Child Support." *Journal of Policy Analysis and Management* 24(2): 329–50.

Holzer, Harry J., Steven Raphael, and Michael Stoll. 2004. "Will Employers Hire Former Offenders? Employer Preference, Background Checks and their Determinants." In *Imprisoning America: The Social Effects of Mass Incarceration*, edited by Mary Pattillo, David Weiman, and Bruce Western. New York: Russell Sage Foundation.

————. 2006. "Perceived Criminality, Criminal Background Checks and the Racial Hiring Practices of Employers." *Journal of Law and Economics* 49(4): 451–80.

————. 2007. "The Effect of an Applicant's Criminal History on Employer Hiring Decisions and Screening Practices: New Evidence from Los Angeles." In *Barriers to Reentry? The Labor Market for Released Prisoners in Post-Industrial America*, edited by Shawn Bushway, Michael Stoll and David Weiman. New York: Russell Sage Foundation.

Hotz, V. Joseph, and J. Karl Scholz. 2001. "Measuring Employment and Income for Low-Income Populations with Administrative and Survey Data." In *Studies of Welfare Populations: Data Collection and Research Issues*, edited by the National Research Council. Washington, D.C.: National Academy of Sciences.

Ioannides, Yannis, and Linda Datcher Loury. 2004. *Journal of Economic Literature*. 42(4): 1056–93.

Juhn, Chinhui, Kevin Murphy, and Robert Topel. 1991. "Why Has the Natural Rate of Unemployment Increased Over Time?" *Brookings Papers on Economic Activity* 2: 75–142.

Katz, Lawrence. 1998. "Wage Subsidies for the Disadvantaged." In *Generating Jobs*, edited by Richard Freeman and Peter Gottschalk. New York: Russell Sage Foundation.

Kling, Jeffrey. 2006. "Incarceration Length, Employment and Earnings." *American Economic Review* 96(3): 863–76.

Kornfeld, Robert, and Howard Bloom. 1999. "Measuring Program Impacts on

Employment and Earnings: Do UI Wage Reports from Employers Agree with Surveys from Individuals?" *Journal of Labor Economics* 17(1): 168–97.

Legal Action Center. 2004. *After Prison: Roadblocks to Reentry*. New York City: Legal Action Center.

Leung, Ambrose, Frances Woolley, Richard Tremblay, and Frank Vitaro. 2005. "Who Gets Caught? Statistical Discrimination in Law Enforcement." *Journal of Socio-Economics* 34(3): 289–309.

Levitt, Steven. 1996. "The Effect of Prison Population Size on Crime Rates: Evidence from Overcrowding Litigation." *Quarterly Journal of Economics* 111(2): 319–52.

Lott, John. 1992a. "An Attempt at Measuring the Total Monetary Penalty from Drug Convictions: The Importance of an Individual's Reputation." *Journal of Legal Studies* 21(1): 159–87.

———. 1992b. "Do We Punish High Income Criminals Too Heavily?" *Economic Inquiry* 30(4): 583–608.

MDRC. 2006. *The Power of Work: The Center for Employment Opportunity Comprehensive Prisoner Reentry Program*. New York: MDRC.

Mincy, Ronald, and Elaine Sorensen. 1998. "Deadbeats or Turnips in Child Support Reform." *Journal of Policy Analysis and Management* 17(1): 44–51.

Nagin, Daniel, and Joel Waldfogel. 1995. "The Effects of Criminality and Convictions on the Labor Market Status of Young British Offenders." *International Review of Law and Economics* 15: 109–26.

Needels, Karen. 1996. "Go Directly to Jail and Do Not Collect? A Long-Term Study of Recidivism, Employment and Earnings Patters among Prison Releases." *Journal of Research in Crime and Delinquency* 33: 471–96.

Neumark, David. 1996. "Sex Discrimination in Restaurant Hiring: An Audit Study." *Quarterly Journal of Economics* 111(3): 915–42.

Pager, Devah. 2003. "The Mark of a Criminal Record." *American Journal of Sociology* 108(5): 937–75.

Pager, Devah, and Bruce Western. 2005. "Discrimination in Low-Wage Labor Markets: Evidence from an Experimental Audit Study in New York City." Paper presented at the Population Association of America Meetings. Philadelphia, PA.

Pettit, Becky, and Christopher Lyons. 2007. "Status and the Stigma of Incarceration: The Labor Market Effects of Incarceration by Race, Class and Criminal Involvement." In *Barriers to Reentry? The Labor Market for Released Prisoners in Post-Industrial America*, edited by Shawn Bushway, Michael Stoll, and David Weiman. New York: Russell Sage Foundation.

Piliavin, Irving, Amy Dworsky, and Mark Courtney. 2004. "Measuring Employment and Earnings Among Low-Income Populations: Survey or Administrative Data?" Unpublished paper, Madison, Wisc.: University of Wisconsin.

Pirog, Maureen, M. Klotz, and K. Byers. 1998. "Interstate Comparisons of Child Support Orders Using State Guidelines." *Family Relations* 47(3): 289–95.

Primus, Wendell. 2002. "Improving Public Policies in Order to Increase the Income and Employment of Low-Income Non-Custodial Fathers." Washington, D.C.: Center on Budget and Policy Priorities.

Raphael, Steven. 2007a. "Boosting the Earnings and Employment of Low-Skilled Workers in the United States: Making Work Pay and Removing Barriers to Employment and Social Mobility." Unpublished paper. Berkeley, Calif.: University of California, Berkeley.

———. 2007b. "Early Incarceration Spells and the Transition to Adulthood." In *The Price of Independence*, edited by Sheldon Danziger, Frank Furstenberg, and Cecelia Rouse. New York: Russell Sage Foundation.

Raphael, Steven, and David Weiman. 2007. "The Impact of Local Labor Market Conditions on the Likelihood that Parolees are Returned to Custody." In *Barriers to Reentry? The Labor Market for Released Prisoners in Post-Industrial America*, edited by Shawn Bushway, Michael Stoll, and David Weiman. New York: Russell Sage Foundation.

Rees, Albert. 1966. "Information Networks in Labor Markets." *American Economic Review* 56(2): 559–66.

Reitz, Kevin. 2004. "Questioning the Conventional Wisdom of Parole Release Authority." In *The Future of Imprisonment in the 21st Century*, edited by Michael Tonry. London: Oxford University Press.

Sabol, William. 2007. "Local Labor Market Conditions and Post-Prison Employment Experience of Offenders Released from Ohio Prisons." In *Barriers to Reentry? The Labor Market for Released Prisoners in Post-Industrial America*, edited by Shawn Bushway, Michael Stoll, and David Weiman. New York: Russell Sage Foundation.

Sampson, Robert, and John Laub. 1993. *Crime in the Making: Pathways and Turning Points in Life*. Cambridge, Mass.: Harvard University Press.

Travis, Jeremy. 2004. *But They All Come Back*. Washington, D.C.: Urban Institute Press.

Tyler, John, and Jeffrey Kling. 2007. "Prison-Based Education and Reentry into the Mainstream Labor Market." In *Barriers to Reentry? The Labor Market for Released Prisoners in Post-Industrial America*, edited by Shawn Bushway, Michael Stoll, and David Weiman. New York: Russell Sage Foundation.

U.S. Congress. Senate. Committee on the Judiciary. 2006. 109th Congress, Session II. September 19, 2006.

Waldfogel, Joel. 1994. "The Effect of Criminal Conviction on Income and the Trust "Reposed in the Workmen." *Journal of Human Resources* 29(1): 62–81.

Western, Bruce. 2002. "The Impact of Incarceration on Wage Mobility and Inequality." *American Sociological Review* 67(2): 526–46.

Western, Bruce. 2006. *Punishment and Inequality in America*. New York: Russell Sage Foundation.

Western, Bruce, Jeffrey Kling, and David Weiman. 2001. "The Labor Market Consequences of Incarceration." *Crime and Delinquency* 47: 410–27.

Wilson, William J. 1996. *When Work Disappears*. New York: Alfred Knopf.

Wooldridge, Jeffrey. 2005. *Introductory Econometrics: A Modern Approach*. New York: South Western.

PART III

Are We at
a Socially
Optimal
Level of
Imprisonment?

John J. Donohue III

9 | Assessing the Relative Benefits of Incarceration: Overall Changes and the Benefits on the Margin

In June 1956 President Dwight Eisenhower signed a bill launching the interstate highway system in the United States. Over the next twenty years, close to 40,000 miles of superhighways were built across America. As the era of massive federal highway building came to an end in the mid-1970s, it was replaced by the next massive public-works project in America: the boom in prison construction. Just as scholars have debated the extent and value of the stimulus to economic growth that followed from the $114 billion spent on road construction, there has been spirited debate over the value of the comparable expenditure devoted to building the vast array of roughly one-thousand-person prisons and other facilities that now warehouse over 2.1 million Americans in federal prisons, state prisons, and local jails (Harrison and Beck 2005). After three decades of prison expansion, approximately 700 out of 100,000 Americans are behind bars; over the period from 1933 and 1973, this figure oscillated between approximately 100 and 120 per 100,000.[1] Except for Russia, which is only somewhat behind the United States, no other country in Europe or Asia incarcerates its citizens at even half the rate of the United States.[2] Figure 9.1 illustrates the steady growth in the U.S. incarceration rate from the mid-1970s until the leveling off at the end of the twentieth century.

THE DEBATE OVER THE INCARCERATION BOOM

The debate over the value, impact, and wisdom of the American experiment in mass incarceration has been highly polarized: one camp strongly opposes the incarceration increase, while the other contends that, if anything, the country would benefit by even further growth in the prison

Figure 9.1   *National Incarceration Rates, 1977 to 2004*

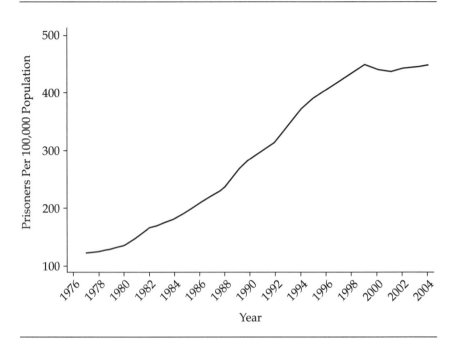

Source: Bureau of Justice Statistics (2005).
Note: This graph only includes state prisoners (excluding local jail inmates and federal prisoners).

population (Donohue 2007; Zimring and Hawkins 1988; DiIulio 1996). Some ardent supporters of incarceration rely on economist Gary Becker's (1968) work on the economics of crime to justify their claims. In Becker's model, increases in the cost of criminal activity will lead a subset of potential criminals—who he argues will rationally weigh the costs and the benefits of potential criminal acts—to choose not to commit crimes. Though Becker did not favor mass incarceration as the optimal strategy for deterring crime, some have used his theory to support increased incarceration, and in many states this approach has become the centerpiece of their anticrime policies. Given the dramatic decline in crime over the last decade and a half, supporters of mass incarceration contend that the high cost of incarceration has been well worth the price.

Critics of the rise in incarceration disagree: they contend that incarceration's net effect is not crime reducing, or they argue that the attendant social costs have not been fully appreciated. Some opponents of mass incarceration argue that there is little proof that increased incarceration deters crime. They argue that, while incapacitation may temporarily prevent criminal activity, the negative consequences for those who are incarcerated may enhance subsequent levels of criminal misconduct and negatively impact the communities to which inmates belong.[3] An innovative study by economists Keith Chen and Jesse Shapiro (2007) raises the possibility that, rather than deterring discharged inmates from future criminality, harsher prison conditions may actually stimulate further criminal activity. Chen and Shapiro exploit the fact that prisoners in their sample are assigned to prisons based on a security-level score to assess the effects of prison conditions on prisoners whose scores lie close to the cutoff points. Inmates on opposite sides of the dividing line are relatively equal in their initial criminality characteristics but are exposed to substantially different prison conditions. The authors find some evidentiary support, admittedly with a small sample, for the view that

> if all inmates were housed in above-minimum rather than minimum security facilities, they would be 41 percentage points more likely to be re-arrested in the year following release. (22)

Political scientist Amy E. Lerman (chapter 5, this volume) provides a psychological explanation for Chen and Shapiro's finding of increased rates of recidivism. Using a similar empirical approach based on assignment to higher-security prisons in California, Lerman finds that, for those with more limited prior criminal involvement, assignment to a higher-security prison has a criminogenic influence on attitudes relating to anger and violence. These two important studies underscore an essential point: crime is too complex a phenomenon to expect a simple "Beckerian" price-theoretic model to have universal explanatory power.[4] Not only can "raising the price" generate unintended negative or offsetting effects, but also, even if Becker's theory is directionally correct, it offers little insight on the five questions that are the lynchpins of determining whether U.S. incarceration levels are optimal:

1. What is the magnitude of any incarceration-induced drop in crime?

2. What is the monetized value of this decrease in crime?

3. What is the marginal cost of incarceration needed to generate these marginal benefits in crime reduction?

4. Does this cost-benefit calculus suggest that a certain level of incarceration is efficient?

5. Could a reallocation of resources to alternative crime-fighting strategies achieve the same benefits at lower social costs?

The current debate on incarceration has been polarized in part because the empirical literature has not yet generated clear and unequivocal answers to these key questions.

THE CORE CONCEPTS UNDERLYING THE OPTIMAL LEVEL OF INCARCERATION

A fundamental concept in estimating the optimal level of incarceration is the elasticity of crime with respect to incarceration—that is, the percentage by which crime will change in response to a percent increase in incarceration (Donohue 2005). More specifically, this elasticity, often symbolized by η, can be defined as:

$$\eta = (\%\Delta C)/ (\%\Delta P)= (\Delta C/C) / (\Delta P/P), \qquad (9.1)$$

where C stands for the number of crimes, and P stands for the number of prison inmates. Once we have an estimate of η, we can continue to the second step in estimating marginal benefits: calculating the number of crimes prevented by incarcerating the marginal prisoner (that is, the last offender entering the prison system). In the literature, this value is usually known as λ, or the marginal effectiveness of incarceration (Spelman 2000b).[5] So, if we want the effectiveness in decreasing crime of incarcerating the last criminal, we let $\Delta P = 1$ in equation 9.1, which yields:

$$\lambda_{reported} = \Delta C = \eta * (C/ P). \qquad (9.2)$$

Since estimates of η usually rely on FBI data on reported crimes, equation 9.2 only captures incarceration's impact on reported crimes as opposed to actual ones. Accordingly, we need to adjust equation 9.2 to account for nonreporting:

$$\lambda_{total} = \lambda_{reported} / R= (\eta/R) * (C/ P), \qquad (9.3)$$

where R represents the fraction of crimes that are reported.[6] To continue, if we multiply λ_{total} by what each prevented crime would have cost society if it had been committed, we get a monetary estimate of the marginal benefit (MB) of incarceration (that is, the benefit from locking up the last offender incarcerated):

$$MB = \lambda_{total} * CPC = (\eta/R) * (C/ P)* CPC, \qquad (9.4)$$

where CPC stands for average social cost of a single FBI Index I crime. Accordingly, MB represents the aggregate monetary cost of all crime prevented by the marginal incarceration. Finally, we can compare this MB to the marginal costs of incarceration (that is, the costs of imprisoning the last offender). If the marginal benefits exceed the marginal costs, then this simple cost-benefit calculus posits that incarcerating the last offender was cost effective.

Although conceptually straightforward, carrying out a cost-benefit analysis is complicated by the fact that we do not have precise estimates of η, λ, nor of the costs of crime and incarceration. We begin with a discussion of the existing estimates of the elasticity of crime with respect to incarceration (η) and the number of crimes averted by locking up one more prisoner (λ), which is derived automatically from the elasticity for any given level of incarceration. Importantly, λ will fall as the level of incarceration grows even if η remains constant; this implies that the marginal benefits of incarceration fall as incarceration grows. Next, we will examine how to monetarily value the reduction in crime that results from increased incarceration. Many vexing issues exist. For example, what is a social cost that should count in this calculus versus what is a mere transfer that should not count? How are intangibles such as pain and fear of crime valued? Are the social costs of murder profitably estimated by a single cost per murder, or are certain murders (perhaps in battles between criminals) less socially costly? After discussing the benefits emerging from increased incarceration, we then explore the costs of incarceration—from the mundane (the operating costs of a prison) to the philosophical (whether the lost utility and lost earnings of prisoners should count as social costs). We conclude by discussing ways in which reallocation of sums spent on incarceration to other crime-fighting approaches might be socially advantageous.

ESTIMATES OF THE ELASTICITY OF CRIME WITH RESPECT TO INCARCERATION (η)

In the next two subsections, we discuss prior estimates of the elasticity of crime with respect to incarceration, and then offer our best estimates of this elasticity.

Literature Overview

Two different approaches have been used to provide estimates of the elasticity of crime with respect to incarceration. The first approach—what economist William Spelman (2000a) calls "bottom-up" research—has mainly focused on estimating λ by surveying criminal offenders. Researchers employing this approach calculate estimates of the annual crime rate of active offenders and then use this rate to determine λ_{total}. Once this value has been obtained, one can estimate η, the elasticity of the crime rate with respect to the imprisonment rate.

In interpreting the estimates from this approach, it is important to note that there are at least two distinct mechanisms through which incarceration affects crime: incapacitation and deterrence. The first mechanism affects crime rates by removing criminals from society so that they are physically unable to commit more crimes.[7] The second mechanism assumes that the threat of incarceration increases the cost to the perpetrator of committing crime, thus deterring potential criminals from engaging in some criminal activity. Bottom-up research only accounts for the effect of incapacitation. In cases where there is a deterrent effect, bottom-up estimates of λ underestimate the marginal effectiveness of incarceration.[8]

A second approach uses econometric methods to directly estimate the elasticity of crime with respect to incarceration. Typically, the researcher runs regressions on large panel databases designed to explain the array of factors that influence crime, including the level of incarceration. Although this approach does not permit separate identification of the deterrence and incapacitation effects, it captures both. Assuming the models are correct, they provide an overall estimate of the impact of incarceration on crime (Liedka, Piehl, and Useem 2006). Table 9.1 summarizes the η estimates of some of the most influential papers.

A review of table 9.1 reveals a disappointing truth for policymakers: the estimates of the elasticity of crime with respect to incarceration do not tightly cluster around a single number, but rather range considerably. The table provides an array of general-crime elasticity estimates, as well as property- and violent-crime-specific estimates and even individual crime elasticities. At the high end (in absolute value), we see estimates of –0.70 for robbery (Levitt 1996) and –0.62 for burglary (Johnson and Raphael 2006). At the low end, sociologist Raymond Liedka, economist Anne Piehl, and sociologist Bert Useem (2006) actually suggest that additional incarcerations beyond the current level will only increase crime (which they attribute to the criminogenic influence of mass incarceration).

As is discussed in further detail in appendix A, the large variation occurs because the various studies are conducted using different econometric approaches and specifications for different data periods. The timing issue is relevant to the important question of whether the elasticity of crime with respect to incarceration is constant over the last thirty years or whether it has changed as the prison population has swelled. Note that a constant elasticity does not mean that the impact on crime from increasing the prison population by one inmate (that is, the marginal benefit of incarceration) will be constant. Remember that the elasticity tells us how much

Table 9.1   Estimates of the Elasticity of Crime with Respect to Incarceration

	Elasticity Estimates	Model Description	Comments
Spelman (1994)			
All index crimes 90% confidence interval	−0.16 [−0.12, −0.20]	Incapacitation Model: based on self-reported criminal behavior of inmates	Does not capture any potential effect from deterrence. Based primarily on Rand's 1978 prison and jail inmate surveys in California, Michigan, and Texas. Incapacitation models usually come up with estimates from about −0.10 to −0.30 (Spelman 2000).
Marvell and Moody (1994)			
All index crimes	−0.16	State-Year Panel Data: 49 states, 1971–89 (1973–1989 for some specifications)	For a variety of reasons, they see their estimates as a lower bound. The −0.16 estimate becomes −0.205 if they run the regression for 1978 to 1989 (a change they attribute to better data for later period). After running the Granger test of causality, they conclude that simultaneity is not a major problem. Nevertheless, in their conclusion, they acknowledge that simultaneity cannot be totally ruled out, so their figures may underestimate the true effect of incarceration. Wilson (1994) is also consistent with these results.
Violent crime (95% confidence interval)	−0.06 ± 0.11^		
Property crime (95% confidence interval)	−0.17 ± 0.06^		
Murder	−0.065 (0.085)		
Rape	−0.113* (0.052)		
Assault	−0.056 (0.053)		
Robbery	−0.260** (0.059)		
Burglary	−0.253** (0.031)		
Larceny	−0.138** (0.026)		
Vehicle theft	−0.200** (0.048)		

Table 9.1   *Continued*

	Elasticity Estimates	Model Description	Comments
Levitt (1996)			
All index crimes	−0.31^	State-Year Panel Data: 50 states and D.C., 1971–1993	Accounts for simultaneity of crime and incarceration by using prison overcrowding litigations as an instrumental variable (regressions actually include ten indicator variables corresponding to changes in prison overcrowding litigation). Since instrument is not perfect, standard errors become much larger. Results are corroborated by Witt and Witte (2000) using national time series.
Violent crime (95% confidence interval)	−0.38* ± 0.36		
Property crime (95% confidence interval)	−0.26* ± 0.24		
Murder	−0.147 (0.373)		
Rape	−0.246 (0.250)		
Assault	−0.410 (0.249)		
Robbery	−0.703* (0.309)		
Burglary	−0.401* (0.172)		
Larceny	−0.277 (0.147)		
Vehicle theft	−0.259 (0.235)		
Becsi (1999)			
All index crimes	−0.087** (0.015)	State-Year Panel Data: 50 states and D.C., 1971–1994	Accounts for simultaneity of crime and incarceration. Runs additional regressions only on murder and vehicle theft because data for these variables are better (less underreporting).
Violent crimes	−0.046* (0.022)		
Property crimes	−0.091** (0.015)		
Murder	−0.063 (0.034)		
Vehicle theft	−0.198** (0.032)		

Spelman (2000) All index crimes	−0.40**(0.15)	State-Year Panel Data: 50 states and D.C., 1971–1997	Accounts for simultaneity using prison overcrowding litigation as an instrument, using Levitt (1996). He also tests a nonconstant elasticity model and confirms his hypothesis that the effect of incarceration grows with scale (results shown here are for constant elasticity model).
Spelman (2005) Violent crimes	−0.44 (state average) 90% confidence interval [−0.13, −0.75]	Texas: County-Level Panel Data, 1990–2000	Study is based on Texas counties, raising issues of external validity. Texas prison expansion was massive, even in comparison to a large national average. There are several advantages to using county-level data. For example, he can include local jail inmates. Addresses simultaneity through an instrumental variable approach. His instruments are three indexed variables: (1) law-enforcement resources, (2) prosecutor and correctional resources, and (3) police civilianization.
Property crimes	−0.26 (state average) 90% confidence interval [−0.12, −0.41]		

Table 9.1 *Continued*

	Elasticity Estimates		Model Description	Comments
Liedka, Piehl, and Useem (2006)			State Panel Data: 50 states plus D.C.: 1972–2000	The elasticity estimate comes from their quadratic elasticity model. In order to get a specific value, we evaluated their results at various incarceration levels. The linear incarceration variable is statistically significant at the 1 percent level and the quadratic at the 5 percent level. Do not account for simultaneity, since they find no evidence that this is a problem.
All index crimes Evaluated at percentiles using all state-year observations of incarceration from 1977 to 2004	50th Percentile	−0.03		
	75th Percentile	0.016		
Evaluated at percentiles using state-year observations for 2004 only	50th Percentile	0.025		For reference, they estimate a constant elasticity model, resulting in an estimate of −0.072(0.044).
	75th Percentile	0.043		

Johnson and Raphael (2007)		State Panel Data: 50 states plus D.C.: 1978–2004	Results shown are from their second four specification (which includes state and year fixed effects and generates the *largest* elasticity estimates). Hence, these results can be interpreted as an upper bound. Since their model is not a log-log model, their regression estimates must be evaluated at a specific prisoner-to-crime ratio to derive an elasticity. The authors choose the sample mean for their evaluation. For our purposes, evaluating the results at the 2005 prisoner-to-crime ratio is more appropriate.
Violent crimes	−0.21		
Property crimes	−0.41		
Murder	−0.38		
Rape	−0.44		
Assault	0.11		
Robbery	−0.39		
Burglary	−0.62		
Larceny	−0.32		
Vehicle	−0.50		

Source: Author's compilation.
Note: Estimates denoted with ^ come directly from Spelman (2005) and not from the original paper.
**statistically significant at the 1% level, *statistically significant at the 5% level [two-tailed]; values in parentheses are coefficients' standard errors.

crime will change when the prison population rises by 1 percent. This means that as the prison population rises over time, a single additional inmate represents a steadily diminishing percentage increase in the level of incarceration. At the same time, as crime falls from the increasing levels of incarceration, a certain percentage decline in crime will imply fewer and fewer crimes averted. Put starkly, when there are 100 million crimes, a 1 percent drop in crime averts 1 million criminal acts; when there are only 100 crimes, a 1 percent drop in crime avoids one criminal act.

To illustrate this point for a given elasticity, we use equation 9.3 to compute the number of crimes averted by an increase of one prisoner for differing levels of incarceration and crime. Table 9.2 illustrates the marginal impact on crime that emanates from the five different constant elasticity estimates from table 9.1, and it shows how the number of crimes averted falls over time. The rows of the table illustrate the impact of the range of constant elasticity estimates as we move from 1977—when the level of crime was below 27 million and roughly 250,000 individuals were incarcerated in U.S. state prisons—to 2005—when there were about 29 million crimes and 1 million more inmates were behind bars than there were in 1977. For economist Zsolt Becsi's (1999) elasticity estimate of –0.087 (row 4, table 9.2), one sees that an additional prisoner in 1977 would be expected to lead to nine fewer crimes; however, one additional prisoner in 2005 would only avert two crimes. For Spelman's (2000b) higher elasticity of –0.4, though, the added prisoner in 1977 would stop a whopping forty-two crimes; by 2005, the number would have fallen to nine.

Table 9.2 foreshadows the overall cost-benefit analysis that is conducted throughout this chapter. First, one must choose the appropriate elasticity, which generates the number of crimes averted from incarcerating one extra prisoner. Second, a dollar value needs to be attached to this reduction in crime. Third, the costs of locking up one extra prisoner must be calculated. Finally, by finding the point at which the marginal cost and benefit of incarceration are equated, an optimal rate of incarceration can be estimated. Once one attaches monetary values to these costs and benefits (for example, say that it costs $30,000 to lock up a prisoner, and the dollar value of the cost imposed by an average index I crime is $10,000), the analysis becomes entirely straightforward. In this case, if two crimes are averted from adding one extra inmate, then it is not cost effective to do so (since the marginal benefit of $20,000 is exceeded by the marginal cost of $30,000). If nine crimes are averted, though, then averting $90,000 in crime costs is a good deal at the price of only $30,000.

Picking the Best Estimate of η

Tables 9.1 and 9.2 illustrate that there is no clear convergence in the estimates of the elasticity of crime across this group of well-designed studies.

Table 9.2   *Marginal Effects on the Number of Index I Crimes from Increased Incarceration Using Constant Elasticities of Crime with Respect to Incarceration (from Five Studies), 1977 to 2005*

| Study | η | Number of Crimes "Averted" by Incarcerating One Additional Prisoner | | | |
		1977	1987	1997	2005
Spelman (1994)	−0.160	−17	−10	−5	−4
Marvell and Moody (1994)	−0.160	−17	−10	−5	−4
Levitt (1996)	−0.310	−32	−20	−9	−7
Becsi (1999)	−0.087	−9	−6	−3	−2
Spelman (2000)	−0.400	−42	−26	−12	−9
Total number of crimes		26,780,518	33,235,831	32,993,370	28,892,802
Total number of state prisoners		256,806	521,289	1,099,347	1,259,905

Source: Author's compilation. Federal Bureau of Investation 2006
Note: The figures listed for each year's crime total are adjusted upward to account for underreporting, as shown in table 9B.6. The expected drop in crime from additional increments of incarceration has fallen sharply since 1977.

As is discussed in appendix A, assumptions about and the treatment of the issue of simultaneity, as well as modeling and data choices, importantly influence the elasticity estimates. Based on a careful review of the literature, Spelman (2000b, 484) concludes that

> our best guess as to the nationwide elasticity should be in the neighborhood of −0.30. Any figure between −0.20 and −0.40 can be defended, and we should not be too surprised to find that the result is anywhere between −0.10 and −0.50.

While this conclusion is reasonable, my own view is that one should lean more towards the lower bound of Spelman's ranges for two reasons. First, although Spelman contends that incarceration becomes more effective as the scale of the level of incarceration increases, Liedka, Piehl, and Useem's (2006) nonconstant elasticity model results, as well as economists Rucker C. Johnson and Steven Raphael's (2006) findings, suggest that the elasticity of crime has been falling as prison populations have risen.[9]

Moreover, the research on the community impact and criminogenic effects of incarceration (Walker and Walker 1987; Chen and Shapiro 2007; Lerman, chapter 5, this volume; Johnson, chapter 6, this volume) suggests that Liedka, Piehl, and Useem's (2006) "collateral damage" argument (discussed further in appendix A) should be taken into account. This would presumably tend to lower the estimated benefit flowing from increasing rates of incarceration.[10]

The other reason that one should lean more towards the lower bound of Spelman's ranges is that three of the four studies which offer crime-specific elasticity estimates (Besci 1999; Levitt 1996; Marvell and Moody 1994) find that the elasticity of murder is lower than the elasticity of other crimes (roughly in the –0.06 to –0.15 range). As so much of the social cost of crime is associated with the crime of murder, applying a general elasticity estimate to the crime of murder may exaggerate the actual benefits of incarceration. This fact militates in favor of using a separate lower elasticity figure for murder or perhaps making a crude downward adjustment to an overall elasticity estimate.

If the elasticity of crime declines as incarceration rises, then elasticity estimates will depend on the incarceration level during the study's sample time period (see table 9.1 for time periods). This implies that early studies based on data before 1990 are likely to find a larger elasticity of crime than identically designed studies using more recent data. This is exactly the case for economists Thomas Marvell and Carlisle Moody (1994) and Liedka, Piehl, and Useem (2006), who generate their estimates using the 1971 to 1989 and the 1972 to 2000 time periods, respectively. As a base model, Liedka, Piehl, and Useem ran a constant elasticity model that is similar in design to Marvell and Moody's. While Marvell and Moody find a general elasticity of about –0.17, Liedka, Piehl, and Useem's results suggest something closer to –0.07. Liedka, Piehl, and Useem attribute their lower estimates in part to their inclusion of additional years of data. In considering the importance of this factor, note that the unweighted incarceration rate (state prisoners per 100,000 population) across the years 1977 to 1989 is 177 (standard deviation of 46), but it jumps to 393 (standard deviation of 59) for the 1990 to 2004 period.[11] In any case, this suggests that, all else equal, recent studies based on incarceration data closer to today's levels are probably more useful for current policy analysis.

In addition, it is important to consider that, because of the nature of available data, all econometric studies listed in table 9.1 use state-prison populations. State-year data for federal prisoners and inmates at local jails is not consistently available, as required for state panel data estimation. In 2004, there were approximately 1,244,311 prisoners under state jurisdiction, 170,535 under federal jurisdiction, and 713,900 serving sentences in local jails (Harrison and Beck 2005). Clearly, a substantial number of incarcerated individuals are not captured by the incarceration variable used in most of the econometric studies. Even if federal-prison and local-jail incarcerations have a smaller effect on crime, they must have some impact on the dependent variable of the models (the FBI index-crime rate). This biases the regression's estimates if federal-prison and local-jail inmate numbers are negatively correlated with crime and positively correlated with the independent variable in the model (that is, state-prison population). This is a reasonable assumption as incarceration levels have been growing overall and in all jurisdictions. Omitting federal and local inmates thus causes the coefficient on the independent variable to be negatively biased; it causes us to overestimate the crime-reducing impact of state-prison population (Harrison and Beck 2005).[12]

Based on this evidence, my best guess for the elasticity of crime with respect to incarceration is highly uncertain; it is perhaps most likely to be between –0.10 and –0.15, but it is conceivably within the broader interval between –0.05 and –0.40. Recognizing the uncertainty and assumptions that surround elasticity estimates, I present results using this broader elasticity range.

Overall Versus Crime-Specific Estimates of η

Rather than identifying a best estimate for the aggregate elasticity of crime with respect to incarceration, one may conceptually prefer to have crime-specific elasticities. Some of the studies presented in table 9.1 have estimated separate elasticities for each crime type, while other studies have run separate analyses for violent and property crimes. Since different crimes involve different economic and social costs, precise crime-specific elasticity estimates could greatly enhance the accuracy of a cost-benefit analysis.

Despite these conceptual advantages, Spelman (2000b) argues against generating crime-specific estimates. One element of imprecision is that the crime-specific models all use the same incarceration variable (state prisoners, regardless of the type of prisoners or reasons for conviction), "making no attempt to disaggregate prison use and obtain a more policy-relevant result" (Spelman 2000b, 477). This makes the estimates imprecise; for example, incarcerating a rapist will not have the same impact on the various index crimes as incarcerating a vehicle thief or a burglar. According to Spelman, "theory is too weak to allow us to distinguish among different crime types, and because the empirical estimates are not statistically significantly different from one another, the most prudent course would be to assume the elasticity for each crime type is about the same, on average" (Spelman 2000b, 484). While crime-specific elasticity estimates should be used with caution, it still is a useful exercise to see how the disaggregated estimates influence the cost-benefit analysis. These results are presented in table 9B.1.

Our ultimate estimates of the optimal level of incarceration in table 9.3 will assume that murders will respond to increases in incarceration in the same proportion as other crimes and will also have high attendant social costs. However, the discussion of in appendix table 9A.2 raises the possibility that murder responds less to incarceration and should thus be treated differently in our analysis.[13] Accordingly, tables 9B.6 and 9B.7 (in appendix B) will assume that the elasticity for the crime of murder is zero (or alternatively that the social benefit of averted murders is zero), and proceed to assess the optimal level of incarceration on this basis. Obviously, because this will reduce the benefit of incarceration, it will lead to a lower estimated optimal level of incarceration. To the extent that one believes that table 9.3 overstates the benefits from incarceration (because the responsiveness of murder to increased incarceration is smaller than for other crimes, or because the social costs are smaller than estimated), then table 9A.3 will help to illustrate the sensitivity of our estimates to a different treatment of murder.

THE BENEFITS FROM PREVENTED CRIMES

Once one has an estimate of the elasticity of crime with respect to incarceration, it is straightforward to compute how much crime is prevented by additional increments to the prison population. In order to move from prevented crimes to prevented losses, though, we need to estimate a monetary cost of crime. This task has vexed economists at least since the Wickersham Commission on Law Observance and Enforcement (Shaw and McKay 1931). More than sixty years later, Franklin Zimring and Gordon Hawkins (1995) argued that economists continue to lack a "concept of the costs of crime that is both relevant and rigorous" for evaluating policy. Nonetheless, it is impossible to allocate crime-fighting resources rationally without some effort to estimate the benefits and costs of crime-prevention policies—including incarceration.

On White Collars, Terrorists, and the Utility of Thieves

The difficulties in estimating the cost of crime result from both theoretical and practical concerns. The practical concerns relate to data availability and the appropriate methodologies for estimating certain aspects of the costs, such as the intangible costs of fear of crime. The theoretical concerns relate to a host of definitional as well as normative issues.

Table 9.3   *Changes in State Prison Population Necessary to Reach Optimality (2005 values)*

(a)	(b)	(c)	(d)
η	Low CPCs	Mean CPCs	High CPCs
A. Optimality Using Marginal Cost = $25,797			
−0.05	−913,903	−158,904	553,662
−0.1	−562,316	790,930	1,891,840
−0.2	62,429	1,838,948	2,827,802
−0.3	503,343	2,069,628	2,703,584
−0.4	763,637	1,982,838	2,377,453
B. Optimality Using Marginal Cost = $35,000			
−0.05	−1,004,002	−439,427	101,332
−0.1	−738,845	312,874	1,210,856
−0.2	−238,279	1,300,062	2,252,358
−0.3	160,316	1,662,828	2,350,620
−0.4	436,217	1,703,113	2,163,553
C. Optimality Using Marginal Cost = $55,000			
−0.05	−1,096,483	−731,827	−377,148
−0.1	−923,725	−215,965	421,394
−0.2	−576,178	597,948	1,429,565
−0.3	−261,704	1,049,606	1,765,169
−0.4	−5,039	1,235,343	1,775,618
D. Optimality Using Marginal Cost = $80,000			
−0.05	−1,147,335	−894,573	−646,615
−0.1	−1,027,016	−524,895	−58,464
−0.2	−776,170	123,627	820,394
−0.3	−532,056	569,753	1,255,355
−0.4	−312,975	824,093	1,398,996

Note: The five depicted elasticities apply to index I crimes. CPC stands for cost per index I crime, using the "high" and "low" CPC costs in table 9.9, as well as an intermediate value, which is the simple mean of the high and low estimates. The values listed in each cell for an attendant combination of η, CPC, and marginal cost of incarceration reflect the difference between the optimal state prisoner count (P^*) and the number of state prisoners in 2005: 1,259,905 (Harrison and Beck 2006), assuming a constant elasticity for all crimes including murder. That is, these figures tell us how many prisoners would have to be added (for positive numbers) or eliminated (for negative values) from the state prison system to reach the point where the marginal costs of incarcerating an additional prisoner equal its marginal benefits. For an analogous table that excludes murder, see table 9A.3.

This chapter does not purport to address the full array of criminal activities. It limits itself to the seven standard index I crimes defined by the Uniform Crime Reports (UCR) listed in table 9.4. As a result, all sorts of white-collar crimes (the property losses from fraud, credit-card abuse, and embezzlement alone dwarf the property losses from robbery and burglary) and "victimless" crimes such as drugs and prostitution are ignored. In addition, while the terrorist acts of September 11, 2001, are estimated to have caused at least $33 billion in lost wages, clean up, and reconstruction (Bram, Orr, and Rapaport 2002), terrorism is not a listed UCR index crime, and the FBI explicitly excludes the victims of the September 11 terrorist attacks in its homicide statistics.[14]

Furthermore, to illustrate a conceptual difficulty in determining the contours of crime costs, consider the following extreme example. A thief steals a sedan from a multimillionaire who happens to own dozens of cars. The car is required by the thief to maintain a job and bring her children to school. How should we account for the illegal transfer of property in this case? This depends on whether one is willing to "give criminals full standing in societal benefit-cost calculations" (Ludwig 2006). Economist Philip J. Cook (1983) argues implicitly for inclusion of criminals' utility in calculations of overall societal well-being. For Cook, social cost—defined as the costs measured against the well-being of all members of society—is the pertinent measure to estimate the costs of crime.[15] The practical consequence of using social costs for cost-of-crime estimates is that any transfers between individuals will be excluded from the cost estimates. Similarly, John Donohue and Peter Siegelman (1998) use the social-cost criteria and exclude increased welfare payments to criminals' families when assessing the costs of incarceration because such payments are mere transfers within society.

Others, including economists William N. Trumbull (1990), Mark Cohen (2005), and Jens Ludwig (2006), prefer to disregard criminals' utility in any social-welfare calculations. Cohen (2005) argues that the value of the stolen car should be included in cost-of-crime figures, as the criminal involuntarily imposes this private wealth reduction. This normative judgment makes a major difference in the costs-of-crime estimates. Economist David Anderson (1999) estimates that transfers account for roughly one-third of the overall costs of crime, thus illustrating the centrality of normative judgments inherent in this exercise. Instead of trying to resolve these normative questions, this chapter illustrates their importance by presenting various estimates of the cost of crime based on different assumptions. The effort to highlight the underlying assumptions and methodologies will enable readers to implement their own normative choices in conducting cost-benefit analyses of incarceration.

Recent studies of the cost of crime (Anderson 1999; Cohen 2005) have

Table 9.4   *Social Costs per Crime (Low Estimate)*

	Cohen, Miller, and Wiersema (1996) ($)	Justice System ($)	Lost Productivity of Offender ($)	Total Low Cost Estimate ($)
Murder	4,100,418	119,200	107,647	4,327,266
Rape	121,339	4,419	3,938	129,696
Robbery	11,158	6,089	5,390	22,637
Assault	13,110	3,436	2,982	19,528
Burglary	600	929	758	2,287
Motor-vehicle theft	558	358	281	1,197
Larceny	140	108	87	335

Source: Author's calculations.
Note: Justice system and lost productivity costs are in present value (discounted at a 5 percent rate), based on NCVS arrest rate for all crimes (except murder, for which the UCR rate is used).

provided comprehensive estimates of all the costs posed by crime, taking into account the perspective of victims, offenders, taxpayers, and all other affected parties. We follow Anderson and Cohen in this approach, presenting specific details on the bearer of the costs whenever possible.

Estimating Intangible Costs of Crime

Crime costs include both tangible and intangible costs. Tangible costs include victims' medical bills, antitheft insurance payments, or expenditures on the criminal-justice system (including court time for criminal matters) that would be tallied in the gross national product (GNP) (Cohen 2005). On the other hand, pain, suffering, and the fear of crime are intangible costs that, while harder to estimate, are social costs of crime. In her 2006 Senate testimony, Mary Lou Leary noted the high percentage of crime victims who develop posttraumatic stress disorder (PTSD). If untreated—and therefore not generating a tangible cost—PTSD reduces the quality of life not only for the initial crime victim, but also for loved ones and friends, in some cases for ten years (Leary 2006). Studies that include intangible costs in their overall cost estimates consistently find that they likely outweigh tangible costs. For example, criminology researchers Ted Miller, Mark Cohen, and Brian Wiersema (1996) found that the intangible costs of a rape victimization are sixteen times the tangible costs.

The primary argument against including intangible costs is the difficulty in accurately measuring them given the absence of market mechanisms that would illuminate valuations through revealed preferences. The main argument for inclusion is that people are willing to pay to avoid becoming crime victims. Consider, for example, the money an average woman would willingly forego to live without the fear of being raped or sexually assaulted. This indicates that people treat the prospect of becoming a crime victim as a real cost. For our purpose, and in line with our comprehensive approach to costs, this chapter tries to estimate and include intangible costs whenever possible.

Four different methods have been used to estimate intangible costs of crime: hedonic pricing, wage-rate differentials for risky jobs, jury awards for tortuous injuries, and contingent valuation.

Hedonic Pricing Estimates   Economist Richard Thaler (1978) derived a framework, now known as hedonic pricing, from economist Kelvin J. Lancaster's (1966) consumer theory and economist Sherwin Rosen's (1974) theoretical model that can be used to estimate the intangible costs of crime. In the crime context, hedonic pricing attempts to gauge the willingness to pay higher property prices to live in a safer neighborhood. With enough controls (that is, size of the house, extras such as having a pool or fireplace, lot size, and local non-crime-related socioeconomic variables), it is possible to estimate:

$$\text{price} = \alpha + \beta * \text{crime} + \Sigma\gamma * \text{property} + \Sigma\delta * \text{local} + \varepsilon, \qquad (9.5)$$

where *price* is the selling price of the house, *crime* refers to the crimes committed in the neighborhood, *property* is a vector of the house and lot characteristics, and *local* is a vector of community characteristics. Estimates of β would give us a sense of how much crime reduces house prices; in other words, it indicates the amount people are willing to pay when choosing where to live in order to avoid crime. Hedonic pricing provides an indirect estimate of intangible costs such as fear of crime or avoidance behavior (for example, not walking down dark streets).

Colinearity across various crime categories makes it difficult to estimate effects of individual crimes with enough precision to unravel their separate effects. Most hedonic regressions are therefore run on either the violent- or property-crime index.[16] One potential shortcoming of the hedonic-pricing regressions is the implicit assumption that the house price is the sum of the house parts (physical or location attributes) without taking interactions into account. Cohen (2005) points out that only a few studies (Hoehn, Berger, and Blomquist 1987) also estimate a local-wage-rate equation in addition to the housing prices.

Compensating Wage-Rate Differential Estimate   Economists have also estimated intangible costs by looking at wage-rate differentials between risky and less-risky jobs to derive the worth of a statistical life (Vicusi 1998, 2000). This research provides estimates of the value that society puts on the increased incremental risk of dying, which can then be used to estimate the costs of crimes that carry some risk of death.

Jury Awards   Cohen (1988) used civil-jury awards to estimate the social costs of similar harms generated by criminal conduct. Combining the statistical-life evaluations and the jury awards, Mark Cohen was able to estimate intangible costs of crime. Mark Cohen, Ted R. Miller, and sociologist Shelli B. Rossman (1994) build on Cohen's initial attempt, ironing out data limitations of the original study. Interestingly, all three approaches— hedonic pricing, wage-rate differentials, and jury-award studies—generate broadly similar cost-of-crime estimates.

Contingent Valuation with Survey Data   The final approach to estimating intangible costs draws on Thomas C. Schelling's (1968) suggestion that in cases in which market prices are not available, one can simply ask people what they think the benefits are worth. Cook and Ludwig (2000) use this so-called contingent-valuation approach in the crime context, in particular to evaluate the cost of gun violence. Essentially, the contingent valuation asks referendum-style questions about the respondents' willingness to pay to change a social condition.[17] More recently, the same contingent-valuation method was used by Cohen and colleagues (2004) to estimate respondents' willingness to pay to reduce violent crime and burglary. They find that the willingness-to-pay estimates are two to seven times higher than previous estimates. In particular, the ratios of willingness to pay over previous estimates for burglary and armed robbery are 5.7 and 7.3, respectively (Cohen 2005).

Serious questions have been raised as to whether these contingent-valuation assessments accurately capture the true willingness to pay, given the fact that we cannot observe actual payments. Moreover, unless one has a random sample of Americans, there is a danger that the answers of unrepresentative individuals can lead to biased estimates of what the average American would be willing to pay. Moreover, we know that criminals are often victims of crime. Applying the per-victim cost as a measure of the social loss when a drug dealer or other criminal is eliminated may be exaggerating the social cost of murder in the United States, which is itself one of the largest components of the cost of crime.

Building on Prior Estimates of the Cost of Crime

Table 9B.2 provides an exhaustive breakdown of the possible factors that need to be considered in estimating the total cost of crime. These fall into three broad categories: costs caused by the criminal act itself, costs from societal reaction to or in prevention of crime, and costs incurred by the offender because of his incarceration. However, gaps in data availability prevent all conceivable costs from being estimated.

Table 9.5 shows the wide range of cost-of-crime estimates from an array of studies. While some of the studies only address portions of the full array of social costs, the estimates for the "general" focus studies that try to capture all costs of crime range from roughly $1 trillion to $2 trillion per year. For our purposes, however, we are ultimately interested in estimating the marginal cost of crime that could be avoided by an enhanced level of incarceration. Expressed differently, we are interested in the marginal benefit (in lowered social costs of crime) resulting from a marginal increase in incarceration. Table 9.2 revealed that adding an additional prisoner to the inmate population in 2005 would be expected to generate between two and nine fewer index I crimes (given elasticity estimates ranging from –0.16 to –0.4). We attempt to provide a monetary valuation to the social benefit of eliminating these two to nine crimes.

What is the social cost of an average index I crime? To generate such an estimate one can compute the average cost of each class of index I crimes and take a weighted average (by frequency of occurrence) across all seven index I categories. The most conceptually straightforward costs included in this calculation are the social costs suffered by the victim of any index I crime. I take these per-crime-category victimization-cost figures from Ted Miller, Mark Cohen, and Brian Wiersema's (1996) study; these figures are presented in the first column of table 9.4. Note that I treat these as lower-bound estimates for two reasons. First, these victimization-cost estimates are substantially lower than the social-cost estimates that were generated by Cohen and colleagues (2004) using the admittedly more speculative contingent-valuation methodology. Second, the value of stolen property is excluded from Miller, Cohen, and Wiersema's estimates; it is assumed to be a mere transfer from the victim to the criminal. Intangible costs, such as diminished quality of life or pain and suffering, however, are included via Cohen's (1998) statistical-life or jury-award method. The comparable upper-bound cost estimates are found in the first column of table 9.6, using the contingent valuation estimates from Mark Cohen and colleagues (2004) and including the cost of stolen goods as a social cost.

To complete the low- and high-end estimates set forth in tables 9.4 and 9.6, the figures in the first column of each table are supplemented with two more quantitatively minor social-cost items: the lost productivity of

Table 9.5 Summary of Studies Estimating the Annual Social Costs of Crime

Study	Focus	Elements Not Included	Time Period (Years)	$ (Billions) in 2006 Dollars
Ludwig (2006)	General		2004–2005	2,040
Cohen, Rust, Steen, and Tidd (2004)	Victim costs of burglary, armed robbery, serious assault, rape, and murder	Opportunity cost of criminals, justice system	2000	534
Anderson (1999)	General	— transfers	1970–1997	2,064 1,334
Collins for *U.S. News and World Report* (1994)	General	Opportunity costs and miscellaneous indirect components	1994	990
Cohen, Miller, and Wiersema (1996)	Victim costs of violent and property crimes	Prevention, opportunity, and indirect costs	1987–1990	608
U.S. News and World Report (1974)	General	Opportunity costs and miscellaneous indirect components	1974	1,176
Cohen, Miller, and Rossman (1994)	Cost of rape, robbery, and assault	Prevention, opportunity, and indirect costs	1987	249
Zedlewski (1985)	Firearms, guard dogs, victim losses, and commercial security	Residential security, opportunity costs, and indirect costs	1976–1983	300
Cohen (1990)	Cost of personal and household crime to victims	Prevention, opportunity, and indirect costs	1985	174
President's Commission on Law Enforcement (1967)	General	Opportunity costs and miscellaneous indirect components	1967	645
Klaus (1994)	National Crime Victimization Survey	Prevention, opportunity, and indirect costs	1993 26	

Source: Adapted and expanded from Anderson (1999).

Table 9.6   *Social Costs per Crime (High Estimate)*

	Cohen, Rust, Steen, and Tidd (2004) ($)	Justice System ($)	Lost Productivity of Offender ($)	Total High Cost Estimate ($)
Murder	11,358,314	127,049	107,960	11,593,323
Rape	277,518	12,014	8,035	297,567
Robbery	271,663	10,754	8,075	290,491
Assault	81,967	6,213	3,636	91,817
Burglary	29,274	1,490	1,216	31,980
Motor-vehicle theft	5,160(a)	285	224	5,669
Larceny	516(a)	217	175	908

Source: Author's calculations.
Note: For Motor-Vehicle Theft and Larceny, we use Miller, Cohen, and Wiersema (1996) estimates (including transfers), since these crime categories are not estimated in Cohen, Rust, et al. (2004). Justice-system and lost-productivity costs are in present value (discount rate is assumed to be 5 percent) based on UCR arrest rate for all crimes.

those incarcerated for such crimes and the criminal-justice costs that accompany an average index I crime.

Lost Productivity Owing to Incarcerating Offenders   One of the benefits of a drop in crime is that fewer individuals need to be arrested, prosecuted, and punished. This involves some obvious savings and some less immediately obvious social benefits. As most individuals who are sent to prison would otherwise be engaging in some socially productive work, the reduction in the need for incarceration gives a form of peace dividend. It eliminates the lost productivity of those individuals who would have committed crimes and then been sentenced to prison. While Miller, Cohen, and Wiersema's (1996) study does not try to estimate this lost productivity of incarcerated offenders, we computed this social cost assuming that the average offender is male and has a high-school diploma but no college education. From the latest available Bureau of Labor Statistics (BLS) data, this offender profile would correspond to an average earning potential of $616 per week. Of course, locking up a criminal only deprives society of his productive efforts if he was actually working; thus, the estimated forgone earnings must be adjusted to reflect the unemployment of criminals, which is higher than that for the noncriminal population (Buonanno 2003).

Although a 2003 Bureau of Justice Statistics report found that 16.7 percent of newly admitted offenders were unemployed, this number overstates the fraction working before prison admission because it excludes individuals not looking for work (per standard BLS definition). Offender employment before admission varied with educational level from 62 percent (for with less than eleventh grade education) to 87 percent (for those with education beyond high school) (Harlow 2003). I adjusted the average forgone earnings from $616 per week to $462 by estimating that only 75 percent of criminals sent to prison are employed. Assuming that wages reflect social value, these forgone wages of $462 per week are a proxy for the lost societal productivity.

Table 9.7 uses data on arrest rates, conviction rates, and sentencing rates, combined with estimates of time served in prison or jail to calculate lost productivity (based on the lost wages) for every offense committed in the respective crime category (see tables 9B.3, 9B.4, and 9B.5 for details). Not surprisingly, murder and nonnegligent manslaughter offenders are responsible for the largest loss in productivity, primarily because of their greater likelihood of capture, conviction, and sentencing (and, less importantly, because of their longer expected sentences).[18]

Miller, Cohen, and Wiersema's (1996) estimates already include figures for the lost productivity of the victim from lost work days, missed school, and house work. As a result, all victim productivity losses are included in our low estimate, and we only need to put these estimates into current dollars to reflect inflation.

Avoided Criminal-Justice-System Costs   The final adjustment to the benefits of avoiding an index I crime is based on the criminal-justice-system costs prevented by increased incarceration (in other words, the costs we are not spending on arresting, processing, and incarcerating criminals due to the reduced crime level from increased incarceration).

Using the previously estimated arrest, conviction, and sentencing rates, we need three items in order to estimate the saved justice-system costs: the distribution of sentences (that is, whether the criminal received a prison, jail, or probation sentence); the estimated time served; and the average cost of the sentence. Daily costs per convicted offender for prison, jail, or probation sentences are conservatively estimated at $70, $67, and $5, respectively.[19] Table 9.8 presents the calculation of prevented criminal-justice-system costs due to reduced crime. Obviously, this is just part of the overall justice costs; Miller, Cohen, and Wiersema (1996) include other costs, such as police and investigative expenditures.

Computing the High Social-Cost-of-Crime Estimate

Combining figures from Miller, Cohen, and Wiersema's study (1996) with the results in tables 9.7 and 9.8 provides a broad array of prevented costs

Table 9.7   Lost Productivity Due to Incarceration of Offenders for Seven Index I Crimes

	Arrest Rate	Conviction Rate	Sentencing Rate (Conditional on Being Convicted)		Days Incarcerated		Total Lost Productivity ($)
			Prison	Jail	Prison	Jail	
	(1)	(2)	(3)	(4)	(5)	(6)	
Murder	0.84	0.70	0.91	0.04	4253	189	107,647
Rape	0.13	0.47	0.59	0.23	1920	154	3,938
Robbery	0.18	0.47	0.71	0.15	1583	191	5,390
Aggravated assault	0.43	0.23	0.42	0.29	1069	139	2,982
Burglary	0.09	0.50	0.46	0.26	529	88	758
Motor-vehicle theft	0.15	0.18	0.37	0.31	353	88	281
Larceny	0.08	0.09	0.36	0.39	374	94	87

Source: Arrest rate is based on NCVS data, except for murder, which is calculated from UCR numbers. The conviction and sentencing rates are based on table 2 of Hill and Harrison (2004). "Days incarcerated" is based on mean sentence and estimated time served. The "total" column is discounted to present value using a 5 percent discount rate.

Table 9.8   Estimating the Avoided Criminal-Justice-System Costs Due to Reduced Crime

	Arrest Rate	Felony Conviction Rate	Sentencing Rate			Cost of Sentence			
			Prison	Jail	Probation	Prison	Jail	Probation	Total
	(1)	(2)	(3)	(4)	(5)	(6)	(7)	(8)	(9)
Murder	0.84	0.70	0.91	0.04	0.05	310162	13785	11400	119,200
Rape	0.13	0.47	0.59	0.23	0.18	139800	11184	8100	4,419
Robbery	0.18	0.47	0.71	0.15	0.14	116571	14091	7650	6,089
Aggravated assault	0.43	0.23	0.42	0.29	0.29	77598	10059	5850	3,436
Burglary	0.09	0.50	0.46	0.26	0.28	39798	6633	5400	929
Motor-vehicle theft	0.15	0.18	0.37	0.39	0.24	26532	6633	3600	358
Larceny	0.08	0.09	0.36	0.31	0.33	27936	6984	5400	108

Source: Author's calculations.

Note: Arrest rate is based on NCVS data, except for murder, which is calculated from UCR numbers. "Cost of sentence" is based on mean time served. The remainder of sentenced time is assumed to be under supervision (same costs as probation). Costs of probation supervision are assumed to be five dollars per day per offender (estimates in the literature vary from one to ten dollars). The "total" column is discounted to present value using a 5 percent discount rate.

reflecting estimates of medical costs, victim services, lost productivity both from the offender and victim, reduced quality of life of the victim, death of the victim, police and investigative costs, and incarceration and nonincarceration sanctions (see tables 9.4 and 9.6 for crime-specific totals). Missing however are estimates for the fear of crime and any costs imposed by changed behavior patterns in order to avoid becoming a crime victim (for example, avoiding certain areas after sundown or taking a cab instead of walking home).

The contingent-valuation method would presumably capture the costs associated with fear of crime and avoidance behavior; however, in other respects we have to guess what the contingent-valuation respondents included in their cost figures, as data exists only on the survey answers and not on the factors that motivated those responses. But it is reasonable to assume, for example, that the average respondent asked about burglaries considers stolen property to be an imposed cost on the victim rather than a mere transfer to the thief. Similarly, when asked about violent crime, one may assume that the respondent includes fear of crime, potential hospital costs, pain and suffering, and an overall reduced quality of life in his valuation. In particular, nonmarket goods (such as fear of crime, and pain and suffering) should be captured by the contingent valuation of crime. Overall then, contingent-valuation estimates seem able to capture several additional cost elements—fear and avoidance behavior—but may blur other distinct cost categories.[20]

Cohen and colleagues (2004) employ the contingent-valuation method to estimate individuals' willingness to pay for crime reduction. This allows them to compute dollar values for specific crimes, which indicates how much society would value a reduction of crime. Using their findings, a second estimate can be constructed by combining the willingness-to-pay estimate with costs that are assumed not taken into account by the respondents. General criminal-justice-system processing costs and lost productivity from a caught, convicted, and incarcerated offender presumably had little influence on individuals' willingness to pay to reduce crime. Table 9.6 presents the per-crime estimate of prevented costs using the contingent-valuation method; table 9.4 presents the analogous estimates of tangible losses based on the aggregation of various costs using jury awards and the value of a statistical life.[21]

The Benefit from Avoiding Index I Crimes

Since our cost-benefit analysis relies on an aggregate elasticity of crime (as opposed to crime-specific elasticities), we need to calculate the average cost of some general or unspecified crime. In other words, with the exception of murder, our lambda quantifies how many crimes are prevented by the marginal incarceration, but they do not tell us what types of crime are prevented. Given this, we need to average the crime-specific cost in a way that gives us the probable cost of an average unspecified index crime (with the exception of murder, which we deal with separately). We derive this value by taking a weighted average of the crime-specific costs of crime, where each cost is weighted by the probability of the particular crime occurring. (The crimes are weighted by an adjusted FBI frequency, where the FBI crime numbers are inflated using the crime's reporting rate obtained from the National Crime Victimization Survey [NCVS].)

Table 9.9 reveals that an average index I crime imposes a social cost of between roughly $5,700 and $27,000. The appendix B reveals that the social cost of the average index I crime would range between $3,350 and $20,000 if murders were excluded.[22] These estimates begin to provide context for the cost-benefit analysis of the incremental incarceration as one compares the number of such crimes that can be avoided with the expense of trying to avoid them. Table 9.2 presents estimates that locking up an extra prisoner would eliminate two to nine crimes. Using the low end of this spectrum and the low estimate for the cost of an average crime, then we see that the marginal benefit (roughly $11,500) is outweighed by the marginal cost (with prisons likely costing more than $25,000 per inmate, per year on average). Conversely, if we accept the higher-end estimates for crimes avoided and cost per crime, then the marginal benefits likely exceed the costs by a substantial margin.

THE COST OF INCARCERATION

Moving on from the monetary estimates of the value of an incarceration-induced reduction in crime, we now turn to the costs of increasing incarceration. As with the cost of crimes, there are several components to the cost of incarceration, and not all of them are easily documented. Factors to be considered include the direct costs arising from the day-to-day prison operations, the lost wages and productivity of inmates, intangible costs such as the value of the inmate's lost freedom, the psychological cost on the family of the incarcerated, and any postincarceration lost earning potential due to a criminal record. Furthermore, there are other potential postincarceration costs, including the costs of increased crime from "prison-hardened" criminals, the increased spread of diseases caught in prison through the reentry community, and the net effects of parental incarceration on the children of inmates.

Operating Costs

Costs of day-to-day prison operations are most easily estimated since they are documented in state budgets and compiled by the Bureau of Jus-

Table 9.9 Average Cost of an Index I Crime Using Weighted Cost of Crime Estimates, 2005

(a)	Reporting Rate (%)	Adjusted Low Cost Estimate ($)				Adjusted High Cost Estimate			
		Low Cost Estimate ($)	Weight	Weighted Cost (Low) ($)		High Cost Estimate ($)	Weight	Weighted Cost (High) ($)	
	(b)	(c)	(d)	(e)		(f)	(g)	(h)	
Murder	100.0	4,327,266	0.0006	2,507		11,593,323	0.0006	6,717	
Rape	38.3	129,696	0.0085	1,106		297,567	0.0085	2,537	
Assault	52.4	19,528	0.0570	1,112		91,817	0.0570	5,229	
Robbery	62.4	22,637	0.0232	524		290,491	0.0232	6,726	
Burglary	56.3	2,287	0.1325	303		31,980	0.1325	4,238	
Larceny	32.3	335	0.7269	244		908	0.7269	660	
Motor-vehicle theft	83.2	1,197	0.0514	62		5,669	0.0514	291	
Average Cost Per Crime				$5,857.26				$26,397.95	

Source: Author's calculations.
Note: To see the detailed derivation of this weighting scheme (as well as two alternative weights that we did not employ), see table 9B.6. The numbers in bold represent the average cost of any index crime, including murder. To see analogous results to this that exclude murder, see table 9B.7.

Table 9.10   *Composition of Operating Expenditures*

	U.S. Aggregate (1000s dollars)	Per Prisoner
Wages, salary, benefits	21,166,199	16,894
Medical care	3,745,103	2,990
Food services	1,362,021	1,088
Utilities	1,134,427	905
All other (supplies, fees, interest on debt, contractual housing services)	4,909,190	3,920
Total	32,316,940	25,797

Source: Hill and Harrison (2004).

tice Statistics. The lost earnings of incarcerated persons can be estimated reasonably well from demographic information about prisoners and Bureau of Labor wage estimates.

Statewide annual day-to-day prison operations expenditures range from less than $10,000 to more than $50,000 per prisoner, with Arkansas at the low end ($9,257 spent annually per prisoner) and Maine at the high end ($50,545 per prisoner) (Bureau of Justice Statistics 2004b).[23] Table 9.10 provides more detail on the composition of operating expenditures. The national average operating cost per inmate is $25,797, of which roughly two-thirds are allocated for salary, wages, and benefits.[24] Many studies have viewed these operating expenditures as the sole cost of incarcerating an additional prisoner, but there are other admittedly less easily quantified costs that should also be considered. For one, the public-finance literature refers to the deadweight loss of taxation—the fact that distortionary taxes dampen economic activity. Some estimate this amount as equal to approximately one-third of the taxes raised. For now, I do not make an additional adjustment for this factor, but it is probably advisable to think of some amount beyond the actual operating costs as an added social burden of incarceration.

Capital Costs

As state prisons already run at near maximum capacity—occupancy levels of state prisons are well over 100 percent capacity in thirty-four states, and they are over 97 percent in an additional eight states (Harrison and Beck 2005)—additional prisoners will likely require prison expansion. Capital expenditures are fixed costs in the traditional sense, and our huge prison construction boom has left us with a situation in which major decreases in incarceration would create excess prison capacity. However, given that state prisons in general do not have any empty cells, capital expenses must be incurred at the margin if there is any call for additional incarceration. Because of this asymmetry, one might want to fully include prison construction costs for assessing increases in incarceration while employing some lesser amount as a measure of the cost savings if incarceration were to decrease. Presumably, a reduction in prisoners in an existing facility will reduce capital costs to some degree because of diminished depreciation owing to less intensity of use. Again, to allow others to assess our findings based on their particular preferences about the pertinent costs, we provide a range of estimates; capital costs are not included in our low estimate of the cost of incarceration, but they are reflected in more inclusive estimates.

The cost for an additional prison cell varies widely by region and security level of the facility. One way of estimating the capital costs is to look at average costs of some current prison construction projects. For example, in 2006 Governor Arnold Schwarzenegger asked California lawmakers to approve nearly $6 billion on new prison construction projects to be able to house an additional 40,000 inmates, a figure of roughly $150,000 for each additional bed (Martin 2006). Six years earlier, the State of Connecticut reported a slightly lower construction cost to house an additional inmate of $125,000 (State of Connecticut General Assembly, 2000).

We use this capital-cost estimate of $125,000 per new bed and assume a prison's lifetime of forty years. The annual capital costs for a newly added prisoner are then slightly over $3,000, or roughly three times the expenditures on food.[25]

Lost Productivity

The lost productivity of incarcerated offenders is a cost associated with increases in incarceration. Productivity is proxied by wage losses of the offender, which amount to an average productivity loss of roughly $25,000 dollars per year of incarceration (assuming the offenders are male with high-school diplomas but no college education, and assuming that 75 percent of offenders were employed before prison). Combining the day-to-day operating costs with capital expenditures and lost productivity indicates annual costs of slightly over $55,000 per prisoner, per year (or $55,797 in 2006 dollars).

Query, though, whether the full value of lost wages should be counted as a social cost of incarceration. The disutility of work is avoided, so presumably this value should be subtracted. Also, the earnings would presumably go at least in part to feeding, clothing, and housing the individual; these amounts are obviated by incarceration (and counted as operating costs of incarceration). The lost tax revenues on legitimate earnings and the amounts that would otherwise have been paid to support others are clearly social losses owing to incarceration. These considerations would indicate using a cost less than the full $25,000 for lost productivity; I estimate this to be approximately $8,000. I therefore will include an intermediate marginal prison-cost estimate of $35,000 in case that the total operating costs, capital costs, and lost productivity estimate of $55,000 is overstated.

Other Costs of Incarceration

In addition to the costs of incarceration that we have included thus far, there are several additional costs that incarceration imposes on the offender or society during or after prison. A criminal record can make it difficult to find a job and thereby dampen future earnings (Holzer, chapter 8, this volume; Raphael and Stoll, chapter 2, this volume). AIDS or tuberculosis caught while in prison certainly harms the prisoner and can impact the community. Children deprived of a father or mother as a result of their incarceration may be placed at greater risk for subsequent behavioral problems (less the benefits of removing any abusive parents) (Johnson, chapter 6, this volume) To the extent that incarceration hardens inmates, Keith Chen and Jesse Shapiro (2007) and Lerman (chapter 5, this volume) suggest that it may increase the future criminality of those returned from prison to the community.

There is also debate over whether the value of the lost freedom of prison inmates should be considered a social cost. Some contend such deprivation is the purpose of incarceration, while others point out that the deprivations and impositions of incarceration still reflect a human loss. In any event, this is another cost that is difficult to quantify even for those who conceptually would like to include it. The size and even the sign of other costs, such as the postincarceration impact on communities, are also sharply debated. Rather than excluding these collateral costs from our analysis, it is useful to add in a reasonable figure to provide an upper bound on the cost of incarceration for the average state (or a more realistic estimate of the cost for a high-operating-cost state). For now, to give a sense of the impact of these other costs, I assume that they increase the marginal cost of incarceration from $55,000 to $80,000. In summary, table 9.3 presents four marginal prison-cost estimates: $25,797; $35,000; $55,000; and $80,000.

THE RESULTS OF A MARGINAL COST-BENEFIT ANALYSIS

As a means to estimate the optimal level of incarceration, we now turn to a traditional cost-benefit analysis according to equations 9.1 through 9.4.

Table 9.11   *Marginal Benefit of the Last Prisoner Incarcerated, 2005 (Using a Static Aggregate Elasticity for Incarceration and Crime Levels in 2005)*

		Total Marginal Benefits		
		Low Estimate ($)	Mean Estimate ($)	High Estimate ($)
(a)	(b)	(c)	(d)	(e)
η	λ	5,857	16,128	26,398
–0.05	1.147	6,716	18,492	30,269
–0.1	2.293	13,432	36,985	60,537
–0.2	4.587	26,864	73,969	121,074
–0.3	6.880	40,297	110,954	181,611
–0.4	9.173	53,729	147,939	242,149

Source: Author's calculations.
Note: Column a shows the elasticity of crime with respect to incarceration that is used to predict the number of crimes that will be averted by locking up one additional prisoner (column b). The remainder of the table converts the reduction in crimes shown in column b into monetary values. The low versus high cost estimates are weighted costs derived for the average crime in table 9.9. Marginal benefits were quite similar if we also extracted motor-vehicle theft from the general elasticity and assigned it an elasticity twice (or even three times) as high. We do not show results for this exercise. λ's are evaluated at 2005 values, when the total number of adjusted index crimes was 28,892,802 (Federal Bureau of Investigation 2006), and the number of state prisoners was 1,259,905 (Harrison and Beck 2006). Table 9B.8 provides analogous results that exclude murder from the benefit calculus.

Though considerable uncertainty remains over the best estimates for the elasticity and costs of crime as well as the costs of incarceration, this analysis uses a range of figures that presumably brackets the true figures. One of the central conclusions is that two factors lead to wildly varying predictions about the optimal rate of incarceration: the imprecision in various key estimates and the influence of certain normative choices.

To begin this analysis, I estimate the marginal benefits of incarceration at an aggregate level; that is, using aggregate elasticity estimates without distinguishing between the different types of crime. The results are presented in table 9.11; the numbers in columns c through e represent the marginal benefits from the incarceration of the last inmate using various estimates. I think that the most accurate aggregate elasticity estimate for 2005 is likely to be between –0.10 and –0.15; however, given the high de-

Table 9.12   *Marginal Benefit of the Last Prisoner Incarcerated, 1986 (Using a Static Aggregate Elasticity for Incarceration and Crime Levels in 1986)*

		Total Marginal Benefits		
		Low Estimate ($)	Mean Estimate ($)	High Estimate ($)
(a)	(b)	(c)	(d)	(e)
η	λ	5,857	16,128	26,398
−0.05	3.338	19,553	53,838	88,124
−0.1	6.677	39,106	107,677	176,247
−0.2	13.353	78,213	215,354	352,495
−0.3	20.030	117,319	323,031	528,742
−0.4	26.706	156,425	430,707	704,990

Source: Author's calculations.
Note: This table replicates table 9.11 using 1986 data on the number of crimes and prisoners, while retaining the same crime-reporting rate values and cost-per-crime figures as in table 9.11 (Harrison and Beck 2006). In 1986, the total number of adjusted index crimes was 32,418,219, and the number of state prisoners was 485,553 (Gilliard and Beck 1996). With higher crime in 1986 (than in 2005) and lower levels of incarceration, the marginal benefit of an additional incarceration is roughly three times higher in 1986 than in 2005—even though we use the same constant elasticities as in table 9.11.

gree of uncertainty, I present results for elasticity estimates ranging from −0.05 to −0.4.

Table 9.11 estimates the benefits of adding an additional prisoner using the marginal benefits equation (equation 9.4), which must be evaluated at specific crime and imprisonment levels (2005 average values are used here). Once again, we see the influence of the fact, stressed in table 9.2, that even under the assumption of constant elasticity, incarceration faces diminishing marginal returns (note that P is the denominator of equation 9.4). All else equal, the impact on crime of an additional prisoner becomes smaller at higher levels of incarceration. To underscore this, we recalculated table 9.11 using sample averages during 1986 (the results are shown in table 9.12). Clearly, the marginal benefits of an additional incarceration in 1986 were significantly higher than they are today, even with the same assumptions about the elasticity of crime with respect to incarceration. This fact of sharply decreasing marginal utility alone suggests caution in advocating additional increases in incarceration.[26]

Of course, looking only at marginal benefits is not sufficient to determine optimality; we need to compare the benefits of the marginal incarceration against its costs. So that we can make the appropriate comparison, it is useful to discuss exactly what is meant by "marginal benefit of the last prisoner incarcerated." Note an important fact about the design of the elasticity models: most of them are at the state-year level. That is, they regress the crime rate on the state-prison rate, which is a yearly snapshot of the state-prison population (the prison rate is usually either once lagged or contemporaneous to the crime variable). Tables 9.11 and 9.12 thus quantify the added benefit of increasing the state-prison population by one for a single year. Hence, the marginal cost analogue is the cost of incarcerating an additional state prisoner during a particular year.

There are several reasonable estimates for the marginal costs: we can estimate the costs at $25,797 per prisoner, per year (if we only include the explicit monetary costs of operating the prison system and use a mean national figure); alternatively, we can use an estimate of $55,000 per prisoner, per year (if we add lost productivity and capital expenditures to the operating costs). An intermediate value of $35,000 might be justifiable for a different set of assumptions about capital costs or offender productivity, or for states with below-average operating costs. Alternatively, the costs of incarceration might go well beyond even the $55,000 estimate for high-operating-cost states or if we attach significant monetary values to some of incarceration's other negative impacts. Among these additional effects is the negative impact on the social fabric of communities and families, the disutility to the prisoner of incarceration, enhanced likelihood of future criminality among inmates, the spread of diseases such as AIDS and tuberculosis, tax distortions that make the social cost of raising a dollar greater than a dollar, and postprison release employment difficulties (Levitt 1996; Holzer, chapter 8, this volume). These additional costs are hard to quantify at the yearly marginal level; however, they could potentially lead to marginal-cost estimates as high as $80,000.

Returning to the classic efficiency condition, optimality is reached when marginal benefits equal marginal costs. Using equation 9.4 to define marginal benefits, and setting that equal to marginal costs (on the present assumption that the elasticity η is fixed over the relevant range of interest, that marginal costs take on one of the fixed dollar values identified, and that total crime costs will vary with the incarceration rate), we get the following equation:

$$MC = (\eta / P^*) * [TC - (TC * \eta * ((P^* - P_0) / P_0))] = MB, \qquad (9.6)$$

where MC is marginal costs, MB is marginal benefits, P^* is the optimal incarceration level, CPC is the cost of crime, and P_0 is the current level of incarceration. We can then solve equation 9.6 for P^*, which can alternatively be represented in terms of the change in incarceration from the current level of incarceration to the optimal level (ΔP). If we note that $\Delta P = P^* - P_0$, then we can rearrange the equation to solve for ΔP:

$$\Delta P = [(\eta * CPC) - (MC * P_0)] / [MC + ((\eta^2 * CPC) / P_0)]. \qquad (9.7)$$

Table 9.3 uses this equation along with the fact that the 2005 national prison population (under state jurisdiction) was 1,259,905 (Harrison and Beck 2006) to calculate how the American prison system would have to change in order to reach optimality for various combinations of our elasticity and cost estimates.

Table 9.3 underscores the point that—based on which figures one adopts for the elasticity of crime with respect to incarceration, the cost of crime, and the marginal cost of an added prisoner—one could justify essentially any conclusion about incarceration, from massive reductions in the number of inmates to dramatic increases.

My own view for a state with average operating costs is that the social cost of incarceration at the margin would be at least $55,000, and it would be reasonable to use something close to the high cost-of-crime estimates (with murder costs eliminated). Under these assumptions, a low elasticity (–0.05) would imply the need to considerably reduce the level of incarceration, while a plausible but larger elasticity of –0.1 would imply the need for substantial increases in the prison population. Optimality would be reached with an intermediate elasticity somewhat above –0.075.

If one were persuaded that the low cost-of-crime figures were more appropriate, then combining any elasticity estimate with prison-cost estimates at $55,000 or above would point toward the need for large reductions in the prison level (except when MC is $55,000 and the elasticity is –0.4, which would be roughly optimal). At the plausible elasticities of –0.05 and –0.1 (and MC = $55,000), the decision to opt for the low cost-of-crime estimates would point towards a drop in the prison population of about 1 million from its 2005 level of 1.26 million.

Substantial increases in the prison population would be necessary for higher cost-of-crime estimates and elasticities above –0.1. Note that even with the highest cost of incarceration, if one uses the high cost-of-crime estimates and an elasticity of –0.2, optimality would call for an additional 820,000 prisoners. If the elasticity were as high as –0.3, it would call for a doubling of the prison population.

Some of the conclusions flowing from table 9.3 are so extreme that they tend to discredit the attending assumptions and estimates on which they are based. Indeed, using a marginal cost of $55,000, the magnitude of the proposed drops in incarceration of close to 1 million for elasticities that are below –0.1 (and a drop of almost 600,000 even for an elasticity of –0.2) suggests either that our current incarceration policy is dramatically inappropriate or that the low cost-of-crime figures are simply unrealistic. Moving down a column in table 9.3 or moving across a row illustrates that a single step can imply very dramatic shifts in the number of prisoners needed to reach optimality (either upwards or downwards). The bottom line is that considerably greater refinement in the estimates of the three categories—the elasticity, the cost of crime, and the marginal cost of incarceration—is needed before strong policy conclusions can be drawn.[27]

EVALUATING THE OPPORTUNITY COST OF INCREASED INCARCERATION

Accordingly, in addition to using a cost-benefit analysis, there is a second hurdle that a policy of incarceration must clear. Specifically, we must consider the opportunity costs of incarceration and the relative efficiency of different ways of allocating crime-fighting resources. Besides incarceration, a variety of additional crime-fighting strategies exist—for example, increasing the police force, changing policing strategies, or spending on education or social programs (Donohue and Siegelman 1998).[28] Given these options, we must ask ourselves whether our very heavy reliance on incarceration is the most effective way of allocating resources from our limited crime-fighting budget. "Unless the government spends in such a way that the marginal benefit (the crime reduction achieved from the last dollar spent) is the same for each activity, society will not be fighting crime in a cost-effective manner" (Donohue and Siegelman 1998, 2).

The large drop in crime in New York City in the wake of very large increases in the police force in the early 1990s suggests that, rather than locking up criminals after they commit their crimes, a more cost-efficient strategy may be to discourage crime with a proactive regulatory approach rather than a post hoc pure deterrence or incapacitation strategy. Economists Donohue and Ludwig (2007) argue that the elasticity of crime with respect to police is likely to be higher (at –0.4) than the elasticity with respect to incarceration. If one recognizes that the number of police officers is lower than the number of prisoners, and the cost of hiring a police officer is roughly equal to the social cost of an added inmate, then this would suggest the attractiveness of switching resources from incarceration toward hiring more police (Donohue 2004a).

However, a full-scale inquiry into the optimal level of incarceration would also have to probe whether shifting resources from prisons to social spending might yield net social gains. Donohue and economist Peter Siegelman (1998) offer a thought experiment designed to spell out "the conditions under which it would be possible to reduce spending on prisons, use the money to fund social programs, and reduce the overall crime rate in the process" (2). That study examined the effectiveness in reducing criminal behavior of certain social programs, such as preschool and early-childhood education, family therapy, programs for juvenile delinquents, and labor-market interventions.[29] After assessing these programs, the authors considered a hypothetical choice between two crime-fighting strategies for the future: "(1) increase the prison population by 50 percent over the level in December of 1993, which seems to be the trend of current policy, or (2) maintain the December 1993 level of incarceration and spend the present value of the saved social resources on crime-reducing social programs" (Donohue and Siegelman 1998, 31).[30] The question was thus if the second policy could achieve the same levels of crime reduction as the first.

To focus the inquiry, Donohue and Siegelman's (1998) study estimated that increasing future incarceration rates for a present cohort of three-year-old children by 50 percent beyond the 1993 level would cost (in present value terms) between $5.6 billion and $8 billion, and future crime rates would be 5 to 15 percent lower than if the incarceration increase had not occurred.[31] Based on an examination of research studies regarding the effects of various social programs, Donohue and Siegelman (1998) concluded that the most promising ones were capable of matching the 5 to 15 percent crime reduction if the equivalent incarceration money ($5.6 billion to $8 billion) were reallocated to such programs. For example, the authors document that if the money were used to fund a national targeted program such as the Perry Preschool (Hohmann, Banet, and Weikart 1979), the volume of crime would decrease by 9.3 percent in the worst-case scenario (if $5.6 billion were invested and assuming that the real-life program would be half as effective as the small pilot study); it would decrease by 20.1 percent in the best-case scenario (using the $8 billion cost estimate and assuming the preschool program would be just as effective as the pilot program).

Importantly, these estimates were based on the assumption that social spending could be targeted towards those most at risk for future criminal behavior. The targeting issue is important because spending the money on children with low risk of committing future crimes leads to only modest benefits, thus costing billions of dollars for little crime-reduction gain. In theory, the targeting problem is solvable if political, legal, and ethical concerns can be addressed. The study showed that even a crude target such as young black males would generate high social benefits if the programs could work in large-scale implementation with reasonable effectiveness. Donohue and Siegelman (1998) thus illustrated that under certain conditions, "increased spending [on] social programs [can] generate crime reductions of the same order of magnitude as the prison spending it replaces" (40). In addition, if one considers that social programs may also have many positive spillovers—such as improving earnings and ed-ucation for some of the most disadvantaged communities in the coun-try—the appeal of social programs becomes further accentuated. It is even more appealing if we consider incarceration's negative spillovers on these same communities (such as on family structure). In summary, con-sidering the question of incarceration from an opportunity-cost perspec-tive reveals a potential inadequacy of the cost-benefit test: even if incar-ceration passes the test, reallocation away from mass incarceration might be a more sound and socially beneficial strategy if similar resources can generate greater or equal crime reductions when allocated to social spending (Greenwood et al. 1996).

CONCLUSION

This chapter cannot provide clear policy predictions concerning the opti-mal level of incarceration. Rather, it provides an exercise of trying to think systematically about the marginal costs and benefits of incarceration in light of the existing literature on prison effectiveness in crime reduction. This can illuminate where we would benefit from more precise estimates of key parameters as well as the importance of resolving difficult philo-sophical questions. Hopefully this exercise will prove valuable as a means of illustrating the areas of our ignorance and the conceptually im-portant issues that need to be resolved in thinking about optimal crime-fighting policy. It would be helpful to further investigate whether utility of prisoners or their families should count; whether utility of victims' families should count (although perhaps this is implicit in willingness-to-pay estimates); whether pure transfer costs should be included in the cost of crime; and whether the important issue of murder victimization should be treated in a more nuanced way to reflect the different social costs attending the deaths of those involved in criminal behavior.

Moreover, if one widens the lens and focuses not only on a narrow cost-benefit calculation of incarceration but also on alternative crime-fighting approaches, there is reason to believe that alternatives to incar-ceration might well be more socially attractive than our current reliance on incarceration as the predominant crime-fighting strategy. This broader inquiry also illustrates why some consideration of the human costs of in-carceration to inmates is appropriate. Consider two equally costly crime-fighting strategies that led to equal reductions in crime, with one leading to 500,000 extra prison inmates and one leading to 500,000 extra children in preschool enrichment programs. Under these circumstances, my belief is that the preschool enrichment strategy should dominate the punitive approach. This intuition supports the view that some measure of the costs borne by prison inmates should be included as a social cost of the punitive approach. With so many inmates suffering from mental illness, alternative and more humane forms of handling such individuals may well be more cost effective if the human toll of mass incarceration is considered in the calculation.

APPENDIX 9A: ESTIMATING THE ELASTICITY OF CRIME WITH RESPECT TO INCARCERATION

Table 9.1 summarizes an array of elasticity estimates that are critical to a calculation of the optimal level of crime. This appendix discusses these studies in greater detail. It offers insights into why there is such variability in elasticity estimates across the various studies, and it discusses the most plausible range of estimates for this elasticity given the current levels of crime and incarceration.

Spelman (1994) provides one of the most carefully conducted incapacitation studies, based primarily on RAND's 1978 prison- and jail-inmate surveys in California, Michigan, and Texas. Similar incapacitation studies have found estimates between –0.10 and –0.30 (Spelman 2000b). However, if marginal deterrence exists, then these studies underestimate the elasticity of crime with respect to incarceration by ignoring this effect. Unfortunately, we do not know enough about the magnitude of any marginal deterrent effect in order to properly adjust incapacitation-based elasticity estimates. On the other hand, there are also factors that could lead incapacitation studies to overestimate the elasticity (Marvell and Moody 1994; Levitt 1996; Spelman 2000b).[32] For example, if crime is conducted in groups or if there is a replacement effect (that is, incarcerated criminals are replaced by new ones who enter the "criminal market" to fill in the space created by incarceration), survey-based research might overestimate the elasticity. Spelman (2000b) tries to adjust for these factors, and he computes an elasticity estimate of roughly –0.16, as indicated in table 9.1.

Thomas B. Marvell and Carlisle Moody, Jr. (1994) conducted one of the first studies to use a state-year panel dataset to estimate the impact of incarceration on crime. After concluding that simultaneity is not a problem (based on their Granger causality test), the authors estimate a state fixed-effect (or first-differenced) model; the log of crime rates (per 100,000 population) is regressed on the log of the state-prison population (per 100,000 population), year dummies, and three control variables related to the age distribution of each states' population.[33] Interestingly, their overall elasticity estimate of –0.16 is exactly the same as the incapacitation effect estimate derived by Spelman. This suggests either that one or both estimates are inaccurate, or the marginal deterrent effect from increased incarceration is zero.

Although Marvell and Moody do not find evidence of simultaneity, and neither do Liedka, Piehl, and Useem (2006), other researchers have deemed simultaneity to be a problem and have attempted to control for it. If simultaneity is present—that is, if crime impacts prison rates in addition to the impact of incarceration on crime—regression results will underestimate the impact of incarceration on crime.[34] Economist Steven Levitt (1996) uses an innovative approach to address this issue. The key insight is that prison-overcrowding litigation is a valid instrumental variable for the level of incarceration. Using this instrument with a state-year panel database, Levitt arrives at estimates of elasticity that are significantly higher than previous ones. This suggests that simultaneity is indeed a problem; not controlling for it significantly underestimates the impact of incarceration on crime. Apart from his two-stage least-square (2SLS) approach and some different controls, Levitt's model is generally similar to Marvell and Moody model. Levitt's variables are first differenced, and he regresses the log of crime rates on the log of incarceration rates (once lagged). Like Marvell and Moody, Levitt runs aggregate regressions as well as regressions for each type of index crime, resulting in crime-specific elasticities. As is frequently the case with this form of estimation, Levitt's 2SLS approach produces much larger standard errors for his coefficients. The 95 percent confidence intervals around his estimates are broad enough to cover essentially all values resulting from other studies.

Recently several studies have been published that use new data sets or employ new analytical methods. For example, Spelman (2005) estimates the elasticity of crime using a Texas county-level panel dataset. He argues that Texas county-level data is more accurate and solves several of the problems associated with more aggregated data sets. Also, working at the county level allows him to collect data for several instrumental variables that he uses to control for simultaneity. As shown in table 9.1, Spelman generates elasticity estimates that are comparable to, but somewhat higher than, Steven Levitt's estimates. The upper end of Spelman's confidence interval for the elasticity of violent crime is –0.75. In my view, this number is too high, but this value may simply reflect the large standard errors that often attend instrumental-variables estimation. There are reasons to be cautious about extrapolating from this study in trying to tease out the causal impacts of incarceration. First, it is based on a single state over a single decade. Second, the particular decade was a period of virtually unparalleled growth in Texas' level of incarceration (as seen in figure 9A.1); also, it was a time when substantial drops in crime were common, even in states that did not resort to such dramatic increases in incarceration. Figure 9A.2 illustrates the sharp monotonic decreases in violent-crime rates in Texas starting in 1991.

Figure 9A. I   *Texas Incarceration, 1990 to 2000*

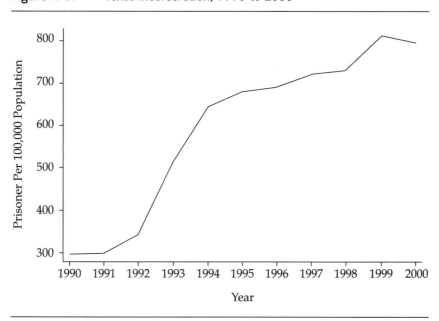

Source: Hill and Harrison (2004).
Note: Only includes state prisoners (excluding local jail inmates and federal prisoners).

A quite different view of the value of incarceration comes from a still more recent study by Liedka, Piehl, and Useem (2006). The authors use a fifty-state panel data set that covers the period from 1972 to 2000, specifically testing whether the elasticity of crime changes as the level of incarceration rises. The study explicitly considers not only the incapacitation and deterrence benefits of increased incarceration, but it also tries to test for a third mechanism—the collateral damage of mass incarceration. The concern is that very high levels of incarceration might "increase crime because of the damage done to communities and the social network of young men and women."[35] Although Liedka, Piehl, and Useem's model is quite similar that to that of Marvell and Moody, and it contains state and year fixed effects, it includes higher-order incarceration variables that allow the elasticity of crime to vary over levels of incarceration.[36] With varying statistical significance, Liedka, Piehl, and Useem's specifications suggest that the elasticity of crime becomes smaller at higher incarceration levels, and it actually becomes positive above some threshold level of imprisonment. They interpret this as support for the collateral-damage

Figure 9A.2   *The Violent Crime Drop in Texas, 1990 to 2000*

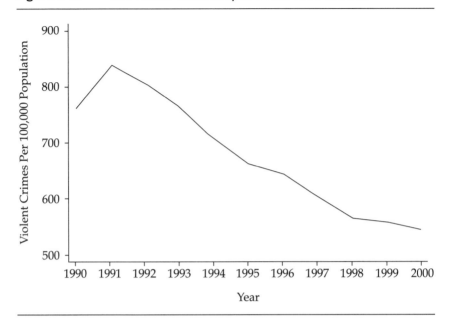

Source: Federal Bureau of Investigation 2006.

hypothesis. The results for their quadratic model, evaluated at various incarceration levels, are shown in table 9.1. Essentially, they suggest that,
over their entire sample period, incarceration had a small dampening effect on crime; however, at the current high levels of incarceration, the adverse consequences of incarceration have caused the sign on the crime
elasticity to turn positive.

How Modeling Choices Influence the Estimates of η

The range of estimated elasticities, albeit problematic for policymakers, is
not surprising to econometricians. There is a great deal of model uncertainty in estimating crime models, and, with widely varying specifications and approaches, the range of estimates is predictably large (Donohue 2004b; Donohue and Wolfers 2006). One approach to resolving this
uncertainty is to adopt a Bayesian model averaging approach, and this
may well be a sensible way to advance this process further (Strnad 2007).

To provide one example of how modeling choices that are frequently not discussed (let alone justified) can reflect very different implicit links between incarceration and crime, consider the evidence presented in table 9A.1. The table shows the average annual growth rate for incarceration and homicide rates, starting in 1977, for the nation and the ten highest and lowest states (ranked by the magnitude of the growth rates in incarceration).[37] The growth rate (b) from a particular state is derived from estimating the following equation:

$$\ln(\text{incarceration rate or homicide rate}) = a + b * \text{year.} \qquad (9A.1)$$

From 1977 to 2004, the incarceration rate grew nationally by 5.5 percent per year; meanwhile, over that same period (albeit ending in 2003), the homicide rate declined an average of 1.3 percent per year (of course obscuring much movement in the homicide rate, which first went up and then down). Leading the way in this prison growth rate were New Hampshire (7.7 percent annually) and Wisconsin (7.2 percent annually). While New Hampshire experienced a robust average annual murder-rate decline of 2.3 percent, Wisconsin actually saw an annual murder-rate growth of about 1 percent over the period from 1977 to 2003. At the other end of the spectrum, North Carolina had the smallest annual percentage growth rate in incarceration (2.3 percent), followed by Maine with a 2.8 percent incarceration growth. Both these states experienced a healthy decline in homicide rates, although Maine's decline of about 2.6 percent per year was almost twice that of North Carolina.

To return to the central issue of the impact of modeling choices, studies that include the natural log of the incarceration rate as their key explanatory variable—as do the econometric studies in table 9.1 with the exception of Rucker Johnson and Steven Raphael's study (2006)—implicitly constrain their estimated impact on crime to be the same across states for equal proportionate changes in the incarceration rate, regardless of overall incarceration levels. However, the data in figure 9A.3 raise questions about this assumption. For example, if we compare the incarceration rate of North Carolina (the slowest growing state in terms of incarceration-rate change) with that of New Hampshire (the fastest growing state), we see that North Carolina still incarcerates prisoners at double the rate of New Hampshire, even after twenty-seven years of much faster prison growth in the latter. Presumably, New Hampshire was sending out a message to potential criminals that the risks of incarceration were growing substantially over this period, which would certainly be relevant to issues of deterrence. Still, in terms of taking bodies off the street, North Carolina was still far ahead of New Hampshire: in 2004, the former state's prison system contained 35,434 inmates, while the latter only had 2,448 (see figure 9A.3 for more detail). It is this larger absolute number of inmates that

Table 9A.1   *Changes in Incarceration/Homicide Nationally and by Selected States*

Geographic Unit	Average Annual Percent Change in Incarceration Rate (1977 to 2004)	Average Annual Percent Change in Homicide Rate (1977 to 2003)
United States	5.54***	–1.281***
States with the ten highest annual percent changes in incarceration		
New Hampshire	7.71***	–2.32***
Wisconsin	7.19***	1.04***
Colorado	7.16***	–2.38***
Washington, D.C.	7.05***	2.88***
Mississippi	7.02***	–1.03***
Idaho	6.92***	–2.76***
California	6.91***	–2.57***
Connecticut	6.91***	–1.33***
Pennsylvania	6.86***	–0.31
North Dakota	6.78***	–0.81
States with the ten lowest annual percent changes in incarceration		
Oregon	4.29***	–3.16***
Nebraska	4.23***	–0.29
Georgia	4.14***	–2.61***
South Carolina	3.72***	–1.91***
Washington	3.60***	–1.64***
Florida	3.46***	–3.71***
Nevada	3.42***	–2.52***
Maryland	3.39***	0.43
Maine	2.85***	–2.645***
North Carolina	2.33***	–1.38***

Source: Author's calculations.
Note: Reported year coefficients are from the following state-year regressions:
ln (incarceration rate) = a + b (year) + e (1977 to 2004)
ln (homicide rate) = a + b (year) + e (1977 to 2003)
Incarceration data include only state prisoners (Hill and Harrison 2006).
*** and ** indicate significance at the 1 percent and 5 percent level, respectively.

is relevant to the likely incapacitative benefit of incarceration: a 1 percent increase in incarceration in North Carolina would take an additional 350 criminals off the street, while a 10 percent increase in New Hampshire would only remove 250. From the perspective of the econometrician, the lesson is that it would not be surprising if different approaches to specifying the effect of incarceration on crime result in very different elasticity

Figure 9A.3   *State Prison Incarceration Rate per 100,000 Persons in Selected States, 1977 to 2004*

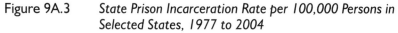

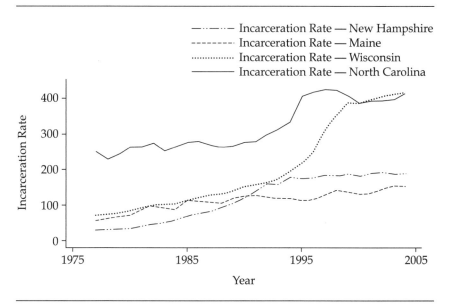

Source: Authors compilation.
Note: Only includes prisoners under state jurisdiction and excludes local jail inmates. Over the 1977 to 2004 period, New Hampshire (the state with the highest prison growth rate) went from 261 state prisoners (30 per 100,000 population) to 2,448 prisoners in 2004 (188 per 100,000). The second fastest growing state, Wisconsin, went from 3,347 (72 per 100,000) to 22,966 (417 per 100,000). For the slow-growth states, Maine went from 637 (58 per 100,000) to 2,024 (153 per 100,000), and North Carolina from 14,250 (251 per 100,000) to 35,434 (415 per 100,000). Nationally, the state-prison population rates per 100,000 rose from approximately 122 in 1977 to 448 in 2004. (Hill and Harrison 2006).

estimates. Logging the incarceration rate will not generate the same result as using the level (or the level as well as the annual change).

There are other ways in which a mere rate of incarceration measure may obscure important crime-fighting differences between states or otherwise fail to reflect the true relationship between incarceration and crime. Spelman (2000b) notes that

some states, such as Hawaii, New York, Massachusetts, and Wisconsin, incarcerate a small proportion of their offenders but hold them for long terms—a de facto incapacitation strategy. Other states, such as Alabama, Georgia, Mississippi, and North Carolina, incarcerate more offenders for shorter terms—a deterrence strategy. If one of these strategies is more effective than the other, this should be reflected in each state's elasticity and marginal offense rate (473).

Furthermore, states also vary in the types of criminals that they incarcerate (for example, drug offenders versus violent offenders), which can also influence the effectiveness of their prison system. Despite these reasons to expect the elasticities to differ among states, most panel studies in table 9.1 estimate a single national aggregate elasticity. Clearly, important policy-relevant information might be lost if the models used are too sparse or too aggregated. In a recent paper, John Pfaff (2007) argues that "even setting aside the problem of endogeneity, the dynamic relationship between crime and total incarceration is complex and . . . ignored" (26) in many of the models studying the impact of incarceration rates on crime. More work is needed to refine the model specifications in light of these dynamic complexities.

One can narrow the range of divergent results shown in table 9.1 by limiting one's focus to only Ordinary Least Squares (OLS) estimates of the elasticity of crime with respect to incarceration. This comparison is presented in table 9A.2. For example, though Levitt (1996) corrects for simultaneity using an instrumental variable, he also provides results for simple OLS regressions that do not correct for simultaneity. Similarly, Liedka, Piehl, and Useem (2006), while focused on developing a nonconstant elasticity model, present results for a constant elasticity specification that resembles that of Marvell and Moody (1994). By comparing overlapping specifications, we can potentially discern certain trends or patterns in the results, even if this exercise cannot resolve the major debates about issues such as simultaneity or nonconstant elasticity.

Table 9A.2 highlights that, even after eliminating major sources of difference by focusing only on OLS estimates, there is still more variation in the elasticity estimates than a policymaker would prefer. With the potential exception of motor-vehicle theft, which seems more responsive to incarceration and is consistently statistically significant, elasticity estimates tend to be in the range of –0.06 to –0.10 (although correcting for simultaneity could well increase these estimates). Though it is difficult to be certain due to large confidence intervals, the elasticity estimates for all index crimes from the simple OLS models seem to decrease in more recent time intervals. This would be consistent with the idea that incarceration becomes less effective with higher overall levels of incarceration. This conclusion is supported by Johnson and Raphael (2007), who find elasticities in the range of Levitt's (1996) for the 1978 to 1990 period, while finding significantly smaller effects for the 1991 to 2004 period. Furthermore, the OLS estimates of the elasticity of murder from studies conducted by

Table 9A.2   *OLS Estimates of Incarceration Elasticities Across Four Studies*

	Marvell and Moody (1994) 1971/1973 to 1989	Levitt's OLS (1996) 1971 to 1993	Becsi (1999) 1971 to 1994	Liedka, Piehl, and Useem Constant Elasticity Results (2006) 1972 to 2000
All index crimes	–0.16(—)	—	–0.087** (0.015)	[1] –0.063(0.046) or [2] –0.072 (0.044) ^
Violent crimes	–0.06 ± 0.11	–0.099** (.033)	–0.046* (0.022)	—
Property crimes	–0.17 ± 0.06	–0.071**(0.019)	–0.091** (0.015)	—
Murder	–0.065 (0.085)	–0.138 (0.177)	–0.063 (0.034)	—
Motor-vehicle theft	–0.200** (0.048)	–0.081* (0.039)	–0.198**(0.032)	—

Note: statistically significant at the 5 percent level; **1 percent level. Levitt's estimated elasticity for motor vehicle theft using OLS (shown in table as –0.081) is far lower than his four estimate of –0.259, which is not far from the ones presented in this table for Marvell and Moody and for Becsi.
^ Liedka, Piehl, and Useem first estimate is for a model that includes only three controls (those in Marvell and Moody 1994), while the second set of results corresponds to a model with a wider set of controls, along the lines of Levitt.
— study does not run the regression in question.

Marvell and Moody (1994) and by Becsi (1999) seem consistently low and statistically insignificant. Indeed, we have yet to see any study that generates statistically significant results for the elasticity of murder. Levitt's OLS estimate for murder is higher, though it is also very far from being statistically significant.

Of course, even while looking at the most similar specifications, these studies still have differences that complicate efforts at direct comparison. To begin with, though Marvell and Moody, Levitt, and Becsi analyze similar time periods, Liedka, Piehl, and Useem's (2006) study extends much further. If the effect of incarceration changes over the sample period, we cannot directly compare results (though differing results can buttress the hypothesis of changing elasticity with levels incarceration). Furthermore, while Becsi and Levitt use similar control variables, Marvell and Moody use a much more limited set of controls. As Liedka, Piehl, and Useem's results show, using the full set of controls leads to somewhat larger estimates of the elasticity. In addition, the definition of some of the main variables is different across studies. Marvell and Moody and Levitt first difference all variables. With one exception, all the studies control for state and year fixed effects (Becsi does not include year dummies).

One feature of all of these studies is that they try to estimate the extent to which a change in incarceration will influence crime in the short term via incapacitation and general deterrence (usually one year after the incarceration increase). These models will be incorrectly specified, though, if the impacts from incarceration are more enduring. Such net long-term effects would reflect the cumulative influence of benign factors such as specific deterrence and rehabilitation, as well as any counterproductive criminal amplification induced by exposure to a criminal population (Chen and Shapiro 2007; Lerman, chapter 5, this volume). If these net long-term effects are undesirable, elasticity estimates based on short-term estimates may give an unduly optimistic picture of the benefits of increased incarceration. Alternatively, if the net long-term effects only buttress the short-term effects, then the current elasticity estimates may be downwardly biased.

ALL STEPS OF COST-BENEFIT ANALYSIS (EXCLUDING MURDER FROM THE AGGREGATE ELASTICITY)

Table 9A.3 computes the changes in incarceration needed to reach optimality under the assumption that either incarceration is ineffectual at reducing murder or the social cost of murder is essentially zero. While it may seem odd that increases in incarceration should reduce other crimes but not murder, note that none of the estimated effects of incarceration on murder depicted in table 9.1 is statistically significant, and most of them have suggested lower elasticities for murder than for other crimes. Still, it seems unlikely that murders would not go down if incarceration increased, even if the estimates in table 9.3 using the same elasticity for all index I crimes may overstate the true level of murder reduction.

The second possible assumption—that the social cost of murder is very low—is again an exaggeration, but it serves as a corrective to the very high estimates of the social cost of murder that we use in the table 9.3 calculations. Since a not inconsiderable number of murder victims are criminals, the social cost of their murder may be considerably lower than the social cost of the murder of an innocent citizen. By computing incarceration optimality both with an exaggerated effectiveness of the benefits of prisons in reducing the social costs of murder and without any regard for this effectiveness, we hopefully bracket the true effect.

Table 9A.3 reveals that if one adopted a low estimate of the cost per crime (CPC), then under any of the combinations of elasticity and cost per added prisoner (MC)—with only one exception—we are above the optimal level of incarceration right now. The one exception is that if prisons are cheap (as shown in panel a of table 9A.3) and highly effective

Table 9A.3   *Changes in State Prison Population Necessary to Reach Optimality (2005 Values, with Murder Excluded)*

(a)	(b)	(c)	(d)
η general	Low CPCs	Mean CPCs	High CPCs
A. Optimality Using Marginal Cost = $25,797			
−0.05	−1,058,287	−410,465	206,160
−0.1	−846,909	363,514	1,374,006
−0.2	−432,768	1,361,053	2,400,065
−0.3	−77,524	1,711,408	2,445,212
−0.4	193,120	1,737,716	2,222,258
B. Optimality Using Marginal Cost = $35000			
−0.05	−1,111,003	−628,489	−163,355
−0.1	−953,099	−25,327	783,555
−0.2	−632,198	865,671	1,831,222
−0.3	−335,799	1,295,861	2,064,135
−0.4	−87,350	1,430,387	1,979,208
C. Optimality Using Marginal Cost = $55,000			
−0.05	−1,164,955	−854,577	−551,423
−0.1	−1,063,080	−447,963	114,152
−0.2	−848,018	246,791	1,050,759
−0.3	−633,268	700,145	1,456,885
−0.4	−433,861	940,192	1,552,589
D. Optimality Using Marginal Cost = $80,000			
−0.05	−1,194,553	−979,902	−768,713
−0.1	−1,123,985	−691,284	−285,037
−0.2	−971,828	−155,247	496,444
−0.3	−813,065	257,915	951,824
−0.4	−656,688	532,054	1,155,009

Source: Author's compilation.
Note: The five depicted elasticities apply to index I crimes excluding murder. CPC stands for an estimate of the average cost per crime. "Low" and "high" cost estimates are described in table 9.9, and the "mean CPC" is the average of the two for each crime type. The number of index I crimes, excluding murder, in 2005 was 28,876,062 (Harrison and Beck 2006). The values listed in each cell for an attendant combination of h, CPC, and marginal cost of incarceration reflect the difference between the optimal state prisoner count (P*) and the number of state prisoners in 2005: 1,259,905 (Harrison and Beck 2006). That is, these figures tell us how many prisoners would have to be added (for positive numbers) or eliminated (for negative values) from the state prison system to reach the point where the marginal costs of incarcerating an additional prisoner equal its marginal benefits. For an analogous table that includes murder, see table 9.3.

($\eta = -0.4$), then further increases in incarceration would be called for in this calculus. Expressed differently, if the true CPC is low, then current incarceration policy could only be optimal if the crime elasticity exceeds –0.3 and prisons are very cheap.

At the other end of the spectrum, now consider the case where costs per crime are high (shown in column d, table 9A.3). In this case, most combinations of elasticity and MC point towards the need for greater levels of incarceration to reach optimality. If the high costs-of-crime estimates are correct, then the only way that current policy could be optimal would be if the elasticity is less than –0.05 (if MC is $25,797), slightly above –0.05 (if MC is $35,000), slightly below –0.10 (if MC is $55,000), and close to –0.15 for the most expensive incarceration cost estimates.

My own view for a state with average operating costs is that the social cost of incarceration at the margin would be at least $55,000, and the high cost of crime might be reasonable. With murder included in the analysis (as in table 9.3), optimality would be reached with an intermediate elasticity close to –0.075. With murder excluded from the analysis (as in table 9A.3), those assumptions and an elasticity of –0.075 would lead us to predict that our prison population should be cut back by perhaps hundreds of thousands. An intermediate assessment that entails some reduction in the social costs of murder from increased incarceration might suggest a need to reduce the prison population by 100,000.

Table 9B.1   Marginal Benefits of the Last Prisoner Incarcerated (Evaluated at Crime and Prisoner Values in 2005)

	Impact of Incarceration		Prevented Crimes' Cost		Marginal Benefits	
	η	λ_{total}	Low Cost Estimate ($)	High Cost Estimate ($)	Lower Estimate ($)	Upper Estimate ($)
(a)	(b)	(c)	(d)	(e)	(f)	(g)
Panel A: Using Levitt (1996) Crime-Specific Elasticities						
Murder	−0.147	0.002	4,327,266	11,593,323	8,452	22,643
Rape	−0.246	0.048	129,696	297,567	6,238	14,312
Assault	−0.410	0.218	19,528	91,817	10,457	49,165
Robbery	−0.703	0.919	22,637	290,491	8,450	108,432
Burglary	−0.401	1.218	2,287	31,980	2,787	38,969
Larceny	−0.277	4.613	335	908	1,547	4,193
Motor-vehicle theft	−0.259	0.305	1,197	5,669	366	1,731
Number of crimes averted = 7.323				Total marginal benefit = $38,295		$239,445

Table 9B.1 *(Continued)*

(a)	Impact of Incarceration		Prevented Crimes' Cost		Marginal Benefits	
	η	λ_{total}	Low Cost Estimate ($)	High Cost Estimate ($)	Lower Estimate ($)	Upper Estimate ($)
	(b)	(c)	(d)	(e)	(f)	(g)
Panel B: Using Marvell and Moody's (1994) Crime-Specific Elasticities						
Murder	-0.065	0.001	4,327,266	11,593,323	3,737	10,012
Rape	-0.113	0.022	129,696	297,567	2,865	6,574
Assault	-0.056	0.030	19,528	91,817	1,428	6,715
Robbery	-0.260	0.340	22,637	290,491	3,125	40,103
Burglary	-0.253	0.768	2,287	31,980	1,758	24,586
Larceny	-0.138	2.298	335	908	771	2,089
Motor-vehicle theft	-0.200	0.236	1,197	5,669	282	1,337
Number of crimes averted = 3.695				Total marginal benefit =$13,967		$91,416
Panel C: Using an Average of the Elasticities of Levitt (1996) and Marvell and Moody (1994)						
Murder	-0.106	0.001	4,327,266	11,593,323	6,094	16,328
Rape	-0.180	0.035	129,696	297,567	4,564	10,472
Assault	-0.233	0.124	19,528	91,817	5,942	27,940
Robbery	-0.482	0.629	22,637	290,491	5,793	74,345
Burglary	-0.327	0.993	2,287	31,980	2,273	31,777
Larceny	-0.208	3.455	335	908	1,161	3,148
Motor-vehicle theft	-0.230	0.270	1,197	5,669	325	325
Number of crimes averted = 5.507				Total marginal benefit =$26,153		$164,335

Source: Author's compilation.
Note: The Panel A estimates using Levitt's crime specific elasticities yield high and low end estimates of the cost per crime averted by adding an inmate that are roughly comparable to the fixed general crime elasticities of between –.3 and –.4, shown in table 9.11 of the text.

Table 9B.2

	Party Who Most Directly Bears Cost	Variable or Fixed Cost (Categorized as Transfer)	Included in Low Cost Estimate (Reason for Exclusion)	Included in High Cost Estimate (Reason for Exclusion)
Costs from criminal act				
Direct Property Losses				
Losses not reimbursed by insurance	Victim	Variable (transfer)	No (transfer)	Implicit
Losses reimbursed by insurance	Society	Variable (transfer)		
Administrative cost: insurance reimbursement	Society	Fixed		
Recovery by police	Society	Variable		
Medical and mental health care				
Costs not reimbursed by insurance	Victim, Victim's family, Society	Variable	Yes	Implicit
Costs reimbursed by insurance	Society	Variable (transfer)		
Administrative overhead of insurance coverage	Society	Fixed		
Victim services	Society	Variable	Yes	Implicit
Expenses charged to victim	Victim	Variable		
Expenses paid by agency	Society	Variable		
Temporary labor and training of replacements	Society	Variable		
Lost workdays				
Lost wages for unpaid workday	Victim	Variable	Yes	Implicit
Lost productivity	Society, Employer	Variable		
Lost school days				
Forgone wages due to lack of education	Victim	Variable	Yes	Implicit
Forgone nonpecuniary benefits of education	Victim	Variable		

Table 9B.2 (*Continued*)

	Party Who Most Directly Bears Cost	Variable or Fixed Cost (Categorized as Transfer)	Included in Low Cost Estimate (Reason for Exclusion)	Included in High Cost Estimate (Reason for Exclusion)
Forgone social benefits due to lack of education	Society			
Lost housework	Victim	Variable	Yes	Implicit
Pain and suffering; quality of life	Victim	Variable	Yes	Implicit
Indirect costs of victimization	Victim	Variable	No (data)	No (data)
Avoidance behavior	Victim	Variable		
Expenditures on moving, alarms, guard dogs, and so on	Victim	Variable	Yes	Implicit
Loss of affection or enjoyment	Victim's family	Variable	Yes	Implicit
Death	Victim's family	Variable		
Lost quality of life	Victim	Variable		
Loss of affection or enjoyment	Victim's family	Variable		
Funeral and burial expenses	Victim's family	Variable		
Psychological injury or treatment	Victim's family	Variable		
Legal costs associated with tort claims	Victim or Victim's family	Variable	No (data)	No (data)
"Second-generation costs"			No (data)	No (data)
Future victims of crime committed by earlier victims	Future victims	Variable		
Future social costs associated with future victims	Society, victims	Variable		
Cost of society's response				
Precautionary expenditures or effort	Potential victim	Variable	No	Implicit
Avoidance behavior	Potential victim	Variable		
Expenditures on moving, alarms, guard dogs, and so on	Potential victim	Variable		

Cost category	Potential victim	Variable		Implicit
Fear of crime	Potential victim	Variable	No	No
Criminal-justice system				
Police and investigative costs	Society	Both	Yes	Yes
Prosecutors	Society	Both	No	Yes
Courts	Society	Both	No	Yes
Legal fees				No Yes
Public defenders	Society	Both	Yes	No
Private	Offenders	Variable	No	Yes
Incarceration costs	Society	Both	Yes	Yes
Nonincarcerative sanctions	Society	Both	No	No
Victim time	Victim	Variable	Yes	Yes
Jury and witness time	Jury/witness	Variable	No	No
Victim services				
Victim service organizations	Society	Fixed	Yes	Yes
Victim service volunteer time	Volunteers	Variable		
Victim compensation programs	Society, offender	Variable		
Victim time	Victim	Variable	Yes	Yes
Other noncriminal programs			No (data)	No (data)
Hotlines and public service announcements	Society	Variable		
Community treatment programs	Society	Fixed		
Private therapy or counseling	Society, offender	Variable	No (data)	No (data)
"Overdeterrence" costs				
Innocent individuals accused of offense	Innocent individuals	Variable	Variable	
Restriction of legitimate activity	Innocent individuals	Variable	Variable	
Actions taken by offenders to avoid detection (for example, kill robbery victims to reduce chance of being caught)	Society, offender, victim	Variable	Variable	

Table 9B.2 (Continued)

	Party Who Most Directly Bears Cost	Variable or Fixed Cost (Categorized as Transfer)	Included in Low Cost Estimate (Reason for Exclusion)	Included in High Cost Estimate (Reason for Exclusion)
"Justice" costs				
Constitutional protections to avoid false accusations	Society		No (data)	No (data)
Cost of increasing detection rate to avoid differential punishment			Society	Variable
Offender costs				
Incarcerated offender costs				
Lost wages	Offender, family	Variable	Yes	Yes
Lost tax revenue and productivity	Society	Variable	No	No
Value of lost freedom	Offender	Variable	No (data)	No (data)
Psychological cost to family or loss of consortium	Family of offender	Variable	No	No
Health impact on community	Society	Variable	No	No
Community cohesion	Society	Variable	No	No
Opportunity costs				
Cost of time spent on illegal activity	Society	Variable	Yes	Yes
Resources devoted to illegal activity	Offender	Variable	No	No

Source: Adapted and expanded from Cohen, Miller, and Rossman (1994).
Notes: "Implicit" indicates that there is no direct cost measured, but we can assume that the average respondent in the Cohen and colleagues (2004) survey was considering it.
Major differences between high and low estimates are highlighted.

Table 9B.3   *Arrest Rates for Index I Crimes*

	Number of Victimizations	Reported Crime UCR		Estimated Number of Arrests		Arrest Rate (Based on NCVS)	Arrest Rate (Based on UCR)
Rape		Murder	16,692	Murder	14,062		0.84
	191,670	Forcible rape	93,934	Forcible rape	25,528	0.13	0.27
Robbery	624,850	Robbery	417,122	Robbery	114,616	0.18	0.27
Aggravated assault	1,052,260	Aggravated assault	862,947	Aggravated assault	449,297	0.43	0.52
Household burglary	3,456,220	Burglary	2,154,126	Burglary	298,835	0.09	0.14
Motor-vehicle theft	978,120	Motor-vehicle theft	1,235,226	Motor-vehicle theft	147,459	0.15	0.12
Theft	13,605,590	Larceny theft	6,776,807	Larceny theft	1,146,696	0.08	0.17
	Source: NCVS 2005, table 91.	Source: UCR 2005, Table 1.		Source: UCR 2005, Table 29.			

Source: Author's computation.
Note: The arrest rate is proxied by the ratio of total arrests to total NCVS or UCR crimes.

Table 9B.4   *Conviction Rates, Given Adult Arrests for Index I Crimes*

	Number of Adults Arrested	Number of Felony Convictions	Felony Conviction Rate
Murder	12,799	8,990	0.70
Rape	23,564	10,980	0.47
Robbery	81,340	38,430	0.47
Aggravated assault	410,892	95,600	0.23
Burglary	201,804	100,640	0.50
Motor-vehicle theft	103,664	18,530	0.18
Larceny (excluding motor-vehicle theft)	1,160,085	105,790	0.09

Source: Paige and Beck (2005).

Table 9B.5   Cost of Prison, Jail, and Probation for Index/Crimes

| | Mean Sentence | | | Estimated % Served | Cost of Sentence | | |
	Prison	Jail	Probation		Prison ($70/Day)	Jail ($67/Day)	Probation ($5/Day)
Murder or nonnegative man-slaughter	225	10	76	63	310,162.5	13,785	11,400
Rape or sexual assault	100	8	54	64	139,800	11,184	8,100
Robbery	91	11	51	58	116,571	14,091	7,650
Aggravated assault	54	7	39	66	77,598	10,059	5,850
Burglary	36	6	36	49	39,798	6,633	5,400
Larceny	24	6	36	52	26,532	6,633	3,600
Motor-vehicle theft	24	6	24	49	27,936	6,984	5,400

Source Author's compilation.
Note: Estimated time served based on prison sentence Durose and Langan (2004).
Remaining sentence is assumed to be under supervision (same cost as probation).
Probation is assumed to cost five dollars per day per offender.
Estimated time served in prison is also used for jail time served.

Table 9B.6 *Three Different Ways of Weighting Crimes in Order to Derive an "Average Cost of Prevented Crime" Estimate*

	Number of Crimes				Possible Weights		
	Reported by FBI	Victim-ization Survey	Reporting Rate (%)	FBI Figures Adjusted for Reporting Levels	Weight 1: Frequency of Each Crime Type (Percentage of All Reported Crimes)	Weight 2: Frequency of Each Crime Type (Percentage of All Victimizations)	Weight 3: Frequency of each Crime Using Adjusted Figures (%)
	(a)	(b)	(c)	(d)	(e)	(f)	(g)
Murder	16,740	16,740	100.0	16,740	0.1%	0.08	0.06
Rape	94,347	191,670	38.3	246,337	0.82	0.96	0.85
Assault	862,220	624,850	52.4	1,645,458	7.46	3.14	5.70
Robbery	417,438	1,052,260	62.4	668,971	3.61	5.28	2.32
Burglary	2,155,448	3,456,220	56.3	3,828,504	18.64	17.35	13.25
Larceny	6,783,447	13,605,590	32.3	21,001,384	58.65	68.28	72.69
Motor-vehicle theft	1,235,859	978,120	83.2	1,485,407	10.69	4.91	5.14
Total	11,565,499	19,925,450		28,892,802			

Source: Author's compilation.

Note: Values are for 2005. Column d is estimated total crime, which is derived by dividing column a by column c, which is the reporting rate from the BJS National Victimization Survey. Hence, it inflates the FBI count of crimes by the reporting rates for each crime type to get an "adjusted count." Thus, like column b, it adjusts for reporting but is not subject to the potential biases of the victimization survey towards certain crime types. Definitions of crime types are somewhat different for the FBI and the BJS; we tried to choose the categories of the BJS crimes that most closely matched the definition of the FBI's seven-index crimes (for example, by FBI categorization, "assault" only includes aggravated assaults). For example, in the case of burglary, the Victimization Survey only includes household burglaries, whereas the FBI includes all types of burglaries (such as commercial). This is another reason to favor the third weight, since it avoids the mismatch (though it does not assume that reporting rates are correct despite the slight categorical mismatch between the two sources).

Table 9B.7 Average Cost of an Index Crime (Excluding Murder) Using Weighted Cost-of-Crime Estimates, 2005

(a)	Reporting Rate (%)	Adjusted Low Cost Estimate				Adjusted High Cost Estimate			
		Low Cost Estimate ($)	Weight	Weighted Cost (Low) ($)		High Cost Estimate ($)	Weight	Weighted Cost (High) ($)	
(a)	(b)	(c)	(d)	(e)		(f)	(g)	(h)	
Rape	38.3	129,696	0.0085	1,106		297,567	0.0085	2,538	
Assault	62.4	19,528	0.0570	1,113		91,817	0.0570	5,232	
Robbery	52.4	22,637	0.0232	524		290,491	0.0232	6,730	
Burglary	56.3	2,287	0.1326	303		31,980	0.1326	4,240	
Larceny	32.3	335	0.7273	244		908	0.7273	660	
Vehicle theft	83.2	1,197	0.0514	62		5,669	0.0514	292	
Average cost per crime				$3,352.06				$19,692.38	

Source: Author's compilation.

Note: This table calculates the cost of a general index crime (but not including murder) using the same figures as table 9.9. These numbers are then used in table 9B.8 to estimate the marginal benefit from increased incarceration, assuming no benefit exists in the form of reduced murders.

Table 9B.8   *Marginal Benefit of the Last Prisoner Incarcerated (Using a Static Aggregate Elasticity for Incarceration and Crime Levels in 2005, with Murder Excluded)*

		Total Marginal Benefits		
		Low Estimate ($)	Mean Estimate ($)	High Estimate ($)
(a)	(b)	(c)	(d)	(e)
η	λ	3,352	11,522	19,692
−0.05	1.146	3,841	13,204	22,567
−0.1	2.292	7,683	26,408	45,133
−0.2	4.584	15,365	52,816	90,267
−0.3	6.876	23,048	79,224	135,400
−0.4	9.168	30,731	105,632	180,534

Source: Author's compilation.
Note: For a description of the underlying calculations, see the equations in the text. l represents the total number of crimes prevented by incarcerating one additional person. Column b shows how many (nonmurder) index I crimes would be averted for the various elasticity estimates in column a. Columns c and d then provide monetary estimates of the column b number of crimes prevented, by multiplying column b by the cost per crime figures computed in table 9B.7. Accordingly, columns c and e provide the low and high cost estimates of the marginal benefits of adding one prisoner to the state prison system. In 2005, the total number of index I crimes, including murder was 28,892,802 (Federal Bureau of Investagation 2006), and the number of state prisoners was 1,259,905 (Harrison and Beck 2006).

NOTES

1. Bernard Harcourt (2007) shows that prior to the massive deinstitutionalization movement in the late 1960s, roughly the same proportion of Americans were institutionalized as today. However, in that period most were kept in state mental hospitals instead of jails and prisons.
2. The rate of incarceration in Russia is 635 per 100,000 (International Centre for Prison Studies 2008).
3. The "incapacitation effect" refers to the idea that imprisoning an individual curtails his criminal activity for the duration of his sentence.
4. Chen and Shapiro's study will need to be replicated on a larger data set to confirm the finding that as one moves from being the "worst prisoner" in a lower-security prison to the "best prisoner" in a higher-security prison, recidivism rates rise. In addition, additional research will be needed to identify whether the psychological effects that Lerman identifies are the product of the harsher prison experience, which presumably can be mitigated, albeit at

some greater risk of escape or interprison violence; or whether they are the presence of the relatively harsher fellow inmates, whose influence may be harder to mitigate.

5. In bottom-up studies, λ usually represents criminals' yearly offense rate (that is, how many crimes they commit per year), which is a slightly more narrow concept than what we call "marginal effectiveness" here (since we also include any deterrent effect of incarceration on crime).

6. Conversely, studies that estimate λ using inmate surveys and self-reports (often called incapacitation models) should not be adjusted for reporting. Survey-based estimates are unaffected by whether a crime is or is not reported. It is the econometric studies that use FBI reported crime data that must be adjusted.

7. As more individuals are locked up, another crime-reducing benefit emerges by removing a group that is often at high risk for crime victimization. To the extent, however, that we merely shift the location of their victimization from the street to the prison (where it may be less likely to be reported), we may be exaggerating the crime-reduction benefits of incarceration. While solitary confinement is an effective incapacitative strategy to protect the inmate from crimes by others and protect others from crimes by the inmate, most prisoners are not subjected to this treatment and instead mix with other prisoners on a daily basis. Considerable unreported criminal violence is inflicted on inmates during these prison interactions.

8. Bottom-up estimates must also be adjusted downward to account for the replacement rate (the rate at which others take on the criminal activity of individuals who have been incarcerated). For example, if a gang member is incarcerated, he may simply be replaced by someone else who commits the same amount of crime. With perfect replacement, a properly adjusted bottom-up estimate of λ should be zero. For market-mediated crimes, such as selling illegal drugs or prostitution, any effort to jail suppliers will lead to wage increases designed to entice replacement workers.

9. Johnson and Raphael calculate their elasticity model across two time periods: 1978 to 1990, and 1991 to 2006.

10. Liedka, Piehl, and Useem call this phenomenon "accelerating declining marginal returns" (2006, 245), which is the exact opposite of Spelman's (2000b) finding of increasing elasticity of crime as incarceration grows.

11. These figures are based on Bureau of Justice statistics that only account for state prisoners, not inmates in federal prisons or local jails. The comparable number for combined state and federal prisoners (not jails) are mean prison rates of 193 (standard deviation of 50) for 1977 to 1989, and 437 (standard deviation of 70) for 1990 to 2004.

12. Ignoring the large and variable share of incarceration provided by federal prisons and local jails conceals other complexities that can be critical for policy evaluation. For example, the cost estimates per inmate do not apply to the full range of facilities. Jails are expensive to run because they involve frequent admissions and discharges, which are high-cost transactions; also, the jails are often small, which prevents economies of scale in building and supervision expenses. Moreover, the focus on index I crimes overlooks the fact

that a considerable proportion of prisoners are incarcerated for drug crimes (particularly in federal prisons). While these incarcerations do appear to reduce the occurrence of index I crimes, their primary goal is to raise the price of drugs. While there are substantial questions about whether these incarcerations achieve their intended antidrug objectives, one could presumably design a more effective anticrime incarcerative strategy if incarcerations were limited to those committing index I crimes. Similar concerns apply to the issue of those incarcerated for white-collar crime, although here the numbers are far smaller than for drug incarcerations.

13. It might seem natural to also look at an independent elasticity for motor-vehicle theft, since it appears to consistently lead to large and statistically significant coefficients. However, we did try a cost-benefit analysis with a separate and higher elasticity (up to three times higher) for motor-vehicle theft; the change in results was negligible and hence the analysis was not included.

14. Accordingly, our estimates of the cost of crime prevention exclude those parts of the homeland-security budget (currently around $40 billion and 11 percent of the total U.S. defense budget) that are used to fight terrorism. The estimates also exclude long-term losses due to increased security efforts after the terrorist attacks, which are estimated to have permanently lowered productivity in the United States by between 0.6 and 1.2 percent (Bram, Orr, and Rapaport 2002).

15. One consequence of Philip J. Cook's definition is that the disutility to prisoners of being incarcerated should count as a social cost. While the issue is complicated, three points should be noted: First, following Cook's approach consistently will raise the estimated cost of imprisonment, while lowering the estimated cost of crime (because the value of stolen goods is not counted). Second, while stolen cash involves a simple transfer from owner to thief, the theft of noncash property frequently leads to some property damage and may move assets into the hands of lower-valued users. This at the least then imposes more transaction costs to sell them back to higher-valued users. Thus, even if one wants to treat theft as a transfer, there will still be some attendant social loss that is not a wash between the deprived owner and the victimizing thief. Third, if we do not consider the utility of prisoners, we might mistakenly conclude, for example, that a mass-incarceration strategy was less costly than a mass-education policy. This obviously raises important normative issues.

16. William Bartley (2000) is one exception to this, but he cautions that colinearity concerns may explain some of the theoretically implausible estimates in various specifications.

17. For example, a question used in Cook and Ludwig's (2000) study reads, "How would you vote on a program to reduce gunshot injuries by 30% that cost $50 more per year in income taxes?" (105). There are several versions of the same question, each with different tax amounts required to pay for the same reduction in injuries. This allows the researchers to create willingness-to-pay schedules of the surveyed population.

18. Although it is well established that past incarceration can lead to underem-

ployment of former prisoners (Holzer, chapter 8, this volume), this lost potential productivity is not accounted for because the impact is not yet quantified at a crime-specific level. Exclusion of underemployment effects will bias the benefit from prevented crime downward. Note however that the same exclusion will bias the cost of incarceration downward even more because it is calculated conditional on already being arrested and convicted. Thus, fully accounting for this factor would make incarceration look less appealing than our current estimates show.

19.   These figures are conservative in that they only account for the direct tangible costs of incarceration estimates.

20.   One cautionary note is that the contingent-valuation questions are based on large reductions of specific crimes (for example, a 30 percent reduction), while a cost-benefit analysis would estimate the impact of a much smaller change in crime.

21.   Differences in justice-system and lost-productivity estimates are caused by using arrest rates based on two different crime-occurrence statistics (from UCR and NCVS).

22.   Murder is treated separately to allow for exploration of the implication that the ability of increased incarceration to reduce crime is lower for murder than for other crimes. Because the social costs of murder are so high relative to other crimes, this difference can substantially impact an overall cost-benefit analysis of incarceration.

23.   In general, northeastern states have the highest costs of incarceration ($37,625 per prisoner), and Southern states have the lowest average costs ($18,768). Local weather conditions and wage levels are among the many factors that explain this wide range of costs. For example, Maine, with only two thousand prisoners in 2004, likely has a higher average per prisoner cost in part because its fixed costs are not spread over a larger inmate population.

24.   This implies daily expenses of about $70 per prisoner. While this estimate makes no provision for other social costs of incarceration, it may not be an entirely unreasonable overall estimate for the states with low operating expenditures. Note that the table provides average costs per prisoner, and we ideally want to capture only marginal costs. One can imagine that adding simply one additional prisoner has a very low marginal cost if prison is not filled to capacity. But perhaps this suggests that we should think of "marginal" in terms of adding (or subtracting) increments of one thousand prisoners. In this case, a state that decides to add one thousand prisoners typically needs to add a new prison. The table 9.10 estimates seem more reasonable when thought of in this light.

25.   One question to consider is whether the table 9.10 interest-on-debt figures capture some of the capital costs that are estimated here directly.

26.   Note that the issue of decreasing marginal benefits from incarceration is distinct from Liedka, Piehl, and Useem's (2006) finding that the elasticity of incarceration becomes smaller at higher levels of incarceration—elasticity itself changes. In these authors' words, this implies accelerating diminishing marginal returns. The analysis in this chapter adopts the more limited assumption of decreasing marginal utility of incarceration (from the assumption of

constant elasticity, which is generated by the log-log regression specification). Similarly, since crime is in the numerator of equation 4, the effectiveness of incarceration is positively related to crime levels. That is, all else equal, incarcerating one more offender will have a smaller benefit in low-crime contexts. Accordingly, the more that crime rates improve, the relatively less effective incarceration becomes.

27. The marginal analysis in table 9B.1 will go awry if there is some major suboptimality in another part of the system. For example, if U.S. drug-enforcement policy leads to massive increases in crime, then table 9B.1 might suggest that greater incarceration is appropriate given this artificially high crime rate. In this scenario, changing drug policy would lower crime, which would automatically lower the estimated benefits of incarceration (thereby reducing the estimated optimal level of incarceration).

28. For example, a study conducted by Lance Lochner and Enrico Moretti (2004) suggests that government efforts to mandate more schooling may dampen crime.

29. The central focus of most of these programs was not to reduce criminal behavior. Rather, they were focused on improving education, earnings, child behavior, and family relations. Nevertheless, many of them also documented the collateral effect of improved criminal behavior in the programs' participants.

30. To underscore the prescience of this prediction of doubling the prison population, note that the total number of state prisoners in December of 1993 was 879,714. This population grew to 1,316,301 in the year 2004, representing an increase of almost 50 percent over the level of 1993.

31. There is wide variation in the estimates of the elasticity of crime and the cost of incarceration. In 1998, Donohue and Siegelman generated lower and upper bounds from then existing estimates. They used those bounds to create the figures of $5 billion to $8 billion costs and 5 to 15 percent crime reduction for the hypothetical situation (implying an elasticity of crime with respect to incarceration of between 10 and 30 percent). The dollar range represented the present value of the future cost of incarceration and was generated by taking today's cohort of three-year-old children as the reference point (mainly because this is the age at which early-childhood programs begin). Hence, the cost of incarceration is the expense that would be required to incarcerate criminals of this cohort in the future, once they reach their high-crime years. However, Donohue and Siegelman also wanted to bring this future cost into the present, which is when the spending on social programs would occur. Therefore, the range of $5.6 billion to $8 billion represented the present value of the future increase in incarceration (with a target incarceration growth of 50 percent).

32. Marvell and Moody (1994) provide a useful discussion about how λs based on surveys and arrest rates should be adjusted in light of various biasing factors and measurement error.

33. The result of the Granger causality test may actually say more about the limited value of the test than about the lack of a simultaneity problem. More plausibly, Yair Listokin (2003) has found that the level of incarceration does

rise mechanically with increases in crime, so the issue of simultaneity is real. Listokin uses abortion rates as an instrument to tease out this mechanical relationship on the grounds that abortion rates in the 1970s influence crime in the 1990s, but they do not influence incarceration in the 1990s except through their effect on crime. Based on this instrumental-variables approach, his paper concludes that the estimated elasticity of prison admissions with respect to crime is exactly one, as the mechanical theory predicts. Note, however, that these results are based on a model whose main dependant variable is prison admission rates, *not* overall incarceration levels. As Listokin acknowledges, prison release rates and other factors "may cause theoretical and empirical deviations from a strictly mechanical (one-to-one) relationship between imprisonment and crime" (2003, 186).

Marvell and Moody (1994) also include lagged dependent and independent variables to control for autocorrelation, and they weight the regressions by the square root of population to correct for heteroskedasticity.

34. Simultaneity will lead to an underestimation of elasticity because incarceration is expected to decrease crime (leading the two series to move in opposite directions), while crime is expected to increase incarceration (tending to cause the two series to move in the same direction). If a study does not account for simultaneity, the estimated effect of incarceration on crime for an ordinary least squares regression will actually be some average of the two effects, and it will thus be biased toward zero.

35. Liedka, Piehl, and Useem (2006) test the nonconstant-elasticity and the collateral-damage hypotheses through three models: a quadratic, a polynomial, and a spline model of incarceration. In addition, they use a Granger causality test to see whether simultaneity between crime and incarceration is a problem. Like Marvell and Moody (1994), they find no evidence of this; consequently, their model does not control for simultaneity.

36. Liedka, Piehl, and Useem (2006) adjust their standard errors to account for first-order serial correlation.

37. The crime statistics come from the Federal Bureau of Investigation's *Crime in The United States* (Federal Bureau of Investigation 2006). Incarceration data comes from Bureau of Justice Statistics (Harrison and Beck 2005)

REFERENCES

Anderson, David 1999. "The Aggregate Burden of Crime." *Journal of Law and Economics* 42(2): 611–42.

Bartley, William. 2000. "Valuation of Specific Crime Rates: Summary." http://www.ncjrs.gov/App/Publications/abstract.aspx?ID=187771.

Becsi, Zsolt. Federal Reserve Bank of Atlanta. 1999. "Economics and Crime in the States." *Economic Review.* First Quarter: 38–49.

Becker, Gary S. 1968. "Crime and Punishment: An Economic Approach." *Journal of Political Economy* 76(2): 169–217.

Buonanno, Paolo. 2003. "The Socioeconomic Determinants of Crime. A Review of the Literature." Mimeo 63, Milan: Universitàdegli Studi di Milano-Bicocca.

Bram, Jason, James Orr, and Carol Rapaport. 2002. "Measuring the Effects of the September 11 Attack on New York City." *Economic Policy Review*: 5–20. New York: Federal Reserve Bank of New York.

Bureau of Justice Statistics. 2006. "Criminal Victimization in the United States, 2005 Statistical Tables." *National Crime Victimization Survey*. Washington: U.S. Department of Justice. http://www.ojp.usdoj.gov/bjs/pub/pdf/cvus0505.pdf.

Chen, Keith, and Jesse Shapiro. 2007. "Do Harsher Prison Conditions Reduce Recidivism? A Discontinuity-Based Approach." *American Law and Economics Review* 9(1): 1–29.

Cohen, Mark. 1988. "Pain, Suffering, and Jury Awards: A Study of the Cost of Crime to Victims." *Law and Society Review* 22(3): 537–555.

———. 1990. "A Note on the Cost of Crime to Victims." *Urban Studies* 27(1): 125–132.

———. 2005. *The Costs of Crime and Justice*. London: Routledge.

Cohen, Mark., Ted R. Miller, and Shelli B. Rossman. 1994. "The Costs and Consequences of Violent Behavior in the United States," in *Understanding and Preventing Violence: Consequences and Control of Violence*, Vol. 4. Albert J. Reiss, Jr. and Jeffrey A. Roth (eds). National Research Council. Washington: National Academy Press.

Cohen, Mark, Roland Rust, Sara Steen, and Simon Tidd. 2004. "Willingness to Pay for Crime Control Programs." *Criminology* 42(1): 86–109.

Collins, Sara. 1994. "Cost of Crime: 674 Billion." *U.S. News and World Report* (January 17), cited in "The Aggregate Burden of Crime" by David Anderson. *Journal of Law and Economics* 42: 611–42.

Cook, Philip J. 1983. "Costs of Crime," in *Encyclopedia of Crime and Justice*. Sanford H. Kadish, ed. New York: Free Press.

Cook, Philip J., and Jens Ludwig. 2000. *Gun Violence: The Real Costs*. New York: Oxford University Press.

DiIulio, John. 1996. "Prisons are a bargain, by any measure." *New York Times*. January 16. A19.

Donohue, John. 2004a. "Guns, Crime, and the Impact of State Right-to-Carry Laws" *Fordham Law Review* 73: 623–52.

———. 2004b. "Clinton and Bush's Report Cards on Crime Reduction: The Data Show Bush Policies Are Undermining Clinton Gains", The Economists' Voice: Vol. 1: No. 1, Article 4, http://www.bepress.com/ev/vol1/iss1/art4.

———. 2005. "Fighting Crime: An Economist's View." *Milken Institute Review*, Quarter 1: 47–58.

———. 2007. "Economic Models of Crime and Punishment." *Social Research* 74 (2): 379–412.

Donohue, John, and Jens Ludwig. 2007. "More COPS." *The Brookings Institution*, Policy Brief #158. Washington: The Brookings Institution.

Donohue, John, and Peter Siegelman 1998. "Allocating Resources among Prisons and Social Programs in the Battle Against Crime." *Journal of Legal Studies* 27(1): 1–44.

Donohue, John, and Justin Wolfers 2006. "Uses and Abuses of Empirical Evidence in the Death Penalty Debate," *Stanford Law Review* 58: 791–846.

Durose, Matthew R., and Patrick A. Langan. 2004. "Felony Sentences in State

Courts, 2002." *Bureau of Justice Statistics Bulletin.* Washington: U.S. Department of Justice. http://www.ojp.usdoj.gov/bjs/abstract/fssc02.htm.

Federal Bureau of Investigation. U.S. Department of Justice. 2006. "Crime in the United States 2005." http://www.fbi.gov/ucr/05cius/.

Gilliard, Darrell K., and Allen J. Beck.1996. "Prison and Jail Inmates, 1995." *Bureau of Justice Statistics Bulletin.* Washington: U.S. Department of Justice. http://www.ojp.usdoj.gov/bjs/pub/pdf/pji95.pdf .

Greenwood, Peter, et al. 1996. *Diverting Children from a Life of Crime: Measuring Costs and Benefits.* RAND. http://www.rand.org/pubs/monograph_reports/MR699-1/.

Harcourt, Bernard. 2007. "From the Asylum to the Prison: Rethinking the Incarceration Revolution—Part II: State Level Analysis." Public Law Working Paper No. 155. http://www.law.uchicago.edu/Lawecon/index.html.

Harlow, Caroline Wolf. 2003. "Education and Correctional Population." Bureau of Justice Statistics Special Report. Washington: U.S. Department of Justice. http://www.ojp.usdoj.gov/bjs/abstract/ecp.htm.

Harrison, Paige, and Allen Beck. U.S. Department of Justice. Bureau of Justice Statistics. 2005. "Prisoners in 2004." *Bulletin of the Bureau of Justice Statistics.* http://www.ojp.usdoj.gov/bjs/pub/pdf/p04.pdf.

———. 2006. "Prisoners in 2005." *Bureau of Justice Statistics Bulletin.* Washington: U.S. Department of Justice. http://www.ojp.usdoj.gov/bjs/pub/pdf/p05.pdf.

Hill, George, and Paige Harrison. Bureau of Justice Statistics. 2004. "Prisoners under State or Federal Jurisdiction." *National Prisoner Statistics Data Series (NPS-1).* http://www.ojp.usdoj.gov/bjs/data/corpop02.csv.

Hoehn, John, Mark Berger, and Glenn Blomquist. 1987. "A Hedonic Model of Interregional Wages, Rents and Amenity Values." *Journal of Regional Science* 27(4): 605–20.

Hohmann, Mary, Bernard Banet, and David P. Weikart. 1979. *Young Children in Action: A Manual for Preschool Educators.* Ypsilanti, Mich.: High/Scope Press.

Holzer, Harry, Steven Raphael, and Michael Stoll. 2007. "Will Employers Hire Ex-Offenders? Employer Checks, Background Checks, and Their Determinants." Forthcoming in *Do Prisons Make Us Safer? The Benefits and Costs of the Prison Boom,* edited by, Steven Raphael and Michael Stoll. New York: Russell Sage Foundation.

International Centre for Prison Studies. 2008. "Prison Brief for Russian Federation." http://www.kcl.ac.uk/depsta/law/research/icps/worldbrief/wpb_country.php?country=118.

Johnson, Rucker. 2007. "The Effects of Increases in Incarceration on Members of Communities that Send/Receive the Majority of Inmates." Forthcoming in *Do Prisons Make Us Safer? The Benefits and Costs of the Prison Boom,* edited by, Steven Raphael and Michael Stoll. New York: Russell Sage Foundation.

Johnson, Rucker, and Steven Raphael. 2006. "How Much Crime Reduction Does the Marginal Prisoner Buy?" Working paper. Berkeley: University of California, Berkeley, Goldman School of Public Policy.

Klaus, Patsy A. U.S. Department of Justice. 1994. "The Cost of Crime to Victims" cited in "The Aggregate Burden of Crime" by David Anderson. *Journal of Law and Economics* 42: 611–42.

Lancaster, Kelvin J. 1966. "A New Approach to Consumer Theory." *The Journal of Political Economy* 74(2): 132–57.

Leary, Mary Lou (Executive Director, National Center for Victims of Crime). 2006. "The Cost of Crime: Understanding the Financial and Human Impact of Criminal Activity." Testimony to the U.S. Senate Committee on the Judiciary. September 19.

Lerman, Amy. 2007. "The People Prisons Make: Effects of Incarceration on Criminal Psychology." Forthcoming in *Do Prisons Make Us Safer? The Benefits and Costs of the Prison Boom,* edited by, Steven Raphael and Michael Stoll. New York: Russell Sage Foundation.

Levitt, Steven. 1996. "The Effect of Prison Population Size on Crime Rates: Evidence from Prison Overcrowding Litigation." *Quarterly Journal of Economics* 111(2): 319–51.

Liedka, Raymond, Anne Piehl, and Bert Useem. 2006. "The Crime-Control Effect of Incarceration: Does Scale Matter?" *Criminology and Public Policy* 5(2): 245–76.

Listokin, Yair. 2003. "Does More Crime Mean More Prisoners? An Instrumental Variable Approach." *Journal of Law and Economics* 46(1): 181–206.

Lochner, Lance, and Enrico Moretti. 2004. "The Effect of Education on Crime: Evidence from Prison Inmates, Arrests, and Self-Reports." *American Economic Review* 94(1): 155–89.

Ludwig, Jens. 2006. "The Cost of Crime." Testimony to the U.S. Senate Committee on the Judiciary. September 19. http://judiciary.senate.gov/testimony.cfm?id=2068&wit_id=5749.

Marvell, Thomas B., and Carlisle Moody, Jr. 1994. "Prison Population Growth and Crime Reduction." *Journal of Quantitative Criminology* 10(2): 109–40.

Martin, Mark. "Governor Seeks $6 Billion for Prison Projects." *San Francisco Chronicle,* August 2, 2006.

Miller, Ted, Mark Cohen, and Brian Wiersema. 1996. *Victim Costs and Consequences: A New Look.* National Institute of Justice Research Report, NCJ-155282. Washington,: U.S. Department of Justice. http://www.ncjrs.gov/pdffiles/victcost.pdf.

Pfaff, John F. 2007. "The Growth of Prison: Toward a Second Generation Approach." *Fordham Law Legal Studies Research Paper No. 976373.* New York: Fordham School of Law. http://ssrn.com/abstract=976373.

President's Commission on Law Enforcement and Administration of Justice. 1967. *Crime and Its Impacts: An Assessment,* cited in "The Aggregate Burden of Crime" by David Anderson. *Journal of Law and Economics* 42: 611–42.

Rosen, Sherwin. 1974. "Hedonic Prices and Implicit Markets: Product Differentiation in Pure Competition." *Journal of Political Economy* 82(1): 34–55.

Schelling, Thomas C. 1968. "The life you save may be your own" in *Problems in Public Expenditure Analysis.* Samuel B. Chase Jr., ed. Washington: The Brookings Institution.

Shaw, Clifford R., and Henry D. McKay. United States Wickersham Crime Commission. 1931. *Social factors in juvenile delinquency.* Washington: U.S. Government Printing Office.

Spelman, William. 1994. *Criminal Incapacitation.* New York: Plenum Press.

———. 2000a. "The Limited Importance of Prison Expansion" in *The Crime Drop in America.* Alfred Blumstein and Joel Wallman, eds. New York: Cambridge University Press.

———. 2000b. "What Recent Studies Do (and Don't) Tell Us About Imprisonment and Crime." *Crime and Justice* 27: 419–94.

———. 2005. "Jobs or Jails? The Crime Drop in Texas." *Journal of Policy Analysis and Management* 24(1): 133–65.

State of Connecticut General Assembly. Legislative Program Review and Investigations Committee. 2000. "Chapter 5: Options to Manage Growth in Prison Populations." *Factors Impacting Prison Overcrowding.* http://www.cga.ct.gov/pri/archives/2000fireportchap5.htm.

Strnad, Jeff, 2007. "Should Legal Empiricists go Bayesian?" *American Law and Economics Review* 9(1): 195–303.

Thaler, Richard. 1978. "A Note on the Value of Crime Control: Evidence from the Property Market." *Journal of Urban Economics* 5(1): 137–45.

Trumbull, William N. 1990. "Who Has Standing in Cost-Benefit Analysis?" *Journal of Policy Analysis and Management* 9(2): 201–18.

U.S. News and World Report. 1974. "Costs of Crime" cited in "The Aggregate Burden of Crime" by David Anderson. *Journal of Law and Economics* 42: 611–42.

Viscusi, W. Kip. 1998. *Rational Risk Policy.* New York: Oxford University Press.

———. 2000. "The value of Life in Legal Context: Survey and Critique." *American Law and Economics Review* 2: 195–222.

Walker, Alan, and Carol Walker, eds. 1987. *The Growing Divide: A Social Audit 1979–1987.* London: Child Poverty Action Group.

Welsh, Brandon C., and David P. Farrington. 2000. "Monetary Costs and Benefits of Crime Prevention Programs," *Prisons,* edited by Michael Tonry and Joan Petersilia. Chicago: University of Chicago Press.

Zedlewski, Edwin W. 1985. "When Have We Punished Enough?" *Public Administration Review* 45 (Special Issue: Law and Public Affairs): 771–79.

Zimring, Franklin, and Gordon Hawkins. 1988. "The New Mathematics of Imprisonment." *Crime and Delinquency* 34(4): 425–36.

———. 1995. *Incapacitation: Penal Confinement and the Restraint of Crime.* New York: Oxford University Press.

Index

Boldface numbers refer to figures and tables.

abortion, 44–45, 337*n*33
African Americans
    arrested for major crimes in U.S.
        cities 1980-2000, percentage of, **81**
    children with an incarcerated parent,
        178
    employability of, impact of criminal
        record on, 249
    employability of all young men and
        incarceration rate, relationship of,
        254–55
    incarceration rate among male,
        5–10
    mass incarceration and less-edu-
        cated, 75–76
    prison time, percentage of males
        who have experienced, 10
    statistical discrimination by employ-
        ers against, 244, 248
    war on drugs and, 84–85, 105*n*9
age, 4–10, 41–45
alcohol: incarceration rates and Prohi-
    bition, 102–4
Alderete, Jaime Calleja, 221
American Friends Service Committee,
    122
Anderson, David, 286–87, 291
Apel, Robert, 125–27
arrest rates
    for drug, violent, and property
        crimes, **80**
    drug crimes and, 79–81
    for index I crimes, **327**
    race-ethnicity and, 80–81

Asians, increase in incarceration rate
    among male, 5–9
"Auburn"/"silent system" of punish-
    ment, 120–21
Ayres, Ian, 333*n*7

Bar Association of the City of New
    York, Joint Committee on New
    York Drug Law Evaluation, 89,
    94–96, 99
Barker, Vanessa, 89
Bartley, William, 334*n*16
Barton, William, 136
Bayer, Patrick, 154
Beck, Allen J., 73, 93
Becker, Gary, 270–71
Beckett, Katherine, 74
Becsi, Zsolt, 276, 280–81, 317
benefits of incarceration
    arguments for, 1, 15–16
    criminal-justice-system costs
        avoided, 293, **295**
    index I crimes avoided, 296–97
    See also cost-benefit analysis of incar-
        ceration; cost of crime
Berk, Richard, 158
Bhati, Avinash, 125–27
blacks. *See* African Americans
Blokland, Arjan, 124–25, 127, 135
Blumstein, Alfred, 73, 79, 84, 93, 102, 128
Bonczar, Thomas, 261*n*27
Bushway, Shawn D., 12, 15–16, 19
Butcher, Kirsten F., 6, 44
Byers, Katharine, 242

Cahalan, Margaret, 100, 102
California
"consensual" or "mixed model" as correctional philosophy of state prisons in, 155
incarceration in, 151–52
new prison construction projects, cost of, 300
Proposition 8, 142
release of parolees in, 170
sentencing policy in, 76
California Department of Corrections and Rehabilitation (CDCR), 16–17, 151, 158–66
Campbell, Donald, 156
Canelo-Cacho, Jose, 128
Carey, Hugh, 90–91
Caulkins, Jonathan P., 106n15
CDCR. See California Department of Corrections and Rehabilitation
Center for Employment Opportunities, 257
Chen, Keith, 156, 271, 301
children with incarcerated parents
behavior problems of, regression results showing, 194–201
characteristics of childhood families classified by parents' most severe deviant behavior offense, 191–92
child family income before, during, and after father's prison release, 188
cross-national comparisons of policies and impacts regarding, 203
cumulative risk of criminal history, incarceration, or early death by race and education, 185, 187
cumulative risk of deviant behavior, criminal involvement, and incarceration, 184–89
data for study of, 181–84
empirical approach to assessing impacts experienced by, 188–93
future research on, 203
impact of parental incarceration by childhood life stage on child behavior problems, 200–201
impacts experienced by, 17–18, 177–81, 202–3
increase in, 178
intergenerational relationship of

parental deviant-behavior history on child behavior problems, 196–97
literature and previous research on, 178–81
outcomes classified by parents' most severe deviant behavior offense, 190
public policy issues raised by, 202–3
child-support collection system, 242–43, 258
Chiricos, Theodore, 141
Cho, Rosa, 251–54, 260n16
Cincinnati Prison Conference, Declaration of Principles, 121
Citizens Crime Commission, 107n19
Cohen, Jacqueline, 79, 102, 128
Cohen, Mark, 286–93, 296
collateral costs of incarceration
for children with incarcerated parents (see children with incarcerated parents)
in earnings and employment (see labor-market outcomes)
estimate of, 301
examples of, 2, 239
literature on, 11
trade-off between state spending on welfare or corrections, 229–30
Collins, Sara, 291
community corrections, 170–71
COMPAS. See Correctional Offender Management Profiling for Alternative Sanctions
Comprehensive Drug Abuse Prevention Act of 1970, 73
consensual/mixed model of correctional philosophy, 155
contingent valuation method, 289, 296
control model of correctional philosophy, 155
Cook, Philip J., 286, 289, 334n15, 334n17
Correctional Offender Management Profiling for Alternative Sanctions (COMPAS), 162–66
cost-benefit analysis of incarceration
benefits from prevented crimes (see benefits of incarceration; cost of crime)
complications and questions regarding, 273

cost of incarceration (*see* cost of incarceration)
identification of issues for, 11–12
marginal benefits of the last prisoner incarcerated, **302–3, 321–22, 332**
murder, exclusion of from aggregate elasticity, 318–20
results of, 301–6
cost of crime
average cost of an index I crime, 296–97, **298**
average cost of prevented crime estimates, weighting crimes to derive, **330–31**
building on prior estimates of, 290–93
complications and limits of estimating, 284, 286–87
computing the high social-cost-of-crime estimate, 293, 296
criminals' utility in social-welfare calculations, question of including, 286
estimating intangible, 287–89
monetary, need for estimate of, 284
social costs (*see* social cost)
tangible, 287
cost of incarceration, 1–2, 297
capital costs, 269, 299–300
collateral (*see* collateral costs of incarceration)
detailed summary of, **323–26**
for index I crimes, **329**
lost productivity of incarcerated offenders, 292–93, **294**, 300–301
operating costs, 297, 299
operating expenditures, composition of, **299**
opportunity costs, 306–8
spending on corrections relative to total spending, increase in, 2
state government spending (*see* state spending on corrections)
See also cost-benefit analysis of incarceration
crack cocaine, 62–65, 70*n*25, 105*n*7
Crime Act of 1994, 78
crime rate
abortion and, legalization of, 44–45
changes in sentencing and enforcement policy and, 33, 36
decrease in, 1
foreign-born individuals and, 44
incarceration rate and, 1–2, 36, 315–16 (*see also* incarceration rate)
in New York, 1960-2005, **87**
by type of criminal offense for 1984 and 2002, **34–35**
criminal behavior
demographic change and, 41–45
as determinant of incarceration rate, model of, 31
deterrence, effect of prison sentences as (*see* deterrence)
drug epidemics and, 59, 62–65
earnings inequality and, 54–61
elasticity of crime and (*see* elasticity of crime with respect to incarceration)
factors that may have altered, 40–41
impact of prison on, philosophies of punishment and, 119–23, 143–45
incapacitation in prison, effect of, 123–29
incarceration rate and, 27, 65–66
peer effects and, 154–55
recidivism (*see* recidivism)
rehabilitation in prison, effect of, 122–23, 129–31
criminal psychology
criminogenic effect of security level assignment, results of analysis of, 165, 167–70
effects of incarceration on, 16–17, 151–52, 170
incarceration effects, literature on, 152–56
inmate security level, classification instrument used for determining, 157–62
measuring, 162–66
policy implications of incarceration's impact on, 170–72
regression discontinuity design for studying, 156–57
Cullen, Francis, 135

death penalty, deterrent effect of, 141
deinstitutionalization of the mentally ill, 45–54, 332*n*1
DeJong, Christina, 136
demographics

age (*see* age)
education (*see* education)
immigrant population, increase in, 68*n*13
of prison populations, **43,** 45–50
race-ethnicity (*see* race-ethnicity)
of the U.S. population and incarceration rates, 41–45
desert, punishment as an offender's just, 120
deterrence
criminogenic effect of, 152–53
death penalty *vs.* life imprisonment as, 141
general, impact on crime of, 138–43
as mechanism for instrumental approach to crime reduction, 119, 123, 131–32, 274
rehabilitation and, boundaries between, 131
risk-assessment tools, negative implications of, 128
specific, impact on crime of, 132–38
specific and general distinguished, 119, 132
DiIulio, John, 154–56
Dinkins, David, 107*n*19
Donohue, John J., III, 12, 20–22, 44, 65, 286, 306–7, 336*n*31
Doob, Anthony, 142
Drug Awareness Warning System (DAWN), 70*n*24
drugs, incarceration rate growth and illicit, 59, 62–65. *See also* war on drugs
Dunlap, Eloise, 62

Earned Income Tax Credit (EITC), 23, 243, 258
earnings. *See* labor-market outcomes
Eastern Penitentiary of Pennsylvania, 120
economic class/status. *See* socioeconomic status
education
children with incarcerated parents and, 184–88
criminality/incarceration and, 42–45
incarceration risk and, 4–10
Eggleston, Elaine, 124
Eisenhower, Dwight, 269

elasticity of crime with respect to incarceration
aggregate estimates, 302–3
definition of, 272–73
how modeling choices influence estimates of, 312–18
literature on/prior estimates of, 273–80
OLS estimates across four studies, **317**
overall *vs.* crime-specific estimates of, 283–84
picking the best estimate of, 280–83
variability in estimates, wide range of, 309–12
Ellwood, John W., 18
employers
empirical studies of incarceration impacts on hiring behavior, 245–49
ex-offenders, views of employability of, 243–44
statistical discrimination against African American males in assessing employability, 244–45, 248
employment. *See* labor-market outcomes
enforcement
arrest rates (*see* arrest rates)
of child-support policies, 242–43
of drug laws in New York City, escalation through politics of disorder, 91–93, 97–98
of drug laws in New York City, pragmatic, 88–89, 94–96
opportunity cost of increased incarceration and, 306–8
See also prosecution

Fagan, Jeffrey, 69*n*20
Farrington, David, 203
Federal Bureau of Investigation (FBI), Uniform Crime Reports (UCR), 33–35
Fogel, David, 122
foreign-born individuals
criminality and the increasing proportion of, 44
percentage of the U.S. population, increase in, 68*n*13

Freeman, Richard B., 55, 69n20, 249–50, 256, 258n2, 259n10
Fryer, Roland G., 63–64, 70n24, 105n7

Gaes, Gerald, 129
Gallagher, Catherine, 129
Garland, David, 75
gender, 4, 180–81
Gendreau, Paul, 135, 153
general deterrence, 119, 138–43
Gibbs, Jack, 135, 141
Goggin, Claire, 135, 153
Golub, Andrew, 62
Gottfredson, Denise, 131, 136
Gottschalk, Peter, 204n3
Gould, Eric D., 55
Governing Prisons (DiIulio), 154
Greenberg, David F., 74, 143
Grogger, Jeffrey, 55, 57, 68n19, 70n24, 105n7, 250–52, 259n10, 260n14
Guetzkow, Joshua, 18

Harcourt, Bernard E., 47, 128, 332n1
Hawkins, Gordon, 284
hedonic pricing, 288
Helland, Eric, 142
Hirsch, Andrew von, 122
Hispanics, 5–10, 75–76. *See also* race-ethnicity
Hjalmarsson, Randi, 136–37, 140, 154, 180
Holleran, David, 135
Holzer, Harry J., 12, 19–20, 23, 242, 245, 248, 254–55, 258n3
homicide rate, changes in selected states of the, **314**
Horney, Julie, 133
Huizinga, David, 133

immigrant population, increase in, 68n13
imprisonment
    alternative crime-fighting options, opportunity costs and need to consider, 306–9
    benefits of a high incarceration rate (*see* benefits of incarceration)
    costs of a high incarceration rate (*see* cost of incarceration)
    criminal psychology and (*see* criminal psychology)

criminogenic effects of, literature on, 152–56
    debate over benefits *vs.* costs of a high incarceration rate, 1–3
    debate over the boom in, 269–72
    identification of issues regarding, 11–12
    impact on crime of (*see* instrumental philosophy of punishment)
    labor-market outcomes and (*see* labor-market outcomes)
    level of (*see* incarceration rate)
    literature on, 11
    of parents, consequences for children (*see* children with incarcerated parents)
    percentage of men who have experienced, 10
incapacitation
    crime, empirical studies of impact on, 123–29
    elasticity of crime and, 274, 309
    as mechanism for instrumental approach to crime reduction, 119, 123
    selective, 127–28
incarceration rate
    age as factor in the increase in, **8–9**
    in California, 151
    changes in selected states of the, **314**
    cost-benefit assessment of (*see* cost-benefit analysis of incarceration)
    crime rate and, 1–2, 33
    deinstitutionalization of the mentally ill and, 45–54
    determinants of, 27–28
    drug markets and, changes in illicit, 59, 62–65
    drug offenders as percentage of prison populations, increase in, 84–85
    earnings opportunities and, effect of changes in, **60–61**
    education as factor in the increase in, **7**
    elasticity of crime and (*see* elasticity of crime with respect to incarceration)
    factors determining by criminal offense for 1984 and 2002, **34–35**
    gender and the increase in, 4
    growth rate in state, 1978-2000, **211**

incarceration rate (*continued*)
  increase to unprecedented levels,
    3–4, 10–11, 27, 29, 269–72 (*see also*
    mass incarceration)
  model of steady-state, 29–32
  "moral offenses" and, 102–4
  national, 1977-2004, **270**
  New York and U.S., 1960-2005, **88**
  optimal level of (*see* optimal level of
    incarceration)
  parole violations and, 39–41
  prison and reformatory, 1880 to
    1980, **101**
  prison and total, 1925 to 1975, **74**
  prison and total, 1950 to 2005, **75**
  public policy choices and (*see* public
    policy)
  race-ethnicity, education, and age as
    factors in the increase in, 4–10
  race-ethnicity as factor in the in-
    crease in, **5**
  in Russia, 332n2
  in selected states, 1977-2004, **315**
  sentencing policy and increase in
    (*see* sentencing policy)
  stability-of-punishment hypothesis,
    73, 100–102
  in state or federal prison, 1925-2004,
    30
  in states for 2000, **211**
  in Texas, 1990-2000, **311**
  trends and variation in states, 210–11
  trends in the behavioral and policy
    determinants of, 32–40
  world, European, and U.S. historical
    figures compared to current U.S.,
    27, 269
inequality, wage, 54–61
inner-city minority populations, 75–76,
  107n20. *See also* African Americans;
  New York City; race-ethnicity
instrumental philosophy of punishment
  deterrence mechanism, impact on
    crime of (*see* deterrence)
  incapacitation mechanism, impact
    on crime of (*see* incapacitation)
  mechanisms for crime reduction, 15,
    119–20, 123, 274
  rehabilitation mechanism, impact on
    crime of, 121–23, 129–31

sentencing policy, as a competing
  approach to, 119–21, 123, 143–44
intangible costs of crime, 287–89
Ioannides, Yannis, 258n3

Jacoby, William, 224–25
Janson, Carl-Gunnar, 203
Johnson, Bruce, 62
Johnson, Rucker C., 17–18, 22, 36,
  69n22, 225, 279, 281, 313, 316–17
Journal of Quantitative Criminology, 124
Juhn, Chinhui, 59, 70n23
jury awards, 289
just desert, punishment as an offender's, 120
Justice Statistics, Bureau of
  experience of time served by race-
    ethnicity, estimates of, 10
  lifetime incarceration risks, esti-
    mates of, 184
  Study Group on Criminal Justice
    Performance Measures, 155–56
  unemployment rate of newly admit-
    ted offenders, 292
  violent victimization rate, declines
    in, 23n1

Kearley, Brook, 131
Kelling, George L., 91
Kempinen, Cynthia, 130
Kessler, Daniel, 142
Kessler, Ronald, 143
Killias, Martin, 153
Kittrie, Nicholas, 122
Klaus, Patsy A., 291
Kleck, Gary, 139
Kling, Jeffrey, 241, 249, 251–54,
  260–61n21, 260nn17–18
Klotz, Marilyn, 242
Koch, Ed, 91–93, 97, 99, 107n18
Kreager, Derek, 133
Kurlychek, Megan, 130
Kuziemko, Ilyana, 130

labor-market outcomes
  aggregate data studies of incarcera-
    tion impacts on, 254–55
  child-support enforcement and,
    242–43, 258
  costs and benefits of incarceration
    on, 19–20, 239–40, 256–57

demand-side empirical studies of incarceration impacts on, 245–49
empirical evidence regarding effects of incarceration on, 245
empirical studies of incarceration impacts on subsequent earnings, **246**
employment of offenders before incarceration, 292–93
increasing criminality and, 54–59
magnitude of incarceration impacts on, 255–56
male incarceration rates, effect of changes in earnings opportunities on, **60–61**
potential impacts of incarceration on, **241**
public policy regarding incarceration impacts on, 257–58
supply-side empirical studies of incarceration impacts on, 249–54
theoretical considerations regarding effects of incarceration on, 240–45
See also socioeconomic status
Lalonde, Robert, 251–54, 260n16
Lancaster, Kelvin J., 288
Laub, John, 124
Leary, Mary Lou, 287
Lerman, Amy E., 12, 16, 22, 271, 301
Levitt, Steven D., 44, 65, 69n22, 142–43, 261n25, 276, 281, 310, 316–17
Lieb, Roxanne, 153
Liedka, Raymond, 274, 278, 281–82, 310–11, 316–17, 333n10, 335n26, 337nn35–36
Lindquist, Matthew, 180
Liska, Franklin J., 47
Listokin, Yair, 336–37n33
local/city governments
jail populations, size of, 27
New York (*see* New York City)
state and federal sentencing policies, implementation of, 76
street crime, "combat" against, 79
Lochner, Lance, 133, 139–40, 336n28
Loeffler, Charles, 135
Logan, Charles, 143, 156
Loury, Linda Datcher, 258n3
Ludwig, Jens, 143, 258n1, 286, 289, 291, 306, 334n17
Lyons, Christopher, 251–52, 260n18

MacKenzie, Doris, 129
Maine, 76, 335n23
Manski, Charles, 137
Marshall, Ineke, 133
Martinson, Robert, 122, 129
Marvell, Thomas B., 143, 275, 281–82, 309–11, 316–17, 336n32, 337n33, 337n35
mass incarceration
accounting for in New York, 93–100
arrest rates and, 79–81
as criminal-justice regime, 75–76
debate over, 269–72
sentencing policy establishes, 76–79
the war on drugs and, 79–85
See also incarceration rate
Matsueda, Ross, 133
McGuire, Robert, 97
mentally ill population, 45–54, 68n18
Michigan, 155
Miles, Thomas, 143
Miller, Ted R., 287, 289–93
Minnesota, 76–77
Moitra, Soumyo, 102
Mollenkopf, John Hull, 92
Moody, Carlisle, Jr., 143, 275, 281–82, 309–11, 316–17, 336n32, 337n33, 337n35
"moral" crimes, the incarceration rate and, 15, 102–4
Moretti, Enrico, 336n28
Murakawa, Naomi, 105n5
Murray, Joseph, 203
Mustard, David B., 55

Nagin, Daniel S., 135, 137, 140
Najaka, Stacy, 131
National Corrections Reporting Program, 33
National Research Council, 130
Needels, Karen, 260n15
New Hampshire, 313–14
New York City
drop in crime after increases in the police force, 306
drug law enforcement, Koch administration expansion of, 91–93, 97–98, 99
drug law enforcement, pragmatic stance on, 88–89, 94–96, 99

New York City (*continued*)
    economic crisis and the politics of
        disorder in, 92–93
    heroin and the violent crime epi-
        demic of the 1970s, 86–87
    Tactical Narcotics Teams (TNT) ini-
        tiative, 107*n*19
    the war on drugs in, 76
New York Executive Advisory Com-
    mittee on Sentencing, 77
New York (state)
    crime rates, 1960-2005, **87**
    escalation of the war on drugs, local
        actions and, 89–93
    felony arrests through the criminal-
        justice system, flows of, **95**
    incarceration rates, 1960-2005, **88**
    mass incarceration and the war on
        drugs in, 75–76
    mass incarceration in, accounting
        for, 93–100
    prison commitments, accounting for
        growth in, **96**
    prison commitments, characteristics
        of new, **98**
    prison commitments, impact of local
        and state-level factors, **100–101**
    Rockefeller drug law, policy and
        politics of, 85–89
    Second Felony Offender (SFO) law,
        86, 88
    sentencing policy in, 77
New York Times, reporting on drug-re-
    lated topics, 90–92
Nieuwbeerta, Paul, 124–25, 127, 135
North Carolina, 313–14
Northpointe Institute for Public Man-
    agement, Inc., 162

Offner, Paul, 254–55
Oliver, Pamela E., 84
opportunity costs of incarceration,
    306–8
optimal level of incarceration
    changes in state prison population
        necessary to reach, **285, 319**
    core concepts underlying, 272–73
    cost-benefit analysis to determine
        (*see* cost-benefit analysis of incar-
        ceration)
    elasticity of crime and (*see* elasticity

of crime with respect to incarcera-
    tion)
    empirical questions underlying,
        271–72
    opportunity costs of incarceration,
        need to evaluate, 306–8
    question of whether we are at, 2–3,
        20–21
    refinement of estimates to draw pol-
        icy conclusions, need for, 304–6
Owens, Emily, 126–27

Pager, Devah, 247
Palermo, George B., 47
Palmer, Ted, 129
Panel Study of Income Dynamics
    (PSID)
    Child Development Supplement
        (CDS), 177–78, 183
    children and parents with a criminal
        history, as a data source on, 184–85
    genealogical design of, 181–82
parental incarceration
    consequences for children (*see* chil-
        dren with incarcerated parents)
    increase in, 178
parole
    community corrections, need for in-
        creased scope of, 170–71
    discretionary boards, abolishment
        of, 76–77
    increase in prison admissions due to
        violation of, 39–41
    mass incarceration and, 78
    reincarceration rate for drug offend-
        ers, 83–84
Paternoster, Raymond, 12, 15–16, 133
"Pennsylvania"/"separate system" of
    punishment, 120
Penrose, Lionel, 47
Personal Responsibility and Work Op-
    portunity Act of 1996, 258*n*4
Petersilia, Joan, 151
Pettit, Becky, 10, 251–52, 260*n*18
Pfaff, John, 316
Piehl, Anne Morrison, 6, 44, 274, 278,
    281–82, 310–11, 316–17, 333*n*10,
    335*n*26, 337*nn*35–36
Piquero, Alex, 123–24, 128, 133–34
Pirog, Maureen, 242
Pogarsky, Greg, 133–34

politics
  of disorder and conservative ascendancy, 91–93
  of "moral panics," 103–4
  of the Rockefeller laws in New York, 86–88
  See also public policy
poverty. *See* socioeconomic status
Pozen, David, 154
President's Commission on Law Enforcement, 291
prisoners
  effects of prison on (*see* criminal behavior; criminal psychology)
  hardening of, 153
  rights of, concerns for, 122
"prisonization," theories of, 153
prisons
  commitment rates, 81–83
  construction boom, expenditure on, 269
  evaluating, 156
  punitive, undesirable consequences of move towards, 172
  state (*see* state prisons)
probation
  cost of for index I crimes, **329**
  future offending and, 135
prosecution
  conviction rates from adult arrests for index I crimes, by type of crime, **328**
  efficiency of in war on drugs, 81–83
  grassroots policing and (*see* New York City)
  opportunity cost of increased incarceration and, 306–8
  See also enforcement
PSID. *See* Panel Study of Income Dynamics
public policy
  children with incarcerated parents, addressing unintended consequences for, 202–3 (*see also* children with incarcerated parents)
  child-support enforcement, 242–43, 258
  community corrections, risk assessment and, 170–71
  as determinant of incarceration rate, model of, 30–32

incarceration impacts on labor-market outcomes, 257–58
  incarceration rate as a consequence of, 10–11, 13–15, 27–28, 33–39, 65–66, 74–75
  optimal level of incarceration and, 304–6 (*see also* optimal level of incarceration)
  parole policy (*see* parole)
  prescriptions for, 21–23
  punitive prisons, questions regarding move towards, 172
  security classification of inmates and, 170
  sentencing of convicted criminals (*see* sentencing policy)
  the war on drugs (*see* war on drugs)
Public Policy Institute of California, 214
punishment
  instrumental and retributive philosophies of, 119–23, 143–45 (*see also* instrumental philosophy of punishment)
  "keeper philosophies" of state prison systems, 155

race-ethnicity
  arrest rates and, 80–81
  changes in the general population regarding, effect on criminality and incarceration of, 41–45
  cumulative risks faced by children with incarcerated parents classified by, 184–89
  incarceration risk and, 4–10
  institutionalization rates for adult women by, **51**
  profiling based on, 105n6
  targeting of "moral" crimes and, 103–4
  the war on drugs and, 84–85
  See also African Americans
Raphael, Steven, 10, 13–14, 23n2, 36, 52, 55, 69n22, 142, 203n1, 225, 242, 245, 248, 250–51, 256, 260n13, 261n27, 279, 281, 313, 316–17
Reagan, Ronald, 87, 92–93
recidivism
  cost of repeat offenders, 258n1

recidivism (*continued*)
  employment of released offenders
    and, 239–40
  incarceration *vs.* probation and,
    153–54
  peer contact/social interactions and,
    154
  rehabilitation programs and, 129–30
  specific deterrence and, 135–38
  third strike threat and, 143
  See also criminal behavior
regression discontinuity, 156–57
rehabilitation
  critiques of, 122–23
  defenses of, 129–31
  deterrence and, boundaries between,
    131
  as mechanism for instrumental ap-
    proach to crime reduction, 119, 121
Reitz, Kevin, 261*n*25
Republican Party, 87–88, 104
responsibility model of correctional
  philosophy, 155
retributive philosophy of punishment,
  119–21, 123, 128, 143–44
Right to Be Different, The (Kittrie), 122
Riley, K. Jack, 105*n*7
risk-assessment, 127–28, 170–71
Rockefeller, Nelson, 86–88
Rockefeller drug laws, 14, 85–89. *See
  also* war on drugs
Rosen, Sherwin, 288
Rosenblatt, Albert M., 106*n*16
Rossman, Shelli B., 289, 291
Ruhm, Christopher, 204*n*3
Russia, incarceration rate in, 332*n*2
Rust, Roland, 291

Sabol, William, 251–52, 260*n*18
Sampson, Robert, 124
Schelling, Thomas C., 289
Schneider, Saundra, 224–25
Schwarzenegger, Arnold, 300
Second Felony Offender (SFO) law, 86,
  88
selective incapacitation, 127–28
sentencing policy
  California, Proposition 8, 142
  Declaration of Principles of the
    Cincinnati Prison Conference, 121
  incarceration rates and, 33, 36–40, 65

indeterminate *vs.* determinate,
  122–23
offenses meriting incarceration, expansion of, 28
philosophies of, 119–23 (*see also* instrumental philosophy of punishment)
punitive reforms, historical development of, 76–78
state-level incarceration rates and,
  74–76
state sentencing structures as of
  1996, **78**
third strike, impact of, 142–43
time served, increase in, 28, 83–84
truth-in-sentencing laws, 77–78
September 11 terrorist attacks, cost estimates for, 286
Sevigny, Eric L., 106*n*15
SFO. *See* Second Felony Offender law
Shapiro, Jesse, 156, 271, 301
Siegelman, Peter, 286, 306–7, 336*n*31
Simon, Jonathan, 171
simultaneity, 16, 309–10
Singer, Richard, 122
Smith, Maurice B., 47
Smith, Paula, 153
social cost
  of an average index I crime, estimat-
    ing, 290–91, 297, **298**
  of crime, studies estimating the an-
    nual, **291**
  jury awards as guide to estimating,
    289
  lost productivity of incarcerated of-
    fenders, 292–93, **294,** 300–301
  as the measure of costs of crime,
    286
  of murder, 318–20
  per crime, **287, 292**
socially optimal incarceration rate. *See*
  optimal level of incarceration
social programs/spending, crime reduction effects of, 306–8
socioeconomic status
  child family income before, during,
    and after father's prison release,
    188
  children with incarcerated parents
    and, relationship of, 186, 188–93,
    193

employment, impact of incarceration on, 19–20
wage inequality, crime rates and increasing, 54–61
See also labor-market outcomes
Song, Lin, 153
Sorensen, Elaine, 254–55
specific deterrence, 119, 132–38
Spelman, William, 65, 273, 275, 277, 280–83, 309–10, 315–16, 333n10
Spohn, Cassia, 135
stability-of-punishment hypothesis, 73, 100–102
state prisons
    crack cocaine and admissions to, 63–65
    incarceration rates in 2000 and changes in incarceration rates 1978–2000, 211
    incarceration rates in selected states, 1977-2004, 315
    "keeper philosophies" of, 155
    mass incarceration in, 74–76 (see also war on drugs)
    percentage of prisoners by type of offense, 85
    size of populations in, 27
state spending on corrections, 18–19, 207–8, 229
    in 2005, 2
    budgetary procedures, effects of, 221–23
    crowding out of other types of spending by, 223–33
    data and methods for analyzing, 213–14
    definitions of spending variables, 234–36
    explaining variation in growth of total, corrections, and noncorrections spending, 220
    explaining variation in levels of total, corrections, and noncorrections spending, 214–20
    growth in, 18, 208–10
    per capita in 2000 and growth in per capita 1978-2000, 212
    percentage of state budget in 2000 and growth in percentage of state budget 1978-2000, 213

trade-off between welfare spending and, 229–30
trends and variation in, 208–13
trends in average, 1977-2002, 210
Steen, Sara, 291
Stoll, Michael A., 13–14, 19, 33, 66n3, 242, 245, 248
Struggle for Justice (American Friends Service Committee), 122
Sweden, child welfare and incarceration policy in, 203
Sweeten, Gary, 125–27

Tabarrok, Alexander, 142
Texas, 155, 311–12
Thaler, Richard, 288
Thistlewaite, Donald, 156
Tidd, Simon, 291
Tittle, Charles, 133
Tonry, Michael H., 104n3, 105n5
Travis, Jeremy, 29, 104n4
Trumbull, William N., 286
truth-in-sentencing laws, 77–78

Ulmer, Jeffrey, 136–37
Useem, Bert, 274, 278, 281–82, 310–11, 316–17, 333n10, 335n26, 337nn35–36

van den Haag, Ernst, 122
Van Kasten, Christine, 136–37
Venkatesh, Sudhir, 69n22
Vera Institute, 107n19
victimization rates, 1
Villettaz, Patrice, 153
Virginia, 128

wage-rate differentials, 289
wages
    crime rates and increasing inequality of, 54–61
    incarceration history and subsequent, 250
    See also socioeconomic status
Waldo, Gordon, 141
Ward, Benjamin, 91–92
war on drugs
    drug offenders as percentage of prison populations, increase in, 84–85

war on drugs (*continued*)
  escalation of in the 1980s, 89–93,
    97–98
  local factors in the prosecution of,
    accounting for, 98–100
  local level implementation of, incar-
    ceration rate and, 74–76
  mass incarceration and, 14–15,
    79–85, 93–100, 102–3
  "moral panics" and parallels to Pro-
    hibition, 15, 103
  prosecution and sentencing in state
    courts, **82**
  prosecution of drug arrests, in-
    creased efficiency of, 81–83
  racial disproportionality in prosecu-
    tion and sentencing, 84–85
  the Rockefeller drug laws, 14, 85–89,
    93–100
  See also crack cocaine
Webster, Cheryl, 142
Weiman, David F., 14–15, 19, 249
Weinberg, Bruce A., 55

Weiss, Christopher, 14–15
welfare spending, 228–29
West, Valerie, 74
Western, Bruce, 10, 74, 247, 249–51,
    254, 256, 259n12, 260n13, 261n27
Western Penitentiary of New York, 121
Wickersham Commission on Law Ob-
    servance and Enforcement, 284
Wiersema, Brian, 287, 290–93
Wilderman, Christopher, 186
Willis, Michael, 70n24, 105n7
Wilson, David, 129
Wilson, James Q., 91, 122
Winter-Ebmer, Rudolf, 55
women, institutionalization rates by
    race-ethnicity for adult, **51**

Yocom, James E., 84

Zedlewski, Edwin W., 291
Zimmer, Lynne, 107n19
Zimring, Franklin, 142, 284
Zoder, Isabel, 153